STRATEGIC ORGANIZATIONAL COMMUNICATION

Cultures, Situations, and Adaptation

CHARLES CONRAD

The University of North Carolina at Chapel Hill

Holt, Rinehart and Winston

New York Chicago San Francisco Philadelphia
Montreal Toronto London Sydney
Tokyo Mexico City Rio de Janeiro Madrid

Acknowledgments *(continued on p. 325).*

Excerpt on p. 28: From *The History of Management Thought* by Claude George, p. 90. Copyright © 1972. Reprinted by permission of Prentice-Hall, Inc. Englewood Cliffs, N.J.

Excerpts on pp. 76 and 101: From "The Hawthorne Studies: A Radical Critique" by Alex Carey. *The American Sociological Review*, 32 (1967). Reprinted by permission of the American Sociological Association.

Interior Design: Barbara Bert
Cover Design: Gloria Gentile

Library of Congress Cataloging in Publication Data

Conrad, Charles.
  Strategic organizational communication.

  Bibliography: p. 312
  1. Includes index.
  1. Communication—Social aspects.   2. Communication in
organizations.   I. Title.
HM258.C63   1985   302.2.   84–22388

ISBN 0-03-061669-7

CBS COLLEGE PUBLISHING
Holt, Rinehart and Winston
The Dryden Press
Saunders College Publishing

To
Helen and Cecil
who gave me a love of knowledge
and
BJ
who has given me knowledge of love.

PREFACE

In an important sense this book originated in SPCH 185, "Organizational Communication Theory," a course I have taught at the University of North Carolina for the past six years. For a number of reasons, this course has been blessed with exceptionally fine students of widely varying backgrounds—juniors and seniors, masters and Ph. D. students from a number of different academic departments, and a large number of "nontraditional" students who are employed on a full-time basis in managerial and/or professional positions. Because of their diversity and sophistication, it has been a recurring challenge to find appropriate reading materials for them. They made it quite clear that they preferred readings that

- Admit that there are very few immutable truths about organizations and organizational communication and that an understanding of organizations can come only by thoughtfully confronting the many sides of complicated issues
- Help people *think through* the meanings of the events and actions that take place around them in organizations and make informed choices about how they should act in the various situations they encounter at work
- Address the kinds of communicative problems members of modern organizations actually face within a comprehensive framework that helps them make sense out of these problems
- Do not treat communication as a "thing" that is separate from the people and patterns of action that make up organizational life

Eventually, their hints and the encouragement of a number of my colleagues persuaded me to attempt to create materials that would fulfill these requirements. As the project progressed, it became *Strategic Organizational Communication.*

This book is based on an assumption that sounds much simpler than it is:

Human beings are inherently choice-making animals, motivated by feelings of hierarchy, creativity, and self-esteem, who both create the social realities within which they live and are guided and constrained by their perceptions of those realities.

The purpose of the chapters in Unit I is to survey the ways in which communicative acts create different types of organizational "realities"—today's popular term for this concept is organizational "cultures"—and how these creations in turn direct and control employees' actions and communication. Each chapter in Unit I concludes with a "postscript," which is designed to stimulate debate (and thought, since thinking and talking seem to benefit one another) about issues that are related to the key concepts presented in the chapters.

The goal of the chapters in Unit II is to provide readers with opportunities to *think through* many of the complicated communication-related problems faced by members of modern organizations. Hopefully, this thinking through will also help them begin to understand how to choose the appropriate communicative strategies with which to confront these problems. My goal is *not* to provide simple, concrete, "cookbook" answers. Instead, I hope to provide readers with experience in using the analytical processes that are necessary prerequisites for selecting among possible strategies.

One final note about the content of this book: Each of the topics that typically are included in discussions of organizational communication— leadership strategies, participatory group decision making, communication networks, and so on—is examined at length at some point in the book. They are not treated in separate chapters because organizing ideas in that way inevitably creates the impression that these dimensions of communication are "things" separate from organizations. The outlines at the beginning of each chapter are designed to aid readers in locating these topics. In addition, a number of important communication-related topics which have not been treated in detail in previous works are examined here—for example, communication and stress, sex roles and power relationships.

This book has occupied two years of my life. No project of this magnitude can be started, much less completed, without the aid and support of a large number of people. Had it not been for the encouragement provided by John Bittner, I would still be thinking about writing it. Without his wisdom, I still would not understand the peculiar "reality" the publishing world has created for itself and for those who enter into it. As the work progressed, a number of the best people and finest minds in our field consented to read and comment on the manuscript. Each made a distinctive contribution to it. I would particularly like to thank Mike Pacanowsky of the University of Utah for his research on organizational culture, his encouragement, and his repeated calls for more examples per square inch; Bob McPhee of the University of Wisconsin— Milwaukee for his insightful criticisms of my initial treatments of Weber's theory of ideal types and of systems-contingency models of organizations; Gabe Buntzman of Western Kentucky University for his help in integrating contemporary organizational theory and organizational communication theory and for his constant reminders that a great many closet logical positivists are alive, well, and doing valuable research on organizations; and Vincent Di Salvo, University of Nebraska; Terrence Albrecht, University of Washington; and Michael Hazen, Wake Forest University, whose comments substantially improved the quality of my ideas and the clarity of my prose.

Finally, I would especially like to thank Janet Ceropski, the coauthor of Chapter 12; Betty Webber Conrad, the coauthor of Chapter 11, whose expertise in stress management made that chapter possible and who suffered more during the development of this book than anyone else; and the editorial staff of Holt, Rinehart and Winston—Anne Boynton-Trigg, Tom Gornick, Jackie Fleischer, and Carla Kay—who did everything good editors should do: they left me alone when I needed to be left alone; they didn't leave me alone when I needed their help; and they forgave me my penchant for forgetting details.

Charles Conrad
Greensboro
May 1984

CONTENTS

UNIT 1

Communication Structure, Process, and Types of Organizations

1

Underlying Concepts

THE STUDY OF ORGANIZATIONAL COMMUNICATION

THE ROLE OF COMMUNICATION IN ORGANIZATIONS

THE FUNCTIONS OF ORGANIZATIONAL COMMUNICATION
The Command Function
The Relational Function
The Ambiguity Management Function

THE THEORY OF IDEAL TYPES

STRATEGIC ORGANIZATIONAL COMMUNICATION

POSTSCRIPT: THE PURCHASING CASE

Don't ask me. I just work here.　　　　　　　　　　　　　　　　**—Anonymous**

At one time or another almost everyone has responded to the question "How did this [disaster] happen?" with a statement like "Don't ask me. I just work here." In some cases the excuse is a legitimate one. Someone other than the person making the statement made a decision or took a step which created a problem. But far too often it is a decision, action, or lack of action by the person offering the excuse that led to the inefficiency or failure. Although the performance of every member of an organization is in many ways influenced by the activities of other members, in the final analysis it is the individuals' choices which decide their destiny in the organization. This book is about the choices and choice-making behaviors of members of formal organizations. It concentrates on *communication* in organizations because it is through communication that individual employees gain the information on which they base choices and exercise the influence which translates their choices into action. The goal of this book is to give readers a sense of how organizational communication is used *strategically*, that is, how individual employees analyze the situations they face at work and choose the appropriate communication strategies to use in those situations. The book assumes that all employ-ees are goal-oriented in some important ways and that if they understand how communication functions in their organization they will be better able to use their communication skills to achieve their objectives and those of their organizations. The book explains when it is appropriate to use a variety of communication strategies, including the denial of responsibility and the claim of ignorance ("I don't know. I just work here"), and more important, when not to use them.

THE STUDY OF ORGANIZATIONAL COMMUNICATION

One of the most important recent developments in the way people look at organizations has been the increasing amount of attention paid to different aspects of communication. Managers and researchers alike have recognized that businesses must maintain at least an adequate level of communication in order to survive, that increasing the effectiveness of communication within a firm contributes to the efficiency of its operation, and that in some cases highly effective communication can increase productivity and eventually profitability. Perhaps more important has been the realization that people who understand how communication functions in a business, who have developed a wide repertory of written and oral communicative skills, and who have learned when and how to use those skills seem to advance more rapidly and contribute more fully to their organizations than people who have not done so.[1] As a result the number of college courses and professional training pro-grams concerned with organizational communication has mushroomed. Of course employees cannnot function effectively unless they possess the tech-nical skills that their positions require. But more and more it appears that being able to recognize, diagnose, and solve communication-related problems is vital to the success of people in even the most technical occupations. Accountants must be able to gain complete, accurate, and sometimes sensitive information from their clients; supervisors of production lines must be able to obtain adequate and timely information on which to base their decisions; managers of different divisions must be able to give their subordinates clear instructions, make sure those instructions are understood, create conditions in which their commands will be carried out, and obtain reliable feedback about the completion of the tasks that they have assigned. In a recent survey of 700 middle managers, almost 85 percent of the respondents reported that it was their subordinates' communication skills (or lack of them) which determined their success or failure in critical situations. Although these managers also noted that factors like their subordinates' job-related expertise and loyalty to their supervisor and organization also had an important impact on their effec-tiveness, it was their ability to communicate effectively that was crucial in most cases.[2]

However, being able to communicate effectively at work requires two kinds of knowledge. First, it requires an understanding of the relationships that exist between communication and the operation of organizations. Since communication processes influence the way an organization operates and are simultaneously influenced by key characteristics of the organization, neither organizations nor organizational communication can be understood adequately if they are examined in isolation of each other.

Second, effective communication depends on employees' understanding how to choose appropriate communication strategies in different situations. This book intends to provide readers with an understanding of *strategic* communication skills—the ability to *analyze* a situation, *select* an appropriate communication *strategy* from a number of available options, and *employ* that strategy in an optimal way. However, understanding strategic communication demands that an individual understand how communication functions in organizations—how it creates and solves problems, how it makes some situations occur and how it prevents others, how it makes some outcomes more probable and others improbable. This chapter will introduce these two most important concepts: the role of communication in organizations and the characteristics of strategic organizational communication. Subsequent chapters will expand each of these concepts and explain how they contribute to the success of complex organizations and their members.

THE ROLE OF COMMUNICATION IN ORGANIZATIONS

Historically, formal organizations have been examined from two very different perspectives. One view has depicted them as the combination of a number of different components, each of which is linked to each other on the basis of some carefully planned and clearly articulated design. People who accept this perspective believe that organizations are designed in three distinct steps. Designing an organization begins with an analysis of a potential *market* and a decision about what products—goods or services—the organization should produce. Designers then decide which *tasks* must be performed in order to produce the desired output and determine how each of those tasks can be completed most efficiently. Finally, designers *organize* the various *tasks* into *structures* and *sequences* which are intended to maximize the efficiency of the total operation. Since many of the components of the organization are people, someone must be assigned the job of seeing that all who are involved in each part of the production process understand the tasks they are to perform, how they are to accomplish those tasks, and the fact that they must accomplish them in a timely and efficient manner if the organization is to function properly. In this perspective, communication is important for *instrumental* reasons. It functions in ways which allow members to share the information necessary for the successful completion of a complex array of interdependent tasks. Although the end products, task requirements, employee skills, or relationships among these components may change when market conditions or technologies change, this perspective assumes that the rational design of an organization will stay relatively constant. At least, the organization will stay stable enough so that the designers can draw a picture, usually in the form of an "organizational chart," which accurately reflects its operation.

Another viewpoint describes organizations as complex, interdependent matrices of ongoing processes, not as a rational, carefully planned combination of interrelated, static components.[3] This distinction is important for two reasons. First, it leads to a view of the members of an organization as actors, not as relatively inert components of the organization. Employees constantly are making choices about how they will act in the variety of situations they face. Second, organizations are networks of interdependent human actors whose actions both create the situations they face and allow them to respond to those situations. Although organizations can be designed by objective, outside planners, their designs constantly are in a state of change. Businesses are composed of large numbers of people who constantly are *monitoring* their own actions and the actions of others, *processing* that information, and *choosing* those courses of action that they think are appropriate. This description of organizations does not imply that their members are either manipulative or Machiavellian, although it would admit that some of them are. Instead, it suggests that people are active agents who have their own reasons for acting as they do. They are not mechanical components of the production process, doing only what they are designed to do in precisely that way in which they are designed to do it. They are choice-making members whose actions are part of a complicated array of ongoing processes.

Within this perspective, communication is important to an organization for two reasons. First, communication is the means through which people acquire the information and develop the criteria by which they decide how to act. Second, communication is the process through which they put their choices into practice. That is, through communication members of organizations learn that there are *precedents* in their organization which constrain their choices, and they learn what those precedents are. Through communication with others, they develop and express the *purposes* which guide their actions. They are able to consider the *potential* effects of different actions only because they are capable of communicating. In addition, it is through communication that members of an organization are able to *coordinate* their actions with other members of the organization. Because the complex array of tasks that must be performed in an organization are interdependent, each member of the organization can perform only if other members do also. In most situations, only a small proportion of the activities of any one employee will be necessary preconditions for the successful action of other employees. However, for each member of the organization, there are some actions that must be taken if the organization is to operate. And, because all members must depend on the actions of some other member(s) in order to do their jobs, they must be able to predict accurately what those other people will do in different situations. Being able to do so requires employees to understand why they act as they do and to recognize that they regularly respond to certain situations in predicatable ways. Communication is the process through which people make sense out of the actions of other people; it is the means by which they are able to understand how they can coordinate their actions with the actions of others. Human action is contextual; it is the result of the choices people make within the situations they perceive themselves to be (see Figure 1.1).

Unfortunately, these two views of organizations and communication often are seen as being mutually exclusive. Scholars who focus their attention on the design or structure of organizations and the *functions* of communication in organizations that have been described in this chapter often overlook the complex *processes* through which people decide how to act at work. Conversely, when scholars concentrate on understanding the relationships between processes of communication and processes of organizing, they often deemphasize the tasks people perform at work and the function communication plays in the completion of those tasks. Understanding strategic organizational communication requires an analysis of both the functions of communication in organizations and the processes through which communication guides the actions of members.

THE FUNCTIONS OF ORGANIZATIONAL COMMUNICATION

In some important ways communication functions as a tool for members of organizations: (1) It allows them to issue, receive, interpret, and act on *commands*; (2) it allows them to create and maintain productive business and

FIGURE 1.1 Processes of Communication In Organizations

Communication Process

Monitoring actions of self and others
Processing information about organizational action
Choosing appropriate actions

Organizational Constraints on Actions

Precedents and norms
Individual purposes
Potential effects of different actions
Need for coordination with others

personal *relationships* with other members of the organization; and (3) it allows them to *manage ambiguity and uncertainty*.

The Command Function

Two types of communication make up the "command" function: *direction* and *feedback*. People perform necessary tasks effectively only when they choose both to initiate action and to limit their actions in clearly prescribed ways. Some members of organizations, usually those given the formal titles of *supervisor* or *manager*, issue messages which tell other members to take action and to limit that action to a particular series of steps to be taken at a specified time and at a specified place. If the person to whom the message is directed does not act, or if the person acts inappropriately, the command function will not be wholly successful. It is inevitable that people will resist commands to some degree. In order to function, organizations must influence people to act in ways in which they otherwise would not act. For instance, few humans would choose on their own to perform seemingly minor, repetitive tasks hour after hour, day after day. But a large proportion of production-oriented organizations could not exist if it was not possible for some people to persuade other people to perform these tasks at a predetermined rate for a predetermined period of time with a minimal amount of creativity. Assembly lines operate successfully only because a complex array of very specific commands are communicated to a large number of people in a way that somehow persuades them to follow those commands exactly. If any worker does a job in a new, varied, unanticipated or creative way, the productivity of the assembly line is reduced. When automobile workers respond to the boredom of their jobs by choosing to install parts backward, upside down, or not at all, the quality of the final product usually is reduced. When they respond by celebrating the end of a monotonous week with a Thursday afternoon (or Thursday through Sunday) visit to a local bar, their ability to follow commands exactly on subsequent days usually is reduced. Although these deviations from expected behavior often do little damage, they create enough problems that most Americans learn at an early age "not to buy a car which was built on Friday." Other types of organizations involve even larger numbers of people whose actions must be initiated and controlled if the organization is to function. Consequently, the *command function* of communication relies on processes of *persuasion* and *influence*. Its effectiveness depends on the availability of some form of influence and some communication strategies through which some members of organizations can persuade other members to act in specific and unnatural ways.

The command function also involves the production of adequate *feedback* about the actions that actually are taken by people who have been issued commands. Supervisors often assume that their subordinates will carry out their commands. This assumption is especially strong when the supervisor has issued a set of routine instructions. Comfortable in the knowledge that their commands will be carried out, supervisors instruct other people to take actions which, when completed, will allow the task that the unit has taken on to be accomplished. If any of the people who are involved in the command process fail to carry out the commands they were given properly or promptly, the supervisors will need to modify the commands that were given to the other people involved. But they cannot make these adjustments unless they receive prompt and accurate feedback about the extent to which each of their commands has been carried out.

Almost all people who have worked in organizations which produce tangible products can remember instances in which they found themselves surrounded by piles and piles of partially finished products because some person or group of people failed to receive, understand, or carry out commands. These situations usually strike the workers who are gazing at the piles as being terribly funny, both because they know that the error is someone else's headache and because they have been allowed to take a lengthy break while waiting for the bottleneck to be eliminated and the unfinished products to reach their stations. Rarely does the supervisor who issued the commands find the situation quite as humorous. The piles of unfinished products do, however, give this supervisor feedback about the effects of the commands. Organizations do seem to function more efficiently when supervisors have access to more timely and less tangible command-related feedback.

Command-related communication typically comes in one of two forms: *publications* and *instructions*.[4] The differences between the two forms are important because employees' reactions to a command are related in part to the form in which it is issued. Organizations produce a variety of formal, written policies and procedures. The published communications have three important characteristics. First, they create the impression that the command is directed to a general audience. No one has been picked out as the recipient; the message seems to be addressed to anyone and everyone. Second, they create the impression that the command is official; that is, it is written by the organization or by someone who represents the organization rather than by any one individual. Finally, they suggest both that the command is a relatively permanent injunction and, indirectly, that the problem it addresses is important and recurring.

In contrast, instructions are oral commands, generally given in a face-to-face encounter and addressed to a single person or clearly defined group of persons. Instructions are highly flexible commands which seem to be transient rather than permanent. They are viewed as being linked to a specific problem which is relatively new, rare, or unprecedented and are from an individual rather than from the "organization." Because *publications* and *instructions* are different forms of commands, they are appropriate to different kinds of situations. The success of any command depends in part on its being issued in the proper form.

In summary, one function of communication in formal organizations is the command function. Because organizations are composed of large numbers of people who play interdependent roles, their actions must be coordinated effectively. Successful coordination is achieved when members initiate the actions they have been directed to undertake. It occurs when some members of the organization communicate in ways that create the kind of situations in which other members of the organization will choose to take the precise actions that are envisioned in the commands. Both the process of creating an appropriate situation and the creation of clear and influential command messages depend on the strategic competence and communication skills of the participants. The command function of organizational communication relies totally on complex processes of constructing, interpreting, and choosing actions in response to a particular type of communication.

The Relational Function

Organizational communication also fulfills a *relational* function. Businesses are composed of human beings who are involved in interpersonal relationships with other human beings. Unlike nonwork relationships, in which people have a relatively wide degree of freedom in deciding who to form relationships with, the structure of formal organizations dictates that each employee must form relationships with a clearly defined group of people. Sometimes, perhaps most of the time, members of organizations are required to form effective "working relationships" with people with whom they never would choose to form personal relationships. For a number of reasons, imposed relationships are less stable and more prone to friction than are "natural" ones.

Like natural relationships, working relationships can succeed only if the parties involved can achieve at least a minimal degree of understanding and cooperation. To do so they must be able to comprehend the meaning of the messages they exchange with each other, assess each others' motivations with some degree of accuracy, and negotiate some agreements about how they will act toward one another. Unless these minimal requirements are met, the development of effective working relationships is impossible. Like all relationships, working relationships inevitably will involve some friction, misunderstanding, and conflict about the proper nature of the relationship. However, in non-working relationships the parties usually develop a degree of commitment to each other and to the continuation of the relationship. Typically they will have voluntarily started the relationship and will have made a number of decisions to continue it in spite of conflicts and frictions because they continue to receive benefits from it. To some degree at least, their commitment is mutual and intrinsic to the relationship. In working relationships, the parties may have very little commitment to the relationship itself. Someone or something else—a supervisor or the organization—initiated the relationship, the parties stay in it because their roles in the organization seem to demand that they continue to work together, and the benefits they receive from it are derived from their place in the organization rather than from the relationship itself.

When people lack an intrinsic commitment to a relationship, it is more difficult to resolve their differences and the degree of communication skills necessary to maintain it is greater. Minor irritations are not overlooked, minor conflicts are not easily resolved, and major disagreements erupt into open confrontation because neither party is as concerned that an open conflict might threaten the continuation of the relationship. Fortunately, and almost inevitably, people do form close personal relationships with some of those with whom they have effective working relationships. Although this means that their work situations will be more pleasant than otherwise would be the case, it also adds a number of complicating factors to the relationship. They must negotiate boundaries between the two dimensions of their relationship, arriving at some mutual agreement that they will communicate differently with each other while at work than they will while in other contexts. In addition, they must cope with the fact that their personal relationship is being observed by a large number of people with whom they have working relationships and that the existence of the personal relationship may further complicate some of their working relationships. "Don't have an affair with your boss, or at least don't let anyone know you are" really is very good advice.

Through processes of communication, working relationships are formed, maintained, and in some cases, transformed into personal relationships. As these relationships begin and develop, the participants in them begin to perceive their jobs, their organization, and their roles in that organization differently. These perceptions combine to define the situations that each individual believes one faces at work. Perceptions provide the *parameters* and *guidelines* within which each individual makes decisions about how to act. These choices influence the character of the relationships with other members of the organization, and these changed relationships influence other members' perceptions of their organization and thus influence their actions. Other members' actions in turn alter the character of their relationship and consequently influence the *parameters* and *guidelines* within which other members make their choices. In a complex matrix of processes, communication, relationships, perceptions, and choices, the "situations" in which people find themselves at work are created.

In addition, the relationships that people form at work influence their performance in complicated and important ways. Employees' perceptions of and satisfaction with the tasks they are asked to perform are affected by the quality of the relationships they form with the people around them. Similarly, their satisfaction with their jobs will influence their ability to form valued and stable relationships with their co-workers. The quality of employees' relationships with their co-workers influences their ability to gain the information and support they need in order to perform their job and influences their willingness to provide the information and support their co-workers need. The nature of supervisors' relationships with subordinates influences their ability to understand the messages they exchange and the probability that any particular command will be carried out. For all these reasons, the relational and command functions of organizational communication are interdependent and interactive. The success of one depends largely on the success of the other.

The Ambiguity-Management Function

The third major function of communication in organizations is the management of ambiguity. Humans are essentially choice-making beings, and their activities at work are essentially choice-making activities. Each day they face a series of decision-making situations. In some of these situations they make choices for the organization; in others their decisions are more personal. Their choice making is complicated by two factors. The first involves the multitude of motivations an individual generally incorporates into decision making. In each organizational choice-making situation, a person simultaneously must consider the effects selecting one of a number of available options will have on one, one's co-workers, and one's organization. In some situations the personal concerns will be more important than the relational or organizational ones; in others, the decision maker will be concerned primarily with the interests of the organization and only indirectly concerned with one's own interests. Since different situations will involve different combinations of self, relationship, and organizational interest, organizational choice-making is a complex and potentially confusing process. If the individual faces a situation which provides clear and explicit guidelines for determining how these interests should be balanced, it is relatively easy to make effective choices. However, choice making typically takes place in situations in which the guidelines for action are either unclear or contradictory. Communication then becomes the process through which an actor manages an ambiguous situation.

Second, organizational choice making is complicated by the ambiguity of the organizations themselves. The objectives of an organization at a particular time often are not clear to its members. In addition, the objectives of a particular unit in the organization or of particular members also may be ambiguous. In organizations which are undergoing rapid change or which exist in rapidly changing environments, these objectives may be particularly confused.

Also, the complex histories of modern organizations complicate the choice making of their individual members.[5] Most situations are not completely unprecedented. The people involved have faced similar situations in the past and can draw on those experiences to help them make effective choices in the new situation. But precedents sometimes hurt choice making more than they help it. Individuals will recall that in similar situations in the past they made a certain choice. They also remember that their choice was followed by a certain good or bad result. They will tend to believe that it was their decision that led to the result. If the outcome was favorable, they will tend to repeat the decision. If the outcome was negative, they will tend to avoid taking any similar course of action. But in most cases, choices made by a single individual are only one part of a complicated series of events and decisions which lead to an observed outcome. Not realizing this, individuals tend to make subsequent choices based on the mistaken belief that it was their choice that caused a particular outcome to occur in the past. In this way the availability of precedents can reduce the quality of the choices that are made.

Precedents complicate choice making in another way. When faced with a decision people tend to search their memories for similar situations. When they discover a precedent they feel a great sense of relief because the new situation suddenly becomes clearer and easier to manage. However, people often discover precedents which really are not precedents at all. They recall past situations that they were able to manage and then define the new situation in a way which makes it seem similar to the past, comfortable situation. Through this process they often overlook important differences between the two.

Organizational choice-making situations are inherently complex and almost always ambiguous. They are simplified and sometimes distorted by characteristically human thought processes. They also are simplified and sometimes distorted by typical communication processes. Members of organizations use communication in two primary ways in their attempts to manage ambiguity. First, they communicate to each other in order to structure, to make sense out of, new situations. They seek out information which will help them gain a perspective on the problem, and they seek out support from others which will confirm their interpretation of the problem and strengthen their commitment to a particular course of action. In addition, they use communication in favor of a particular way of looking at the problem and in support of a preferred option. Through communication with other members of the organization they are able to create a shared, mutual understanding of what a problem is and how it should be addressed. If the information they gain through communication has been sufficient, relevant, and accurate, and if the shared perspective that they have created has been appropriate to the problem, communication will have improved their decision making.

But if the information gained has been inadequate in any significant way, or if the perspective that has been adopted by the people who were involved in the communication is flawed in any important respect, the availability of communication will have reduced the quality of the decision and further complicated choice making in the future. In the latter case, organizational communication has been used to *reduce* ambiguity artificially; it has not been used to *manage* ambiguity successfully. Sometimes processes of communication allow members of organizations to make foolish decisions and become comfortable with and strongly committed to them. In other instances communication allows members to make choices which satisfy their needs and the needs of their organizations. In some cases organizational communication even may provide the basis for making the best possible decisions. A variety of processes inevitably influences the potential effectiveness of the ambiguity-management function of organizational communication.

Communication fulfills three major functions in formal organizations—a *command function*, a *relational function*, and an *ambiguity-management function*. For any organization to succeed, each of these functions must operate at or above some minimal level of effectiveness. For any individual members of an organization to perform their roles successfully, they must be capable of using a variety of communication skills to issue effective commands and respond adequately to commands issued by others, to develop and sustain efficient working relationships, and to manage ambiguity strategically. However, some kinds of organizations are designed in ways which lead their members to rely most heavily on one of these three communication functions. Some organizations rely most heavily on the *command* function, others on the role of communication in the management of *relationships*, and others on the effective management of *ambiguity*.

The chapters which make up Unit I of this book describe three different "ideal types" of organizations and the role of communication in each. Every organization must have adequate command, relational, and ambiguity-managing communication. However, the relative importance of these three functions varies in the three different types of organizations (see Table 1.1). "Traditional" organizations, the type that will be discussed in Chapters 2 and 3, rely most heavily on the command function of communication and less heavily on the other two. Human relations and resources organizations (Chapters 4 and 5) depend on effective relational communication. Some versions of this type also rely heavily on the command function. In most versions the ambiguity-managing function has a limited role. The final type, "systems-contingency" organizations, relies heavily on ambiguity-managing communication. In this type, relational and command functions are important in some situations and less important in others. In fact, it is the assumption that command and relational communication must be combined in different proportions in different situations that distinguishes the systems-contingency type from the traditional and human relations and resources type. The purpose of the remainder of this chapter is to explain the concept of the "ideal type" of organization that will be developed in more detail throughout Unit I.

FIGURE 1.2   The Functions Of Communication in Organizations

The Command Function	*The Relational Function*
Directing and limiting action	Creating and sustaining "unnatural" relationships
Maintaining adequate performance feedback	Negotiating boundaries of work relationships
Using publication and instructions	Determining and defining organizational roles

The Ambiguity-Management Function

Balancing organizational interests and self-interest
Managing precedents and traditions
Creating shared perspectives

TABLE 1.1   Organizational Types and Functions of Communication

Traditional	Human Relations and Resources	Contingency	
Low	Mixed	High	*Ambiguity Manangement*
High	Low or High	Mixed	*Command*
Low	High	Mixed	*Relational*

THE THEORY OF IDEAL TYPES

The ideas of the German sociologist Max Weber have been an important part of the study of organizations for decades. In America Weber is best known for his analysis of bureaucracy and bureaucratic organizations and for his discussion of the relationships between the characteristics of a culture and the uses of three different types of leadership—traditional, rational-legal, and charismatic authority. An equally important but less well-known component of Weber's work is the overall perspective that he took in studying organizations, the theory of "ideal types." This perspective rests on a particular set of assumptions about the nature of organizations and the appropriate means of studying them. His ideas provide a method through which employees can understand their organizations and make effective decisions about how to act in them.[6]

Weber's primary assumption was that organizations are composed of human actors who are enmeshed in interdependent activities and who continually are making decisions about how to act. Their choices are based on the meanings they attribute to the actions of others and on their interpretations of the organizational situations in which they are involved. When people enter formal organizations they bring with them a long history of monitoring their actions and the actions of others, of processing the information they obtain, and of choosing from among a number of options. People from a particular culture develop ways of monitoring, perceiving, and acting which are very much like one another. These perceptual "filters" are not identical, of course, because every individual has had unique experiences and has been part of a particular group of relationships with others. To some extent all members of a culture will have developed their own beliefs about what actions are "normal" and proper and about what meanings can be attached to different messages. However, within all this diversity and individuality lies a common core, a culture-bound framework for making sense out of people's actions and of deciding how to act in response. It is this common interpretive schema that defines a culture and distinguishes it from other cultures.

When employees from a particular culture come together within a formal organization they bring with them a common way of interpreting and responding to one another. But once they come together, their interpretive frameworks begin to change in subtle but important ways. Humans develop their interpretive frameworks through their experiences with other people. Relationships formed with people at work provide us with additional experience communicating with and making sense out of the communication of others. As a result, people drawn together in a formal organization begin to form new "mini-cultures" at work. These new ways of interpreting and acting both retain the basic framework of the employees' general culture and reflect the more specific frameworks that develop through working relationships. The complicated interrelationship that exists between the broad patterns of action that characterize a society and the patterns that develop within an organizational "culture" was the basis of Weber's theory of ideal types.

Weber argued that researchers can understand organizations if they can understand how actors (employees) in them interpret their surroundings and choose among the wide variety of different courses of action that are available to them. The study of organizations should begin with careful observations of the choices that employees make. Eventually these observations will reveal that different groups of employees use different sense-making schemes. Researchers will begin to recognize that members of some organizations typically interpret and act in ways which are different from those in which people act in other organizations. At some point these observers will begin to construct mental images of organizations whose employees share the same basic interpretive frameworks.

For example, employees may perceive that their organization is like an army—a formal structure with a clearly defined administrative staff which, for some as yet unexplained reasons, is obedient to commands issues by superiors. This type of organization would function properly only if it exhibited a number of necessary characteristics:

1. Each member of the staff occupies a specific position in the organization which has clearly defined, written duties and a clear place in the hierarchy of the organization.

2. Each person knows who the supervisor is, who the subordinates are, and how each of them fits into the heirarchy of the organization.

3. Each employee is selected on the basis of qualifications for the job, determined by some "objective" measure like educational background or a score on an examination; works under a contract which can be terminated if performance is inadequate; and can be promoted to a more responsible or higher paying position only on the basis of performance or seniority.[7]

Of course, there may be no "real" organization anywhere which has all these characteristics. Because this type of organization is an abstraction, which represents the perceptions of a number of different groups of employees, it exists only in the mind of the observer; it is an "idealized" example of a particular "type" of organization. It is an image of how a certain type of organization should be designed and how it ought to operate, not a summary of the characteristics and operations of a group of real organizations. But these mental conceptions of ideal types can be useful for researchers. If researchers or managers or any other members of a real organization understand how different types of organizations should be designed and operated, they can use that knowledge to detect and solve problems in their own organization. To do so, they would examine their organization, looking for features of its design or operation which do not correspond to the necessary features of the most relevant ideal type. Armed with perceptions of the essential features of a number of different types, the researcher or manager can discover cases in which the members of the organization do not choose to act in the ways that are necessary for the organization to function efficiently. Once these discrepancies are discovered the observer can make careful decisions about how to alter the organization or change the conditions under which the members make decisions about how to act. When these changes are implemented, the real organization will begin to operate more like the ideal type to which it is most closely related.

Unfortunately, these are very abstract ideas. A summary of them might increase their clarity. Weber's approach to the study of organizations rests on his theory of ideal types. It suggest that an observer can begin to understand how an organization operates by attempting to understand how its members interpret and respond to the situations they face in the organization. The observer then can design the organization to increase the probability that its members will choose to act in precisely those ways that are in its best interests. Employees always will make their own decisions about how to act. They are human, and consequently they will continually be involved in observing, processing, and responding to their surroundings. But they make their choices based on their interpretations of the situations they face. Both their perceptions and many of the key characteristics of the situations they face can be created strategically through communication. However, appropriate situations can be created only if the people who design organizations know the elements that must be included. The search for these necessary features begins with the construction of a group of ideal types of organizations. Observers ask "What kinds of organizations do employees' interpretive frameworks suggest are possible?" and then construct a list of features necessary for each of these "mythical" organizations to operate most efficiently. The most important features will involve the conditions under which employees will choose to *initiate* and *limit* their actions in desired ways. Among these necessary features will be certain characteristics of *organizational communication*. After observers have delineated the features of each ideal type of organization, they can begin to examine existing organizations, searching for points at which the real organizations differ from the ideal type. If they can detect important differences and determine the reasons for them, they can begin to isolate problems in the real organization and develop strategies for reducing them.

Of course, Weber assumed that most of the "observers" would be scholars involved in academic research. But his perspective can just as readily be used by employees. The social psychologist Fritz Heider once argued that human beings think like researchers think; that the same analytical tools that theorists use to understand the world around them can be used by other people to understand their environment and to decide how to act in the situations they face. Heider's notion that people are "naive theorists" suggest that all theoretical perspectives, of which Weber's theory of ideal types is one, are based on our interpretations of reality and can be used by us to understand the realities that surround us.[8] This assumption underlies the ideas that will be presented throughout the book. If readers can understand how communication functions in different types of organizations, they can examine their own organizations, determine how communication functions there, and choose the best communicative strategies for responding to the situations they face. Equipped with an understanding of how communication functions in different types of organizations and explanations of why communication functions differently in real organizations, readers can intelligently observe their own organizations and ask themselves these questions:

1. How does communication operate in my organization?
2. How must people, including myself, act in order for this organization to operate successfully?
3. Why do they sometimes act in those ways and sometimes act differently?
4. How can I act in order to make the organization work more effectively and to make the greatest contribution to its success and to my advancement?

These are the kinds of questions Weber suggested that researchers must ask; the answers provide the kind of information from which organizational theory is made. More important, they are the kinds of questions that members of organizations must ask themselves before they can choose the best communication strategies to use in different organizational situations. Through understanding how different types of organizations operate and why a particular organization functions differently, the "naive theorists" who make up an organization can adopt the best available communication strategies.

STRATEGIC ORGANIZATIONAL COMMUNICATION

For more than two thousand years communication scholars have argued that people communicate most effectively if they adopt the communication strategies that are most appropriate to the situations they face. Plato's intellectual rival, Gorgias, argued that knowing how to adapt to different situations was the only kind of knowledge that was available to human beings and, consequently, should be the focus of education. Some equivalent to Gorgias' concept of adaptation, an idea he labeled *kairos*, has been important to the study of human communication since his time.[9] Historically, training students in the art of adapting their communication to different situations has involved two steps: (1) teaching them to analyze the situations they face and choose the best strategies for those situations, and (2) equipping them with the repertoire of communication skills needed to implement those strategies. This book will concentrate on providing readers with the first kind of knowledge. It will

FIGURE 1.3   **Processes and Functions of Organizational Communication**

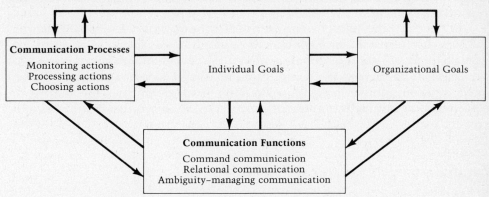

examine the myriad of features which make up organizational situations, explain the kinds of communication in which employees must be competent if they and their organizations are to function effectively, describe the strategies through which they can gain the information necessary for them to adapt intelligently to the situation they face at work, and provide guidelines for choosing the optimal communication strategies to use in those situations. Although it will discuss a variety of communication skills and suggest when and how those skills might be used by members of organizations, it will not attempt to provide detailed training in the skills themselves. Throughout the book the focus will be on explaining the strategic uses of organizational communication.

Unit I is composed of six chapters. This chapter has introduced the key concepts that underlie the remainder of the book. Chapters 2 through 6 will examine the communication processes necessary to the operation of three ideal types of organizations: traditional, human relations and resources, and systems-contingency. Each of these topics will be organized around Weber's theory of ideal types. They will begin with a description of the ideal type and the function that communication must play in it and conclude with analysis of how and why communication processes in real organizations often differ from those envisioned in the ideal type.

Unit II develops the idea of strategically selecting communication strategies in greater detail. Chapter 7 examines the relationships between organizational communication and organizational power. It will explain why power is a crucial element of all organizational situations and how members of organizations can analyze power relationship as a first step in choosing appropriate communicative strategies. Chapter 8 surveys the communicative skills that newly hired employees must use to make sense out of and manage the new situations that they face. Chapter 9 focuses on the analytical processes through which members of organizations can choose the most productive communicative strategies and introduces the idea that organizes the remainder of the book—the concept of the comic and tragic frames.

Chapters 9 through 12 examine three of the communication-related problems most often faced by members of modern organizations: the causes and management of organizational *conflict,* the sources and solutions to organizational *stress,* and the complicated relationships among *sex role stereotypes* and communication in organizations. In all three cases the focus is on understanding and adapting strategically to the situations that employees face.

The Purchasing Case

Jane Doe is an ambitious young "middle manager" who has been with her current firm for about a year. She is in charge of a unit which produces a key component used in the construction of the firm's most important product, a video game. The company is a very old-fashioned one in some respects. Everyone has clearly defined, written responsibilities and is expected to follow the chain of command when doing anything not clearly within one's job description. One morning Jane's best worker told her that one of the companies which supplies the materials used in the component made by their unit is about to file for bankruptcy and is willing to sell their remaining stock at one-half its usual price. Jane immediately called the supplier and learned that the tip was correct, but that it had contacted a number of other firms and planned to sell the material on a first-come-first-served basis. Jane then went to her supervisor, who told her that (1) the company's policy was that all purchases must go through the purchasing department, (2) purchasing would take two to three weeks to process the request, (3) Jane's unit did have enough discretionary money available to make the deal, and (4) since Jane's supervisor had had trouble with the supervisor of the purchasing department before, she would have to handle the situation.

If you were Jane,

1. What information would you try to gain before making a decision?
2. How would you go about getting it?
3. How would you make the decision?
4. How would you communicate your decision to the people involved?
5. Why would you do these things in those ways?

Notes

1.   These conclusions are supported by the results of a series of surveys of college graduates who majored in speech communication that were recently conducted by the Speech Communication Association and the International Communication Association.

2.   Cal Downs and Charles Conrad, "A Critical Incident Study of Effective Subordinancy," *Journal of Business Communication*, 19 (1982), 27–38.

3.   This perspective has been developed most effectively by Karl Weick, *The Social Psychology of Organizing*, 2nd ed. (Reading, Mass: Addison-Wesley, 1979).

4.   Bonnie Johnson has presented similar ideas in *Communication: the Process of Organizing* (Boston: Allyn & Bacon, 1977).

5.   James March and Johan Olsen, *Ambiguity and Choice in Organizations* (Bergen: Universitetsforlaget, 1979).

6.   Weber's concept of bureaucracy will be explained further in Chapter 2; his discussion of "authority" will be summarized in Chapter 5. His concept of ideal types is explained most clearly

in Robert McPhee, "An Ideal-type 'Theory' of Organizational Coalitions" (paper presented at the Conference on Interpretive Approaches to Organizational Communication, Salt Lake City, 1981), and Stewart Clegg, *Power, Rule and Domination* (London: Routledge and Kegan Paul, 1975). The assumption that organizations are made up of complex connections of human actors is central to a number of contemporary views of organizations. The most important of these perspectives are explained in Anthony Giddens, *Central Problems in Social Theory* (Berkeley: University of California Press, 1979), and Stewart Clegg, *The Theory of Power and Organizations* (London: Routledge and Kegan Paul, 1979).

7.   These are necessary features of Weber's ideal bureaucratic organization. They are summarized in Morton Albrow, *Bureaucracy* (London: Pall Mall, 1970).

8.   Fritz Heider, *The Psychology of Interpersonal Relations* (New York: John Wiley, 1958).

9.   George Kennedy, *Classical Rhetoric in Its Christian and Secular Traditions from Ancient to Modern Times* (Chapel Hill: University of North Carolina Press, 1980).

2

The Traditional Type of Organization

THE DEVELOPMENT OF THE TRADITIONAL IDEAL TYPE
Frederick Taylor and Scientific Management
The Bureaucratic Theorists

NECESSARY CHARACTERISTICS OF THE TRADITIONAL TYPE OF ORGANIZATION

PROBLEMS IN MODERN TRADITIONAL ORGANIZATIONS

POSTSCRIPT: "TAKE THIS JOB AND SHOVE IT"

The foreman should never be authorized to enforce his discipline with the whips if he can accomplish the result with words. **—Varro of Rome, c. 100** B.C.

If the words of command are not clear and distinct, if orders are not thoroughly understood, the general is to blame. **—Sun Tzu of China, 500** B.C.

One shall put every petition in writing, not permitting that he [a worker] petition orally. **—Instructions to Egyptian managers, c. 2000** B.C.

As these ancient comments suggest, neither the study of organizations nor of communication in organizations are terribly new topics. By the time human beings had joined together into families and clans, they had become involved in the primitive economic activities of hunting and gathering, both of which required them to communicate with other workers. Still later, after humans had become farmers, they developed more complex organizations with more complicated communication needs. With farming came villages and the need to govern groups of people; with villages came the concepts of citizenship and community welfare, which created the dual needs of defense and the successful management of the village's economy.

23

As villages became city-states, it became necessary for their managers to plan the operation of the society and to keep permanent records of the rules and procedures that they developed. The oldest written documents still in existence deal with three topics—religon, management, and government—a combination which makes great sense when one realizes that the earliest managers also were governors and priests. In fact, the oldest written documents yet discovered are 5,000-year-old Sumerian "balance sheets," scripts which recorded financial transactions and kept track of the wealth and debts of citizens. The Sumerian manager-priests believed that their souls would continue to live after their deaths; they evidently hoped that written communication would allow their wealth to live on. As ancient religious and political civilizations grew and expanded, their needs for effective economic organizations and effective organizational communication multiplied. As early as 2000 B.C., leaders recognized the importance of communication. Pharoah Ptah-hotep instructed his sons and the managers who worked for him in the importance of effective listening skills, the need actively to seek advice and information from their subordinates, the importance of "staying informed" about what was taking place around them, and the necessity of clearly explaining each worker's tasks and documenting these instructions in writing. The Chinese emperors Yao and Shun (c. 2300 B.C.) also actively searched for ways of opening communication channels between themselves and the peasants in the countryside and advocated consulting their subordinates about the problems faced by the government. By the time of Christ, Greek and Roman scholars had at least suggested many of the key concepts of modern organizational theory and organizational communication theory. But it was the growth of the nation-state and the mercantile system which created separate roles for governors, managers, and priests, and it was the large and complex firms of the Industrial Revolution which led to the first careful studies of formal organizations.[1]

Before the Industrial Revolution, the Western world was dominated by a domestic system of production. Small groups of workers, almost always families, obtained some necessary equipment and produced something (usually textiles) for a small local market. Since every member of these family organizations performed simple, repetitive tasks within sight of every other member, the communication needs of these "organizations" were minimal. Coordinating the activities of family members was simple: technological advancement and sophisticated managerial techniques were neither needed nor possible. But eventually these family businesses started to "put out" their products, contracting with local merchants to purchase their goods at an agreed-upon price. At some point these merchants started to provide the families with both the raw materials they needed to make their products and with a market for their finished goods. Family entrepreneurs had become employees. They no longer were involved in a cooperative family enterprise in which each member shared profits and losses. Instead they were "hired help" whose interests coincided with those of their employers only to a limited degree. They soon learned they could increase their profits by weaving their cloth less tightly. This minor change in quality allowed them to work faster, producing more cloth, *and* to sell the raw materials they saved on the black market. In spite of strict laws against it, this kind of fraud became so widespread that it ended the "putting-out" system.

The history of the putting-out system is important because it reveals three concepts central to the "traditional" type of organization: (1) All other things being equal, employees will act in ways which are consistent with what they perceive is their own self-interest; (2) in order to be successful, organizations must be able to make workers *accountable* for both the quantity and quality of their output; and (3) supervisors must be able to obtain accurate and reliable information about the activities of their subordinates.

With the invention of power-driven machinery, home production was replaced very rapidly by large factories. The cost of the new machinery was far beyond all but a few families, and improvements in transportation enabled factories to have access to a large enough market for all their production. Although very little attention was paid to management in these early factories, the concepts of division of labor, planning, job design, controlling employees, creating acceptable working conditions, and rewarding employees in ways which would increase their productivity were discussed by the managers of the late 1700s. The first systematic design of an organization took place during an expansion of the Soho Engineering Foundary in Great Britain in 1800. Equipment purchases, factory layout, job design, and incentive systems all were based on carefully obtained information. One of the primary concerns of the designers of the Soho plant was worker's *performance* and *accountability*. A very detailed accounting system was created so that supervisors could have access to accurate and up-to-date *information* about the performance of their subordinates. In addition, a combination of weekly wages and bonuses based on the number of items produced by each worker was designed and implemented. Because this wage system was very complicated, the designers realized that it would be successful only if it could be translated into a formula simple enough to be *easily and clearly communicated to workers*. Thus, as early as 1800, practicing managers recognized that workers' *accountability* could be achieved only if organizations had systems of effective command communication. Supervisors must be able to make their subordinates understand what their jobs entail, how the jobs are to be done, and how they will be rewarded for performing their tasks well. These rudimentary concepts of management and task-related organizational communication subsequently were developed in greater detail by advocates of the traditional type of organization.

The remaining sections of this chapter will summarize the development of the traditional type of organization, describe the factors necessary for traditional organizations to succeed, and explain why modern traditional organizations find it difficult to create and sustain these necessary features. Chapter 3 will examine the aspects of communication necessary for traditional organizations to function effectively and explain why it is difficult for them to maintain communication at adequate levels of effectiveness.

THE DEVELOPMENT OF THE TRADITIONAL IDEAL TYPE

At the beginning of the twentieth century large, complex organizations still were relatively new. The people who owned and operated these organizations had few reliable models available on which they could base their managerial decisions. Of course, each of them had had some experience in business and could manage by hunch or intuition. They also could try to apply some lessons that had been learned by commanders of military units, not because their organizations were like armies but because armies were virtually the only kind of large, complex organizations which existed prior to the Industrial Revolution. However, neither of these guidelines was adequate. Individual managers' past experiences often provided distorted methods for coping with current situations. People's memories often omit or redefine their failures and over-emphasize their successes. Even if their memories were both objective and accurate, the strategies and practices that had succeeded in one situation might be wholly inappropriate to new situations. Similarly, the lessons learned in military organizations had only a limited application to the textile factories of the Industrial Revolution. Even in 1900 flogging workers was frowned on and deserters from New England factories rarely were punished by death. Military discipline and much of military operations simply did not fit the factory situation.

Armed with little reliable information, managers often acted in ways which were arbitrary and capricious. Their treatment of workers often, perhaps even usually, was inhumane by today's standards. Their decision making suffered from a lack of concern for efficiency, a virtual absence of reliable information, and an ever-present ability to blame the workers for the disastrous outcomes of their intuitively correct but nonetheless foolish decisions. The early organizational theorists developed ideas and methods which were designed to eliminate the causes of poor decision making and improve the quality of labor-management relations.

A large number of people were involved in these efforts. In general they can be placed into one of two groups. One group, the "scientific managers," were concerned with improving organizations "from the bottom up." They focused their attention on the tasks being performed by production workers at the bottom of the organizational hierarchy and on the way that those workers were treated by their supervisors. The second group, the "bureaucratic theorists," attempted to improve organizations "from the top down." They concentrated on the activities of employees who were not directly involved in production but instead had sizeable administrative responsibilities. Both groups had the same primary concern—replacing the arbitrary, capricious, and intuitive practices of contemporary organizations with systematically designed, objective, fair, and equitable systems of management and supervision. The traditional type of organization they envisioned was a carefully designed alternative to the inefficient and inhumane operations of the complex organizations which existed in their day.

Frederick Taylor and Scientific Management

Frederick Taylor was a practicing manager whose observations of the unfairness and inefficiencies of the factories in which he worked led him to think seriously about the nature of organizations and the role of management and manager-employee relationships.

> He saw, for example, that management had no clear concept of worker-management responsibilities; that virtually no effective work standards were applied; that no incentive was used to improve labor's performance . . . that managerial decisions were based on hunch, intuition, past experience, or rule-of-thumb evaluations . . . that workers were ineptly placed at tasks for which they had little or no ability or aptitude; and, finally, that management apparently disregarded the obvious truth that excellence in performance and operation would mean a reward to both management and labor.
>
> It was at this time, too, that he experienced the typical struggle between foremen and workers over the quantity of output. At first he attempted to employ the usual methods of the time—some persuasion and a lot of force—with the usual outcome of bitterness, resentment, and an air of division and struggle.[2]

Probably the most striking problem Taylor observed was the phenomenon of "systematic soldiering." Most of the factories of Taylor's time employed some kind of loosely structured "piece-rate" incentive system—workers were paid bonuses for producing above a certain standard rate and/or were paid a wage based on their individual output. Frequently, however, these systems worked so well that some employees were being paid more than other workers in a particular geographic area. Employers responded to this difference by cutting the piece rates that they paid their employees in order to bring their workers' incomes back into line with the typical wage rates of the area. Thus, in the long run, workers were "rewarded" for their increased output by having to work harder to gain the same income. Seeing this, the workers responded to rate cutting by reducing their effort to the minimal acceptable standard. As Taylor explained, the worker "accepts the cut, but he sees to it that he never makes enough . . . to get another cut." In this way, workers became "soldiers," exer-

FIGURE 2.1 Systematic Soldiering

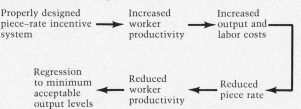

ting only the minimum amount of effort and creativity necessary to keep their jobs. The workers did so because it was in their best interests to do so. With rate cutting, "soldiering" maximizes workers' income while minimizing their effort.

Based on a long series of observations, Taylor developed a theory of management for production-oriented firms which sought to reduce the inefficiencies of poorly designed organizations *and* increase the motivation of workers. His model was based on two concepts: (1) a "complete mental revolution," a total change in attitudes about management and labor-management relations; and (2) a systematic and scientific procedure for designing organizations and employees' reward systems.

Taylor's "Great Mental Revolution" Three attitudes formed the basis of Taylor's great mental revolution. The first was that managers were responsible for carefully designing each component of their organizations in accordance with information gained through systematic and careful research. Taylor's contemporaries typically made decisions based on their beliefs about how something had "always" been done. Taylor's ideas were radical in two ways: They asserted that "scientific" principles of experiment and analysis should replace intuition, and they implied that managers were at least as responsible for the success or failure of an organization as were their workers.

Taylor's second key concept was that businesses would prosper, not by artificially limiting employees' wages, but by employing systems which appropriately increased their earnings. He reasoned that workers, like anyone else, make sensible choices about how to act based on their perceptions of their own self-interests. Since it always is in their self-interests to do everything possible to maximize their income while minimizing their effort, managers had a sensible basis on which to design wage systems. Managers should determine the most efficient ways of performing the tasks required of their units, encourage their workers to perform their tasks in precisely those ways, and reward them with increased income and greater status when they used those means to increase their output.

The final, most important, and least remembered concept in Taylor's model was the creation of a cooperative relationship between labor and management. Through the increased efficiency that would result from scientifically designed tasks, organizations, and reward systems, firms would be able to increase the income of *all* their employees and to reduce their prices, thus benefitting all consumers. When a large number of firms employed the principles of "scientific management," the prices of most consumer goods would be reduced, the real incomes of all citizens would be increased, and the nation's standard of living would improve. Since cooperation between labor and management thus would lead directly to increased economic benefits to both groups, their own self-interests would lead to a reduction of the intense labor-management hostility that characterized organizations of Taylor's time. Taylor expressed this concern most clearly in a speech delivered in 1915, two weeks before his death:

To the workman has come, practically right off as soon as scientific management is introduced, an increase in wages amounting from 33 to 100 percent, and yet that is not the greatest good that comes to the workman from scientific management. The great good comes from the fact that, under scientific management, they look upon their employers as the best friends they have in the world. . . . The workmen, after many object lessons, come to see and the management come to see that this surplus can be made so great, providing both sides will stop pulling apart, will stop their fighting and will push as hard as they can to get as cheap an output as possible, that there is no reason to quarrel. Each side can get more than ever before. The acknowledgement of this fact represents a complete mental revolution.[3]

During the brief time immediately after firms employed scientific management, Taylor's concept of labor-management cooperation was realized. But during the 1930s this situation changed, primarily because of the success of his system. Taylor had assumed that as firms became more efficient, their income "pie" would grow and thus the piece of the pie that was distributed to each employee also would increase in size. But as "scientifically managed" firms became more successful, workers began to demand a larger proportion of the income pie. Issues over the proper distribution of increased profits eventually reduced the labor-management harmony that had characterized early uses of scientific management and led to intense opposition to Taylor's ideas by organized labor.

These concepts—scientific design of organizations, motivation through increased economic rewards and individual self-interest, and cooperation between labor and management—formed the basis of Taylor's new theory of organizations. He believed that his ideas could be implemented through four techniques, each of which depended on successful communication between supervisors and workers. Unfortunately, over time Taylor's techniques were used by managers who had not been part of his "mental revolution" and who failed to realize that effective superior-subordinate communication was essential for the successful use of those techniques.

Implementing Scientific Management: Taylor's Four Principles Taylor's first principle involved *scientific job design*. Workers, he reasoned, had a great storehouse of knowledge about how tasks could be most efficiently accomplished. Through past experience they had learned that some ways of performing a task required less time and effort than did other ways. But their knowledge was neither refined nor complete. They had been given little opportunity to experiment with different methods and had had little chance to share their information with other workers or with their supervisors. Scientific job design begins when supervisors seek out the store of knowledge possessed by their subordinates. It is completed when they use all that knowledge to design scientifically their subordinates' tasks so that the tasks can be accomplished with minimum time and effort. They then refined the design of the tasks through a process of "time-motion study," in which the supervisor or a consultant carefully observed workers completing each task, broke the process down into its elements or motions, and then redesigned it so that the number of movements necessary to complete the task was minimized. Partly because Taylor was able to use the time-motion study to redesign the relatively simple task of shoveling coal in a way which remarkably increased worker efficiency, and partly because his successors, Frank and Lillian Gilbreth, successfully applied the technique to a wide variety of tasks, time-motion studies became the most widely used of Taylor's ideas. However, the technique eventually was used without consulting workers, often by outside consultants who were perceived by the workers as a threat to their jobs. Both in the 1930s and today time-motion studies often were and are resisted by workers, especially when there is a lack of trust in management. However, if these studies are used in the way that Taylor suggested, in a context of openness and consultation with workers, very little employee resistance is encountered.[4]

Taylor's second principle was the *scientific selection* of workers. Managers were responsible for carefully studying their workers in an attempt to determine the characteristics which made it easiest for an individual to perform a particular task. They then were to hire workers based solely on the extent to which they possess those characteristics. Workers who were too short or too tall, too weak or too strong, would not be placed in jobs which were difficult for them to perform.

Taylor labeled his third principle "Bringing Together the Science and the Man." The concept had two components: training workers adequately and rewarding them for their productivity. Selection and training would equip workers with the capacity to feel a sense of *achievement* from their work; incentive systems would allow them to gain economic and status-related rewards from their work. Two excerpts from Taylor's 1915 speech explain this principle:

> Select and train your workmen all you may, but unless there is some one who will make the men and science come together, they will stay apart. The "make" involves a great many elements. They are not all disagreeable elements. The most important and largest way of "making" is to do something nice for the man who you wish to make come together with the science. Offer him a plum, something that is worthwhile. There are many plums offered to those who come under scientific management—better treatment, more kindly treatment, more consideration of their wishes, and an opportunity for them to express their wants freely. That is one side of the "make." An equally important side is, whenever a man will not do what he ought, to either make him do it or stop it. If he will not do it, let him get out. I am not talking of any mollycoddle. Let me disabuse your minds of any opinion that scientific management is a mollycoddle scheme. . . . Under the new system, if a man falls down, the presumption is that it is our fault at first, that we probably have not taught the man

right, have not given him a fair show, have not spent time enough in showing him how to do his work. . . . Under the new, the teacher [supervisor] is welcomed; his is not an enemy but a friend. He comes there to help the man get bigger wages, to show him how to do something.[5]

Through a *combination* of careful selection, effective communication of the best means of completing a task (training), supportive *and* directive supervisory communication, and adequate incentives, both workers' productivity and labor-management cooperation could be enhanced.

Taylor's final principle concerned division of work. Before Taylor, workers were assumed to be responsible for any errors or inefficiencies. Taylor argued that workers and managers were partners in the production process, that errors and inefficiency were the responsibilities of both groups, and that when managers made mistakes, workers had just as much right to demand improvement as managers did when workers made errors. He envisioned the creation of a team relationship between labor and management which would be characterized by democracy and cooperation. Of course, the cooperation was to be based on the mutual self-interest and economic reward that came from increased organizational efficiency. Techniques like time-motion studies,

FIGURE 2.2   Dimensions of Scientific Management

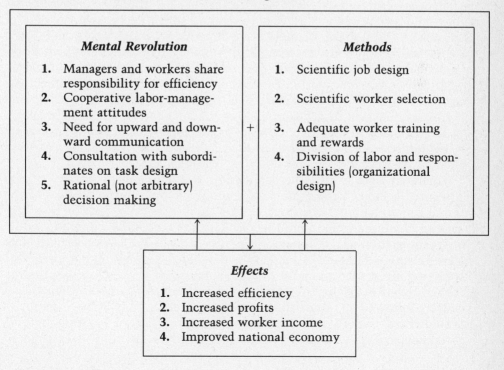

Mental Revolution

1. Managers and workers share responsibility for efficiency
2. Cooperative labor-management attitudes
3. Need for upward and downward communication
4. Consultation with subordinates on task design
5. Rational (not arbitrary) decision making

\+

Methods

1. Scientific job design
2. Scientific worker selection
3. Adequate worker training and rewards
4. Division of labor and responsibilities (organizational design)

Effects

1. Increased efficiency
2. Increased profits
3. Increased worker income
4. Improved national economy

scientific selection of workers, and rational decision making by supervisors were important elements of scientific management. But the techniques were to be implemented within an organizational context which was humane, democratic, efficient, and rewarding.

Unfortunately, most modern descriptions of Taylor and his system are not very flattering. He often is depicted as a cold and uncaring, almost an inhumane, autocrat who viewed workers as subhuman cogs in a giant industrial machine who cared only about economic gain. Taylorism often is viewed as a dishonest system which allows unscrupulous managers to manipulate and dehumanize their workers. Admittedly, a large number of managers used Taylor's techniques in manipulative and dehumanizing ways. But Taylor's system was designed to reduce the arbitrary, unfair, and capricious treatment of workers that characterized the organizations of his era. The combination of selection, training, and rewards that he proposed was intended to meet workers' needs for a sense of achievement, social status, *and* economic success and security. Taylor's combination of centralized decision making, shared rewards, efficient organizational design, and active task-related communication between labor and management made scientific management attractive to many political and business leaders who were unquestionably concerned with the well-being of workers. One of the earliest converts to Taylorism was the Russian revolutionary V. I. Lenin. World War I and the Bolshevik revolution had virtually destroyed the Russian economy. Although Lenin believed that centralized government would be unnecessary in a Communist state and eventually would "wither away," he also recognized that effective management of businesses was vital to the recovery of the Russian economy. Based on Taylor's concepts, Lenin proposed a doctrine of "democratic centrism," in which workers provided task-related information to a centralized group of managers through the Communist party. Taylorism was acceptable to Lenin precisely *because* it combined centralized decision making, economic efficiency, and workers' participation in decision making. Unfortunately, scientific management largely failed in the Soviet Union, primarily because Lenin's successors were so suspicious of all American ideas.[6] Eventually, Taylor's ideas were resisted by Western workers for different reasons.

American labor fought the application of Taylor's ideas, partly because they wanted a larger proportion of the profit pie and partly because of the distorted way in which Taylor's successors applied his system. The most important problems stemmed from their tendency to accept his techniques while rejecting the mental revolution on which they were based. Taylor showed great concern for the well-being of his employees. His followers did not share this concern and often tried to apply the techniques that he developed within an unchanged labor-management atmosphere. For example, time-motion studies often were followed by rate cutting, which led to the same kinds of hostilities and "soldiering" that Taylor had hoped to eliminate.[7] Taylor's *system*, with its focus on cooperation and open yet controlled communication—was replaced with the *techniques* he advocated. Without the system and the values it included, economic reward systems became ways to manipulate workers, standardization of tasks led to workers being treated as less than human parts of the production machine, and time-motion studies were used to benefit management alone. One of the most consistently recurring paradoxes of new theories about organizations and organizational communication is that people often try to apply the techniques included in the theories while refusing to accept the beliefs and values that are necessary elements of them.

The Bureaucratic Theorists

Taylor and the scientific management group primarily were concerned with making the people at the bottom of their organizations more efficient and productive. Other theorists of Taylor's generation were concerned with the people at the "top" of the organization, the administrative staff. The most important of these theorists were Henri Fayol and Max Weber. Fayol was a contemporary of Taylor, but his ideas largely were overlooked for three decades because of the popularity of Taylor's model. His work is important because it provides the first broad and general theory of management and because it provides a very early analysis of the functions of communication in complex organizations.

Henri Fayol Fayol argued that managing is a normal and universal human activity. The administration of any organization includes six key activities, he argued, the last of which is the most important:

1. Regulating technical processes
2. Purchasing and marketing
3. Obtaining and using capital
4. Protecting employees and property
5. Accounting
6. Managing

"Managing" consists of five key activities, *planning, organizing, commanding, coordinating,* and *controlling.* Although Fayol did not view planning as a communicative activity, he did recognize that it depends on the availability of timely and accurate information. The four other elements of managing directly involve communication:

> *Organizing* includes explaining employees' duties clearly, controlling the use of written communication, and providing clear and effective statements of managerial decisions.
> *Commanding* involves conducting periodic assessments of the organization's operation through systems of performance feedback (usually

aided by organizational charts) and conducting conferences with employees in order to *direct* and *focus* their efforts.

Coordinating depends on making certain that all employees understand the nature and limits of their responsibilities.

Controlling involves administering rewards and punishments and persuading employees that their rewards are based on the quality of their performance.

Today Fayol is best known for two additional ideas: the hierarchical (pyramid-shaped) organization chart, with its concept of vertical communication following the chain of command, and a modification of this chart, typically called "Fayol's bridge."

In the organization that Fayol envisioned, communication was to be task-oriented, relatively open between supervisors and their subordinates (of which there usually were five or six), and normally restricted to the chain of command, especially if the communication involved people other than a sub-

FIGURE 2.3   Chart of a Traditional Organization with Fayol's Bridge

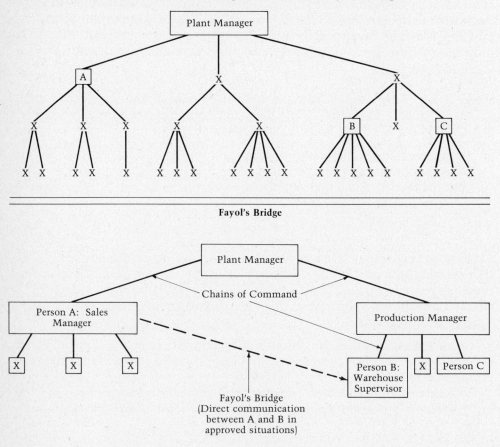

ordinate and immediate supervisor. However, Fayol recognized that there are times when following the chain of command is not wise. For instance, people may face crises in which they need information from other employees who are located in other parts of the organization's hierarchy. By the time a request for information reaches the other person and a response is received through "normal" channels, it might be too late to use the information. The crisis would have passed without the subordinate taking any action. Fayol suggested that in times of legitimate crisis, employees should be allowed to bypass the chain of command and communicate directly with other employees. They could form a temporary communication "bridge" across the formal hierarchy of the organization. Supervisors would still be able to limit and control their subordinates' communication, but the "bridge" also would allow employees to gain and transmit information rapidly during crises.

Fayol recognized that even in formal hierarchical, traditional organizations, effective and efficient communication is essential to their operation. He believed that "once an enterprise was organized, its employees would need commands [communications] from the manager to know what and how to perform; that their actions and functions required managerial coordination to bind and harmonize their efforts; and finally, that the manager would of necessity have to control their activities."[8]

Max Weber Weber primarily was interested in the relationships between a culture and the institutions—religious, political, and economic—that its members create. Although he believed that societies and their organizations are alike in many ways, their most important similarities involve (1) the ways in which they are structured, (2) the processes through which their members make decisions, and (3) the means through which their members' activities are influenced and controlled. As was suggested in Chapter 1, today Weber is known primarily for his lengthy discussions of the type of organization which seemed to him to best "fit" the cultures of Western democracies, the "bureaucratic" organization. [9]

Weber observed that

1. Bureaucracies are composed of a complex *matrix of formal positions* which are defined by a group of *specialized duties* for which their occupants are *selected* on the basis of their *technical expertise* and are *evaluated* by their supervisors based on their *performance* in carrying out their duties.

2. Some of these positions involve the actual *production* of the goods or services sold by the firm; others are *administrative staff* positions whose occupants are responsible for maintaining the organization, particularly its *lines of communication.*

3. These positions are arranged in a *hierarchy*, usually shaped like a pyramid, in which the supervisors are directly responsible to the supervisor directly above for their actions and for those of their immediate subordinates. They also are responsible for ensuring a free flow of job-related information from their subordinates to their supervisor.

Officers are to base decisions on their rational assessment of the facts of a particular case. Their decisions are to be guided *solely* by the *written policies* and rules of the organization. They are to maintain impersonal and detached relationships with their clients, supervisor, and subordinates so that they will be able to keep their personal feelings or concerns from biasing their decisions. All actions, decisions, and rules are formulated and recorded in writing, even when it is normal or even necessary to carry on oral discussions. Employees maintain a contract with their organization which specifies that they will receive a salary (and usually a pension) in exchange for carrying out their duties and promises that they will be promoted when their performance and/or seniority warrants such action. Although employees may terminate the contract at any time, they gain tenure in the organization after successfully completing a probationary period. As long as they perform their duties adequately, they can expect to remain in the organization until they choose to retire.

Employees' actions are controlled by the formal and informal rules of the organization. Weber noted that as people mature, they acquire a variety of beliefs through communication with their parents and other members of their society. These beliefs form the basis of their decisions about how to respond to the commands they are given by others. In some cultures, people believe that the hierarchies and hierarchical relationships which exist in their society are legitimate because they "always" have existed. In these societies and in the organizations which are part of them, some people are dominant and others are subordinate because they have inherited a specific position in the hierarchy. The subordinate people choose to follow the instructions of their superiors because their positions in the society (organization) make it legitimate for them to do so and illegitimate for them to do otherwise. "Children, obey your parents" and "Because I [parent] said so" are commands which, as they typically are interpreted in Judeo-Christian cultures, succeed because of the child's belief that the parent's position is a sufficient reason to comply with the command. This *traditional authority*, Weber's first kind of authority, works well in stable, hierarchical cultures and organizations. It is less successful when it leads supervisors to become so secure in their positions that they become arbitrary and capricious in their treatment of their subordinates or when the society is in a process of change. The character Tevye in *Fiddler on the Roof* found life frustrating when his daughters decided to ignore this "traditional" base of authority and make decisions and adopt beliefs which he opposed. Tevye's Russia was in the midst of radical social change, a change which upset traditional superior-subordinate relationships and undermined traditional authority. When he sang "Tradition," Tevye reflected his reliance on a form of authority which no longer was relevant; when he said "on the other hand," he reflected his recognition that his culture was making fundamental changes.

In other situations and cultures, people respond to the commands of leaders who seem to them to embody some divine or supernatural force. Weber's second form of authority, charismatic authority, is most effective with subordinates who perceive that the mission of an organization is to change society; it is an inappropriate source of influence with people who are involved in mundane, day-to-day tasks of running a bureaucracy.

Weber's third kind of authority, that on which bureaucratic organizations are based, relies on subordinates' willingness to obey established rules of behavior. Individuals learn that these rules are necessary for the success of their organization and that the rules protect them from arbitrary or harmful treatment by their superiors. These are organizations or societies which are "societies of law, not men." A formal, impersonal (and thus objective), written code of rules forms the basis of legal authority. This form of influence is legitimized by the contracts employees form with their organization and by the pressures imposed by other members who have accepted the rules and act in accordance with them. Although supervisors in bureaucracies may have other sources of influence over the actions of their subordinates, *technical rules* and *group norms* legitimize their commands.

Weber's bureaucratic ideal type of organization, with its tight hierarchy, limited communication, and legal, written rules of action rapidly became the model for governmental agencies and formal organizations. Although it is clear that no real organizations correspond *perfectly* to the ideal described by Taylor, Fayol, and Weber, it also is clear that the model has been applied so often that new employees entering an American organization today will find themselves in a situation which resembles the traditional ideal in many important respects. Procedures and policies will be documented in writing, job-related communication will flow through the chain of command, positions will require specialized skills and will be filled at least in part because applicants possess a particular kind of expertise, and decision making will be centralized near the top of the organization. Consequently, understanding the characteristics of this type of organization and being able to anticipate and respond appropriately to the communicative problems which typically occur there will be crucial to the success and advancement of most new employees. Using the organizational structure suggested by Weber's theory of ideal types, the remainder of this chapter and Chapter 3 is designed to provide the information necessary for understanding and adapting to communication in traditional organizations.

NECESSARY CHARACTERISTICS OF THE TRADITIONAL TYPE OF ORGANIZATION

Weber suggested that an organization designed in accordance with any particular ideal must possess a number of key characteristics if it is to succeed. If the ideas of the scientific managers and the traditional organizational theorists are combined—as they were on a grandiose scale by practicing managers after 1920—four features are necessary for success:

1. There will be workers available to the organization who
    a. Expect and are satisfied by jobs which fulfill their economic needs and provide only limited opportunity to develop the status and

feelings of achievement that come from the successful completion of challenging tasks

b. Expect to spend most of their careers in the same firm because they have few adequate alternatives available elsewhere

c. Realize that they can readily be replaced by other workers who can easily be recruited from the lower levels of their firms or from the external labor force.

2. Supervisors will maintain effective working relationships with their subordinates, create and sustain open channels of task-related communication, and treat their subordinates in a fair and objective manner consistent with the policies, procedures, rules, and reward systems of the organization.

3. Thinking activities (coordination and planning) will be isolated at the top of the organization, and only the *minimum necessary* amount of independence and autonomy will be allowed employees at the bottom of the hierarchy.

4. Each employee will be assigned routine and specialized tasks; each supervisor will be responsible for seeing that subordinates perform their assigned tasks exactly as they are designed to be done.

As long as the culture from which an organization draws its employees "creates" a pool of potential employees with these characteristics, traditional organizations can expect to have a relatively prosperous, satisfied, and productive labor force. As long as the managers within a traditional organization make wise strategic decisions, maintain the organization's design, and sustain appropriate kinds of relationships with their subordinates, they can expect their organizations to operate efficiently and productively. However, if either the culture changes or the operations of their organizations begin to depart from the traditional ideal, problems will develop.

PROBLEMS IN MODERN TRADITIONAL ORGANIZATIONS

Some of the problems facing today's organizations stem from improper applications of the traditional model. Even in Taylor's time supervisors often abused the techniques of scientific management. Favoritism, arbitrary and unfair treatment, and inefficiencies combined to increase labor-management hostility. As Taylor and Weber both recognized, without labor-management cooperation based on shared economic interests and impartial and equitable treatment, traditional organizations are inherently unstable and potentially inefficient creations.

Other problems result from the traditional model itself.[10] Some of these stem from changes that have taken place in the cultures of the Western democracies since 1945, the most important of which involves the education of workers. In Taylor's day only a small proportion of the work force had completed even eight years of formal education. Today only a tiny proportion has *not* completed eight years of formal schooling. Most have finished high school, and a very large percentage have college degrees. In August 1983, one-quarter of employed Americans held bachelor's degrees, the first time in history that such a high proportion of the work force had college educations. Highly educated workers expect to have jobs which utilize their creative talents and training in decision making. They have been taught to be concerned with noneconomic rewards, thus presenting new motivational challenges to supervisors. Supervisors already understand the implications of these changes. One supervisor from General Motors exclaimed, "The old-type tactics of being a supervisor don't work with these guys. In the past a man didn't need much motivation to do a job like this—the paycheck took care of that. But these guys, they're different."[11] During the same forty years, other social changes have occurred. A smaller and smaller proportion of the population is involved in production tasks. Today only about 20 percent actually make consumable goods; the remainder produce services or are involved in administrative activities. In many Western democracies (although this is less the case in the United States), the specter of unemployment is not particularly threatening. Social support programs promise at least a tolerable standard of living for temporarily unemployed persons.[12] One of the most popular country music tunes of the 1970s reflected this change in circumstance. Hundreds of workers at all levels were both alienated and secure enough to tell their bosses to "take this job and shove it. I ain't workin' here no more."

In all Western democracies a variety of entrance barriers—requirements for union membership, state or professional licensing requirements, active and passive discrimination against women and members of minority groups—reduce the "replaceability" of employees of all ranks and specialities. In addition changes in social norms and values have reduced the influence granted to supervisors because of their formal rank or position. Increased geographic and career mobility have eliminated the expectation that an individual employee will spend an entire career in the same organization. In short, the features which made traditional organizations appropriate for Western democracies rapidly are disappearing. As a result job satisfaction and productivity are now quite low; absenteeism and voluntary turnover are rapidly growing problems, especially among educated but underemployed workers.[13]

During this era of tremendous social and economic change, traditional organizations have responded in ways which further complicate their situations. They rely on two rather simple techniques for both efficient production and control of their employees. The most important of these is scientific job design, the process of dividing complex tasks into their component steps and selecting and training employees for these small, simple tasks. When these tasks are arranged in sequential steps, as in the "miracle" of Henry Ford's assembly line, efficiency is maximized. As an added benefit, control is enhanced. Because workers perform tasks which require few skills, they can be easily replaced and must adjust the pace of their activities to the pace of the machine. Arrayed along an assembly line, they are given little or no opportunity to communicate with one another. This keeps them from sharing grievances, comparing the way they are treated by management, or making plans for collective action.[14] By the mid-1960s most production workers were involved in this kind of routine, repetitive, "de-skilled" activity. By the mid-1980s most white-collar workers will be involved in similar jobs.

Although "de-skilling" increases productivity for a time, it also decreases job satisfaction and increases labor-management hostility. For decades organizations attempted to offset this growing dissatisfaction by relying more heavily on the second technique of increasing productivity and control in traditional organizations, economic reward systems. It is not accidental that the most routinized sectors of our economy, automobile manufacturing, for example, pay the highest average wage rates. High wages may temporarily increase both job satisfaction and control (because highly paid workers face certain reductions in their standard of living if they quit, and unemployed workers see those jobs as being highly attractive). Eventually they also tend to reduce profits, forcing management to search for ways to increase productivity. However, traditional organizations rely on technological advances and segmentation of tasks for increased productivity. The use of technological advances requires capital; task segmentation creates workers' frustrations, which can only be offset within the traditional model by increased economic rewards. Eventually tasks become so routinized that productivity based reward systems no longer make sense, since it is the speed of the assembly line rather than the employees' efforts that determines output. At some point performance-based reward systems tend to be replaced by hourly wage systems, which separate performance and rewards. Wage rates continue to escalate; job satisfaction and productivity continue to decline. Firms begin to face production costs so great that their products and services will be competitive only in a market that is made up exclusively of firms which have similar characteristics, wage rates, and histories.

If technological advances suddenly slow or competition from firms with different characteristics suddenly increases, profits are reduced and the capital needed for using technological advances disappears. Increased efficiency depends almost completely on the further de-skilling of tasks. If all these conditions occur simultaneously, as happened in the American automobile industry during the late 1970s, the survival of traditional organizations becomes a questionable proposition. If upper management also makes a few important but unwise decisions, as has been the case for a number of American airlines during the early 1980s and was true of American automobile manufacturers' assessments of the impact of the Arab oil embargoes on consumers' preferences, the combination of pressures may make survival impossible. Inherent in the underlying assumptions and design of traditional organizations is the problem of cycles of de-skilling, alienation, overreliance on economic reward systems, further de-skilling, and so on. When supervisors also misuse the techniques of scientific management, workers' alienation and inefficiency become serious problems.

Unlike the problems created when managers abuse the traditional model, these cycles are built into the operations of traditional organizations. Abuses of the model could be reduced by improving the operation of traditional organizations through better regulation of supervisors' activities, more explicit rewards and profit-sharing plans, and so on. But cycles of alienation and response can be broken only by changing the system itself: by introducing noneconomic reward systems, creating less-alienating tasks, adopting different means of controlling employees, gaining sufficient control of the market so that increased costs can continually be passed on to consumers and competition is minimized, and "hoarding" technological breakthroughs. Some of these solutions are both difficult to implement and risky. Others require fundamental changes in the design and operation of traditional organizations and capitalist economies. None deals directly with the added strains that the alienation-response cycle places on communication.

As the cycle continues, decision makers need access to more varied and accurate information. Staying abreast of technological changes, market characteristics, capital costs, political events, and labor-management relations becomes progressively more important as management is pressured from below by workers' alienation and labor costs and from above by competitive pressures. Decision making becomes a more complicated activity as the "margin for error" available to decision makers is reduced. Perhaps the most important dilemma facing traditional organizations is one of communication:

> The elements of traditional organizations that are necessary for efficient production and control of workers create cycles which impose increased pressures on traditional systems of communication. *But* it is the communication structure of traditional organizations that is their most vulnerable element.

This dilemma and its implications will be the focal point of Chapter 3.

"Take This Job and Shove It"

While I was writing this chapter my mind kept flashing back to images of automobile assembly lines. Because of my father's job I have spent much of my life around cars and around people who build and repair them. For each of the abstract concepts discussed in this chapter, I've heard story after story that make them concrete and alive.

Systematic soldiering didn't die with Frederick Taylor, but today it takes on some different twists. Research and development departments create and deliver new, more efficient computerized machines to assembly lines. The new machines simplify workers' jobs even more than previously, and they produce auto parts more rapidly and with fewer workers. Assembly-line workers aren't stupid. They realize that the new machines threaten their jobs, their sanity, and their incomes, because when a new machine is installed, a new piece rate is established. So they have an absolute incentive to sabotage the new equipment. Some sabotage is simple and not very artistic—just let the machine break down by not adjusting it (all new machines need to be adjusted before they "run to specs," that is, produce parts which meet specifications) or help it to break down. Some sabotage is more creative. George had a sense of the ironic. He sabotaged new machines by disconnecting their governors (devices which keep them from running too fast). While the new machine was being repaired, the old one was started up again. He ran it as fast as possible (as Taylor recognized, all workers know how to perform their tasks more efficiently than they normally perform them) and even "helped it" along by crediting some of the parts he had made with the new machine to the old one. Then, when the research and development people compared the output of the machines at the end of the month, they found that the new machine wasn't nearly as much of an improvement as they had projected. When he was particularly successful, George created objective statistical data which demonstrated beyond a doubt that the old machine was more cost effective than the new one. The happiest day he had ever had was during one July when the big bosses chewed out the smartass college boys from research and development right in front of everyone for their inaccurate estimates, cost overruns, and shoddy technology.

Everyone was bored at the plant; most found ways to cope with it. Some were on cocaine or speed; many smoked pot on breaks; virtually everyone drank. "Don't buy a car made on Monday [or Friday or Thursday after checks come out]." Other tactics added creativity to boring, repetitive jobs. Jane was in quality control. At first she measured every piston to be certain that it was the proper size, shape, and so on. But this took time, which made her supervisor get on her back, which gave her headaches. It also was useless because when she sent parts back they were almost always returned with a pink slip telling her to send them on anyway. Eventually she figured out that a certain number of pistons were expected to be defective (1 out of 100 if I remember correctly). No one cared if she rejected a good one or failed to reject a bad one as long as she rejected about 1 out of every 100. So she learned to reject the correct number rather than the correct pistons. At first she counted them and threw out every 100th one. Soon she figured out that they come down the line spaced at the same intervals, so that when number 1 was in front of her, number 100 was next to a bracket that held the conveyor belt to the ceiling. When work started in the morning she would tie a red handkerchief around the bracket. Then she'd take one piston out of the row and throw it in the reject box. She would watch the conveyor until the gap that was left in the row passed the handkerchief. When it did she knew that is was time to reject another one. All the while she would compose music in her head, and on breaks she would go out to her car and play her guitar. She's still there, I think. (By the way, the abstract, theoretical explanation for this problem is that unlike Japanese firms which control quality by regulating the production *process*, American firms do so by regulating the products themselves.)

Supervisors knew what was going on. To become a foreman (no women had ever been promoted in this plant) you either had to be a troublemaker or make lots of mistakes. Troublemakers were promoted in order to coopt them. Once they became management the workers wouldn't follow their lead and they became less of a threat. Screwups were promoted because foremen can do less damage to expensive, computerized equipment than workers can. Foremen and workers had "arrangements": They'd leave one another alone as long as they didn't do anything to get one another in trouble. After all, George had learned the governor trick from his foreman. Sometimes the unspoken deal would break down. The foremen would begin to enforce the rules strictly even if they had nothing to do with the worker's offense. Docking workers for being late from lunch was a favorite punishment. (Lunch "hour" was 18 minutes long. No one could clean up, eat, and get back in that amount of time.) Rules were used in exactly the way that they shouldn't be—arbitrarily, capriciously, and ineffectively. But that is another story, one for another chapter.

Notes

1. Claude George, *The History of Management Thought* (Englewood Cliffs, N.J.: Prentice-Hall, 1972), p. 52. The quotations from ancient managers that introduced this chapter and some of the historical summary in this chapter are from this work.

2. Ibid., p. 90.

3. Frederick Taylor, "The Principles of Scientific Management," in *Classics of Organizational Theory*, ed. Jay Shafritz and Philip Whitbeck (Oak Park, Ill.: Moore, 1978), pp. 12–13.

4. Edwin Locke, "The Ideas of Frederick W. Taylor: An "Evaluation," *The Academy of Management Review*, 7 (1982), 14–24.

5. Taylor, "Principles of Scientific Management," pp. 15–16, 19.

6. Daniel Wren, "Scientific Management in the U.S.S.R.," *The Academy of Management Review*, 5 (1980), 1–12.

7. Locke, "Ideas of Frederick W. Taylor."

8. George, *History of Management Thought*, p. 114.

9. This summary is based on Max Weber, *The Theory of Social and Economic Organization*, ed. Talcott Parsons (New York: Macmillan, 1947). A more complete summary is available in Peter Blau, *On the Nature of Organizations* (New York: John Wiley, 1974).

10. See Harry Braverman, *Labor and Monopoly Capitalism* (London Monthly Review Press, 1974), or Ivar Berg, *Education and Jobs* (New York: Praeger, 1970). An extensive survey of job satisfaction in America was reported in U.S. Department of Health, Education, and Welfare, *Work in America* (Cambridge, Mass.: M.I.T. Press, 1972).

11. Quoted by Judson Gooding in *The Job Revolution* (New York: Macmillan, 1972), p. 119. Similar comments and illustrations are presented by Barbara Garson, *All the Livelong Day* (London: Penguin, 1977).

12. Jurgen Habermas, *Legitimation Crisis* (Boston: Beacon, 1970).

13. U.S. Department of Health, Education, and Welfare, *Work in America*; Berg, *Education and Jobs*.

14. U.S. Department of Health, Education and Welfare, *Work in America*; Richard Edwards, *Contested Terrain* (New York: Basic Books, 1978).

3

Communication Problems and Traditional Organizations

Organizations are made up of a number of complicated interlocking systems. The traditional type of organization is composed of three primary systems—task design and implementation, formal communication following the chain of command, and employee control. The final sections of Chapter 2 explained that a number of necessary features must be present in real traditional organizations for their component systems to function properly. Organizations have problems whenever one or more of these necessary features is absent or when the implementation of one of the component systems imposes unmanageable pressures on one or more of the other systems. Problems arise in traditional organizations when the operation of their control and reward systems reduces the margin of error available to the organization's decision makers. Effective decision making requires even more effective formal communication. But communication systems can function effectively in traditional organizations only if a second set of necessary features are present.

1. There must be sufficient amounts of information flowing from subordinates to the top of the pyramid. Three kinds of "upward" communication are crucial:
   a. *Special expert information* about how best to perform a particular task which subordinates possess and supervisors must use in designing jobs
   b. Information about the extent to which supervisors' *orders have been carried out*
   c. Information about the *job-related problems* encountered by subordinates, especially when these problems involve other units of the organization.

This information must be accurate, timely, and both complete and concise. As information flows up the chain of command, each person must interpret the messages that are received and pass on only those items which are both accurate and useful to the supervisor. If this "filtering" process is not carried out, the people at the top of the hierarchy will be overwhelmed with information and their decision making will suffer. If the filtering is too complete, large amounts of relevant information will not be available to the decision makers and their decisions also will be harmed.

2. There must be effective communication from the top of the hierarchy to the bottom. This "downward" communication will consist of job-related messages which provide each subordinate with *clear and accurate information* about what they are to do and not to do, how they are to perform their assigned tasks, and the identity of the person to whom they are directly responsible. *All* these messages must be presented as coming from the organization itself rather than from an individual supervisor. *Some* of these messages will contain policies and procedures which are relevant to a number of subordinates and thus *must* be communicated *in writing*.

3. Employees must be given any information which will encourage them to act in conformity with the desires of the organization. Rules and reward systems must be clearly explained, and informal norms of behavior must be effectively transmitted.

If any of these communication processes break down, the traditional organization will function at less than optimal efficiency. If the margin of error available to the organization is small, the gap between this optimal level of efficiency and the actual level of communicative effectiveness may threaten the survival of the organization.

NECESSARY COMMUNICATION FEATURE 1: EFFECTIVE VERTICAL FLOW OF INFORMATION

As was suggested in Chapter 1, traditional organizations rely most heavily on the command function of communication. However, traditional theories of organizations paid only limited attention to processes of communication, partly because the early theorists tended to take effective communication for granted and partly because they envisioned organizations which would limit communication in two important ways: It would be almost wholly task-related; it would follow a hierarchical chain of command in which each supervisor was responsible for interpreting the messages received and sending only necessary and relevant information on up or down the chain. The combination of a rigid formal hierarchy and centralized decision making and the necessity of limiting the amount of vertical communication creates a fundamental paradox for traditional organizations. A pyramid-shaped hierarchy means that the managers who make decisions for the organization and who issue the commands rarely are in direct contact with the employees who carry out the commands or originate feedback about their performance. These managers can do their jobs well only if they receive timely, accurate, and relevant information on which to base their decisions; if their commands are received, understood, and carried out by their distant subordinates; and if they receive prompt and accurate feedback about the subordinates' responses to their commands. In traditional organizations, vertical communication substitutes for direct supervision.

But if information did flow freely through the chain of command, the upper-level managers soon would be overwhelmed. Imagine a mythical organization in which each supervisor has only four subordinates, there are seven levels in the organization's hierarchy, and each person in the organization produces only one message per day to be sent to the top of the hierarchy. If every message is passed up, the managers at the top would receive 4,096 messages per day. So at each level some messages must be screened out and others must be abbreviated. But if each person in the chain of command screens out only one-half the information received, 98.4 percent of the information sent up the chain never would reach the people at the top of the hierarchy.[1] Consequently, the hierarchical structure of traditional organizations requires employees simultaneously to (1) rely on formal channels of communication for the information they need and (2) restrict the flow of information through these channels. It is this paradox that makes it difficult to fulfill consistently the command function of organizational communication. Although these problems exist in all organizations, they are particularly acute in traditional ones.

Hierarchies as Barriers to Information Flow

Two general features of vertical communication in organizations—*structural distortion* and *trained communication incapacity*—impede the flow of information. When a message is communicated from one person to another, it is interpreted by each of the people involved. The words that make up the message are meaningless until some human being attributes meaning to them. Even if the persons to whom a message is sent attempt to pass the message on to another person exactly as it was received, they inevitably will transfer the meanings that they attributed to the message. A number of factors suggest that the message they send on will differ from that which was sent to them.

There are five recurring sources of differences between messages received and messages sent. During the process of interpretation, messages are

1. *Condensed*—the messages sent on are shorter, simpler, and less detailed than those received.

2. *Accented*—the messages are simplified into good or bad, all or none, or other extreme terms.

3. *Assimilated*—the messages are transformed so that they are similar to information that was received in the past and/or that the person expects to receive in the future.

4. *Whitewashed*—the messages are made to fit the interpreter's attitudes and values.

5. *Reductively coded*—the messages are combined with other information to form a sensible overall picture, especially when the message is complex or ambiguous.

All messages carry with them some degree of ambiguity, some degree of uncertainty about how the receiver should interpret them. Before deciding how to respond to a message receivers must make sense out of it. In doing so, they transform its content. But they also absorb some of the ambiguity, some of the uncertainty about what the message means. Processes of interpretation simultaneously clarify and alter the meanings of messages.[2] Since the information is exchanged repeatedly as it moves through the chain of command, the amount of alteration is increased and the amount of absorbed uncertainty grows. If an organization is structured in a traditional hierarchy, messages will be exchanged many times before reaching the people who will use the information they contain. This structural source of distortion takes place whether the information is flowing up or down the hierarchy.

The concept of *trained communication incapacity* is based on an idea originally developed by the economist Thorstein Veblen. He noted that as economies become more complex, people begin to occupy progressively more specialized roles in them. As the members are trained in more and more technical a set of skills they become less and less capable of performing other tasks, both because they lack the information and training necessary to perform those tasks and because they eventually become incapable of learning the alien skills or adopting the alien patterns of thought. They are trained to be incapable. This idea can be illustrated quite easily by choosing a bright professor at random, removing an obvious part from the engine of a car (a battery or coil wire, for example), and observing the attempts to figure out why it will not start. Even if someone then clearly and carefully explains the functioning of an automobile engine and of the part that has been removed, the professor often will be at a loss in understanding what has happened. In some cases, the new information will be processed and a solution will be found. In others, the professor's intellectual skills will not be transferable to the new topic and no solution will be available. (By the way, this example is for illustration only. It is not a suggested class or individual activity.)

In organizations a kind of "trained incapacity" influences communication. As people become more accustomed to performing their roles in the organization, they begin to interpret the communication they receive in a manner appropriate to that role. Personnel officers interpret messages in terms of what they imply about future needs for hiring, firing, or training employees; financial officers attribute meaning to messages based on the economic impact that they imply; and so on. As their training and experience progress, they become less capable of taking the perspectives of other members of the organization when they interpret messages or when they construct messages to be sent to those other people. As a result of successfully adapting to their roles in the organization, people develop perceptual sets which keep them from easily understanding the perceptual sets of others. This phenomenon exists across different units of an organization and across different levels in the hierarchy. Supervisors perceive messages differently than their subordinates, even when they once held their subordinates' position in the organization. As a result, in most organizations, misunderstanding is more common than understanding.

These somewhat depressing results have been observed in a series of studies. Robert Minter found that in 63 percent of the superior-subordinate exchanges that he studied, there was less than a fifty-fifty chance that the two parties shared the same information. Norman Maier found that supervisors and subordinates often did not even agree on whether or not they had met with each other during the past week.[3] In general, supervisors perceive that their subordinates are much better informed than they really are and as a result pass less information on to them than they need to have. People incorrectly perceive that others understand their own perceptions and needs for information and inaccurately assume that they understand the perceptions and needs of the others.

Trained communication incapacity is complicated further by the tendency for people who occupy specialized organizational roles to create their own languages. As they become literate in the artificial language of their position or unit, they become less capable of translating their ideas into a language that other people can understand.[4] An increasingly frequent complaint heard by communication consultants is that people in specialized areas—and today the most frequent complaints seem to involve computer operations—cannot be understood by people outside their units and that specialists do not make an effort to be understood. Although these complaints probably are not wholly accurate, they do reflect the difficulties that non specialists encounter when attempting to communicate with specialists. In fact, some recent research indicates that effective specialty units often assign someone (usually the manager of the unit) the specific job of communicating, or translating, to people outside the unit.

Trained communication incapacity is most probable in traditional organizations. Employees are selected for specific, clearly defined positions; are trained for those particular positions; and are told to communicate only with their immediate subordinates and supervisors. Each of these steps isolates them in their own communicative worlds and contributes to the development of position-specific perceptual sets and languages. Thus, two general features of organizations—structural distortion and trained communication incapacity—reduce the quality of the information flowing through the chain of command. In addition, a number of personal and interpersonal factors also influences the degree to which members of organizations effectively fulfill the command function of organizational communication.

Interpersonal Barriers to Upward Information Flow

Decision making in all organizations, and especially in traditional organizations, depends on the movement of adequate amounts of accurate information. Unfortunately, a number of nonstructural factors reduces the amount and accuracy of upward communication. The *amount* of *vertical* communication is restricted by the size of an organization, the actions of supervisors, and the characteristics of subordinates. Larger organizations have proportionately less information flowing upward than smaller ones, especially at the upper levels of the hierarchy. People tend to shy away from communicating with people who have greater status than themselves. If the organization accents the status differences that exist across its various levels, the amount of upward communication is reduced. If status differences are deemphasized, and if subordinates are encouraged to communicate to their superiors, trained in communication skills, and rewarded for upward communication, the effects of status differences may be offset. But supervisors often discourage their subordinates from communicating with them, either overtly, by in some way communicating "I don't want to hear about it now," or indirectly, by failing to acknowledge or act on the information provided. Subordinates who lack trust in their supervisors and/or who desire promotions send little information up the chain of command, apparently because they fear reprisals and assume that if their supervisors do not know what is going on they are less likely to respond negatively.[5]

The *accuracy* of information sent up through an organization also is limited by a number of factors. As a general rule, little negative information flows up through the chain of command. Information is distorted even more when (1) there are sizeable differences in power or status between two people;

(2) there is little trust between them; (3) a subordinate wants to advance to a higher position in the organization and/or wants to be recognized for past advancement; or (4) a subordinate does not believe that a supervisor will help in advancement, especially if the subordinate also believes that the supervisor will have an important impact on that advancement.[6] The distorting effects of these factors seem to be present even when the subordinate and supervisor generally communicate in a free and open fashion.

In addition, information is distorted when it is provided at the wrong time, particularly when it arrives too late to be incorporated into decision making. Communicating through the chain of command is very time-consuming, as any student who has needed to change a registration for a course or searched for a "lost" student-aid check is painfully aware. In traditional organizations employees expect to spend their careers with the firm. But often advancement is limited by the fact that as they move up through the pyramid, there are fewer and fewer positions to which they can be promoted. Their aspirations often are frustrated. When organizational roles and relationships are formalized and distinct, differences in power and status limit the development of trust between supervisors and their subordinates. It is precisely in this kind of climate that the upward flow of adequate amounts of timely information is least probable. The structure of traditional organizations exacerbates the factors which reduce the effectiveness of vertical communication.

Barriers to Effective Downward Information Flow

One of the most consistent findings in research on organizational communication is that subordinates want their supervisors to "keep them informed" and feel that they receive too little relevant and useful information from their supervisors, especially about events, policies, and changes which directly influence them or their jobs. This perception evidently has two causes. First, supervisors generally do not provide their subordinates with sufficient amounts of job-related information. Although some supervisors convey as much as 80 percent of the available relevant information to their subordinates, others provide as little as 4 percent. Downward communication is selected, filtered, and interpreted in much the same way as upward communication. In addition, when supervisors believe that they are responsible for giving their subordinates only the absolute minimum necessary amount of information, an even higher proportion of downward communication is filtered out. Often even critically important information is withheld from subordinates. The manager of my neighborhood grocery store first learned that his and twenty other nearby stores were going to be closed from reading an article in the morning newspaper. His superiors had chosen to keep this information secret, even from the people who would be most effected by it.

However, subordinates also help to create the impression that they are not kept informed. In general, the more information they receive the more information they believe they have to have.[7] Consequently, until some point of extreme information overload is reached, employees may always feel that they are not "kept informed," regardless of what their supervisors do.

Another problem related to downward communication is one of clarity. Instructions and policies must be clear, specific, and understood if they are to be implemented correctly. Although a variety of factors impede subordinates' understanding of instructions, two potential problems are very important to traditional organizations. First, traditional organizations tend to rely on written communication. Although written messages have a number of potential advantages, they also are easily misunderstood.[8] Because writing takes substantial time and effort, written messages generally include less detailed information than do messages delivered orally. For example, rarely do memos contain explanations of the rationale underlying a policy or command. A lack of detailed or explanatory information allows subordinates to interpret messages quite broadly, and misunderstanding may result. If, however, written messages include great amounts of detail, subordinates may be overwhelmed with information and therefore will be forced to use their own perceptual sets to interpret the message. In either case, since subordinates generally perceive things differently than their supervisors do, they will tend to interpret messages differently than their supervisors intended. And since supervisors' perceptions differ from those of their subordinates, they will find it difficult to construct messages which their subordinates can understand easily. When misunderstandings do occur and responsibility for the communication breakdown is assigned, employees are given added incentive to rely even more on written communication in the future. Putting things in writing and keeping a copy is tedious and time-consuming, but it does allow a person to "cover his ass" (shift responsibility to someone else) when breakdowns occur.

This problem is complicated further by the tendency for organizations which rely on written messages to develop norms which discourage subordinates from confessing that they are confused and asking for clarification. When the message deals with controversial or sensitive issues, both supervisors and subordinates tend to be defensive and the pressures against seeking clarification are magnified. In general, understanding of command-oriented messages is greatest when *both* written and face-to-face oral communication is used. But in highly formal, traditional organizations, downward communication is written communication, and norms of behavior discourage the use of the combined mode.[9]

Second, supervisors may either overtly or covertly discourage their subordinates from seeking clarification of their instructions. Their nonverbal cues may communicate messages like "I don't have time to explain it now" or "you should be able to figure some things out for yourself." If supervisors respond to questions or requests for more information with brief, hurried answers delivered in a tone of voice which conveys annoyance or by instructing the subordi-

FIGURE 3.1   Factors Which Distort Vertical Communication

Structural	Personal and Relational

1. Processes of interpreting messages
    Condensation
    Accenting
    Assimilation to past
    Assimilation to future
    Assimilation to attitudes and values
    Reduction
	1. Power, status differences between parties

2. Number of links in communication chain	2. Mistrust between parties

3. Trained communication incapacity
    perceptual sets
    language barriers
	3. Subordinates' mobility aspirations

4. Large size of the organization	4. Inaccurate perceptions of information needs of others
5. Problems in timing of messages	5. Norms or actions which discourage requests for clarification
6. Problems inherent in written communication	6. Sensitivity of topic

nate to ask someone else for the information, they again create the impression that subordinates should not seek clarification. Even those supervisors who report that they want their subordinates to seek clarification and initiate task-related communication seem to communicate subtly that they really do not want their subordinates to do so.[10] Characteristics of written messages, the different perceptual sets of supervisors and subordinates, and the dynamics of supervisor-subordinate communication processes all serve to reduce the clarity and understanding of downward communication.

Potential Solutions to Problems of Vertical Communication

The discussion of the necessary features and characteristic problems of vertical, command-related communication presented thus far may lead readers to draw the premature conclusion that successful command communication in traditional organizations is as rare as a white gorilla. Of course, this is not true. A large proportion of modern organizations are very much like the traditional ideal, and the vast majority have successful command communication. This success can be attributed to two factors.

First, some organizations have minimal needs for rapid and accurate task-related communication. Traditional organizations thrive in stable situations. If tasks can be planned, defined, and coordinated with only an occasional modification; if decision-making situations are routine, predictable, and precedented; and if the environment surrounding the organization is calm and stable, the problems related to vertical communication may not have a serious effect on the functioning of the organization. Second, feedback can be formalized, subordinates can learn to understand commands through trial and error, and the delays and distortions inherent in communicating through the chain of command can be offset or compensated for. Organizations do not need perfect communication in order to function successfully; neither do they require optimal amounts of communication. Instead, they must have at least a *minimally adequate* degree of effective command communication. This level of satisfactory communication may be quite low for organizations characterized by stability and predictability.

However, communicative and decision-making processes cannot be separated from other aspects of organizational functioning. Traditional organizations can tolerate some inefficiencies and breakdowns in communication and decision making because there is a margin of error between perfect and satisfactory effectiveness. As suggested in Chapter 2, both external competition and cycles of workers' alienation and increasing economic rewards can "squeeze" margins for error. As long as increased labor costs and the expenses associated with communication breakdowns and unwise decisions can be passed on to an organization's consumers in the form of increased prices, margins can be maintained. But if external pressures limit an organization's ability to shift the costs of internal inefficiencies, it must absorb them internally. The short-term strategies often used by traditional organizations to absorb these costs—delaying capital investments, increasing the degradation of tasks, taking more intransigent positions in response to labor's wage demands—all tend to reduce the margin for error available in the long term. The two key characteristics of traditional organizations—formal communication coupled with centralized decision making, and task efficiency and control through task simplification and economic reward systems—combine to reduce further an organization's ability to cope. When the *situation* also changes, as it did suddenly for America's largest airlines during the early 1980s, the inherent dynamics of traditional organizations may take a heavy toll.

Fortunately, the people who make up organizations generally are flexible and creative. They often find ways to compensate for even the most serious problems faced by their organizations. Raymond Miles has summarized this idea effectively:

> All this is more than just a lengthy way of saying that organizations do not actually work exactly as they are or were designed to—which is, of course, a well-documented fact. . . . People violate their positional constraints for

many reasons. They do so because of their own needs and desires—for security from threat and pressure, to develop or modify social ties, to satisfy needs for recognition and esteem, and so forth. They also do so simply because their position appears [to be] unclear or unworkable. . . . Thus, organizations not only may work less well than they were designed to work because of the interaction of people and their positions, but they also work much better than they have the right to perform. . . precisely because people do not accept their roles, relationships and responsibilities as immutable.[11]

People compensate for the problems of command communication faced by traditional organizations in at least four ways. (1) They compensate for problems of filtering and interpretation by actively seeking information from a number of other people, by building *redundancy* into their own communication. (2) They compensate for potential distortions of information through *counter-biasing*, in which they determine the source of a message, assess the probable biases that come into play as the information is transmitted to them, and adjust their interpretations and uses of that information accordingly. (3) Over time they learn that some kinds of communication breakdowns tend to *recur*, and they *formalize means of preventing* them or *compensating* for them when they do occur. (4) And perhaps most important, they *develop informal communication* ties which can compensate for the problems of formal vertical communication. These informal ties emerge naturally, almost automatically, and unless they are actively suppressed by the organization, do so inevitably. They arise because people need information that they cannot or do not receive through the formal chain of command and because they need to form and maintain interpersonal relationships with other employees.[12] Employees learn who has the information they need in order to do their jobs and they discover ways of getting in touch with those people. They discover people with whom they can form meaningful friendships, and thereby compensate for the isolation and dehumanization that often are part of traditional organizations. In actively meeting their own needs they inadvertently fulfill the needs of their organizations.

NECESSARY COMMUNICATION FEATURE 2: MAINTAINING CONTROL IN TRADITIONAL ORGANIZATIONS

People naturally act in ways which meet their needs, but often their natural actions do not meet the needs of their organizations. But organizations can create conditions within which it is probable that employees will choose to act in desired ways. Creating these conditions is the goal of organizational reward systems and one of the most important command-related functions of communication. The need for control in successful organizations has been recognized by theorists since the time of the pharoahs. Amatai Etzioni has explained this ever-present problem:

> Organizations are unlike natural social units, such as the family, ethnic group or community. . . . [The structure, focus on performance and size of organizations] . . . make informal control insufficient. . . . Organizations require formally institutionalized allocation of rewards and penalties to enhance compliance with their norms, regulations and orders. Most organizations most of the time cannot rely on most of their participants to carry out their assignments voluntarily. . . . The participants need to be supervised. . . . In this sense, the organizational structure is one of control, and the hierarchy of control is the most central element of the organizational structure.[13]

In traditional organizations, control is accomplished through *rules, norms,* and *systems of reward and punishment.* Effective communication is essential to the success of each.

Rules, Norms, and Communication

Rules and rule enforcement are the dominant means of control used in modern organizations.[14] Members of organizations will choose to obey formal rules only if they (1) understand the rules, (2) see the rules as legitimate, and (3) perceive that the rules are supported by appropriate sanctions. To succeed, rules must be articulated clearly and communicated effectively. They must be expressed in clear and precise terms and be both general enough not to be seen as "nitpicking" and specific enough to define some behaviors as vital and others as forbidden. They also must be appropriate to the kinds of situations faced by employees. Perhaps the best recent example of rules which did not meet these requirements were those established by the Occupational Safety and Health Administration (OSHA). When OSHA's rules were too specific (for example, the heights of toilets in millimeters) or too confusing, people responded with hostility and/or disobedience. When they were inappropriate to the situation (flush toilets in farmers' fields), they were ridiculed and violated. Widespread disobedience forced OSHA to revise or abandon many of the most inappropriate of its rules. Eventually the belief that the organization was incapable of developing effective rules was in part responsible for Congress' decision to restrict its powers of enforcement.

Rules will be seen as legitimate only if they are believed to apply equally to everyone in the organization, are fairly and objectively enforced, and are produced by the organization rather than by a single individual. In addition, rules can seem to be illegitimate if they are applied outside an appropriate range of activities. For example, rules about employees' private lives will be resisted unless the employees perceive that their employer has a legitimate right to enforce such rules. At one time employees, especially managerial and supervisory personnel, gave their organizations the right to control much of their private lives. In recent years the range of appropriate outside activities seems to have narrowed. Employees now often refuse to accept company rules about where they should live, how they should spend their income, or what they should do with their leisure time. Municipal employees refuse to live within their city's boundaries, employees reject dress codes, and priests are beginning to reject canon law concerning celibacy and marriage. Union workers negotiate for contract clauses which allow them to choose the holidays they will celebrate (with pay), to arrive at work at times which best fit their outside lives, and so on. These changes do not mean that employees no longer obey those rules that they perceive are legitimate. Rather, the range of actions over which they grant their organization the right to enforce rules has changed.

Finally, rules must be linked directly to sanctions—*punishments* or *rewards*. The concept of punishment is not often discussed in organizational research, in part because of the negative values that our society attaches to the concept and in part because legal and contractual constraints have reduced its use in modern organizations. However, punishment has been linked favorably to improved job performance in certain circumstances. To have these favorable effects, punishment must follow the objectionable action as immediately as possible, involve relatively intense sanctions, be administered by supervisors who have good interpersonal relationships with the offender, be objectively applied to all employees, and be accompanied by a clear explanation and justification of the sanction. Punishment must be used as a motivational tool and not as a mechanism through which supervisors can get revenge. Generally it is most effective if it involves a denial of an expected reward rather than the imposition of a negative consequence. Cancelation of an upcoming merit raise works better than a reduction in an employee's current salary, for instance.[15]

Even if these requirements are met, motivating employees through systems of rules has a number of negative side effects. Rules may be *too effective* in leading employees to restrict their actions, encouraging them to follow rules rigidly even when doing so impedes the functioning of the organization. Rules must not be so specific nor obeyed so rigorously that they deny employees the flexibility that they need. Recognizing this, employees often rebel against rules or against their organizations by following rules strictly. Recently, municipal police forces, who cannot strike lawfully, answered *every* call, ticketed *every* jaywalker, arrested anyone driving 27 in a 25 mph zone, and in so doing paralyzed their cities and court systems. During the imposition of martial law in Poland in 1981 workers rebelled by following rules to the letter. In both cases the employees realized that malicious obedience can paralyze an organization or country. They chose to rebel in the only available way, by visciously obeying rules.

People also may respond to rules by processes of "regression," reducing their performance to the minimum acceptable standard allowed by the rules. The goal of rules is to increase conformity, to reduce individual deviations from the actions envisioned in their design. But rule enforcement also may reduce deviations that would be valuable for an organization. Following rules to the letter prevents people from experimenting with new ways of doing their jobs. Without experimentation they cannot discover more productive and efficient approaches. Regression also reduces the overall level of performance in an organization because it means that highly productive workers eventually reduce their productivity to average levels. The popular phrase "it may be a stupid rule, but do it anyway" reflects the tendency for rules systems to create regression.

Finally, people may respond to the enforcement of rules with withdrawal or open rebellion. The former leads people to be progressively less involved in and committed to their jobs; the latter may culminate in sabotage. A friend of mine once rebelled against rules regarding the speed of an assembly line by placing right-side motor mounts backwards in the Oldsmobiles he was assembling. Because V-8 engines rotate clockwise, it usually is difficult to detect this change in "design" . . . not until some hapless buyer accelerates rapidly. Less serious forms of sabotage—placing small bolts or nuts in hubcaps so that wheels will rattle when they turn—and more serious forms—mixing various foreign substances into the meat that will be ground into hot dogs or sausages—all serve the same purpose. They allow employees to rebel against control systems with little chance of being detected. Both withdrawal and sabotage reduce the quality of individual and organizational performance.[16] If rules and sanctions are not communicated effectively, they will fail. But even if they are communicated perfectly they still may not meet the needs of the organization.

Rules are most effective with people who feel that they are an integral part of their organization and who are psychologically involved in their work groups. All social groups have norms of behavior, and in all social groups members exert significant pressure on other members to conform to these norms. If informal norms are consistent with the formal rules and reward systems of an organization, they reinforce more formal means of control. In most cases, rules, rewards, and norms are mutually supportive. Organizations tend to select people who are sufficiently like their current employees to find it easy to accept the norms of their work groups. White, Protestant males hire white, Protestant males for a number of reasons, one of which is that they already know "how to behave." If people are hired who do not conform to the organization's norms, these outsiders soon leave the organization. But most newcomers do conform. As Max Weber noted years ago, people become socialized when they enter an organization. They learn which actions are expected of them and which are frowned upon. The socialization process is streamlined when the organization has norms consistent with those of the culture from which it recruits its members. The natural norms that children learn while growing up are translated into the organizational situation. If, while they were children, new employees learned to be "seen and not heard," they will find it easier to accept organizational norms which support passive behavior. The power of norms and socialization processes is so great that organizations rarely need to exercise formal rules.[17] But new employees can learn these rule-supporting norms only through informal communication from "older" members of the organization. If supervisors discourage the informal communication through which norms are shared, the socialization process may be delayed or

FIGURE 3.2   Constraints on Action in Traditional Organizations

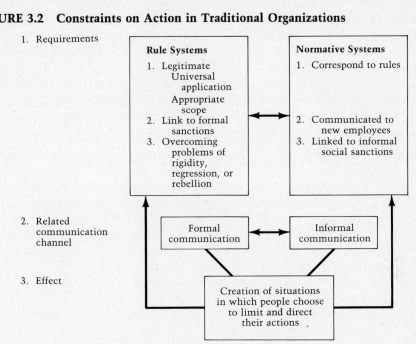

stopped. For either formal rules or informal norms to create the conditions which will lead people to limit their actions in desired ways, effective formal *and* informal communication links must be present.

Reward Systems and Communication

Traditional organizational theorists recognized that people base choices about how to act on their perceptions of the rewards they are likely to receive from their actions. Frederick Taylor assumed that if production employees believed they would receive substantial and fair economic rewards for performing their tasks in the most efficient way and expending maximum effort in attempting to complete those tasks, their performance would improve. Weber assumed that if administrative employees believed their efforts would assure them of (1) lifetime employment, (2) adequate pensions, and (3) promotions and salary increases, their performance would be enhanced. More recently, organizational theorists have developed more complex theories of the relationships among employees' expectations, perceptions of fairness (equity), rewards, effort, and performance. The common assumption underlying these theories is that people make choices about how to act within contexts defined by past choices, perceptions of the current situation, and expectations of the potential effects of the different courses of action. Human action thus is a constant, ongoing process which takes place in a constantly changing scene. The assumption underlying all organizational reward systems is that some members of an organization can act in ways which will increase the probability that other members will choose to act in "desired" ways.

One of the clearest and most valuable models of the factors and processes which underlie reward systems is the *expectancy theory* proposed by Lyman Porter and Edwin Lawler. Three major ideas define their theory:

1. The *purpose* of reward systems is to create situations in which employees will choose to expend high levels of effort in performing their assigned tasks. Although a number of factors other than the effort they expend will influence the quantity and quality of their performance (for example, their skills, training, equipment, access to information), increasing their effort is the goal of reward systems.

2. Employees' efforts depend on their perceptions of the value of the rewards they may receive, the degree to which effort is necessary for the receipt of rewards, and the fairness of the reward system.

3. Reward systems depend on the availability of *four kinds of information:*

    a. Information which indicates that employees' efforts have been rewarded adequately in the past

    b. Information which leads them to *expect* their efforts to be rewarded appropriately in the future

    c. Information which leads them to believe that the rewards they receive are and will continue to be fairly and equitably distributed

    d. Information which indicates that the employees' successes or failures are consistent with their images of themselves.

Thus, the success of a reward system depends on its being both appropriately designed and supported by communication that fulfills a number of requirements.[18]

The Necessary Features of Reward Systems

Reward systems are designed to increase the effort employees expend at work and thus, when coupled with efficient job design and effective training, to increase the quantity and quality of their performance. This is an important point because recent research has indicated that the features of organizations which encourage effort and productivity may not be those which generate high levels of morale and job satisfaction. For instance, Edwin Locke's extensive survey of research on job satisfaction and productivity concluded that "both logic and research suggest that it is best to view productivity and satisfaction as *separate outcomes* of the employee-job interaction, and to expect causal relationships between them only in special circumstances."[19] Consequently, the aspects of organizational structures and communication which generate high levels of performance are different from those which create high levels of job satisfaction. The remainder of this chapter will discuss reward systems designed to increase performance. Chapters 4 and 5 will examine satisfaction-oriented reward systems and the relationships among communication, satisfaction, and performance.

The Valence of Rewards   The first requirement for performance-oriented reward systems is the availability of rewards which employees perceive as both substantial and important. Pay seems to be the one reward which most often has these characteristics. It is most important to employees whose incomes are low, whose tenure in the organization has been brief, whose commitment to the firm is low, and who feel that their pay is appropriate when they compare it to that received by other workers. Overall, reward systems based on pay have been successful in improving performance.[20] The opportunity for promotions and the enhanced status that accompany pay increases also seem to be important to most people, especially those who have a high need for achievement.

Performance feedback also seems to be a salient reward for most people. Verbal recognition (praise) is an important correlate of improved performance and also seems to increase job satisfaction. It succeeds if it informs subordinates that they are doing their jobs correctly or efficiently and therefore encourages them to continue to use the same approaches. Although the idea that praise is rewarding is not particularly new, its visibility has increased during recent years because of the increased use of "behavior modification" systems of management.[21]

The Connection Between Rewards and Performance   Reward systems influence effort only to the extent that workers believe their increased effort will be rewarded *and* that the rewards will be related directly to their performance rather than to friendships or biases. To create this expectation, organizations must devise reward systems which do link rewards to performance, and supervisors *must persuade* their employees that the rewards they are given (or not given) are determined solely by their effort and performance. This is, of course, a very difficult task. First, it demands that someone persuade employees that they have been and continue to be responsible for their performance. Since there is clear and consistent evidence that people tend to attribute their successes to themselves and/or to factors within their control, and their failures to others and/or factors they cannot control, it is quite difficult to meet this requirement. The problem has been addressed most explicitly in the design of the complex goal-reward-feedback systems which will be explained in the final section of this chapter.

Second, people must believe that it is either their individual performance or the performance of a group over which they have influence that determines the rewards they receive. "System rewards," those based on the length of time an employee has been in the organization or merely on membership in the organization (for example, across-the-board salary increases or gifts of turkeys at Christmas), do not generate increased performance for precisely this reason.

At most, systemwide rewards increase job satisfaction and loyalty to the organization, neither of which consistently or significantly increases individual performance. In most cases they encourage people to work at the minimum level required to stay in the organization. In some cases they may even be counterproductive. Marginal or poorly motivated workers who are rewarded beyond the level warranted by their performance will be encouraged to stay in the organization, whereas highly motivated workers will be encouraged to look elsewhere for employment. In time, low-producing employees begin to expect rewards in spite of their performance. If system rewards are reduced or discontinued, these workers will be alienated and their satisfaction further reduced. This possibility makes it difficult for firms to shift away from system rewards to performance-producing rewards. In time the organization may have only poorly motivated, unproductive employees who are also dissatisfied.

Finally, system rewards also may be adapted inappropriately to the motivations of particular groups of employees. Research with college professors, for example, has found that although monetary rewards are motivating for younger, untenured professors, they are less motivating for older, perhaps more loyal employees. If across-the-board percentage-based salary increases are given, the lion's share of the reward budget will go to those employees who will be least motivated by them.[22] Employees choose to increase their efforts when the situations they face suggest that they can expect to receive appropriate and significant rewards for doing so. System rewards do not create these expectations.

Another problem is the necessity of persuading workers that the rewards they will receive are substantial enough to be worth the extra effort that obtaining them will require. This is the factor which makes it difficult to use grades as motivational tools. To succeed, grading systems must define higher than normal grades (in theory, A's and B's) as (1) rare, because if a large number of people receive them their value is reduced and (2) achievable, because if they require exceptional effort students will conclude that they are not worth the trouble. In fact, motivational grading systems are similar to organizational reward systems in a number of ways. If grades become system rewards (everyone gets A's and B's) they will fail to motivate, and they will tend to attract and hold low-performing students in those courses in which they are used. If they can be obtained for less effort in a competing organization (in this case, in another course), their motivational effects in a particular organization (course) will be altered.

The final complication is that employees must believe that increasing their efforts will lead to increased rewards in both the long term and the short term. Taylor was very much concerned with "systematic soldiering," the regressive behavior that resulted when organizations responded to increases in output by cutting the per-unit rate of rewards. "Soldiering" occurs when people expect rate cutting to occur. Reward systems encourage employees to increase their effort only if they believe that it is in their self-interest to do so, *both* in the short and long term. Thus, for reward systems to succeed, they must be supported by communication which persuades employees that rewards will be contingent on *their* actions, that they will be substantial, and that they will continue to be provided in the long term. Employees also must be persuaded that the reward system is equitable.

Equity Theory, Communication, and Reward Systems Perhaps the most important theories of human action to be developed in the last thirty years are a series of perspectives generally labeled *exchange theories*. A recent extension of the exchange theory paradigm is *equity theory*, first proposed by J. Stacy Adams. Although it is not possible to describe either exchange theory or equity theory in any detail in this book, one component is particularly relevant to communication and reward systems.[23] This is Adams' concept of "distributive justice," the notion that people evaluate the net gains they receive from being involved in a relationship or organization by comparing its rewards to the costs they incur in order to gain those rewards. While making this comparison, people also compare their net gains to those received by other people. They will be motivated by the rewards they receive only if their net gains seem to be adequate *and* equitable when compared to those received by others. If they believe that their rewards are not equitable, they will feel emotional pressure to alter the situation.

When applied to organizational reward systems, equity theory suggests that people will compare their efforts to the rewards they receive *and* to the efforts expended and rewards received by other members of their organization and members of other organizations. If they feel they are being treated inequitably, that is, if they feel that their net gains are lower than those of other employees, they will feel emotional discomfort and will seek to resolve it by reducing their efforts, attempting to increase their rewards, leaving the organization, or rationalizing the inequity by changing their perceptions of what net gains other people are receiving. Thus, for reward systems to succeed, someone in the organization must convince each employee that he or she is receiving an equitable reward. This task may be achieved overtly, by providing workers with information supporting the conclusion that they are being equitably rewarded, or covertly, by withholding the information the employees need to make comparisons with others. It is quite difficult to employ the first strategy with any degree of success, a point that professors remember every time they try to respond to a student's complaint that "I worked much harder than so-and-so and received a lower exam grade." It is equally difficult to implement the second strategy, although organizations often try to do so by creating rules which forbid employees from discussing their raises (or salaries) with other employees. The primary effect of these rules seems to be to encourage employees to obtain the forbidden information, since their very existence creates the impression that employees are being treated unfairly. The rules thus give employees an incentive to share salary information covertly with each other. As a result, most employees eventually learn what their peers are receiving. In fact, the tendency for such rules to fail may provide the best evidence to support equity theorists' assumption that people are very much concerned with "distributive justice."

The Communicative Requirements of Reward Systems   This analysis of the dimensions of organizational reward systems indicates that their success depends largely on the effectiveness of communication. Three major communicative requirements must be met:

1.   Workers must be *persuaded* that the rewards they receive are significant and will continue to be available in significant amounts in the future. Supervisors must be able to gain reliable information about the extent to which their subordinates share this belief.

2.   Workers must *receive immediate, clear, and comprehensive feedback* about the quantity and quality of their performance. Without this feedback they will be unable to choose the most effective tactics with which to perform their assigned tasks and will not have the kind of information available to encourage them to continue to exert high levels of effort.

3.   Employees must be persuaded that the *rewards* they receive have been, are, and will continue to be (a) *based on* their *effort* and *performance* and (b) *equitable*.

Although these communicative requirements can be fulfilled in a number of ways, the most comprehensive recent attempts to implement them have come in the form of goal-setting and feedback systems (commonly called *management by objectives*.)

The assumption underlying management by objectives is that the necessary features of reward systems can be met most completely if organizations design and implement strategies which (1) provide employees with performance goals, (2) evaluate their efforts in terms of these goals, and (3) reward them for their goal achievement through a long-term, cooperative process. The two most important components of these systems are the negotiation of accepted goals and the shared evaluation of performance.[24]

In general, goals are most successful in improving performance if they are (1) difficult but achievable, given the talent, training, and materials available to the employee; and (2) as specific and tangible as possible. The positive effects of goals are enhanced when employees are allowed to participate actively in setting their goals. However, the effects of participation depend on a number of features of the communication that takes place during the negotiation of goals. First, the discussion must give employees a better understanding of the role they play in the organization and a clear indication of what their specific goals are. When roles are clarified and employees and their supervisor better understand their role in the organization, they will have less role-related stress and performance will improve. Second, open discussion of goals should give employees a better understanding of how they should go about achieving the goals. They will be better able to focus their efforts on the most important parts of their jobs and determine the most effective means of accomplishing their tasks. Finally, participation in goal setting may increase an employee's willingness to accept the goals that are set and will allow their supervisors to express confidence in their ability to achieve the goals. However, each of these factors depends on the quality of the communication between a subordinate and supervisor during the goal-setting process. Unless goals, strategies, and roles are clarified and unless the subordinate accepts the goals and means of achieving them, participatory goal setting will have little if any impact on performance.

Another major component of management-by-objective reward systems is feedback about employees' performance. Feedback can stimulate increased performance only if it is combined with effective goal setting. The effects of feedback also depend on effective superior and subordinate communication during evaluation sessions. Research performed over the course of forty years and in an amazingly large number of different organizational situations indicates that (1) supervisors and subordinates evaluate the quality of the subordinate's performance differently, (2) they attribute the performance to different factors, and (3) supervisors artificially inflate their evaluations of poor-performing subordinates in anticipation of discussions of performance. Since agreement on evaluations *and* the causes of good or bad performance is necessary to the success of reward systems, these are serious problems. They can be offset somewhat by developing and using evaluative criteria which are quantifiable or in some way independently verifiable. But in situations where goal achievement cannot be measured by examining tangible output, the success of goal-feedback systems depends on effective communication between supervisors and their subordinates, both during evaluation sessions and in day-to-day interaction. If subordinates generally are satisfied with the quality of the communication they have with their supervisor, if they have found that their supervisor typically provides accurate and reliable information, and if they have been persuaded that their supervisor is trustworthy, they are more likely to accept performance evaluations. Thus, through a complex process, supervisor and subordinate communication establishes a context in which perceptions of performance and its sources can be shared, goals can be established and clarified, feedback can be interpreted and used, and superior and subordinate communication can be improved.[25]

A central tenet of the traditional ideal organization is that employees will be most productive and will contribute most to the goals of their organization if they expect to be rewarded appropriately for their efforts. For this ideal to be realized in operating organizations, employees must perceive that they will receive significant and salient rewards, that these rewards will be contingent on their performance, that the quality of their performance is within their control and thus is their responsibility, and that rewards will be equitably distributed. Their actions will contribute most efficiently to the goals of the organization if they are guided and encouraged through effective systems of goal setting and performance appraisal. Although a number of personal and organizational factors influence the degree to which employees hold the per-

Communication Structure, Process, and Types of Organizations

FIGURE 3.3   Expectancy-Equity Theory

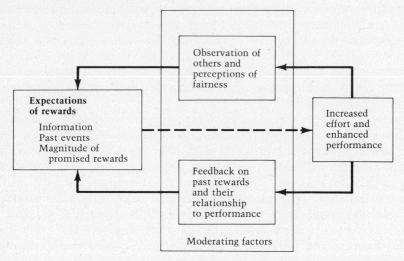

ceptions necessary for the success of reward systems, they will have little impact unless they are supplemented by effective communication. Perceptions are created through processes of communication; actions are directed toward organizational goals only when employees are persuaded that choosing to act in particular ways will allow them to gain desirable rewards. Effective command-related communication is a vital part of motivating workers through systems of reward.

CONCLUSION

The traditional ideal type of organization is based on two primary assumptions: (1) Tasks and organizations are rationally and scientifically designed in ways which will maximize their efficiency; (2) situations can be created in which employees, in their own self-interest, will choose to act in ways which further the goals of the organization. The first assumption can be implemented successfully only if the people who design the organization and its components and guide its everyday operations have access to timely, accurate information about the functioning of the organization and are able to communicate commands to their subordinates successfully. This command function can be fulfilled only if the potential barriers to effective vertical flow of information can be avoided or offset to a satisfactory degree *and* only if managers are able adequately to resolve the dilemma produced by the need to limit and control communication and the need to stay informed about what actually is going on in their organization.

FIGURE 3.4   Reward, Rule, and Normative Systems

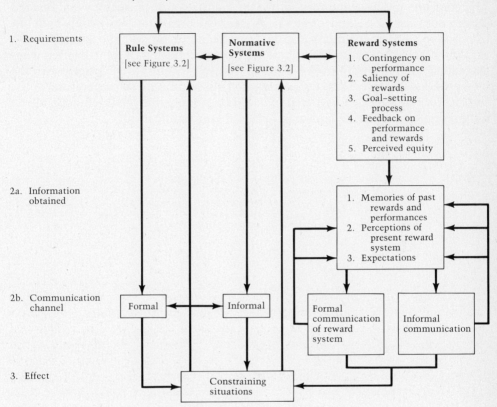

The second assumption can be fulfilled through the successful communication of formal rules and informal norms and the creation of the expectation that some actions will be rewarded and that others will not be. Creating and sustaining the perceptions that underlie the success of rule, norm, and reward systems require a continual process of communication between supervisors and their subordinates.

People make choices about how to act based on their interpretations of past events, current situations, and future actions. If members of organizations remember that choosing to follow organizational rules and norms led to desired rewards and that this relationship between actions and outcomes held true for all members of the organization, and if they believe that an equitable distribution of rewards based on performance will continue in the future, the self-interest of most employees will be served by choosing to act in ways desired by their organization. Of course, the traditional ideal does not assume that all individuals will act in identical (or even in desirable) ways in any particular organization. The complexities of human beings and the complicated character of human choice making make it unwise to assume that any group of persons will perceive, process, and respond to their situation in the same way. But the model does assume—and observations of real organizations which have attempted to implement the traditional ideal tend to support the assumption—that the probability of an individual employee's choosing to act in desired ways is greatest when the employee perceives that self-interest is congruent with the interests of the organization. Creating and sustaining these perceptions is the central task of supervisory personnel. It is a responsibility which depends on the presence of effective command-related communication.

THE ADVANCEMENT CASE

Almost everyone can remember playmates from their childhood who got ahead by shamelessly ingratiating themselves with the powers that be. For me it was Susie S. (not her real name), the little twit who spent her entire grade school career polishing apples, tattling on the rest of us, and engaging in a variety of other sordid activities. Fortunately, we grow up and enter organizations in which ingratiation has to be more subtle if it is to succeed.

One of the hardest lessons for young professionals to learn is how to create the kind of visibility that is vital for organizational success. One of the realities of organizational life is that competent people are promoted only if the people who make promotion decisions believe that they are competent. Although it is difficult to become visible, especially in large, complex organizations, it is not impossible. The first source of aid is sponsor relationships, contacts with senior people who notice a bright young prospect and take steps to keep his or her name circulating among the powerful. The second aid is the informal communication networks that exist in the organization—the pattern of communicative links that ensures that when a sponsor mentions a young employee's name to one person, that person will mention it to another person, and so on. The final aid is comprised of signal events—opportunities for a young professional to demonstrate competence in public and thereby signal his or her promotability to others. But these aids are useless unless a young employee knows how to use them.

A second reality of organizational life is that newcomers must both cooperate and compete with their peers. Most organizations promote from within, which means that a line supervisor will become Supervisor of Production if and only if she or he is perceived as being better than the other supervisors. Assistant personnel directors become personnel directors only after winning a battle to develop an image which is more impressive than that created by their peers. So, inevitably peers compete with one another. They also must cooperate. Part of being promotable is being able to work effectively with others. Often succeeding in a task requires the cooperation of one's peers. If these are not reasons enough to cooperate, there is the simple reality that if you are not promoted, one of your peers will be. That means that she or he then will be your supervisor. Life will be much, much easier if your relationships with that person have been cooperative ones. And that is the rub—how can you make yourself "visible" without alienating your peers? One of my former students explained the trick that is involved while recounting his first two years as a line supervisor. The key, he said, is subtlety, subtlety and the ability to resist seeing your peers as enemies.

"I once observed," he explained, "the first two years in their new organization of two young M.B.A.s. One of them was an adult version of Susie S. The other was a quiet confident young adult. June was the essence of tact; Susie the epitome of tacky. Susie took every possible opportunity to blow her own horn.

She got an article about herself published in the company newsletter; she took credit for everything good that happened in her unit regardless of who actually was responsible; she invited everyone who was anyone to lunch and bored them to tears with her exploits. Once she learned that there were defects in the titanium alloy that we were using to make some airplane parts. Instead of telling the rest of us, she sat on the information while we ran the parts. She shifted her own crew's work schedule around so that they ran everything else first. Then, after we'd wasted a week, she went to quality control and asked them to check on the density of the materials. Quality control found the problem and reported it to the production supervisor. The rest of us got chewed out and had to work overtime for two weeks to get caught up. At the monthly performance meeting she even had the gall to brag about her line's superior productivity for the month. She still has the January performance plaque on the wall in her office. This kind of stuff works for a while (you should have seen the production vice-president at the performance meeting), but not for long. Eventually the top management will find out about her approach (the information is going through the grapevine now, the rest of us made certain of that), and if they do not find out, the rest of us will find some other way to get her.

"June operates differently. Her group always seems to be finding more efficient production techniques. Sometimes what they do is really simple—like when they figured out that shortening the handle on the drill presses would take less motion and keep pressers from getting tired as rapidly as they used to. Sometimes it is more complex—like when they made changes in the whole layout of the plant that reduced injuries 23 percent. But *always* what she does benefits the rest of us, too. So we envy her but like and respect her, especially for the mileage that she gets out of her ideas. She does not talk much, but she *always* goes into meetings well prepared. She is articulate, makes clear and effective proposals, and handles questions as if she wrote them. I think she was a debater in high school; I also wish she had become a lawyer. She will be our next production supervisor. I'm sure of it, and I don't really mind."

Notes

1. Anthony Downs, *Inside Bureaucracy* (Boston: Little, Brown, 1967).

2. Richard Blackburn, "Dimensions of Structure: a Review and Reappraisal," *The Academy of Management Review*, 7 (1982), 59–66; Raymond Miles, *Theories of Management* (New York: McGraw–Hill, 1975).

3. John Campbell, "Systematic Error on the Part of Human Links in Communication Systems,"*Information and Control*, 1 (1958), 334–369. Also see Herbert Simon, *The New Science of Management Decision* (New York: Harper & Row, 1960).

4. Harold Guetzkow, "Communication in Organizations," in *Handbook of Organizations*, ed. James March (Chicago: Rand–McNally, 1965), pp. 534–573; Michael Tushman and Thomas Scanlan, "Boundary Spanning Individuals," *Academy of Management Journal*, 24 (1981), 289–305;

Thomas Allen, Michael Tushman, and Denis Lee, "Technology Transfer as a Function of Position in the Spectrum from Development to Technical Services," *Academy of Management Journal*, 22 (1979), 694–708.

5. These studies are summarized in detail in W. Charles Redding, *Communication Within the Organization* (New York: Industrial Communication Council, 1972).

6. Guetzkow, "Communications in Organizations"; Peter Monge, Jane Edwards, and Kenneth Kirstie, "The Determinants of Communication and Communication Structure in Large Organizations,"in *Communication Yearbook 2*, ed. Brent Ruben (New Brunswick, N.J.: Transaction Books, 1978), pp. 311–334; Samuel Bacharach and Michael Aiken, "Communication in Administrative Bureaucracies," *Academy of Management Journal*, 3 (1977), 365–377; Karlene Roberts and Charles O'Reilly, "Failures in Upward Communication: Three Possible Culprits," *Academy of Management Journal*, 17 (1974), 205–215.

7. Guetzkow, "Communications in Organizations."

8. Problems of misunderstanding also are examined in Chapter 4 of this book. Characteristics of written and oral messages are summarized in Chapter 1.

9. Redding, *Communication Within the Organization*; Daniel Katz and Robert Kahn, *The Social Psychology of Organizations* (New York: John Wiley, 1978).

10. Cal Downs and Charles Conrad, "A Critical Incident Study of Effective Subordinancy," *Journal of Business Communication*, 19 (1982), 27–38.

11. Miles, *Theories of Management*.

12. Guetzkow, "Communications in Organizations"; Richard Farace, James Taylor, and John Stewart, "Criteria for Evaluation of Organizational Communication Effectiveness," in *Communication Yearbook 2*, ed. Brent Ruben, pp. 272–292. These factors will be examined in detail in Chapter 4.

13. Amatai Etzioni, "Organizational Control Structures," in *Handbook of Organizations*, ed. James March, p. 658.

14. Katz and Kahn, *Social Psychology of Organizations*, p. 297. This section is based in part on pages 307–331 of this book.

15. Richard Arvey and John Ivanevich, "Punishment in Organizations," and Henry Sims, "Further Thoughts on Punishment in Organizations," *The Academy of Management Review*, 5 (1980), 123–138.

16. See the summaries of research by Merton, Gouldner, and Dahrendorf that are provided in Katz and Kahn, *The Social Psychology of Organizations*.

17. Processes of socializing new employees are examined in Meryl Reis Louis, "Surprise and Sense–making in Organizations," *Administrative Science Quarterly*, 25 (1980), 226–251.

18. Edwin Lawler, *Pay and Organizational Effectiveness* (New York: McGraw–Hill, 1971).

19. Edwin Locke, "The Nature and Causes of Job Satisfaction," in *Handbook of Industrial and Organizational Psychology*, ed. Marvin Dunnette (Chicago: Rand–McNally, 1976), p. 1,333. More recent research is summarized in Arthur Brief and Raymond Aldag, "The 'Self' in Work Organizations," *The Academy of Management Review*, 6 (1981), 75–88.

20. John Campbell and Robert Pritchard, "Motivation Theory," in *Handbook of Industrial and Organizational Psychology*, ed. Marvin Dunnette (Chicago: Rand–McNally, 1967) pp. 63–130. Also see Charles Greene, Philip Podsakoff, "Effects of Withdrawal of a Performance–Contingent Reward on Supervisory Influence and Power," *Academy of Management Journal*, 24 (1981), 527–542.

21. In a now–famous series of studies "at Emery Air Freight," Edward Feeney applied a system of behavior modification in an attempt to improve workers' performance. His system involved three steps: Supervisors specify a "standard" level of performance, preferably in quantifiable terms; workers are provided with immediate feedback about how their performance relates to this standard; and workers are given positive feedback when their performance exceeds the standard and encouragement when their performance falls short. After implementing this system, average productivity at Emery improved significantly. Although Feeney's studies now have been criticized on a number of grounds, the most important attack for the concept of reward valence is Locke's argument that feedback itself, rather than the positive nature of the feedback, produced the increases. See Edwin Locke, Karyll Shaw, Lise Saari, and Gary Latham, "Goal Setting and Task Performance: 1969–1980," *Psychological Bulletin*, 90 (1981), 125–152.

22. Katz and Kahn, *Social Psychology of Organizations*, pp. 412–414.

23. These models have been summarized very effectively by Michael Roloff, *Interpersonal Communication: the Social Exchange Approach* (Beverley Hills, Calif.: Sage, 1981).

24. Locke et al., "Goal Setting."

25. Lawrence Hanser and Paul Muchinsky, "Performance Feedback Information and Organizational Communication," *Human Communication Research*, 7 (1980), 68–73; Linda Smircich and R. Chesser, "Superiors' and Subordinates' Perceptions of Performance," *Academy of Management Journal*, 24 (1981), 198–205; Arthur Brief, "Differences in Evaluations of Employee Performance," *Journal of Occupational Psychology*, 50 (1977), 129–134.

4

The Human Relations Type of Organization

THE DEVELOPMENT OF THE HUMAN RELATIONS TYPE OF
   ORGANIZATION
Origins of the Human Relations Type
Completion of the Human Relations Type

NECESSARY FEATURES OF THE HUMAN RELATIONS TYPE

POSTSCRIPT: HUMAN RELATIONS AND THE STRUCTURE OF
   ORGANIZATIONS

*If thou art one to whom petition is made, be calm as thou listeneth. . . .Do not
rebuff him before he has . . . said that for which he came. . . .It is not [necessary]
that everything about which he has petitioned should come to pass, [but] a good
hearing is soothing to the heart.*   **—Pharoah Ptah-hotep to his managers, 2700 B.C.**

*If a leader maintains close relationships with his soldiers they will "be more eager
to be seen performing some honorable action, and more anxious to abstain from
doing anything that was disgraceful."*   **—a lesson learned by Alexander the Great
from the Persian King Cyrus, c. 325 B.C.**

By the late 1920s workers, managers, union representatives, and organizational
researchers began to voice concerns about the traditional model of organizing.
During the following two decades these concerns grew in frequency and intensity, until by 1940, a great many people were actively seeking new and
different ways to design and operate businesses. During the 1930s a group of
industrial psychologists, led by Fritz Roethlisberger and Elton Mayo, and two
organizational theorists, Mary Parker Follett and Chester Barnard, proposed the
key ideas which were to lead to the development of the needed alternative. The

73

result of their efforts was an ideal type of organization which was designed around the individual identities and needs of employees and which assumed that cooperation and supportive interpersonal relationships were the keys to organizational effectiveness. This *human relations* movement, as the model eventually was labeled, rapidly gained followers and soon replaced the traditional model as the dominant idea in organizational theory. In what may be the most important article ever published in *Reader's Digest*, Stuart Chase asserted that if only American organizations would accept the ideas of the human relations theorists, our economy would be revived and our nation transformed.[1]

This chapter will describe the development of the human relations ideal and the role that communication plays in these organizations. Chapter 5 will evaluate the communication-related problems faced by these organizations and explain the processes through which the key ideas of the model were modified or abandoned.

THE DEVELOPMENT OF THE HUMAN RELATIONS TYPE OF ORGANIZATION

Ten years before the birth of the human relations movement, the ideas of the traditional organizational theorists had gained the same kind of sudden, widespread acceptance. In both cases the sudden popularity of the new ideas can be understood only if one also understands the social and economic situations in which they were developed. Frederick Taylor had seen organizations run by managers who had little real understanding of why they managed as they did and staffed by masses of workers who were alienated and angered by the arbitrary and capricious actions of their supervisors. The early human relations theorists lived in a social and economic situation very different from the one that had spawned the traditional model. And, like Taylor, they observed organizations in which workers continued to be alienated by abuses of management.

Abuses of the traditional model stemmed primarily from managers' resistance to the mental revolution that Taylor recognized as the key to the model. When workers increased their performance in traditional industries, managers often responded by cutting their pay rates or raising the standards that they had to exceed in order to receive bonuses. In still other cases, supervisors exploited their workers by constructing pay systems which were so complex that they could not be understood. Workers and union representatives were so angered by these practices that they forced an end to most of the incentive systems Taylor and his successors had inspired.[2] In short, the cooperative labor-management relationship that Taylor predicted did not come to pass, nor did the concepts of fair and impersonal treatment that were important parts of Max Weber's theory of bureaucracy. The use of carefully designed reward systems of the type developed by the traditional theorists rarely occurred. "Rational" and "scientific" ideas of management and leadership were distorted so completely that they eventually were used to justify the belief that workers were only mechanical parts of the production process. The idea that employees were to be treated impersonally, which was intended to eliminate arbitrary and capricious treatment by supervisors, was distorted to imply that they should be treated as nonpersons.[3]

Social and economic changes also stimulated interest in finding an alternative to the traditional model. The growth of labor unions and the growing hostility between workers and management soon led to the creation of two separate and hostile camps. The increasing education of the population created a work force that was capable of having more control over their jobs than ever before and one that also wanted to obtain more than economic rewards. The disastrous effects of the Great Depression led many people to doubt the viability of capitalism and the effectiveness of its institutions, including privately owned and administered businesses. When combined, these developments created a climate in which alternatives to traditional ideas about how societies and their organizations should be designed and run were actively sought and carefully considered. Into this new climate stepped a group of professors whose research and ideas provided a very attractive alternative.

Origins of the Human Relations Type

The spark which ignited the human relations movement was the publication of the results of the now-famous series of studies made by a group of Harvard psychologists at the Hawthorne Plant of the Western Electric Company in Cicero, Illinois, between 1927 and 1932. During its first year the Hawthorne study was much like the studies of task efficiency that had been conducted by followers of the scientific management movement. The Harvard group's initial objective had been to determine the optimal level of illumination to be provided workers who assembled electrical components. Surprisingly, productivity increased both in the experimental group, where lighting was decreased, and in the control group, where no changes were made. In subsequent studies it became clear to the researchers that (1) until the lighting was reduced so low that workers could not see what they were doing, changes in illumination had no significant effect on productivity; and (2) workers perceived that the level of lighting had been changed when told that it had been, even if no actual changes had been made. These "screwy" (Roethlisberger's term) results led to a second series of "controlled" experiments in which five women were placed in a separate room and told to assemble telephone relays under a variety of different working conditions.

The data gathered in this and subsequent studies served as the basis of the three radical conclusions that the Hawthorne researchers eventually drew:

1. Workers who are involved in a friendly, relaxed, and congenial work group with supervisors who listen to them, are concerned about their needs, and are supportive are more productive than other workers, even when other working conditions are not particularly favorable.

2. Workers' satisfaction with the social and interpersonal relationships they have with their peers significantly influences their productivity, and workers feel substantial pressure from their peers to conform to the norms of their work group.

3. Researchers can accurately understand workers' (subjects') actions only if they understand the meanings that the workers attribute to their surroundings and the actions of others in their work environment. It was the first and second of these conclusions that spawned the human relations movement, but it is only the third conclusion that consistently has been supported by subsequent research. However, the extent to which the first two conclusions were accepted by managers and researchers alike cannot be questioned. As Alex Carey noted as late as 1967, "reputable textbooks still refer almost reverentially to the Hawthorne studies as a classic in the history of social science in industry."[4]

At about the same time that the Hawthorne studies were first publicized, Follett and Barnard were developing similar ideas. Both these writers accepted many of the basic tenets of the traditional school of organizing. But unlike the traditional model, which concentrated on the structure of the tasks performed, Follett and Barnard were concerned primarily with improving the quality of relationships between supervisors and workers and increasing the job satisfaction of all employees. Follett believed that managers could be most effective in motivating their subordinates if they understood and used the principles of modern (which meant Freudian at that time) psychology. The key to leadership, she argued, was the capacity to give orders which would not be resisted by workers. She admitted that the primary concepts of traditional command-related communication were sound—orders must be clear and specific, must seem to be logical and appropriate, and must be "legitimate" in the sense that Weber used that term.

However, workers may choose to not comply with even those orders which are clear, rational, and legitimate. First of all, compliance depends on a supervisor's ability to communicate commands in a way which allows subordinates to retain a sense of personal pride, self-respect, and autonomy. Second, workers will comply with orders only when they believe that they have freely chosen to do so. They will resist orders when they feel that they have been coerced into doing so. They will believe that they have made a free and open choice when (1) they have been trained to make appropriate choices, (2) they have made similar choices so frequently in the past that they have developed habits of obedience, and (3) the order originates from an immediate supervisor with whom they have formed a good relationship and who has given orders in ways which spare the feelings of the subordinate.

All people, Follett argued, incorporate a variety of beliefs, values, and feelings in their responses to communication from other people. Because some of these internal pressures make them want to comply with an order and some make them want to violate it, internal conflicts are stimulated whenever an order is given. Psychologically sensitive supervisors recognize this fact and explain their orders in ways which help their subordinates resolve these internal conflicts. For example, subordinates who like their supervisor and want to comply with orders also need to feel that they are in control of their life. Wise supervisors will present an order to this kind of subordinate in a way which expresses their liking for the subordinate, involves the subordinate in the construction of the order, and indicates to the subordinate their confidence in his or her ability to figure out how best to implement the command. In this way, sensitive supervisors create a situation in which subordinates could resolve their internal conflict by obeying the order.

When supervisors combine careful training, the creation of positive habits, and appropriately communicated commands, they can form a work group which is coordinated, close to one another, and mutually supportive. If supervisors also recognize that organizations and the norms of work groups evolve and change over time and adapt their leadership to those changes, they can retain the kind of climate in which their subordinates will choose to comply with their orders. Follett's ideas are important for two reasons. First, her focus on supervisor-subordinate relationships, consideration of the psychological needs of workers, concentration on the long-term process of creating productive working climates, and recognition of the importance of supportive, face-to-face communication between workers and management laid the groundwork for both the human relations model of organizing and the academic discipline of industrial pyschology. Second, her ability to incorporate new ideas about leadership and motivation into the general framework provided by the traditional theorists provided a valuable transition between the traditional and very different human relations models. Because she accepted many of the concepts managers had become comfortable with, it was easier for them to accept the more radical ideas that she developed.

Like Follett, Barnard concentrated on the role of the professional manager in formal organizations. His most widely recognized work was *The Functions of the Executive;* his most important ideas involved the role of *communication systems* in organizations and the power of the *informal organization.* Barnard wrote that organizations are complex systems of coordinated activities which depend on the abilities of an executive who must (1) create and maintain a system of communication among members of the organization, (2) stimulate the activities and effort needed to make the system operate, and (3) define the goals of the organization and each of its units. Organizations depend on managers to make decisions, and managers depend on the availability of accurate information to make good decisions. Although each of these ideas was part of the traditional model, Barnard elevated them to a much higher level of importance. In fact, he asserted that "in an exhaustive theory of organizations [he felt that his work was only part of a complete theory], communication would occupy a central place, because the structure, extensiveness, and scope of organizations are almost entirely determined by communication techniques."[5]

Not only did Barnard recognize the importance of formal, task-related communication in the success of organizations, but also he was one of the first modern scholars to acknowledge the existence and importance of informal communication and the informal organization. He believed that societies, or cultures, are large informal organizations. They do not have a formal structure and they do not require or sanction any particular kinds of relationships among their members. But they allow people to form relationships from which they gain important kinds of satisfactions, and they teach people the norms of conduct necessary for the society to continue to function cooperatively. Formal organizations arise within these large informal organizations because, in all societies, a number of political and economic activities must be carried out, and formal organizations are necessary for the efficient completion of these activities. But as Weber had realized, formal organizations can exist only because the society has created a situation in which some members of those organizations can legitimize their right to control the activities of other members.

Once formal organizations are formed, another more specific kind of informal organization, a mini-culture, emerges within the formal organization. People form interpersonal relationships with other employees, creating a network of relationships that is much like the network which makes up their formal organization. Through these smaller informal organizations, workers maintain their own identities, gain a sense of self-respect, and exercise control over their lives at work. By communicating with other members of their informal organizations, workers obtain and provide valuable information about their firm and people in it. Often, and unfortunately, managers and executives either ignore the existence of these informal organizations or become afraid of them and try to suppress them. According to Barnard, experienced managers often said that

> "you can't understand an organization or how it works from its organizational chart, its charter, rules and regulations. . . . Learning the organization ropes" in most organizations is chiefly learning who's who, what's what, why's why of its informal society. . . . In fact, informal organization is so much a part of our matter-of-course intimate experience of everyday association . . . that we are unaware of it, seeing only a part of the specific interactions involved. Yet it is evident that association of persons in connection with a formal or specific activity inevitably involves interactions that are incidental to it.[6]

It is through informal ties that employees gain rewards from their membership in a formal organization. Through informal communication they express and share their satisfactions and dissatisfactions with work. Since people will choose to remain in a formal organization only if they receive greater rewards from it than they could receive from other organizations, the informal organization is an important factor in the success of a formal organization. Without informal organizations, workers would have little incentive to be part of and contribute to a formal organization.

Barnard's work made two important contributions: It stressed the important role that communication plays in the functioning of formal or-

FIGURE 4.1   Barnard's Formal and Informal Organizations

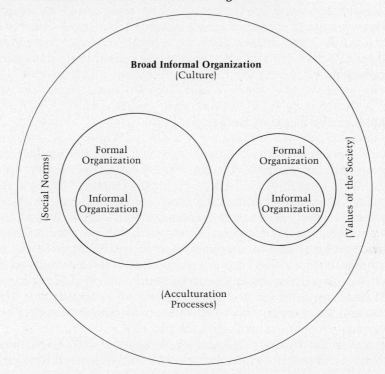

ganizations, and it helped people recognize that informal communication is (1) always present in organizations, (2) an important source of rewards for employees, and (3) a crucial aspect of the operation of formal organizations. While Follett was introducing managers to the key psychological concepts of resistance, self-esteem, and interpersonal support, Barnard was introducing them to the sociological concepts of rewards, group membership, and informal ties. However, like the traditional theorists before them, Follett and Barnard saw communication primarily as a command and task-related function. They continued to accept Weber's suggestion that the flow of communication in bureaucratic organizations must be restricted to the chain of command.

When considered as a unit, the work of the early human relations theorists introduced managers and organizational researchers to a revolutionary set of ideas:

1. Members of organizations are complex, thinking beings rather than mechanical parts of an organizational assembly line.

2. Their decisions about how to act are influenced by a complicated set of personal feelings, interpersonal relationships, and social pressures.

3. Communication processes are central elements of the ongoing process of sustaining a formal organization.

These researchers provided a rough description of a type of organization in which managers strategically create cooperative and supportive situations in which employees could coordinate their activities to receive a variety of non-economic rewards. They did not draw a complete picture of this new type of organization, but they did provide a framework which their successors were able to complete.

Completion of the Human Relations Type

The history of organization theory and organizational communication theory represent two distinct phases of thought. The boundaries between them always have been a little blurred, both because each phase retained many of the ideas of the previous phases and because the ideal type of organization described in each has always been just that, a theoretical construct which never really existed.[7] However, the early years of each phase are remarkably alike. They begin when managers and/or theorists become frustrated with the existing theories, either because they are not successful when put into practice or because they do not make sense when examined carefully. These frustrations eventually lead to calls for the development of new attitudes about organizations and the people who work in them and new strategies or mechanisms for putting the new attitudes into practice.

The traditional model originated in frustration with the arbitrary, inhumane, and inefficient managerial practices of the Industrial Revolution and culminated in calls for a complete mental revolution on the part of managers and the use of rational solutions to their problems. Similarly, the human relations model originated in concerns about the dehumanizing excesses of the traditional model and a realization that workers were not the mechanical, wholly economic creatures they had been assumed to be. It proposed a second "mental revolution," in which managers and theorists would adopt more accurate and humane views of the complicated human worker, would become more employee-centered, and would use a series of new managerial and motivational techniques. The most important of these new techniques involved changes in the content and methods of supervisor-subordinate communication. Although each of the later human relations theorists developed his or her own terms for these concepts, three major themes were woven through all their work: (1) Relationship-oriented attitudes and communication are important, (2) non-economic aspects of job satisfaction are significant, and (3) maintaining a "supportive" climate in work groups is necessary for them to function successfully.

Relational Attitudes and Communication The early human relations movement was motivated by a new set of assumptions about the nature of human beings and their work. These commonly held assumptions were summarized quite clearly in Douglas McGregor's comparison of traditional (*Theory X*) and

FIGURE 4.2   McGregor's Theory X and Theory Y

Theory X	*Theory Y*
1. Workers must be supervised as closely as possible, either through direct oversight or by tight reward and/or punishment systems.	1. People usually do not require close supervision and will, if given a chance to control their own activities, be productive, satisfied, and fulfilled.
2. Work is objectionable to most people.	2. Work is natural and enjoyable unless it is made to be offensive by the actions of organizations.
3. Most people have little initiative, little capacity for being creative or solving organizational problems, do not want to have responsibilities, and prefer being directed by someone else.	3. People are ambitious, desire autonomy and self-control, and can use their abilities to solve problems and help their organizations meet their goals. Creativity is distributed "normally" across the population, just as is any other characteristic.
4. People are motivated by economic factors and a need for security.	4. People are motivated by a variety of needs, only some of which involve economics or security.

human relations (*Theory Y*) ideas about organizations. According to the assumptions of Theory Y, human beings are complex, creative people who will expend substantial skill and effort in constructive work if they are given opportunities to do so. These opportunities are created by a very specific set of supervisory behaviors and complex, challenging, and rewarding tasks. The later human relations theorists concentrated on the first of these features (supervisory behaviors), and their successors, often called "human resources theorists," concentrated on both.

Two series of studies eventually led to the development of a complete list of desirable supervisory behaviors. The first group was conducted by members of the Survey Research Center of the University of Michigan under the direction of Rensis Likert. These studies compared the attitudes and activities of employee-centered and job-centered supervisors. Their goal was to determine the factors which contributed to the effectiveness of different managers. In general, Likert's group found that high-producing organizations and units of organizations had supervisors who

   1. Focused their primary attention on the human aspects of their subordinates' problems *and* on endeavoring to build effective work groups which had high performance goals

2. Communicated a kind of contagious enthusiasm about achieving those goals and did not place "unreasonable" pressure on their subordinates to meet the goals

3. Supervised "generally" (or "loosely") rather than closely, making their objectives clear to their subordinates and also giving them substantial lattitude and freedom to do their jobs as they saw fit

4. Expressed genuine concern for their subordinates and their personal problems

5. Actively encouraged their subordinates to participate in decision making

6. Were technically competent in their jobs

Likert indicated what an employee-centered supervisor was by reprinting one such supervisor's description of himself:

> One way in which we accomplish a high level of production is by letting people do the job the way they want so long as they accomplish the objectives. I believe in letting them take time out from the monotony. Make them feel that they are something special. . . . If you keep employees from feeling hounded, they are apt to put out the necessary effort to get the work done in the required time. I never make any decisions myself. . . . I don't believe in saying that this is the way it's going to be. . . . My job is dealing with human beings rather than with the work. . . . The chances are that people will do a better job if you are really taking an interest in them. Knowing the names is important and it helps a lot, but it's not enough. You really have to know each individual well, know what his problems are.[8]

Similar ideas and results emerged from a second series of studies, which were conducted by Edwin Fleishman and his associates at Ohio State University. These studies compared the performance of work groups led by supervisors who communicated "consideration" to their workers with that of groups led by supervisors who focused on "initiating structure." *Consideration* involved behaviors which expressed mutual trust, respect, and a certain degree of warmth and rapport between the supervisor and subordinates. It did not involve superficial "pat-on-the-back" or "first name" gimmicks but emphasized a deeper concern for the group members' needs. *Initiation of structure* included behaviors which emphasized the goals of the organization, deemphasized the needs and goals of the workers, eliminated any shared decision making or assignment of tasks, and involved continual pressure for increased output. The results of the Ohio State studies, like Likert's, indicated that consideration was positively related to performance, at least up to a certain point.[9]

When combined, the ideas and research of McGregor, Likert, Fleishman, and their associates suggest that superior-subordinate relationships in human relations organizations would differ from those in traditional organizations in two important ways. First, supervisors in the former would adopt employee-centered, relationship-oriented attitudes and values. Second, they would communicate with their subordinates in ways that would put those new values into practice. But both attitudes and actions must be changed. Without improved communication, a change in supervisors' values will have no impact on the involvement, effort, or performance of their subordinates. The success of human relations organizations thus depends on supervisors' developing two different, but related, kinds of relationship-oriented communication skills.

First, supervisors must learn to be supportive. In a now-famous essay, Jack Gibb described the characteristics of supportive communication and of its opposite, defensive communication. Gibb concluded that communication creates feelings of discomfort and defensiveness when either its content or the way in which it is presented makes people feel that they are

1. Being *judged* (even praise creates discomfort if it is excessively strong or too public)
2. Being *manipulated* or *controlled* too tightly or inappropriately
3. Being *tricked*, especially into believing that they are having an important impact on decisions or playing an important role in the organization when they are not
4. Being subjected to *cold, impersonal, uncaring* treatment
5. Being treated as an *inferior*, relatively useless person
6. Being "preached at" by a smug or "know-it-all" supervisor

A supervisor's communication creates feelings of personal worth and comfort to the extent that it is descriptive and objective rather than evaluative; focuses on working together to solve important problems; is spontaneous and an accurate expression of the supervisor's true attitudes rather than an attempt to manipulate the subordinate; reflects the belief that the subordinate is capable and competent; and expresses appropriate degrees of tentativeness, doubt, and openness to questioning (see Figure 4.3). When successfully and consistently used, supportive communication increases the level of trust between a supervisor and subordinates and creates the perception that the supervisor is considerate or employee-centered.[10]

A second, related dimension of communication is the creation of an open climate. Although the concept of openness is difficult to define, it depends on

FIGURE 4.3   Gibb's Communication Climates

Styles of Communicating Which Create Defensiveness	*Styles of Communication Which Are Supportive*
Evaluative	Descriptive
Controlling, manipulative	Focusing on tasks
Strategic	Spontaneous
Neutral, lacking concern	Empathic
Superior	Showing equality
Certain	Qualificative, tentative

subordinates' feeling that their supervisor encourages them to initiate communication on either personal or work-related topics *and* that they will not be punished when they do so even if the information reflects negatively on themselves, their work, or their supervisor. An atmosphere of openness is created when supervisors actively encourage their subordinates to communicate with them and when they are careful to evaluate only the content of the messages and not the subordinates themselves. If supervisors attack or fail to acknowledge the existence and competence of their subordinates (a process that communication theorists have labeled *disconfirmation*), openness will be reduced.[11]

Consequently, it seems that the potential success of the human relations model of supervisor-subordinate relationships depends on two key aspects of relational communication: (1) creating an atmosphere of mutual trust, respect, and support, and (2) encouraging open communication. But unless supervisors also adopt attitudes and values which are appropriate, relational communication can become merely a new and different way of manipulating subordinates. The tendency for managers to adopt human relations communication strategies without accepting the underlying values of the model—a phenomenon so widespread that it has been given a name of its own (*pseudohuman relations*)—eventually generated a strong backlash of opposition to the human relations movement among managers and organizational theorists alike.

The Central Place of Job Satisfaction in the Human Relations Type   In general, human relations theorists assumed that humane supervisory attitudes and appropriate communication strategies would lead to increased individual and organizational performance. The causal relationship they envisioned is relatively complex (see Figure 4.4). Although the theory eventually was justified on the grounds that human relations strategies would improve job satisfaction (which is an important goal in and of itself), the initial justification of the model was that of improved performance and productivity.

Human relations strategies would increase satisfaction, it was assumed, because they fulfill employees' noneconomic needs. Two of the most influential foundations of this assumption was the model of human motivation proposed by psychiatrist Abraham Maslow and a series of studies by Frederick Herzberg and Chris Argyris. Maslow's "hierarchy of prepotent needs" is by now known to almost everyone. As a brief review, Maslow's experience as a psychotherapist led him to believe that humans have five different kinds of needs,

FIGURE 4.4   The Causal Relationships of the Human Relations Model

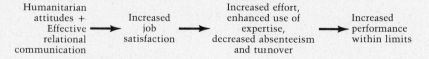

Humanitarian attitudes + Effective relational communication → Increased job satisfaction → Increased effort, enhanced use of expertise, decreased absenteeism and turnover → Increased performance within limits

physiological (expressed in feelings of hunger, thirst, lust, and so on), *safety* (freedom from danger, harm, and fear that physical needs will be denied), *social* or *belongingness* (expressed in a desire for meaningful relationships with other people), *esteem* or *ego* (achievement and recognition), and *self-actualization* (a concept Maslow has never explained clearly but which seems to be related to the feeling that one has done or is doing what one is meant to do). These needs are arranged in a hierarchy of dominance from the most basic or potent (physiological) to the least basic (self-actualization). Maslow said that the upper-level needs are not salient to most people until their lower-level needs are met. Although the lower-level needs do not have to be fulfilled completely before the upper-level ones become important, and although the relative salience of the different needs varies among individuals, times, and situations, most people will find that their lower-level needs will be met more completely than their higher-level ones. Although Maslow never explicitly applied his model to motivation of workers, it has become the basis of a number of need-satisfaction theories, the most important of which were Herzberg's "motivator-hygiene" theory and Argyris' concept of integrating individuals into the organization.

Herzberg started his research by asking a group of two hundred engineers and accountants to describe "critical incidents," events in which they had felt especially satisfied or dissatisfied with their jobs. He then classified these incidents into two groups, those in which the subjects reported satisfaction and those in which they reported dissatisfaction. Looking for frequently mentioned sources of satisfaction or dissatisfaction, he eventually developed two groups of factors; *motivators* (satisfiers) and *hygiene* (dissatisfiers). A summary of these categories is presented in Figure 4.5.

From the results of his research Herzberg argued that (1) satisfaction and dissatisfaction result from different factors and (2) these factors operate in different ways. Hygiene factors are related to physical, safety, or social needs and motivate people by giving them opportunities to avoid pain. When these needs are not met, people feel discomfort; when they are met, the discomfort is reduced but no additional pleasure is experienced. Motivators (or satisfiers) are related to personal growth (ego or self-actualization) and when provided are pleasurable. However, when they are denied, people do not feel frustration or pain. Although neither of Herzberg's conclusions have been supported consistently by subsequent research, his two-factor theory was accepted as support for both the assumption that noneconomic needs significantly influence workers' satisfaction and the belief that enlarging and enriching workers' jobs will increase their satisfaction.[12]

Argyris extended Maslow's model to develop a theory of how people become alienated from their jobs and from the organizations in which they work. His most important ideas were expressed in five "propositions":[13]

1. The "upper-level" needs of normal, psychologically healthy people are not consistent with the characteristics of traditional organizations. These inconsistencies are frustrating.

FIGURE 4.5   Maslow's Hierarchy of Needs and Herzberg's Two Factors

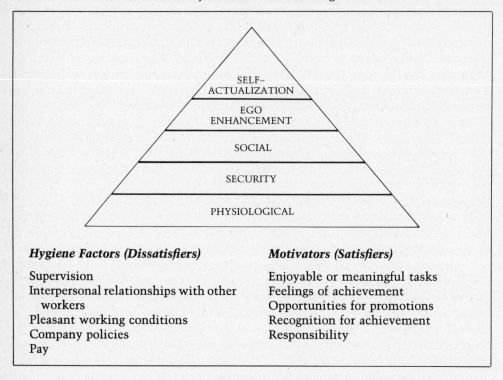

2.   Frustrations are increased when organizations rely on formal rules for control, when supervisors become overly controlling and directive or refuse to allow their subordinates to set their own goals and means of achieving them, when jobs become too narrow or specialized, and when managers use human relations communication strategies to manipulate their employees.

3.   The competitive climate within organizations will lead employees to rivalry, hostility, and a narrow, short-term, and individualistic perspective instead of a cooperative, organization-centered view.

4.   Employees will adapt to these situations by engaging in a number of defensive reactions (for example, daydreaming, being aggressive, or withdrawing), becoming apathetic, forming informal social ties with other frustrated workers and concentrating their attention on those ties rather than on their work, leaving the organization, or attempting to advance in the organizational hierarchy to positions which are less frustrating.

5.   The more mature and healthy individuals are, the more probable it is that they will be frustrated and respond in these ways.

The key to Argyris' theory is the belief that human beings actively interpret their surroundings and choose actions which are appropriate responses to their situations. If they have opportunities to grow and fulfill their need for self-actualization, they will choose to act in ways which also meet the needs of their organization. But if their situations frustrate those needs, they will act in ways which do not meet the needs of the organization.

Of course, neither Maslow's model nor the research conducted by Herzberg and Argyris explicitly tested the causal relationships among job satisfaction, effort, and performance, which were the basis of the human relations model. But their work generated such concentrated attention of ways on increasing workers' satisfaction that human relations theorists largely accepted or assumed the validity of those causal links. After all, the work of Mayo, Likert, Fleishman, and their associates had demonstrated a relationship between human relations strategies and performance. It was assumed that the rest of the causal chain could be supported intuitively by their research. Unfortunately, more recent and more precise research has not provided consistent support for the assumed causal relationships.

Establishing an Appropriate Organizational Climate The first and second elements of the human relations ideal involved an emphasis on relationship-oriented superior-subordinate communication and an assumption that human relations strategies would contribute to workers' satisfaction and organizational performance. The final element is the notion that the success of human relations strategies depends on the creation and maintenance of a particular kind of organizational "climate." Human relations theorists repeatedly emphasized that the communication strategies they advocated were not enough in and of themselves. They would increase satisfaction and performance only if they were employed where cooperative and supportive interpersonal relationships are normal and expected. The term typically applied to this overall pattern of attitudes, expectations, and norms of supervisor-subordinate communication is the *organizational* or *communication climate*. If human relations strategies are employed in an open and supportive climate, members of the organization will interpret the communication they receive from others as humane and honest and will respond favorably. But if the strategies are used in a closed and defensive climate, they often will be interpreted as offensive attempts by managers to manipulate their subordinates and will cause reduced satisfaction and performance.[14] Although there is substantial disagreement about what a supportive climate is, there seems to be a consensus that it is created through four processes: (1) establishing a pattern of effective relational communication (as it was defined earlier in this chapter), (2) encouraging active channels of informal communication, (3) creating a system of group rewards, and (4) adopting some form of participatory decision making or "power sharing."

Active Informal Communication Networks Barnard realized that informal organizations and informal channels of communication emerge in all organizations. They will continue to exist and will become valuable assets to managers unless managers actively attempt to suppress or destroy them. As the ancient quotations at the beginning of Chapter 2 indicated, the importance of maintaining effective formal channels of communication has been recognized for centuries.[15] But formal communication channels need to be supplemented by informal ones. Each member of an organization is instructed to transmit certain kinds of information to certain people and to seek certain kinds of information from other people. When people communicate through these formally prescribed channels, they do so more from their willingness to follow instructions than from their own needs for information or personal contact. Informal channels of communication, in contrast, emerge because people find that they often need to gain or provide information to people with whom they have not been told to communicate or because they are attracted to or enjoy communicating with those people.

Informal channels exist because of their unique advantages and because of the weaknesses inherent in formal channels of communication. Formal channels allow people to handle predictable, routine situations quite well. Because they tend to be filled with written rather than oral messages, they are effective means of transmitting broad, general kinds of information. But communicating through formal channels is a slow, laborious process which involves long delays between the time a worker first sends a message and the time a reply is received. Consequently, formal channels are inefficient means for meeting unanticipated communication needs, for managing crises, for effectively communicating complex or detailed information, or for sharing personal information.[16] Because these are inevitable aspects of formal communication channels, workers develop informal communication with other members of their organization.

Informal communication ties have a number of important characteristics. First, they are "emergent" rather than imposed on people. This means that it takes time for them to become established and that they must continue to be used or they will disappear. People form links with other people because they discover that they need information from them or that they need to communicate information to them. Since the people often are working in different parts of the organization and have different backgrounds, tasks, and experiences, it takes time for them to find one another and a substantial number of conversations for them to begin to understand each other. Sometimes the two people will be members of units which develop their own, unique technical languages. For instance, members of personnel departments often develop code words and jargon which are completely different than those used by the people in computer operations. Before these people can form informal communication ties they have to, literally, learn the foreign language that is used by the other person. For similar reasons the two people must continue to communicate with one another on at least a fairly regular basis or they will forget the language and perceptual sets used by the other person. Just as the effects of foreign language courses wear off, learning the language of different employees also deteriorates. Unless there is some "steady state noise" in the informal communication channel that two people have created, the communication

FIGURE 4.6   Formal and Informal Communication Links

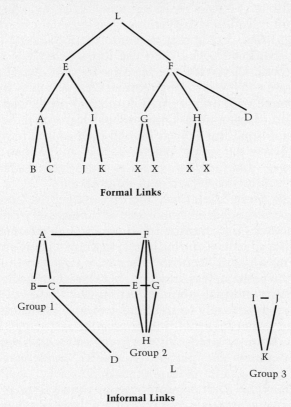

Formal Links

Informal Links

link eventually will dissolve. Then, when a crisis occurs in which they need to communicate with each other, they will find it very difficult to do so.

Second, informal communication links are complex and overlapping. Every person has a number of communication needs. For each need, the person will form informal links with a certain group of people who have the information or personality necessary to fulfill that need. Eventually, people form a group of links which allows them to share information about organizational policies, another group for information about personnel changes, another for insight into organizational politics, and so on until they have formed links for all their communication needs.

Fortunately, these separate sets of links often overlap. An employee will discover that a particular person has access to reliable information about a number of important topics. These individuals will become key sources of information for the employee. In addition, these key links usually are attractive sources of information for other members of the organization. Although any employee can become a key link in the informal communication network, these people usually have high levels of formal status, are satisfied with their jobs, and are sensitive to the informal norms of the organization. And, because these key links also have formal positions in the hierarchy, formal and informal channels of communication also overlap. An individual may learn something through informal links, decide that that information should be passed on to supervisors or subordinates, and then use formal channels to transmit the information to them. Of course, the opposite kind of interchange also takes place. Messages are conveyed through formal channels with instructions that they are to be shared with only a small number of people and passed on only through the chain of command. Other people learn of these organizational secrets through informal links, even though they cannot formally (officially) admit that they know the secret. When informal and formal communication links are combined—and they always are to some extent—they form complicated, mutually reinforcing networks of information.

As the early human relations theorists suggested, informal communication ties have a number of important advantages. Two of them already have been mentioned: First, information flows through informal channels very rapidly, a particular advantage during crises. In a now-classic study Keith Davis found that during a quality-control crisis in a large firm, the information needed to solve the problem was disseminated almost immediately and almost completely through informal communication links.[17] For this reason supervisory personnel generally rely on informal communication during crises. The second advantage is that informal communication is "richer" in content than formal communication. It almost always involves vocal, face-to-face communication, which allows the parties to receive immediate feedback and clarification and provides information through nonverbal cues not available in written communication. Oral communication allows large amounts of information to be exchanged with a minimal expenditure of effort. Writing takes time and carries substantial costs, so much so that people tend to avoid it unless it is absolutely necessary. In some cultures the relative energy advantage of oral communication is enormous because the written language is so complex.

The third advantage of informal links is that this kind of communication is very accurate, even when it consists of rumors. Informal links are, by definition, beyond the control of upper management. Frequently, messages whose accuracy cannot be verified by management flow through these channels (these messages usually are labeled *rumors*). Rumors are created when members of organizations are confused or uninformed about topics which interest them. They attempt to make sense out of the situation by constructing explanations which seem to be plausible. Since they cannot do this with the small amount of information received through formal channels, they "fill in" their explanation with extraneous information, some of which may be untrue or inaccurate. Then they share their completed explanations with other employees in an attempt to determine whether or not it really does make sense. The others use the explanation to form their own explanations of what is going on and then share these explanations with others. In this way a rumor is born and spread. Because rumors are beyond the control of supervisors, and because they sometimes are false, managers often become "paranoid" about them and attempt to prevent them by suppressing the informal communication links through which they are passed. Although this reaction is understandable, it usually is counterproductive. It inaccurately assumes that informal communication is less accurate than formal communication. In Chapter 3 a number of reasons were given to explain why information is distorted as it flows through formal communication channels. Distortions occur when a message is exchanged between people who have different degrees of power, status, and rank. Because informal communication typically goes through short chains and because it allows people temporarily to ignore status and power differences, it does not suffer from the sources of distortion which plague formal communication. As a result, informal communication may not be any less accurate than formal communication.[18]

The fact that informal links tend to avoid the tensions and constraints that are inevitable when people of different ranks communicate with one another provides another asset for the organization. Through his twenty-year study of bureaucratic organizations, Peter Blau found that informal communication channels both allow people to gain advice and assistance without having to admit formally or publically that they need it and give people opportunities to "think out loud" about new ideas or experiences. This process really is consultation in disguise because it creates "nonverbal communications from listener to speaker [which] indicate to the latter whether he is on the right track. . . .Talking out loud reduces the anxiety engendered by difficult problems and thereby improves the ability to solve them . . . and the experience of being consulted by colleagues tends to increased self-confidence."[19] Thus the presence of informal communication links can improve both the quality of problem-solving activities and interpersonal relationships by increasing each participant's status and morale. If management suppresses informal communication this advantage is eliminated.

In addition, suppressing informal communication links may keep people from gaining information necessary to disconfirm or correct rumors. If managers succeed in suppressing or destroying informal channels—and the fact that informal channels exist in prisons, prisoner-of-war camps, concentration camps, and occupied countries suggests that they never can be destroyed completely—this self-correcting function cannot take place. Members of the organization will be forced to rely on formal channels of communication, which often carry distorted information; fail in crises, when accurate information is most important; and create the confusing or ambiguous situations which spawn inaccurate rumors in the first place.

Thus, instead of trying to succeed in the impossible and often counterproductive objective of suppressing informal communication ties, managers should recognize their inevitability and learn to use them strategically. Sometimes people with little formal power have access to a wealth of valuable information about employees' attitudes, performance, and morale. Sometimes these people go to great lengths to obtain "private" information, as illustrated by a number of the characters in the recent movie *9 to 5*. Now, not too many people sneak into bathrooms and sit on toilets with their knees drawn up around their chins in order to eavesdrop unobserved. But employees do find a variety of ways to obtain "secret" information, and supervisors can benefit from having access to those people and the information they possess. They also can use their links to informal networks to disseminate information they believe their subordinates should have but cannot release through formal channels. They can release "trial baloons" and obtain employees' reactions while never having to admit in public that the proposal was even being considered. Thus, in spite of the tendency for managers to develop rumor paranoia, informal communication consistently has been shown to be an important and valuable part of formal organizations.

Group Rewards and Group Pressures   One of the two most important findings of the Hawthorne studies was that pressures imposed by some members of a work group on other members have a significant effect on the actions of those members. In many production-oriented firms, including the Hawthorne plant, employees are paid on the basis of a piece-rate system, in which each employee's production is compared to an average or expected rate for the group as a whole. During the observations of the bank wiring room of the Hawthorne plant, Mayo and his associates noticed what every new worker learned within a week or so of being hired. If any member of the work group violated the informal production norms of the group, either by being too productive or by not being productive enough, the other members pressured that person to come "back in line." If any member "squealed" to a supervisor about these pressures, or if any supervisor tried to force a group to change its behavior, the pressure to conform intensified. Each of these responses is predictable, since employees expected that the behaviors of the "deviants" eventually would lead management to take actions which were not in the workers self-interest—the cycle that leads to systematic soldiering. Conforming to the pressures also is predictable, both because it is in the deviant members' self-interest to do so and because deviants often are isolated by the rest of the group and therefore lose the satisfaction gained from communicating with other people. Organizations could use these pressures to their advantage, the Hawthorne researchers reasoned, if they created work groups in which supervisors were supportive and cooperative and rewards were based on group rather than individual performance.

A number of such systems have been developed since the 1930s. The most widely used of these was first proposed by a steelworker and union leader, Joseph Scanlon. At the center of the *Scanlon plans*, as they came to be called, was an open suggestion system through which workers could make recommendations for changes to increase the productivity of their groups or the quality of their product. Each unit of the firm included a "production committee," which screened the suggestions made by workers in its unit, implemented those which were reasonable and feasible, and communicated any worthwhile organizationwide suggestions to a committee higher in the hierarchy. In addition, a bonus system was established through which each worker received a monthly reward based on the increased productivity of the *entire organization*. Scanlon's plans succeeded so remarkably in his steel mill and in the other firms in which it was applied that he spent the remainder of his career on the staff of M.I.T. as a labor-management consultant. Although the Scanlon plans failed in some firms, their forty-year history has been one of frequent success. They are important because they have been a successful effort to create the kind of situation envisioned in the human relations model.[20]

Power Sharing and Participatory Decision Making   The final element of the communication climate depicted in the human relations type of organization is the equitable distribution of decision-making power throughout all levels of the organization. Sharing the power traditionally given to upper management is to be accomplished through some system that encourages workers to participate in organizational decision making.

The impact of distributing power equally is illustrated best by research conducted in a number of countries by Arnold Tannenbaum and his associates. They found that in a wide variety of organizations in both capitalist and socialist countries, employees perceive that the people at the top of the hierarchy exercise far more influence over decisions than people who are lower down. If one adds up the amount of influence that each member of the organization perceives that he or she has, some organizations will have greater total amounts of perceived power than other organizations. From these data the Tannenbaum group reasoned that perceived power is not like a pie, which has a fixed size and must be divided up among employees. It is more like an

FIGURE 4.7   Tannenbaum's Power Curves

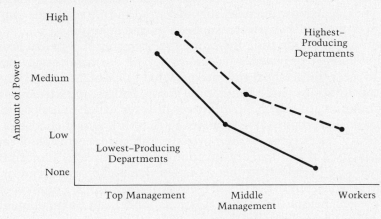

expanding balloon (or an expandable pie), which can be enlarged continuously, allowing every member to obtain a larger and larger piece. A more elegant way of expressing this idea comes from "game theory." Power is not a "zero-sum game," a situation in which when one person gains something, other people invariably lose something. Instead, it is a "mixed motive" situation, in which everyone can gain something simultaneously.

Tannenbaum and his associates found that high-producing departments and firms tended to have larger "power pies" than low-producing firms or units (see Figure 4.7).[21] Thus, organizations could profit from strategies designed to increase employees' perceptions that they are able to influence decisions. By encouraging employees to participate in decision making, organizations will gain their expertise and better decisions will be made. By participating in decision making, employees will gain a greater sense of autonomy and self-worth. However, to achieve these goals, participatory decision-making programs must incorporate the following five features:

1. Subordinates must wish to be involved in decision making, must be involved in complex tasks, and must be given substantial control over how they will complete those tasks.

2. Supervisors must be willing to allow their subordinates legitimately to participate in decision making, to listen and respond to their ideas, and to encourage them to contribute.

3. The issues being discussed must be important to the participants (workers usually believe that any decisions which directly affect them or their jobs are important and that decisions about more general company policies are less important).

4. All the participants must have expertise and information relevant to the problem being discussed.

5. There must be clear organizational policies and norms which support the concept of participatory decision making.[22]

Unless each of these features is present, participatory decision making may generate poor decisions, alienate subordinates, and increase the gap in perceived power that exists between supervisors and subordinates.

In summary, by the time the human relations ideal type had been developed completely, it provided a picture of a type of organization which was designed to meet the personal and interpersonal needs of individual employees. The key contributions of the Hawthorne group, Follett, and Barnard—the concept of communicating with subordinates in ways which enhanced their self-esteem and created cooperative climates so that they would choose to comply with necessary restrictions on their actions, plus the recognition of the power and potential uses of informal organizations and pressures for conformity—had been refined and expanded to incorporate a comprehensive series of human relations strategies. But like all ideal types of organizations, a number of factors must be present before the human relations model can be implemented successfully in real organizations.

NECESSARY FEATURES OF THE HUMAN RELATIONS TYPE

The human relations type of organization differs from the traditional type in two important ways. First, it assumes that each member of an organization will adopt the attitude that organizations are cooperative enterprises made up of people whose needs for social support and feelings of self-worth, autonomy, and creativity must be met. Second, it entails a recognition that these attitudes can be taught and nurtured only in an organizational climate characterized by free, open, and supportive communication. The human relations type is similar to the traditional model in that it retains the hierarchical structure of bureaucratic organizations. Consequently, the organizational charts and *formal* communication channels of traditional and human relations organizations would be very much alike. But the patterns of communication and the beliefs about human beings and work which are accepted by its employees would be very different.

To function successfully, a human relations type of organization would have to possess *four necessary features*:

1. Members would believe that human beings are *complex, thinking,* and *productive* beings and they would act toward each other in ways which reflect these beliefs.

2. Supervisors would create an *atmosphere* of *mutual trust* and *open communication* between themselves and their subordinates and would strive to establish a climate in which there is free and open communication among all members of the organization.

3. High levels of *job satisfaction,* achieved at least in part by effective *relational communication,* would be maintained, leading to increased *effort* and enhanced organizational *performance.*

4. *Power* would be *shared* by all members of the organization, usually through communication systems which encourage participation in decision making.

Early efforts to apply the human relations model in existing organizations indicated that the use of these strategies actually could create satisfying and productive work environments. However, over time and with more sophisticated research has come the realization that these conditions are very difficult to create and sustain. Perhaps more important, even if the conditions are present, the increased performance and productivity promised by the model may not come to pass. Chapter 5 will compare real and ideal human relations organizations and examine the many factors which make it difficult to apply the model successfully.

Human Relations and the Structure of Organizations

In general, the ideal type of organization described by human relations theorists retained the pyramid-shaped formal organizational structure that was part of the traditional type of organization. However, some of the human relationists did suggest making some changes in the structure of organizations, one of which involved broadening the "span of control" of supervisors. In the traditional model, supervisors are responsible for a relatively small number of subordinates (usually four to six). With this limited range of responsibility, supervisors could observe their subordinates very closely, making certain that they carried out their orders. But if, as the human relations theorists suggested, supervisors granted their subordinates more autonomy, allowed them to determine the best means of accomplishing their assigned tasks, and supervised them "loosely" rather than closely, they could be given a much broader span of control. And if they were assigned more subordinates, they would have to grant them more autonomy and self-control. Consequently, flattening (or *decentralizing*, to use a fancier term) the hierarchy of an organization would make it possible to employ human relations strategies and would reinforce the use of those strategies (see Figure 4.8).

FIGURE 4.8   Centralized and Decentralized Organizational Hierarchies

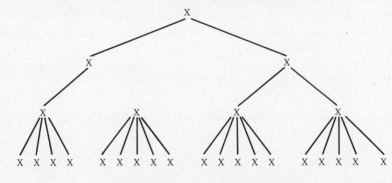

Traditional, Tall, or Centralized Organization

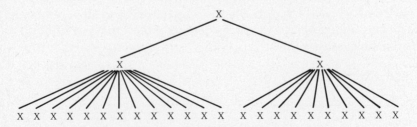

Human Relations, Flat, or Decentralized Organization

The second structural change was proposed by Likert. He suggested that organizations should be structured around multiple overlapping groups instead of being made up of the separate units of the traditional organizational hierarchy. Each group would make any decisions which effect it or its members. In addition, each group would be linked to every other group with which they needed to cooperate by a "linking pin," an employee who was a member of both work groups. In this structure each group could better understand the needs and problems of the other groups because one of its members was a part of those groups. They could minimize the problems of trained communication incapacity and language barriers (discussed in Chapter 2) because someone always would be available who understood the perceptual sets and jargon of the other groups. Unnecessary intergroup conflict could be reduced because communication breakdowns between the groups would be less frequent. Communication between the groups could be improved because the supervisor of a work group no longer was solely responsible for communicating with the other groups. Group decision making would be enhanced because each linking pin would have access to different kinds of information as a result of his or her contact with the other groups. When combined, these features made up a radically new organizational structure, one labeled *System 4* by its creator (see Figure 4.9).

FIGURE 4.9   Likert's Multiple Overlapping Groups

Ⓧ Linking pins.

Notes

1. Stuart Chase, "What Makes the Worker Like to Work," *Reader's Digest*, (February 1941), 15–20.

2. Raymond Miles, *Theories of Management* (New York: McGraw-Hill, 1975).

3. Warren Bennis, "Beyond Bureaucracy," *Trans-action*, 2 (1965), 31–35.

4. Alex Carey, "The Hawthorne Studies: a Radical Criticism," *American Sociological Review*, 32 (1967), 403–416. As Chapter 5 will indicate, neither of these first two conclusions is supported by a careful reading of the Hawthorne results.

5. Chester Barnard, *The Functions of the Executive* (Cambridge, Mass.: Harvard University press, 1938).

6. Ibid. The concept of organizational mini-cultures is developed by Michael Pacanowsky and Nick O'Donnell-Trujillio, "Organizational Communication as Cultural Performance," *Communication Monographs*, 50 (1983), 126–147.

7. Thomas Kuhn, *The Structure of Scientific Revolutions* (Chicago: University of Chicago Press, 1970), argues that this kind of developmental process characterizes science in general.

8. Rensis Likert, *New Patterns of Management* (New York: McGraw-Hill, 1961), p. 7.

9. See the articles by Edwin Fleishman and his associates in the first and second editions of *Studies in Personnel and Industrial Psychology*, ed. Edwin Fleishman (Homewood, Ill.: Dorsey, 1961 and 1967).

10. Joseph Sgro, Philip Worchel, Earl Pence, and Joseph Orban, "Perceived Leader Behavior as a Function of Trust," *Academy of Management Journal*, 23 (1980), 161–165.

11. Fred Jablin, "Superior-Subordinate Communication," in *Communication Yearbook 2*, ed. Brent Ruben (New Brunswick, N.J.: Transaction Books, 1978), pp. 293–310.

12. Edwin Locke, "The Nature and Causes of Job Satisfaction," in *Handbook of Industrial and Organizational Psychology*, ed. Marvin Dunnette (Chicago:Rand-McNally, 1976), pp. 1,297–1,342.

13. Chris Argyris, *Personality and Organization* (New York: Harper & Row, 1957).

14. Research on organizational climate is summarized in M. Scott Poole and Robert Mc-Phee, "Bringing Intersubjectivity Back in: A Change of Climate," in *Interpretive Approaches to Organizational Communication*, ed. Linda Putnam and Michael Pacanowsky (Beverley Hills, Calif.: Sage, 1983).

15. Also see Richard Cyert and James March, *A Behavioral Theory of the Firm* (Englewood Cliffs, N.J.: Prentice-Hall, 1963), p. 104.

16. Noel Tichy, Michael Tushman, and Charles Fombrun, "Social Network Analysis for Organizations," *Academy of Management Review*, 4 (1979), 507–519.

17. Keith Davis, "Management Communication and the Grapevine," *Harvard Business Review* (Sept.-Oct., 1953) 43–49.

18. Everett Rogers and Rekha Argawala-Rogers, *Communication in Organizations* (New York: The Free Press, 1976); and Jerry Wofford, Edwin Gerloff, and Robert Cummins, *Organizational Communication* (New York: McGraw-Hill, 1977).

19. Peter Blau, *On the Nature of Organizations* (New York: John Wiley, 1974), p. 7.

20. Rogers and Argawala-Rogers, *Communication in Organizations*, p. 42.

21. Arnold Tannenbaum, "Control in Organizations," *Administrative Science Quarterly*, 7 (1962), 17–42.

22. Research supporting these conditions is summarized in Bernard Bass and V. J. Shakleton, "Industrial Democracy and Participatory Management," *Academy of Management Review*, 4 (1979), 393–404; John Ivanevich, "An Analysis of Participation in Decision Making Among Project Engineers," *Academy of Management Journal*, 22 (1979), 252–269; Abraham Zalzenik, "Power and Politics in Organizational Life," *Harvard Business Review* (May-June 1970), pp. 47–60; James Lee, "Behavioral Theory vs. Reality," *Harvard Business Review* (March-April 1971), 20–25, 157–159; and Walter Nord and Douglas Durand, "What's Wrong with the Human Resources Approach to Management?" *Organizational Dynamics* (Winter 1978), 13–25.

5

From Human Relations to Human Resources

Most behavioral theorists have "known" for years how an organization and its management style should be changed to bring about tremendous improvement in morale and productivity. Executives, managers and administrators . . . appear, at least to the theorists, to have adopted their "findings" almost not at all.
—James Lee, 1971

[Our] results clearly indicated that the foreman is more responsible to the day-to-day climate in which he operates than to any special course of training he may have been given. *—Edwin Fleishman, commenting on the Ohio State University studies, 1955*

By the late 1950s the human relations ideal had been fully developed. By the late 1960s it had largely been replaced by a related but substantively different ideal, the *human resources* model. Although there were a number of reasons for the modification of the human relations model, the most important involved the cost of implementing the model and the complications involved in attempts to apply it effectively. This chapter will summarize the factors which limit the applicability of the human relations ideal and explain why it eventually was supplanted by a different ideal.

LIMITATIONS OF THE HUMAN RELATIONS TYPE OF ORGANIZATION

For an organization to function as envisioned in the human relations model, a complex kind of relational communication must be developed and maintained. It must reflect high levels of consideration between supervisors and their subordinates. Consideration is achieved when there is open communication, supportive interpersonal relationships, and a climate of mutual respect and trust. Through effective relational communication, employees come to feel that they are important parts of their organization and that their jobs are an important and meaningful part of their lives. Unfortunately, a number of characteristics of organizations and their employees makes it difficult to either create or sustain this kind of communication climate. Other factors make it improbable for the existence of supportive relationships to enhance individual performance or organizational productivity. Still other factors limit the favorable effects of sharing organizational power.

Limits to Supportive Communication

Perhaps the best place to start is at the concept's beginnings—the research performed at the Hawthorne Western Electric plant.[1] These studies initially were interpreted as providing support for two conclusions: (1) giving workers opportunities openly to communicate their feelings and needs to supportive supervisors increases their productivity because it increases their morale, and (2) pressures imposed on workers by their peers influence their actions at work. Although the first conclusion was restated throughout the Hawthorne studies, the key evidence for it came from observations of the five women employees in the Relay Assembly Room experiment. In this phase of the research a number of aspects of the work situation surrounding the women were varied systematically. These factors included the simplicity of the tasks they were asked to perform, the number of hours worked, the number and duration of the rest pauses allowed, the consideration and supportiveness of their supervisors, and the basis on which their income was computed. The last feature involved the addition of a reward system based on group performance somewhat like that of the Scanlon plans. By the end of two years, the group's performance had increased by 30 percent, an improvement that Elton Mayo and his associates attributed to the "more relaxed, friendly attitudes" created by supportive supervisory communication.

However, as Alex Carey has pointed out in great detail, this inference is based on highly questionable reasoning. For example, in stage I of the experiment, the simultaneous adoption of considerate supervision *and* the group-oriented monetary reward system led to an increase in output of 30 percent. In stage II the incentive system was introduced alone, and output immediately increased by 12 percent; when it was withdrawn, output immediately decreased by 17 percent. In stage III, supportive supervision without the incentive system led to no increase in total output. These data suggest, *at most*, that friendly supervision increased output *when combined* with a group reward system. A more accurate conclusion would seem to be that changes in the economic reward system alone led to the increased performance observed in these studies.

A closer inspection of the impact of "friendly" supervision provides an even clearer conclusion. Stage I of the research began with the selection of five experienced, willing, and cooperative (and thus atypical) employees from the Hawthorne plant. Soon after friendly supervision began, the women started talking to each other so much that their work started to suffer. Eventually four of them were reprimanded for "talking too much." The reprimands failed to reduce the talking, and the supervisors eventually were forced to adopt a group of "stern disciplinary rules." After eight weeks of enforcing these rules, during which talking continued and production either remained stable or fell, two of the five women were fired and replaced by two other women who were "experienced and . . . desirous of participating in the test." The two new workers immediately produced at a rate greater than that of any of the original five at any time during the test. Soon after one of the new workers joined the group her mother died, leaving her as the primary source of financial support for her family. From that point on she played a strong disciplinary role within the group and was the most productive worker of the five.

In the midst of all of these changes, working hours and rest pauses also were varied. However, during this entire period "free and friendly" supervision was continued, and it was this factor, the Hawthorne researchers concluded, that explained the increased output.

Unfortunately, this explanation was offered with little supporting analysis. For example, since the workers had been consulted about the frequency of rest pauses before they were changed, the researchers concluded that it was the consultation rather than the pauses themselves which produced the results. Using statistical procedures not available to the Hawthorne researchers, Richard Franke and James Kaul found that 79 percent of the improved output in the Relay Assembly Room could be attributed to improved discipline, an additional 14 percent could be attributed to the effects of the worsening Depression on workers' attitudes (when unemployment increased, the workers became more concerned about the possibility of being fired and their output increased), and an additional 4 percent could be explained by increased rest periods. When the effects of improvements in the quality of the raw materials also is considered, the maximum possible effect of supportive supervision alone is reduced to less than 3 percent of the total increase in output. Carey accurately summarized the results of the Hawthorne studies: "The results of these studies, far from supporting the various components of the 'human relations approach,' are surprisingly consistent with a rather old-world view about the value of monetary incentives, driving leadership and discipline."[2] Franke and Kaul's observation that "quantitative analyses of the data from Hawthorne, as well as empirical studies in the decades subsequent, unfortunately do not support a contention that improvements in human relations lead to improved economic performance"[3] support Carey's conclusion.

In short, both the Hawthorne research and later studies indicate that supportive communication has only a minimal positive effect on employees' performance. Evidently, if supportive communication is to favorably effect performance, it must be used in conjunction with a series of other strategies, including a focus on productivity and discipline and an appropriate system of economic incentives. This conclusion seems to be accurate when either employees' productivity or job satisfaction is the desired outcome. In a now widely accepted and replicated study, Donald Pelz found that subordinates were satisfied with supervisors who used human relations strategies only when these supervisors also had sufficient influence with their supervisors to obtain economic rewards and promotions for their subordinates.[4] When combined, these results seem to support Rensis Likert's early observation that organizational performance will be enhanced by the use of supportive communication *only* if it is accompanied by communication which emphasizes high levels of performance. This conclusion served as the basis of the human resources model which will be discussed in the final section of this chapter.

The *effects* of open and supportive communication climates thus seem to be influenced by a number of factors. In addition, the *ability to implement* models of open and supportive communication also is limited by a number of variables. First, characteristics of human beings and human relationships place limits on open communication. Communication scholars have long recognized that people often choose not to reveal their ideas, feelings, or knowledge to others. They prefer to engage in closed rather than open communication. People withhold private, personal information for a variety of reasons. *Males* seem to refuse to "self-disclose", because they fear that doing so will reduce their ability to *project the image* of themselves that they want to create or reduce their *ability to control* another person or situation. *Females* avoid self-disclosure because they fear that others may use any information they reveal *against them* in ways which will hurt them or their relationships with others. Members of both sexes, even in "natural" interpersonal relationships, seem to realize that engaging in open communication, especially about sensitive or personal matters, makes them more vulnerable. Consequently, they choose to avoid free and open communication.[5]

This natural tendency not to communicate openly is exacerbated by the competitive nature of Western society, the broad "informal organization" which Chester Barnard discussed. Formal organizations long have been dominated by competitive, defensive atmospheres. In order to implement the human relations ideal, supervisors must attempt consciously to create cooperative, supportive climates. But to create this kind of climate, they must overcome the effects of competitive social and organizational norms which sanction secrecy and the withholding of information and perpetuate the illusion that "misrepresentation is necessary to achieve or maintain power in our society."[6] Human relations theorists advocate a number of techniques to offset the competitive, manipulative, and closed communication practices that people learn through normal processes of acculturation. Regardless of the specific form these mechanisms take—sensitivity training, T-groups, interpersonal skills workshops—they involve reeducating key members of an organization. Any training which attempts to change deeply ingrained patterns of action tends to be resisted by people because they have become accustomed to those patterns. This resistance is both inevitable and to be expected, as psychotherapist Abraham Zalzenik explained:

> Very frequently, particularly in this day and age of psychologizing conflict, obsessive leaders "get religion" and try to convert others into some new state of mind. The use of sensitivity training with its attachment to "openness" and "leveling" in power relationships seems to be the current [1970] favorite. What these leaders do not readily understand is . . . [that] . . . to force openness through the use of group pressure in T-groups and to expect to sustain this pressure in everyday life is supremely ritualistic. People intelligently resist saying everything they think to other people because they somehow have a deep recognition that this route leads to becoming over-extended emotionally and, ultimately, to sadistic relationships.[7]

In short, being open involves taking risks. Openness is resisted because people recognize that those risks exist in all interpersonal relationships. In organizational relationships the risks and the bases for resistance are even greater. Just as managers resisted Frederick Taylor's great mental revolution, employees have resisted the great mental revolution of the human relations movement. They seem to perceive that adopting its key elements may be against their own self-interests, and they choose to act accordingly.

Organizational politics and power relationships also limit the extent to which members will engage in open communication. For the career-oriented professionals who hold supervisory positions in organizations, gaining power is seen as a crucial prerequisite for success.[8] Although power can be obtained in a number of ways, it is closely related to an individual's or group's ability to form and maintain valuable coalitions and to control the limited resources available within an organization. In the highly competitive environment of formal organizations, it often is an individual's ability strategically to withhold or distort information that gives an advantage. If one member of an organization can obtain otherwise secret information about a key issue, the people who will make decisions about that issue, and the decision-making processes they will use, that person may be able to use the information to his or her advantage. Information is an important source of power in organizations. If one shares information with others, one reduces one's power and may reduce one's potential for success. The norms and political realities of organizations thus usually reward people for closed, not for open, communication.

Consequently, when supervisors attend training sessions which emphasize the human relations skills of open and honest communication, they rarely continue to use those strategies for long after returning home.

I once spent the first evening of a week-long training session in "humanistic management" with a depressed vice-president of a pharmaceutical firm who had by 6:00 P.M. consumed more than his quota of alcohol. He explained that he had once before attended this program, had learned that working relationships need not be competitive and mistrustful, and had gone home refreshed and with a new optimism and outlook on work and life. Soon after he met with his subordinates, told them all about what he had learned, and introduced his new "open door" philosophy of management. He would be available to any of them at any time of the day or night to help them with any problem. His unit would, from that point on, have weekly meetings in which they would all share freely any feelings, problems, and solutions that they might have. He even redecorated his office and rearranged the furniture so that he no longer would talk to people across his large, imposing desk.

At the first weekly meeting he talked about his insecurities—revealing that the new chemists he had hired recently were far more up to date on important topics like side effects of drugs and long-term assessment procedures, and he felt threatened by them. He had not planned to be this open in the meeting, but no one else seemed to be willing to talk and this kind of revelation was just what had occurred during the last three days of the training program. Soon afterward everyone in the firm seemed to know about his new self and about his concerns about the new chemists. Communications channels already were beginning to open up. But slowly, almost impreceptably, things began to change.

Instead of accepting his open-door invitation people started to avoid him. His supervisors—the same people who had forced him to go to the seminar in the first place and had spent $3,000 for it—began to drop hints about not rocking the boat. One morning he came to work and found that his office had been rearranged and the desk moved back to its old position. In his six-month appraisal meeting his boss expressed concern that he was losing the toughness needed for upper management and that one of his subordinates had been appointed director of the lab that he was hoping to head. Eventually he caught on and started to revert to his old, traditional ways of supervising. The difference was that he now felt guilty about it. He *knew* that openness and cooperation were the keys to managerial effectiveness.

That was ten years ago. He recovered from the lost promotion and eventually rose to the rank of vice-president. He now knew that middle managers were sent to this seminar on a rotating basis, not because anyone wanted them to change as a result of the experience. It was a junket, a vacation, a well-earned and tax-deductible rest. But for him, the memories of his first visit made it improbable that this one would be restful in any way.

Because people are sensitive to the situations they face at work and are capable of adapting realistically to closed, competitive environments, they tend to reject concepts of free and open communication even when their training has led them to accept the values which underlie the practices. Now, none of this discussion is meant to indicate that free and open, supportive communication is either wrong or inevitably ineffective. It is meant to suggest, as Edwin Fleishman's comment at the beginning of this chapter does, that the competitive realities of organizational power and politics make the use of human relations communicative strategies difficult indeed. Also, it is unlikely that managers' behaviors will change in the directions advocated by the human relations ideal until their organizations and our society make a fundamental shift away from values which sanction competition to values which support cooperation.

Limits to Power-sharing, Participation, and Group Communication

The most frequently discussed approach to increasing and equalizing perceived power in organizations is involving subordinates in decisions which will affect them or their jobs. Usually participatory decision making is implemented through an increased use of problem-solving groups made up of both subordinates and their supervisors. Making decisions in groups is time-consuming and costly for organizations, but advocates of participation argue that these costs will be more than offset by (1) the increased morale that results when subordinates' needs for social interaction, autonomy, and self-actualization are fulfilled through participation in decision making; and (2) the improved quality of the decisions when the expertise of subordinates is brought to important organizational problems. There are, however, a number of factors which limit these positive effects. Some of them are related to the internal characteristics of participatory group decision-making processes. Others are a function of the situations in which such decision making is used.

Group Decision Making: Dimensions, Processes, and Potential Problems
Three aspects are particularly important to participation: communication networks, stages of decision making, and pressures to conform.[9] An almost bewildering number of laboratory studies have examined the impact of different kinds of group "networks" on the satisfaction of group members and the quality of their decisions. The concept of *group communication network* is really quite simple. It is a depiction of the people who make up a group and their typical patterns of communicating with one another. Communication networks reflect the frequency, type, and value of the information exchanged

among members of groups. In general, research has involved artificially creating groups which use the communication networks that theoretically are
possible and then comparing the quality of the decisions and the satisfaction
achieved in each type of group. Figure 5.1 depicts some of these possible networks and the title usually given to each.

When people are placed in centralized networks (the wheel or Y), where
they funnel information to and through a key individual, they tend to solve
simple problems quickly and efficiently. However, members of these groups
usually are not very satisfied with their groups, both because the peripheral
members do not feel involved in the process and because the central member
often becomes overloaded with information, often feeling that he or she is
solely responsible for the group's success or failure. In addition, centralized
groups make a relatively high number of errors, presumably because there is
little opportunity for peripheral members to monitor and correct inaccurate
information or mistakes in judgement. However, if the simple tasks assigned
to these groups also are routine, the error rate tends to be reduced; processes of
trial and error eventually lead to effective decision making.

For more complex and/or less routine decisions, groups using decentralized networks tend to make better decisions because they provide an opportunity for all group members to use their expertise to generate valuable and
innovative solutions. Decentralized networks also allow members of the group
to detect and correct errors or weaknesses in the ideas presented by other
members. Decentralized networks allow members to be involved in decision
making. If they want to participate, their opportunity to communicate and
their satisfaction with the process is increased.

FIGURE 5.1 Communication Networks in Decision-Making Groups

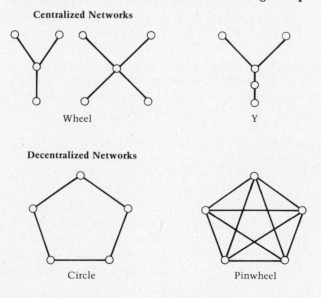

However, it is very important to recognize that the results of these controlled laboratory studies are only partially applicable to the situations faced by decision-making groups in organizations, primarily because of the way in which laboratory studies are designed. First, the types of networks imposed on subjects in these studies may not exist in real organizations. Second, the communication that takes place in the laboratory groups usually is private, occurring between pairs of participants without being overheard by anyone else. In organizational groups, communication rarely is private and generally is influenced by the presence of other people. The results of laboratory studies also suggest that communication patterns often differ according to the size of a group. Since laboratory studies usually involve groups of three, four, or five people, their results may not be relevant to the larger decision-making groups that usually are found in organizations. Perhaps most important, laboratory studies tend to use "zero-history" groups, ones made up of people who have not been together previously and who probably never will be together again. Since members of organizations base decisions about how to communicate partially on their past experiences with other members of their groups and with work groups in general, and partially on their expectations of further experiences, they may communicate very differently in organizational groups than in laboratory groups.[10]

Finally, although the principles discovered in laboratory studies generally have been replicated over and over again, it is almost impossible to make any statement about group communication networks without having to admit that there is at least one study which contradicts it.[11] However, laboratory studies are important because they indicate that the positive effects of participatory decision making on morale and the quality of decisions depend in large part on the communication patterns that emerge, and also, that a number of situational factors may influence the effectiveness of participatory processes.

Once decision-making groups are formed and given a task to perform, they tend to progress through a predictable series of stages, the second aspect of group decision making. Although the boundaries between these stages generally are blurred and the exact nature of the progression is still in dispute, there is consistent evidence that group decision-making processes involve (1) attempts to define the problem, (2) generation of a number of possible solutions, (3) evaluation of each alternative, and (4) selection of a final solution. Subordinates perceive that they have had some influence over the decision-making process if they are allowed to participate in stage 3, more influence if they participate in stage 2, even more if involved in stage 4, and the most if they participate in all four stages. Evidently, involvement in creating options and in making the final decision contributes most to subordinates' feelings of autonomy and power and thus has the greatest impact on their satisfaction. However, Raymond Miles' studies of the attitudes of supervisors about participatory decision making indicate that they are willing to allow their subordinates to be involved in stages 2 and 3 but not in stage 4.[12] For a number of reasons supervisors seem to want to make final decisions themselves, especially if they ultimately are responsible for their outcomes. But if they do, the morale-enhancing effects of participatory decision making are reduced.

The third aspect of group decision making, which is particularly important to participatory strategies, is conformity. General research indicates that pressures to conform and cohesion are crucial determinants of the success of group decision making. When all members of a group actually participate in decision making, they begin to feel comfortable with each other; become more supportive of one another; and become more committed to the group, its members, and the decisions it reaches. When groups are cohesive they become less threatening to new, reticent, or relatively powerless members, and it becomes more possible for every member to participate. Cohesion and involvement are important because the members of close groups are more likely to carry out the decisions the group makes and to defend the group and its decisions when they are questioned or attacked by outsiders. And the more cohesive a group is, the easier it is for its members to understand its goals, to sacrifice their own needs and goals to the larger objective, to obtain social rewards from participating in the group, and to accept its norms. In a complex cycle, participation, cohesion, group norms, and individual rewards mutually reinforce each other to create a situation which is satisfying to members of the group.

However, cohesion may also reduce the effectiveness of decision-making groups. Participatory decision making is superior to individual or nonparticipatory decision making only to the extent that it allows a wide range of expertise and information to be presented during the decision-making process. However, in all groups (and especially in highly cohesive groups) pressures develop which may reduce the range and quality of the information presented and thus eliminate the relative advantage of group decision making. Groups may develop "norms of concurrence," which pressure members into agreeing with other members rather than seeking the best solutions. If an individual member dissents from the group's position or questions the assumptions the other members of the group seem to share, the other members often respond by arguing with, ignoring, or in extreme cases, expelling that individual from the group. When dissent is suppressed, the group is robbed of precisely the kind of information exchange that is the key to effective group decision making. As a result, groups may make "extreme" decisions—ones which unquestionably continue precedents and existing policies or which are inordinately risky. Since cohesion generates high levels of commitment to decisions and high levels of motivation to implement them, participation may lead groups to do all they can to implement foolish decisions and to ignore or distort feedback indicating that their decision was unwise.[13]

Cohesive groups also may develop an illusion of invulnerability. Their members consistently support its decisions and rarely are exposed to any negative information about its choices. In organizational settings, the members of a group begin to see themselves as separate from and better than the members of other work groups. The competitive orientation that develops tends to increase intergroup conflict. In time, the errors cohesive groups make and the conflict they have with other groups may generate dissension within the group. Members of the group may respond to this dissension by even more intensely suppressing disagreement, which increases cohesion and its disadvantages. In a continuing cycle, groups may become less and less capable of making good choices and contributing to the success of their organizations.

In summary, laboratory studies of participatory group decision making indicate that participation may be a mixed blessing. It may increase satisfaction, commitment, and the quality of decisions made about complex problems. But it also may lead to poor decisions, increased organizational conflict, and low levels of satisfaction with the process. The communication processes which are crucial elements of successful participatory decision making also are key factors in its limitations.

Participation and Power Sharing: Barriers in Organizational Settings   In addition to the potential problems which arise from group communication processes, the positive effects of participatory decision making are limited by the characteristics of organizations. The first of these involves the preferences of workers themselves. There is, for example, recurring evidence that many workers, especially blue-collar workers, do not wish to participate in decision making because they would rather not share the responsibilities that accompany shared power. For example, in socialist Yugoslavian factories efforts to share power often have failed, more because of labor's resistance than because of managers' opposition. Participatory decision making is not particularly attractive because workers gain the social rewards available through participation from non-work-related aspects of their lives. In addition, to some managerial personnel (those who have low needs for power, control, independence, and affiliation with others), participation seems to be not particularly attractive. In other words, in cultures where norms support traditional hierarchical relationships which involve significant differences in power, employees do not necessarily gain satisfaction from participation in decision making. The key assumption underlying participatory decision making is that all human beings possess a number of higher-order needs and that they will be satisfied with their jobs only if those needs are met by the tasks they perform and the relationships they form at work. This assumption seems to be inaccurate. Some people, because of acculturation processes, the richness of their outside lives, or their personal preferences, do not value the opportunity to share power. They would rather not participate in decision making, even if the decisions are related to them and their jobs. They have more than enough opportunity to influence decisions made in their families, lodges, churches, or civic organizations. With these people, the use of participatory strategies rarely will increase morale and, if imposed against their will, may alienate them, reducing their satisfaction and performance.[14]

Among workers who do value the opportunity to participate in decision making, there is a trade-off between that satisfaction and the quality of the decisions made. Power-sharing strategies have two objectives: increasing members' satisfaction and improving the quality of the decisions. To achieve the first goal, each member must actually participate in the decision-making process. Feelings of autonomy and self-worth (Abraham Maslow's higher-order needs) are created by the *act of communicating* and by receiving communication from others that suggests one's ideas are worthy of being considered. The morale-building effects of participation are greatest when each member participates in substantial and approximately equal amounts. If each member has high and relatively equal levels of information and expertise relevant to the problems being discussed, equal amounts of actual participation will improve the quality of the decisions made by the group. And when organizations use participation properly, they will create decision-making groups composed of people who have relevant expertise, vested interests in the decision being made, and a role in implementing the group's decisions.

However, if there are significant differences in the amount of problem-related information and expertise possessed by each member of the group, participation will lead to better decisions only to the extent that the more expert members participate more than the less expert members. But if some of the members participate very little, their needs will not be met and their satisfaction with the process and their commitment to carrying out the decision will be reduced. If the less expert members do participate actively, the more expert members may be alienated from the group because their expertise is not being used and their needs for recognition, influence, and autonomy will not be met. Presumably, over a long time and a large number of decisions, every member of the group occasionally will be among the most expert members. Thus every member need not be involved in every decision in order to be satisfied by the process. However, although this balancing effect may occur in the long run, in the short term, participatory decision making may alienate group members and actually may reduce the quality of group decisions.

Participatory strategies can alienate other people for many additional reasons. Perhaps the most important type of alienation involves people with high levels of expertise or a high position in the formal hierarchy. In most modern organizations, supervisors have become supervisors at least in part because they have a desire for power and an ability to obtain and use it to their advantage.[15] Once they have advanced to a high level in the organization, they are able to gain substantial rewards from their position—salary, status, and most important, the legitimate right to exercise power over other employees. People are able to maintain positive self-images by comparing themselves, their positions, and their achievements to others. For people who value power and who are in positions which involve power, their images of themselves are tied in very important ways to their belief that they have and deserve to have more power than others. Power-sharing strategies, including participatory decision making, are designed to reduce the power "gap" that exists between supervisors and their subordinates. If the strategies succeed, they threaten the superiority, and thus the self-esteem and self-images, of powerful people. Thus, it is precisely those people whose relative power is reduced by participatory strategies who hold power most dear and have the greatest personal and practical incentives to hold on to the power they have gained over the years.[16]

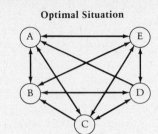

Optimal Situation

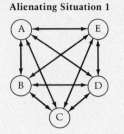

Alienating Situation 1

1. Circumstances

   All members have equal topic-relevant expertise
   All members recognize that each of them has equal expertise
   All participate in equal amounts

2. Effects

   High-quality decisions with complex or unprecedented tasks
   High morale/satisfaction and commitment to decisions
   Minimal problems with conformity

1. Circumstances

   B and C have more topic-relevant expertise than A, E, or D
   B and C realize their greater expertise
   All members participate equally

2. Effects

   Lower quality decisions
   Increased probability of alienation and sabotage by B and C
   Low morale/satisfaction and commitment to the group's decision for B and C in short term
   High morale/satisfaction/commitment for A, E, and D in the short term; low morale/satisfaction/commitment for A, E and D in the long term

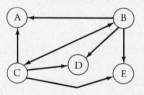

Alienating Situation 2

1. Circumstances

   B and C have greater topic-relevant expertise than A, E, and D and realize it
   B and C participate to a substantial degree; A, E, and D receive information from B and C but have little input or influence

2. Effects

   Adequate decisions; high-quality decisions if B and C possess all the relevant expertise of A, E, and D
   Reduced morale for B and C because of the imposition of a participatory system
   Low morale/commitment for A, E, and D because of violated expectations
   Increased potential for resistance or sabotage by A, E, and D

Power holders may resist sharing their power in a number of ways. Some of these methods may be overt: refusing to use participatory strategies, using them only for trivial issues, acting in ways which split the group or otherwise impeding its ability to make effective decisions, refusing to carry out the group's decision, or sabotaging the decision after it is implemented. Other forms of resistance are more subtle. The most effective of these is to withhold valuable information from the people who make up the group. The success of participation depends on the availability of accurate and relevant information. Because of the positions that they occupy in the formal hierarchy of the organization, supervisors have greater amounts of information and a better ability to take a broad perspective than do their subordinates. For example, supervisors usually are better able to anticipate the effects of a particular course of action on the organization as a whole.

As the human relations theorists have shown, people who are threatened or defensive tend to withhold or distort information. Power-sharing strategies threaten the more powerful and knowledgeable members of organizations. Since possessing information, especially secrets, is an important source of power, participatory decision-making strategies increase the potential for supervisors to withhold or distort information. By doing so, they can lead their group to low-quality decisions. Since they are privy to information which is not available to others, they also can predict accurately that the group's decision will fail. When their self-fulfilling predictions come true, their expertise and competence as they are perceived by the other members of the group are enhanced and their ability to control the group's decisions in the future is increased. Power holders can use participation to increase their influence and enlarge the power gap that exists between themselves and their subordinates.

Powerful members of organizations also can use the opportunity for free and open communication provided by participation to increase their power. In a series of studies of power-sharing strategies in European firms, Mauk Mulder found that in addition to having greater access to information, supervisors also have greater communication skills than their subordinates. They are more persuasive, argue positions more effectively, and are more adept at interpreting other members' communication and responding appropriately. When placed in participatory arrangements, these advantages allow them to influence the views of other members of the group. In time a "power elite" develops. Although the makeup of this elite seems to be determined by the personal communication skills of the group's members, it also is related to their formal positions in the organization. Eventually, less-powerful members communicate less and less and more-powerful members begin to dominate the decision-making process. Thus, the *opportunity* for more-open communication, which is the strength of participatory strategies, may lead to increased differences in the power of supervisors and subordinates rather than to a sharing of power.[17]

Participation also may alienate other members of the organization. People who have high levels of problem-relevant expertise but lack oral communication skills often are frustrated by group decision-making processes. They realize that they are less able to articulate their ideas than are other members of the group and that this keeps them from having as much impact on decisions as their level of expertise leads them to expect. People with high levels of communication anxiety also may find participation to be very threatening and may respond by withdrawing from the discussion. The group loses their expertise, and their satisfaction with the group and with work is reduced. In less-participatory arrangements, these people would have opportunities to communicate privately and directly with a single supervisor. Since nonparticipatory systems allow them to plan and even to rehearse their messages for a single, known listener, their anxiety and difficulties with spontaneous, open group communication may be reduced. For them, nonparticipative decision making may be more satisfying and may allow them to use their expertise best to benefit the organization.[18]

Participation also may alienate every member of a group because of the additional stress that it creates. One of the primary functions of traditional organizational hierarchies is to control the amount of communication that people send and receive. These limits help the organization by ensuring greater control of its members, and they help the members by reducing the communication load that they have to manage. When participatory strategies are used, everyone who is involved is required to increase communication activities. Especially during periods when their job places extreme demands on them, employees may not be able to handle the increased communication and the time it takes away from other activities. The communication overload that results from participatory decision making is a particular problem for people who play roles like the linking pins in Rensis Likert's System 4 model. The problem is even greater when employees, for whatever reasons, wish to participate *less* than they are required to do. When employees have either less opportunity to participate than they desire or more than they wish, they feel higher levels of stress and have lower-quality performance than when their involvement in decision making matches their preferences.[19]

Participation also may increase stress because it increases the amount of close contact among employees. As was suggested in Chapter 1, organizations impose relationships on people which lack many of the stabilizing features of natural interpersonal relationships. People often find that their jobs force them to interact with other people with whom they otherwise would not communicate, and they often manage the resulting tensions by reducing their contact with these people to the minimum level necessary for their jobs. Participation forces them to increase their contact with each other. Although this increased contact may allow them to overcome their differences by learning more about each other, it also may increase their hostility by forcing them to spend time with people they do not like. If the participatory situation also creates pressures to discuss openly personal and professional concerns, it may blur the boundaries individuals have formed between their "working" and "personal" relationships, further increasing their frustrations and hostilities. Since it was the implementation of participatory decision making which upset the employees' system of reducing frustration by minimizing contact, they may project their anger onto the participatory system and seek to regain their former stability by sabotaging it.

Finally, power-sharing strategies may require so much additional time and effort that they cost more than they contribute in increased satisfaction and performance. This is especially true during the early phases of their implementation. As a result, even when upper management is strongly committed to the philosophy underlying power sharing, organizations tend to abandon participatory systems.[20]

Overall, research on power sharing and participation seems to support two conclusions:

1. Outside of organizations, participatory group decision making may increase members' satisfaction by fulfilling their higher-order needs, providing that

    a. Each member actually gets to participate to the extent desired and in the most important stages of the decision-making process[21]

    b. It actually does generate better solutions to complex problems, group cohesion does not lead the group to extreme solutions, and there is a balance between each member's contribution and expertise

FIGURE 5.3 Factors Limiting the Success of Power Sharing Through Participation

---

Problems Inherent in Group Decision Making

Use of participation where individual decision making is adequate or advised
Problems of cohesion and conformity
Trade-off between involvement and expertise

Sources of Alienation

Reduced relative power of powerful employees
    Threat to self-esteem
    Threat to position and security
Violated expectations about opportunity to influence decisions
Personal factors
    Inadequate match between desire and opportunity to participate
    Communication anxiety or low level of communication skills
Increased communication overload and stress
Increased pressures from imposed relationships

High Organizational Costs

Time
Energy
Start-up costs

---

2. In organizations, participatory group decision making will be productive only to the extent that it does not alienate employees (especially those with high levels of formal power) and increases productivity enough to offset its costs.

These comments on the *limitations* of participatory decision-making systems are intended to be just that—an indication that their positive effects depend on a large number of factors. In a great many cases organizations have adopted participatory systems and found that both morale and productivity have increased significantly. But these successes occurred because steps were taken to offset the limitations and problems of the system. Middle and upper managers were involved actively in its design and implementation. Steps were taken to assure all participants that sharing influence and responsibility would not make them more vulnerable. Groups were formed carefully in order to ensure a relatively equal distribution of expertise, and all employees were trained in group communication skills and provided access to problem-relevant information. Evaluations of the systems were delayed until after a realistic period of time had passed and were based on sufficiently broad criteria. In examining the factors which limit the success of participatory systems (or any other communicative systems) it is important to understand both the potential payoffs and the problems and limitations.

Limits to the Relationships Among Communication, Satisfaction, and Performance

Human relations theorists assumed that there is a four-stage causal relationship by which relational communication improves individual performance: Considerate, open, and supportive communication will increase job satisfaction, which will increase workers' involvement in, concentration on, and commitment to their jobs, which will improve their performance. In addition, open communication will improve the quality of the information available, the quality of decisions, and eventually, organizational performance (see Figure 5.4). Effective relational communication also may encourage people to make desirable but risky changes, which sometimes may increase productivity. Relational communication will have especially favorable effects on the performance of younger or newer employees because they need large amounts of information about how to do their jobs and substantial amounts of emotional support.[22]

Of course, the factors which have been discussed throughout the first sections of this chapter indicate that there are major limits to each of these causal relationships. Since the factors which make up the "organizational" side of the equation that is presented in Figure 5.4 already have been discussed in some detail, the following sections of this chapter will look at the "individual" side. Three specific causal relationships will be discussed: the link between relational communication and job satisfaction, between satisfaction and performance, and between relational communication and performance.

FIGURE 5.4   The Satisfaction-Performance Relationship in Human Relations Theory

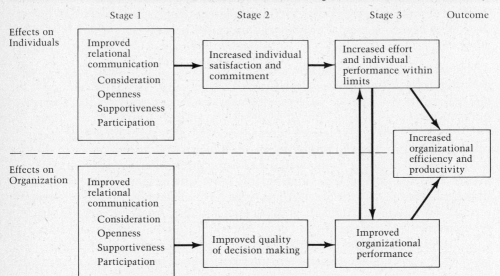

Relational Communication and Job Satisfaction   Dimensions of relational communication consistently have been found to be related to job satisfaction. The relationship is especially strong when subordinates' satisfaction with their supervisors is considered. Of course, this finding makes sense because superior-subordinate relationships are so important to overall job satisfaction. Supervisors who are perceived as employee-centered; supportive; understanding; tolerant of disagreement; and willing to listen to their subordinates, who provide them with information, and involve them in legitimate decision making have more satisfied subordinates. The impact of effective relational communication on job satisfaction has been shown to be quite small from a practical standpoint, but it does seem to occur consistently regardless of the specific characteristics of the research. The relationships also seem to be strongest with subordinates who are near the bottom of the organizational hierarchy and for people who need large amounts of information to do their jobs well.[23] As the human relations theorists suggested, effective relational communication seems to be an important factor in the extent to which workers feel that their higher-order needs are fulfilled. Thus, the first link in the individual side of the communication-performance equation seems to be correct: Relational communication is satisfying to employees.

Job Satisfaction and Performance   The second causal link, between employees' satisfaction and their effort and performance, also makes intuitive sense. If people are happy at work, they *should* be more committed to their organization and to their role in it, and thus *should* want to work harder in order to make sure that their organization is a success. Unfortunately (at least for the employees' supervisors), workers often do not respond as they "should" to satisfying work situations.[24] They may not be motivated to work harder when they are satisfied, and even if they do want to work harder, they may not translate their new attitudes into action. Although there have been some exceptions to the rule, four decades of research on the relationship between job satisfaction and performance has not found strong or consistent relationships between the two. In fact, this research seems to indicate either that high performance causes high satisfaction (presumably because workers feel pride from their success) or that other factors influence both satisfaction and performance. If employees strongly value productivity for its own sake (they accept the "Protestant work ethic") or if they believe they will receive other rewards from high levels of performance, they tend to be both satisfied and productive. If they do not hold these beliefs, they tend to be both dissatisfied and relatively unproductive regardless of the nature of the organizational climate in which they work.

However, even where workers are highly committed to their organization and its success and where external rewards are unimportant, satisfaction does not seem to lead to increased effort or performance. In a study of an Israeli cooperative farm (kibbutz), David Macarov found neither that job satisfaction improved performance nor that people who worked hard were more satisfied than people who did not.[25] Whatever the relationship between job satisfaction and performance may be, it does not seem to be the simple causal relation envisioned by the human relations ideal. In short, the world seems to be relatively full of people who smile a lot and do very little or who smile not at all and do a lot.

Since these findings run counter to intuition they have been hard for managers and researchers to accept. With the exception of the Hawthorne studies, research before 1955 found little relationship between satisfaction and performance. In 1955 Arthur Brayfield and W.A. Crockett[26] found no significant relationship between the two and provided a cogent explanation of their findings. They argued that workers' lives involve a large number of interpersonal relationships and fulfilling situations. Work and work relationships are only a small part of their lives. Employees' decisions about how to act at work are based on a complex group of considerations which are related to their entire life situation. Their choices also are related to their own, individual values and goals. In some instances, they may choose to perform at abnormally high levels even if they are not satisfied with their work situations. Unskilled employees working in autocratic organizations with no opportunity for advancement or sense of personal fulfillment and few employment opportunities may be both very dissatisfied and very productive because they are afraid of losing their jobs. People who have few employment opportunities because of their sex, lack of education, or disabilities or who are working during a severe economic recession may also be productive. For instance, the most productive worker in the Hawthorne plant's Bank Wiring Room seemed to have these characteristics.

Conversely, people who have extensive noneconomic rewards in their lives outside of work may choose to expend only the minimum amount of effort necessary to keep their jobs and the income they provide. For them work largely is irrelevant to their upper-level needs. Their effort and performance will be unrelated to the noneconomic dimensions of job satisfaction. In fact, there is rather clear evidence that the desire for work which fulfills upper-level needs is important only to educated, middle or upper socioeconomic groups. The "intuition" which led human relations theorists to assume that satisfaction leads to increased commitment, effort, and performance may just be an expression of middle-class academic values and beliefs. What may be intuitively acceptable to professors and their students may be largely irrelevant to other people.

It also may be that people simply do not expect their jobs to meet their upper-level needs. Thus they choose to act in certain ways independent of their work.[27] Whatever the reason, the lack of a relationship should not be surprising. A long series of studies of the relationships between people's beliefs and their actions indicates that we often do not behave in ways consistent with our attitudes. The belief that charity is good often does not generate donations, that bigotry is bad does not prevent discrimination, or that excess calories are unhealthy does not stop the sale of cakes and ice cream.[28] Even when people do hold a particular belief (for instance, "I should work hard"), they may choose to act in ways incongruent with it. When the belief is a general one ("I am satisfied with my job") and the behavior is very specific and only indirectly related to the belief (expending effort at work), the probability that an employee's actions will be consistent with the belief is even lower. In short, research on both the general relationship between beliefs and behaviors and the more specific relationship between job satisfaction and performance fails to support the simple causal relationship that was included in the human relations model. Humans are complicated, choice-making animals whose decisions about the amount of effort they should spend on any particular activity are based on a myriad of personal considerations. As a result, work often is not what we do.

It is important to note that job dissatisfaction has consistently been linked to the important performance-related variables of absenteeism and turnover.[29] Of course, a number of factors influence employees' decisions about such things: obligations to their employers or to people who depend on them for financial support, level of financial need, and availability of other jobs, for example. Perhaps 80 percent of voluntary decisions to change jobs are related to workers' perceptions of the overall economic situation and their expectations about future changes in the economy. If the economy is bad, absenteeism and turnover are lower; if it is good, they are higher. An additional 10 to 15 percent can be attributed to job dissatisfaction. When social and economic conditions allow workers substantial employment options, their decision to be absent or to resign will be related to their level of job satisfaction. They will say "take this job and shove it" only when they are free to do so.

When employees perform tasks important to the operation of the organization which cannot easily be performed by others, their absenteeism may reduce the overall performance. When the costs of searching for and training replacement personnel are high, voluntary turnover may be harmful to an organization. But if absences allow a worker to be rejuvenated and thus to work more efficiently upon returning to work, or if an individual worker is expendable, absenteeism and turnover may not hurt an organization. In fact many organizations—government agencies and industries that have slack periods during the year—have systems which actually encourage absenteeism (taking "leave without pay") during times of reduced workload. By allowing their employees temporarily to escape the pressures of work, these industries increase job satisfaction and reduce absenteeism and turnover during peak times. Thus, although satisfaction is related to absenteeism and turnover, it may or may not be related to organizational performance, depending on a number of intervening factors. Overall, there seems to be only a small amount of evidence that strategies which increase either job satisfaction or communication satisfaction cause increases in performance. At most, the relationship which does exist depends on a large number of extraneous influences.

Summary: Communication, Satisfaction, and Performance As the complicated relationships depicted in Figure 5.5 indicate, the relationships among communication, satisfaction, and performance are far more tenuous and complicated than the human relations ideal would suggest. Some of these compli-

FIGURE 5.5   The Observed Relationships among Communication, Satisfaction, and Performance: The Individual Side of the Equation

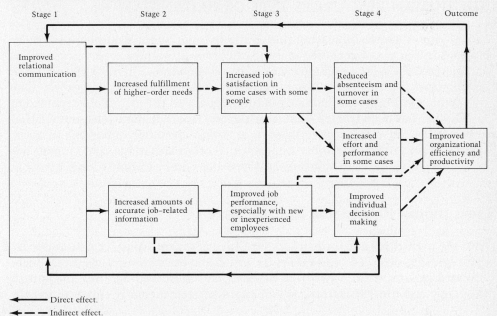

cating factors involve the nature of organizations and the tasks that employees perform. When accurate, rapid exchange of information is necessary for a worker to do a job well, effective relational communication can improve performance. When, for whatever reasons, people must make quick, complex, unprecedented, and risky decisions, relational communication can help. Consequently, in some organizations and in some situations, improved relational communication will be positively related to individual and organizational performance. In other situations, the relationship will be less important.

Additional complicating factors involve the nature of human beings. Workers are complicated, choice-making beings. They often do not act as either human relations theorists or supervisors believe they *should* act. Sometimes they will choose to expend high levels of effort even though they are not satisfied with their jobs. Conversely, they may choose to expend only the absolute minimum amount of effort even when they are in highly satisfying work situations. In fact, it may be in organizations which have the most supportive, participatory, and satisfying relational communication that employees choose to be least involved and least productive. Human workers seem to make complicated and often unexpected decisions based on their own unique interpretations of an almost limitless number of considerations. Rarely do they choose to act in ways which fit the rather simple predictions of the human relations model. In the years after the publication of the Hawthorne studies, both managers and researchers began to realize these facts, and theorists started to develop more complex and accurate pictures of the actions and communication of members of organizations.

THE HUMAN RESOURCES TYPE OF ORGANIZATION

Faced with evidence indicating that workers incorporate a number of considerations into their own choice making, theorists attempted to develop models of organizations which included each of these elements. Their efforts led to the development of two more complex theoretical types of organizations. One type, which attempted to include simultaneously all the factors that seemed to be relevant, has been labeled *human resources*. Another approach assumed that although all these factors are important, some are more important in some situations and others are most important in other situations. This model has been labeled the *systems-contingency* type and will be examined in Chapter 6.

From Human Relations to Human Resources

Both the traditional and human relations type of organization were proposed by theorists who objected to the ways in which the businesses of their eras were designed and operated. Taylor and his associates observed that the concepts of efficiency and mechanization, which characterized the early stages of the industrial revolution, had been implemented in ways that allowed managers to be arbitrary and capricious in their decision making and in their treatment of subordinates. They proposed radical new "scientific" theories designed to reduce or eliminate the dehumanizing excesses of existing organizations. The early human relations theorists observed these changes and found that they too had been used in ways which dehumanized workers and created intense conflict between labor and management. In this sense, both models were proposed to correct the excesses in application of the previous model.

The human resources type also was based on a reaction to the previous (human relations) model. However, it was not a reaction to the ways in which the model had been applied in real organizations. Instead, it was based on the realization that the human relations ideal had rarely been applied in any organization. Objections were based in part on the fact that it had been developed by professors, not acting managers. Before 1950 or so, organizational theories were developed by practicing managers, who attempted to bring their experience into some overall framework which could be applied by other managers. After 1950, models of organizations tended to be developed by academics and were based largely on values drawn from philosophical investigations or the results of laboratory studies from the new fields of psychology and sociology. In one of the most comprehensive critiques of the human relations ideal yet written, Strauss concluded that it was based on a set of assumptions about human behavior and motivation consistent with the egalitarian values of the academic world but rarely consistent with the values of workers or the realities of organizations.[30] Specifically, academics tended to overemphasize the importance of job satisfaction and higher-order needs to employees and underemphasize the role of pay. More important, these values may have led researchers to interpret their findings inaccurately, to ignore factors which limited their relevance or instances of contradictory results, and to overlook serious flaws in the research.[31]

Practicing managers seem to have applied the concepts of the human relations ideal in a more realistic way. Miles' fifteen-year study of managerial attitudes found that managers adopted a peculiar version of the human relations model.[32] When asked how they should act toward their subordinates, managers generally endorsed the major tenets of the human relations model—subordinates should be encouraged to participate in decision making, communication should be open, and organizational climates should be supportive. However, these same managers doubted that their subordinates had sufficient judgment, responsibility, and self-control actually to make good decisions or to work well when given much autonomy. In addition, managers seemed to believe that using human relations strategies would improve job satisfaction and morale but to doubt that they would have a favorable effect on performance. But since high morale helps make subordinates more cooperative, managers were willing to engage in effective relational communication. Of course, this version of the human relations model violates many of the humanistic assumptions and values on which the model is based, but it reflects quite accurately the limits and problems of participation and relational communication discussed in this chapter.

In contrast, when managers were asked how they should be treated by their supervisors, they espoused a very different group of attitudes. They perceived that they were at least as capable, creative, ingenious, flexible, and willing to change as their supervisors. They believed that their complete and active participation in decision making would lead to both increased morale and improved organizational performance. They saw themselves as valuable reservoirs of talent and expertise which their supervisors were not using. Managers described an ideal organization for themselves very much like the *human resources* ideal. This model includes

1.   High levels of concern for both organizational performance and people
2.   Organizational structures which allow all employees to be involved in decision making (for example, Likert's System 4)
3.   Tasks designed to utilize fully the skills and capacities (the "resources") of each worker
4.   Open, formal and informal channels of task-related communication
5.   Clearly established performance goals which guide employees' actions while allowing them substantial autonomy in choosing the means of achieving their goals
6.   An array of tangible and intangible rewards linked to goal attainment in challenging, productive jobs.

The best-known version of this composite human resources model was developed by Robert Blake and Jane Srygley Mouton and labeled the *managerial grid* (see Figure 5.6).[33] Members of organizations differ, this model assumes, in terms of their concern for people (interpersonal relationships and relational communication) and for production (organizational performance and command communication). Organizations are most successful when their managers act in accordance with high levels of concern for both people and production. However, since most supervisors are more concerned with production than with people, this optimal situation can be obtained only if they are persuaded that the composite approach (9,9 on the chart) is best and are trained in the leadership (communication) skills necessary to put the new attitude into practice.

Overall, communication functions in just about the same way in the human relations and human resources ideals. There are, however, three differences in emphasis. First, with the exception of Likert's model, the structure of an organization was only a secondary part of the human relations model. In contrast, the human resources model assumes that changing both communication processes and organizational structures is necessary for the maximum use of human capacities. Second, the human resources model sees command and relational communication as equally important; the human relations model accented the latter.

FIGURE 5.6 Blake and Mouton's Managerial Grid

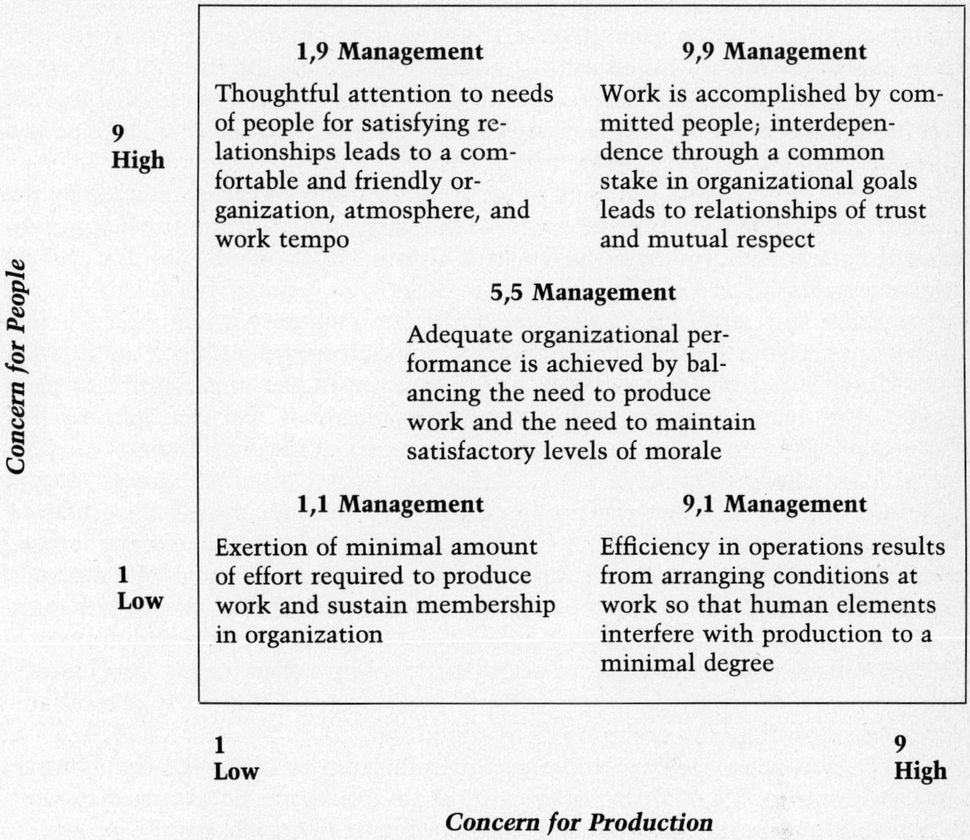

Concern for People

**9
High**

1,9 Management

Thoughtful attention to needs of people for satisfying relationships leads to a comfortable and friendly organization, atmosphere, and work tempo

9,9 Management

Work is accomplished by committed people; interdependence through a common stake in organizational goals leads to relationships of trust and mutual respect

5,5 Management

Adequate organizational performance is achieved by balancing the need to produce work and the need to maintain satisfactory levels of morale

**1
Low**

1,1 Management

Exertion of minimal amount of effort required to produce work and sustain membership in organization

9,1 Management

Efficiency in operations results from arranging conditions at work so that human elements interfere with production to a minimal degree

**1
Low**

**9
High**

Concern for Production

Adapted from "Grid Organizational Development," *Personnel Administration* (January-February 1967).

Finally, in the human resources model, improved superior-subordinate communication and structural change are combined with strategies of "job enlargement" or "job enrichment." Although both Maslow and Frederick Herzberg claimed that people's upper-level needs are frustrated by repetitive and boring jobs, the concept of redesigning tasks so that they challenge workers' capacities was deemphasized in the human relations model. But job "enrichment"—providing assignments which allow workers to use their abilities fully—became a crucial element of the human resources model. Effective communication is crucial to the success of job enrichment in three ways. First, enrichment increases satisfaction only if workers are given tasks complex enough to challenge them but simple enough for them to succeed. If a job is too complex it is frustrating, not satisfying. If it is too simple it is boring. Successfully matching tasks to individual workers requires a high level of open communication and feedback between supervisors and their subordinates.

Second, communication also is important because people seem to determine how "rich" their jobs are both by monitoring what they actually do and by listening to other workers' comments about it. Unless people believe that their tasks are stimulating, they will not be. People develop these beliefs when others tell them that they envy their jobs. In other words, successful job enrichment requires both careful job design and communication that leads people to believe that their jobs are rich.[34]

Third, the positive effects of job enrichment seem to be influenced by the overall communication climate of the organization and the quality of superior-subordinate communication. Supportive communication and prompt and accurate performance feedback from supervisors are crucial for the increased satisfaction and performance that can come from job enrichment and enlargement. Supervisors also must receive timely and accurate feedback about their subordinates' performance in enriched jobs. Even in the most complex, challenging jobs, there are some relatively boring elements. For example, writing examinations is one of the least stimulating parts of most professors' jobs. As a result, many of them give the task a low priority, procrastinate as long as possible, and eventually write mediocre exams. But since evaluating students' learning is important for improving the content and design of courses, writing good examinations is an important element of the job. In industrial settings, employees with stimulating jobs also seem to ignore the necessary but mundane elements. As a result, their performance suffers. For job enrichment to succeed in increasing individual performance, supervisors must successfully communicate the importance of every element of the job and must gain reliable feedback regarding the completion of each one.[35]

The actual tasks that people perform do seem to influence their morale and satisfaction. This effect occurs only if their jobs are (1) designed in ways which are appropriate to the desires and abilities of each employee and (2) accompanied by appropriate communication about the challenge provided by the task and feedback about the employees' performance. Like many components of the human relations and human resources models, job enrichment strategies can succeed only if they are supported by successful communication. Their impact can be destroyed by ineffective or defeating communication processes.

CONCLUSION

Chapter 4 concluded with a summary of the features necessary for the successful implementation of the ideal type of organization described by the human relations theorists. During the last twenty years it has become increasingly clear that there are few organizations which have these characteristics, except for brief periods immediately after efforts to change were applied. This is true partly because members of organizations resist human relations strategies and partly because organizations who have employed them have found that in both the short and long runs the costs of implementation exceed the benefits gained from increased job satisfaction and performance. Figure 5.7 summarizes the necessary features of the human relations ideal and the factors which limit organizations' capacities to put its elements into practice.

Basically, the limitations of the human relations model lie in its under-estimation of the individuality and complexity of human workers and their amazing capacity to act in unanticipated ways. Need-fulfillment theories of human motivation—even the more complex models proposed by Maslow and Herzberg—assume that the complex array of feelings and concerns which people incorporate into their decisions about how to act can be reduced to a small number of innate characteristics which are salient to every person in roughly the same degree. The unique, active processes through which human beings make these choices are assumed to be essentially alike for all people. Individual differences in employees' perceptions of their work environments; the relative importance they attach to the myriad of goals, desires, emotions, and expectations which enter into their decision making; and the rich repertories of actions available to them in every work situation are subsumed in the theorists' assumption about what human beings are like.[36] Whereas the traditional ideal type incorrectly assumed that all the communication needs of workers could be predicated, formalized, and controlled, the human relations ideal inaccurately presumed that employees are sufficiently alike to allow accurate predictions of their responses to improved relational communication.

Perhaps more important, both the traditional and human relations models oversimplified the nature of the situations in which employees make their choices. Robert Katz and Daniel Kahn have borrowed the concept of "partial inclusion" from social psychologist Gordon Allport to explain why workers often do not behave as organizational theorists think they should.[37] At any time in one's life a person is part of a large number of different formal and informal organizations. In church, place of business, bowling league, family, and so on, a person forms and maintains a great many relationships with a large number of people. By communicating with these people, a person is able to achieve the goals and fulfill the desires that are important. It is the total effect of being part of all these relationships that influences a person's choices about how to act within any particular relationship, including, of course, relationships at work.

However, both the traditional and human relations models assume that employees are divorced from all but their work. Traditional organizations were—*are* probably is a better word—designed for people who leave their concerns for everything other than economic needs and professional status at the door of their organization when they enter it in the morning and deposit monetary concerns at the door when they leave at night. Of course, this notion is inaccurate. To some degree people expect and desire a variety of rewards from all their relationships.

Factors outside the work situation also influence the importance of economic rewards. The new woman added to the Relay Assembly Room of the Hawthorne plant decided to push herself and her co-workers to perform more efficiently because of her concerns for people who had no role in Western Electric. Her decision had little to do with the supportive climate she found

FIGURE 5.7   Necessary Features and Limiting Factors of the Human Relations Ideal

The Human Relations Ideal	*Limiting or Compromising Factors*
1. All members of the organization believe that all their associates are capable, complex, thinking beings.	1. One believes that only oneself is a capable, complex, thinking being.
2. Supervisors successfully create climates of mutual trust, respect, and free and open communication.	2a. People generally avoid openness, especially if it involves self-disclosure.
	2b. Organizational power and politics reduce sharing of information or feelings.
	2c. Open climates may increase stress because of imposed relationships.
3. Job satisfaction, increased through effective relational communication, leads to increased effort, individual performance, and organizational productivity.	3a. Relational communication does not increase satisfaction; satisfaction does not lead to increased effort. To succeed, relational communication must be accompanied by extrinsic rewards and a performance focus.
	3b. People gain relational rewards from nonwork associations and often do not seek them at work.
4. Power can be shared and effective decisions can be made through systems of participatory decision making.	4a. Participatory decision making is effective only in certain situations and when certain kinds of communication processes are present and key problems are avoided.
	4b. People usually resist reductions in their power because they threaten their identities and self-esteems.
	4c. Persons with high status and expertise emerge as the central figures in decision-making groups, thus decreasing the amount of participation and eventually increasing gaps in power.
	4d. Being allowed to participate in decision making is resisted by some people and not desired by others.
	4e. Participation may increase stress by creating communication overload.

within the Relay Assembly Room; it had everything to do with the financial situation of, and her commitment to, her family. During the period of rapid economic growth that occurred between 1950 and 1973, employees in Western industrial firms turned down opportunities for overtime work so frequently that management eventually pressured unions to add compulsory overtime clauses to their contracts. The nature of the economic rewards these employees received had not changed (although inflation and a progressive income tax did reduce the absolute value of the income gained by working overtime), but their function in employees' decisions about how to allocate their time had.

In contrast, the human relations ideal assumed that people left nothing at the door, that each of their needs would be salient to their satisfaction and performance at work. It also assumed that general social pressures and acculturation processes which support competitiveness and hierarchical relationships could be overcome or offset by changing organizational structures and training workers in human relations attitudes and skills. Years earlier Max Weber and Chester Barnard had realized that different forms of influence and control could be legitimized only within the beliefs and norms of a culture. Human relations theorists failed to recognize that just as strategies of power must be legitimized to be effective, strategies of power equalization also must be demonstrated to be consistent with social norms and expectations. There was even less acceptance among human relations theorists of the observation that people might not value or expect the fruits of the human relations movement because of the rewards received from nonwork relationships. There was little recognition that the characteristics of a culture and a general socioeconomic situation will affect workers' willingness to accept human relations strategies.[38] Even during the economic boom from 1950 to 1973, firms generally abandoned efforts to apply the ideals of human relationism and based decisions on competitive, economic grounds. During the recession of the later 1970s and early 1980s, there seems to have been a wholesale abandonment of human relations and resources strategies for more traditional approaches to organization, communication, and motivation.

Two lessons have emerged from attempts to implement the traditional and human relations types of organizations. The first is that both communication in organizations and employees' choices about how to act are complex, ongoing processes which can be understood fully only when their dynamic, ever-changing nature is considered. The second is that organizations must be viewed as their members view them—as complicated systems composed of individual and interdependent human actors who are imbedded in and influenced by the broader social, cultural, and economic situation. These two lessons are the basis of the still developing systems-contingency type of organization, which will be examined in the following chapter.

Implementing the Human Resources Model: The Japanese Experience

One of the most striking developments of the last thirty years has been the virtual transformation of Japanese industry. Once known for the production of inexpensive, low-quality, and short-lived goods (an Arabic word for such products is *japania*), Japanese firms are now envied for their efficiency, productivity, and the quality of their output. As a result of these changes, Japan is a dominant force in the traditionally American industries of electronics, automobile manufacturing, and steel fabrication. Suddenly in the late 1970s, American managers started to notice the transformation of Japanese industry. During the 1980s American businesses have become very much interested— *obsessed* probably is a more accurate term—with finding ways to duplicate Japanese managerial practices. Although a number of general economic factors are responsible for much of Japan's success, improvements in the efficiency of Japanese industries also result from their ability to implement successfully the human resources model.

Key features of Japan's culture (the broad "informal organization" that Barnard argued is so important to the success of any approach to management) have made it possible to apply the principles of the human resources ideal. The Japanese population is very homogeneous. Employees, workers and managers alike, have similar backgrounds, beliefs, values, and past experiences. Firms hire employees from the same schools, which further increases the similarities of their workers. As a result, managers see their workers as being very much like themselves in ability and expertise. This perception is almost the opposite of the attitudes that Miles discovered in his studies of American managers. Since Japanese workers are virtually assured of lifetime employment in the same firm and are promoted on the basis of their seniority, managers have no reason to feel threatened by competent and successful subordinates. Because supervisors and subordinates have so much in common, they have relatively few problems understanding each other's communication. When all these factors are combined—as they are in most Japanese manufacturing firms—they minimize or eliminate all the pressures which lead supervisors to resist power sharing and participation.

Homogeneity of the work force also makes it easier for senior members of organizations to communicate informal norms of behavior to new workers. When employees are hired by Japanese firms they go through extensive indoctrination sessions designed to create emotional ties between the workers and their company. Soon after beginning work they are linked up with an older employee, who begins to communicate the values of egalitarianism, achievement, and harmony which characterize Japanese firms. When these processes are combined with the security of lifetime employment and such almost constant activities as singing the company song and reciting the company's slogans, the new workers soon become part of an organizational "family" whose norms and emotional ties are very much like those of the worker's own family.

The characteristics of Japanese family life are transferred to the workplace in another important way. Traditionally, Japanese families include a clearly defined, unquestioned superior member. This traditional hierarchy is preserved in Japanese firms. Although Japanese businesses have adopted participatory systems to a very large degree, they are designed to maintain the "superior" place of supervisors. Thus, the homogeneity of the work force and the key characteristics of Japanese culture combine to support systems which retain some elements of both the traditional type of organization and the human relations type.

The version of participatory decision making most often used in Japanese firms and most envied by American managers is the *quality control circle* (QCC). These are small groups of workers from the same unit of an organization who meet regularly to identify and solve problems faced by the group. QCCs usually are led by a first-line supervisor, who along with the subordinates, has been trained in interpersonal and group communication skills. QCCs meet weekly and discuss any problems or concerns, personal or job-related, of their members. Employees make suggestions for improving productivity, morale, or quality control, which if accepted, are rewarded with cash bonuses and awards. Suggestions are implemented immediately if they involve only the immediate work group. Other suggestions are communicated by the supervisor to QCCs higher in the hierarchy. Supervisors are responsible for maintaining a cooperative atmosphere and open communication among members of their work group and are expected to help maintain close social ties among their employees.

Cooperation, consultation, and open communication also help link the various levels of the organization. Managers and union leaders share information and cooperate in solving organizational problems. Kazero Nishiyama provides an example from the Nissan Motor Company:

> Twice a year Nissan Motor Co. . . . holds a Chuo Kieiekyogikai (Central Management Council) between top management and the top union leaders to jointly review past performance, to discuss the major problems of production, marketing and management, to analyze current market conditions and competition, and to decide on common goals. At this meeting, the top management voluntarily reveals the "management data" and presents new management proposals. The Union, in turn, submits its counter-proposals on work conditions and suggestions for improving production efficiency. And in an atmosphere of complete trust and cooperation, management and labor jointly work out specific goals that are mutually agreed upon. Then, these goals are communicated down to the lower levels of management and the rank-and-file of the labor union.

The QCC system also facilitates communication between upper and middle managers, who are expected to base policy decisions on scientifically gathered and analyzed information rather than on precedent or intuition. They also are encouraged to take a long-term, growth-oriented perspective in their decision making. To fulfill these expectations, upper-level managers must have access to the information their subordinates have available. Because first-line supervisors are responsible for communicating the suggestions made by their QCCs to middle managers, the system improves vertical communication and increases the visibility and authority of lower-level and middle-level managers. Even the Japanese language contributes to open vertical communication. Because the Japanese *written* language is even more tedious, time-consuming, and frustrating to use than the English language, it increases the relative advantage of oral over written communication (discussed in Chapter 1). As a result, Japanese supervisors rely far more on interpersonal, face-to-face communication than do American managers.

To summarize, QCCs work in Japanese organizations precisely because they incorporate a unique set of conditions which allow human resources strategies to succeed. Cultural factors combine with lifetime employment and job security to foster cooperation, reduce conflict and competition, and support the sharing of power. Reward systems and informal norms which support high levels of performance and quality are communicated successfully to employees through "rich" face-to-face channels. QCCs have been especially successful in businesses where jobs are complex and the costs of poor quality are high. Japanese firms seem to have developed a unique combination of concern for production, concern for people, rational decision making, open communication, cooperative climates, job security, and reward systems within a culture which largely supports the ideals of the human resources model.

Of course, if any of these features is absent, participatory systems are less effective. In businesses, or in societies, which lack a history of labor-management cooperation, job security for all employees, supervisors whose power is not threatened by successful subordinates, supportive social norms, and appropriate tasks, QCCs will be less successful and more difficult to implement. The primary lesson of Japan's success is that human resources systems work well when a complicated set of organizational, cultural, and economic factors favor them, and they work less well when any one of these features is absent.

Notes

1.   Alex Carey, "The Hawthorne Studies: a Radical Critique," *American Sociological Review*, 32 (1967), 403–416: J. M. Shepard, "On Alex Carey's Critique of the Hawthorne Studies,"*Academy of Management Journal*, 14 (1971), 23–32; Richard Franke and James Kaul, "The Hawthorne Experiments: First Statistical Interpretation," *American Sociological Review*, 43 (1978), 623–643; W. J. Wardwell, "Critique of a Recent 'Put Down' of the Hawthorne Studies," *American Sociological Review*, 44 (1979), 858–861; Richard Franke, "The Hawthorne Studies: a Re-View," *American Sociological Review*, 44 (1979), 861–867.

2.   Carey, "The Hawthorne Studies," p. 416.

3.   Franke and Kaul, "The Hawthorne Experiments," p. 638.

4.   Ralph Stogdill, *Handbook of Leadership* (New York: The Free Press, 1974); also see Fred Jablin, "A Re-Examination of the 'Pelz Effect,'" *Human Communication Research*, 6 (1980),

211–227. The relationships among communication, satisfaction, and performance will be examined later in this chapter.

5. Lawrence Rosenfeld, "Self-Disclosure Avoidance," *Communication Monographs*, 46 (1979), 63–74.

6. Ibid., p. 64.

7. Abraham Zalzenik, "Power and Politics in Organizational Life," *Harvard Business Review* (May–June 1970), 57.

8. Walter Nord and Douglas Durand, "What's Wrong with the Human Resources Approach to Management?" *Organizational Dynamics* (Winter 1978), 13–25; Jeffry Pfeffer, "Power and Resource Allocation in Organizations," in *New Directions in Organizational Behavior*, ed. Barry Staw and Gerald Salancik, (New York: St. Clair Press, 1977), pp. 235–265. See Chapter 7 for a more detailed discussion of power, politics, and communication in organizations.

9. A fine summary of this research is available in M. E. Shaw, *Group Dynamics* (New York: McGraw-Hill, 1971).

10. Richard Farace, Peter Monge, and Hamish Russell, *Communicating and Organizing* (Reading, Mass.: Addison-Wesley, 1977).

11. Barry Collins and Bertram Raven, "Group Structure," in *Handbook of Social Psychology*, ed. Gardner Lindsay and Elliot Aronson, (Reading, Mass.: Addison-Wesley, 1969), vol. 4.

12. Raymond Miles, *Theories of Management* (New York: McGraw-Hill, 1975). Also see Michael Wood, "Power Relationships and Group Decision-Making in Organizations," *Psychological Bulletin*, 79 (1973), 280–293.

13. Irving Janis, *Victims of Groupthink* (Boston: Houghton Mifflin, 1972).

14. Peter Dachler and Bernhard Wilpert, "Conceptual Boundaries and Dimensions of Participation in Organizations," *Administrative Science Quarterly*, 23 (1978), 1–39; Wood, "Power Relationships;" William Strauss, "Some Notes on Power Equalization," in *The Social Science of Organization*, ed. Harold Leavitt (Englewood Cliffs, N. J.: Prentice-Hall, 1963).

15. Jeffry Pfeffer, "Power and Resource Allocation." Also see Pfeffer, *Power in Organizations* (Marshfield, Mass.: Pitman Publishing, 1981); Mauk Mulder, "Power Equalization Through Participation?" *Administrative Science Quarterly*, 16 (1971), 31–38; and Mauk Mulder and H. Wilke, "Participation and Power Equalization," *Organizational Behavior and Human Performance*, 5 (1970), 430–448.

16. Nord and Durand, "What's Wrong with the Human Resources Approach," p. 17.

17. Mulder, "Power Equalization"; Mulder and Wilke, "Participation and Power Equalization"; Tom Burnes, Lars Karlsson, and Veljko Rus, *Work and Power* (Beverly Hills, Calif.: Sage, 1979).

18. James McCroskey and Virginia Peck Richmond, "The Impact of Communication Apprehension on Individuals in Organizations," *Communication Quarterly*, 27 (1979), 55–61.

19. John Ivanevich, "High and Low Task Stimulating Jobs: A Causal Analysis of Performance-Satisfaction Relationships," *Academy of Management Journal*, 22 (1979), 206–222. The effects on stress of being a linking pin will be examined in more detail in Chapter 10.

20. Nord and Durand, "What's Wrong with the Human Resources Approach," p. 20.

21. Likert believed that the optimal level of participation is slightly greater than the amount each employee expects to have.

22. Charles O'Reilly and John Anderson, "Trust and Communication of Performance Appraisal Information," *Human Communication Research*, 6 (1980), 290–298; John Hatfield, Robert Gatewood, William Boulton, and Richard Huseman, "Moderating Effects of Worker Characteristics on the Communication-Performance Relationship" (paper presented at the International Communication Association Convention, Minneapolis, 1981).

23. Paul Muchinsky, "Organizational Communication: Relationships to Organizational Climate and Job Satisfaction," *Academy of Management Journal*, 20 (1977), 592–607; G. T. Goodnight, D. R. Crary, V. W. Balthrop, and M. D. Hazen, "The Relationships Between Communication Satisfaction and Productivity, Role Discrepancy and Need Level."

24. Edwin Locke, "The Nature and Causes of Job Satisfaction," in *Handbook of Industrial and Organizational Psychology*, ed. Marvin Dunnette (Chicago: Rand-McNally, 1976), 1,297–1,342; Cynthia Fisher, "On the Dubious Wisdom of Expecting Job Satisfaction to Correlate with Performance," *Academy of Management Review*, 5 (1980), 607–612; W. J. Goode and I. Fowler, "Incentive Factors in a Low Morale Plant," *American Sociological Review*, 14 (1949), 618–624; Hatfield et al., "Moderating Effects of Worker Characteristics."

25. David Macarou, *Incentives to Work* (Beverly Hills, Ca.: SAGE, 1981).

26. Arthur Brayfield and W. A. Crockett, "Employee Attitudes and Employee Performance," *Psychological Bulletin*, 52 (1955), 415–422.

27. This situation may change in the near future because so many college graduates are becoming underemployed (working in unskilled or semiskilled jobs). As students who have learned these "academic" values begin to occupy positions near the bottom of organizations, the gap between academic values and workers' values should narrow. See K. D. Duncan, M. M. Gruneberg, and D. Wallis, *Changes in Working Life* (New York: John Wiley, 1980).

28. Martin Fishbein and Icek Ajzen, *Belief, Attitude, Intention and Behavior* (Reading, Mass.: Addison-Wesley, 1975); Robert McPhee and Donald Cushman, eds., *Message-Attitude-Behavior Relationships* (New York: Academic Press, 1980), especially the chapter by David Seibold.

29. Karlene Roberts, Charles Hulin, and Denise Rousseau, *Toward an Inter-Disciplinary Science of Organizations* (San Francisco: Jossey-Bass, 1979).

30. Strauss, "Some Notes on Power Equalization."

31. Harold Koontz, "The Management Theory Jungle Revisited," *Academy of Management Review*, 5 (1980), 175–187; Richard Nehrbass, "Ideology and the Decline of Management Theory," *Academy of Management Review*, 4 (1979), 427–431.

32. Raymond Miles, "Human Relations or Human Resources?" *Harvard Business Review* (July-August 1965), 43–161; also see Bernard Bass and V. J. Shackleton, "Industrial Democracy and Participatory Management," *Academy of Management Review*, 4 (1979), 393–404.

33. Robert Blake and Jane Srygley Mouton, *The Managerial Grid* (Houston: Gulf, 1964); "When Scholarship Fails, Research Suffers," *Administrative Science Quarterly*, 21 (1976), 93–96.

34. James Shaw, "An Information-Processing Approach to the Study of Job Design," *Academy of Management Review*, 5 (1980), 41–48; Edward O'Connor and Gerald Barrett, "Informational Cues and Individual Differences as Determinants of Perceptions of Task Enrichment," *Academy of Management Journal*, 23 (1980), 697–716.

35. Daniel Brass, "Structural Relationships, Job Characteristics and Worker Satisfaction and Performance," *Administrative Science Quarterly*, 26 (1981), 331–348; Robert Vecchio, "Worker Satisfaction and Performance," *Academy of Management Journal*, 23 (1980), 479–486; John Ivanevich, "The Performance to Satisfaction Relationship," *Organizational Behavior and Human Performance*, 22 (1978), 350–365.

36. Locke, "Nature and Causes of Job Satisfaction."

37. Daniel Katz and Robert Kahn, *The Social Psychology of Organizations* (New York: John Wiley, 1978).

38. Zalzenik, "Power and Politics."

39. Much of the information for this section was derived from Randy Hirokawa, "Improving Intra–Organizational Communication: A Lesson from Japanese Management," *Communication Quarterly*, 30 (1981), 35–40; Kazero Nishiyama, "Japanese Quality Control Circles" (paper presented at the International Communication Association Convention, Minneapolis, 1981); and Richard Pascale, "Communication and Decision–Making Across Cultures," *Administrative Science Quarterly*, 23 (1978), 91–110.

40. Nishiyama, "Japanese Quality Control Circles."

6

Systems-Contingency Types of Organizations

In high and far-off times, organizational theorists pronounced that there was one best way to organize, although these universalists did not agree whether this best was scientific management, human relations, or good leaders. Universalistic theorists currently are as hard to locate as steam engines.   **—organizational theorists, c. 1979**

Anyone who has struggled through the concepts, perspectives, and research in the first five chapters of this book probably felt like the mythical Theseus trapped in a Minoan maze (or to use a more modern metaphor, like a laboratory rat caught in an unending "run.") The virtue of both the traditional and human relations and resources ideal organizations was their simplicity. If one assumes, as those theorists did, that human beings are motivated by an identifiable group of needs or drives and that human communication functions in

133

regular and predictable ways to meet or frustrate those needs, it is possible to construct organizations which are efficient and satisfying. But when the ideals were put into practice, it became clear that human workers often chose not to act as the theorists assumed they would or should. It also became clear that achieving high levels of effective organizational communication is not a simple task. To confound the situation even more, researchers also found that traditional organizations sometimes succeed and sometimes fail and that some applications of the human relations and resources ideal are effective, whereas other organizations with the same characteristics are ineffective. Although some organizations are characterized by effective communication, other organizations, designed and operated on the same principles, are beset by communication breakdowns.

Making sense out of all these exceptions and all the confounding variables described in Chapters 1 through 5 seems to require the development of some broad, overall *framework* which could be used to integrate this bewildering maze of concepts. Explaining the differing success of organizations which appear to be identical seems to require some *perspective* to account for these variations. The framework was provided by *general systems theory*. The perspective eventually was labeled *contingency theory*.

GENERAL SYSTEMS THEORY: COMMUNICATION AND ORGANIZATIONS

The basic outline of general systems theory was proposed by the German philosopher and biologist Ludwig von Bertalanfy.[1] It was applied in a complete form to the study of formal organizations by the American scholars Talcott Parsons, Daniel Katz, and Robert Kahn. Systems theory is based on the three concepts of *wholeness, boundary, and process*.

The theory asserts that every system is composed of a number of separate and interdependent parts (subsystems). Each subsystem acts in ways which simultaneously influence the actions of each other subsystem and of the larger system. Each subsystem monitors information provided by the actions of the other subsystems (input); processes that information, changing it in some way (throughput); and then acts on its interpretations of that information (output). Because the subsystems are interdependent and because every subsystem in some way influences every other subsystem, it is impossible to understand the actions of a system by breaking it down into its component parts (subsystems) and examining them separately. All the subsystems and their influences on each other must be examined simultaneously. Because the subsystems are interdependent, the whole system is more than just the sum of its parts.

The concept of system *wholeness* is complicated further by the notion that every system is imbedded in a group of larger systems (suprasystems) and that every subsystem is made of a number of smaller, interdependent subsubsystems. For example, system theorists would view the loading crew of a freight-handling company as a system made up of a number of subsystems (workers, worker relationships, supervisor-worker relationships, and so on) which are made up of smaller subsystems (each worker's perceptual processes, tasks, information-processing activities, memories of the past, anticipations of the future, family, church, and social ties, and so on). And they would view the loading crew as only one part of the production suprasystem of the organization, which is only one part of the freight company (supra-suprasystem), which is part of the even larger trucking industry, and so on. At any given point in time, the actions of any of the many related elements of the organization (the loading crew, for example) may be influenced by the actions of any of the many interrelated subsystems or suprasystems (see Figure 6.1). Although this schema certainly is not simple, it does provide a *framework* in which all the individual, organizational, and societal factors that were discussed in Chapters 1 through 5 can be included. The ability simultaneously to consider a large number of complicated, interrelated factors in a single *wholistic* model is the greatest strength of general systems theory.

FIGURE 6.1 Levels of Systems

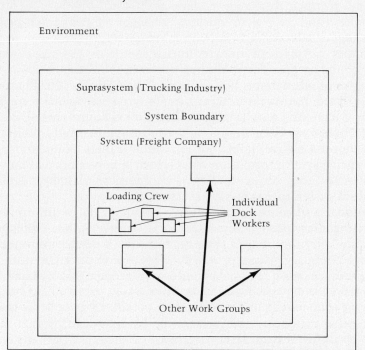

Components of the Individual Worker as a System

Task characteristics   Perceptual processes   Memories and anticipations

Valuation of various rewards   Interrelated organizational and nonorganizational roles

Emotional responses   Information processing abilities/activities

The second key concept of systems theory concerns system *boundary*. For the sake of clarity assume that the system depicted in Figure 6.1 is the corporation (freight line) mentioned in the previous example. A "boundary" defines the limits of the system. Although this concept often is thought of in concrete terms (the physical walls of the building, for example), it really is an intangible barrier. Inside this barrier, elements of the system (the subsystems) communicate more with one another than with elements outside the barrier. Systems (organizations) differ in the degree to which their boundaries are "permeable." Some organizations are very open and have permeable boundaries. A substantial amount of information flows between their subsystems and systems outside their boundaries. Other organizations are very closed, with little information flowing across their boundaries. Think, for example, of the differences in permeability of two large, southern fraternal organizations—the Southern Presbyterian Brotherhood and the Ku Klux Klan.

Open organizations generally have either a large number of *boundary role elements*, people who maintain communication with outsiders, or a small number of very active boundary role elements. These people perform four crucial functions for the organization. First, they provide other elements in their organization with useful information from the surrounding environment.[2] They obtain *strategic* information about the organization's *inputs* (raw materials, personnel, and so on) or *outputs* (changes in consumer tastes, competitors' pricing, or advertising strategies). Piedmont Airlines, one of the major success stories in American industry during the 1980s, has prospered in part because its boundary spanners obtained accurate information about the coming deregulation of airline fares and routes and its probable effects on the firm's operations. Based on this information, Piedmont's management made a series of *strategic* decisions—purchasing smaller, fuel-efficient planes; developing a series of "hubs" for their flights; and choosing potentially profitable routes while abandoning highly visible but unprofitable ones. Boundary spanners also gather *managerial* information, that which involves normal day-to-day operations. Finally, they obtain *technical* information, including data on advances in product design or production technologies.

Second, boundary spanners control the dissemination of information throughout their organizations. In some ways they protect other employees from the information environment of their organzation. If all the information obtained by active boundary spanners was communicated throughout an organization, its communication channels would soon become jammed and the members would face serious problems of communication overload. So boundary spanners act on some of the information they obtain, store or delay transmission of some other messages, and interpret or summarize still other messages. They help to absorb the uncertainty created by the organization's environment. For instance, some evidence suggests that one of the reasons why Braniff Airlines, in the same environment faced by Piedmont, made less-successful strategic decisions was in part because its decisions makers were innundated with information, especially as the company's situation deteriorated further. If so, their boundary spanners may have been fulfilling the information-gathering function quite well while fulfilling their information-controlling function not well at all.

Third, boundary spanners protect people inside the organization from outsiders who would like to influence their behavior. When I recently moved to a new city I encountered severe problems in my efforts to begin delivery of a Sunday morning newspaper. For each of seven consecutive weeks I woke, prepared morning coffee, walked the one-half mile to the end of our lane, discovered the newpaper was missing, walked home, and called the newspaper's circulation department to request the delivery of my morning newspaper. Each time I spoke with a surprisingly pleasant person who assured me that a newspaper would be delivered immediately and the problem would be corrected. Eventually it dawned on me that my pleasant telephone contact was serving in the role of a boundary spanner, insulating the influential members of the circulation department from irate customers. (This story does have a happy ending. After making my discovery I vowed to defeat the boundary-spanning system. During my next telephone call I obtained the home phone number of the supervisor of the circulation department. The next Sunday I arose a little early, at approximately 6:30 A.M. After making certain that my newspaper was nowhere to be found, I called the supervisor, awakened him and his wife, and requested that he intervene on my behalf. I also promised that I would call him 15 minutes earlier every Sunday morning until the problem was corrected. It took one more week. The moral of the story: Boundary spanners play crucial roles for organizations, but they can be outsmarted.)

Fortunately, effective boundary-spanning people emerge rather naturally in virtually all organizations. J. S. Adams (the person who applied equity theory to organizational behavior) noted that boundary spanners and buffering processes develop almost automatically as organizations grow and develop. Those subsystems which most frequently have to deal with new information from outside the organization develop the kinds of communication patterns and networks they need to cope with environmental changes. Units which do not often need to manage change develop very different communication processes. They can do so because they are protected from the disorganizing effects of change by multiple levels of buffering boundary spanners.

The final crucial function played by boundary spanners is representing the organization to outsiders. Boundary spanners legitimize their organization by presenting evidence that the organization is striving to meet the outsiders' needs. And they *influence* the activities and attitudes of outsiders through carefully planned and executed persuasive communication. Of course, the functions played by boundary spanners are not independent of one another. They obtain information about how outsiders view their organizations, appropriately diffuse that information throughout the relevant parts of the organization, and persuade the outsiders that the organization has adapted to or is in the process of adapting to their concerns. Information gathering, information diffusion, buffering, and image management all are interrelated elements of the boundary spanners's organizational role.

The first two key concepts in general systems theory were *wholeness* and *boundary*. The final key concept is *process*. Unlike the traditional and human relations and resources ideals, which tacitly assumed that the structure of communication in an organization could be designed and then imposed on its employees, the systems model focuses on the *processes* through which patterns of communication emerge and are sustained and modified by the actions of employees. Systems theory adopts the principle of *equifinality* as a means of explaining why organizations often develop quite different patterns of communication. The concept itself is quite simple: In complex situations a number of different processes and avenues can be used to reach the same objectives. The application to organizational communication is a bit more complicated. It assumes that employees naturally develop communication processes which meet what they perceive are their needs and the needs of their organizations. When these patterns of communication are repeated over and over again, they begin to become stable parts of the organization. These continually emerging patterns are important because (1) they place constraints on the actions of members of the organization, and (2) they allow the organization and its component subsystems to meet their needs for information. Of course, the communication structures which emerge in one organization may be very different than those which emerge in another, even when the two organizations are very much alike in most other respects. Organizations and units of organizations tend to develop their own "personalities," their own cultures. They can do so and continue to function successfully because systems are equifinal.

The framework provided by general systems theory and its central concepts of wholeness, boundary, and equifinaliy has spawned a large number of "contingency" theories of organizing. They differ from both the traditional and human relations and resources models in two important ways. As previously indicated, although their universalistic perspectives differed from one another in important ways, they shared two underlying assumptions. The first assumption was that human being all share the same essential characteristics. Although they are complex beings, humans have a limited number of needs which can be arranged in some known order of priority. Consequently, organizations can be designed to meet these known needs successfully. The second assumption was that human beings are rational, goal-directed animals and that their creations, including their organizations, reflect their essential rationality.

Contingency theories can be understood most easily if they are divided into two groups. The members of the first group have in common a willingness to abandon, or at least to relax, the first assumption that underlies the universalist models. These contingency theories assert that human beings are so complex, the factors which influence their organizations so varied and interrelated, that any model which reduces their actions to a small number of core needs is unrealistic. The second group shares a willingness to relax both this assumption and the assumption that employees and organizations are rational entities. Some people and some organizations sometimes may confront problems through seemingly rational processes. They develop objectives, define problems, seek out the information they need to arrive at logical solutions, and then choose the most reasonable course of action. But very few organizational situations are like the Starship Enterprise; very few organizational decision makers are like the wholly rational Mr. Spock. Their needs are so complex, their goals so mixed and inconsistent, the information they need so difficult to obtain, that they act in ways which differ quite a lot from the rational decision-making ideal. But the nonrational processes often succeed. Consequently, there is, according to this view, no "one best way" to use information or make decisions.

The remainder of this chapter will survey some of the existing examples of these two groups of contingency theories. The first group will be considered under the title "The Contingency Ideal;" the second, under the title "Communication, Rationality, and the Management of Ambiguity."

THE CONTINGENCY IDEAL

Unlike the traditional and human relations and resources models, the systems-contingency type still is being developed. Although the work of contingency theorists is moving slowly and progressively toward a complete picture, very few researchers have attempted to transform the abstract and complicated concepts of systems theory into a comprehensive contingency theory. Instead, theorists have used a smaller number of the key concepts of the framework as the basis of less-than-fully-developed models of task design, leadership skills, and communicative processes. Although these contingency theories differ from one another in some ways, they all assume that organizations and units of organizations will be successful only to the extent that their characteristics are adapted appropriately to the demands imposed on them by their subsystems and suprasystems. In a sense, each of the contingency models that will be described in the following sections of this chapter "slices" across the multiple subsystems, systems, and suprasystems that make up an organization and focuses on one or two factors in the process. The first of these considers the organization and its relationship to its environment.

Contingency Theory 1: Environments and Communication Systems

Some existing organizations and some units of other organizations seem to be very much like those depicted in the traditional ideal. Decision making is centralized at the top of the organizational hierarchy, the use of informal communication channels is discouraged, task-related communication follows the chain of command, and employees are granted little autonomy and are rewarded for following prescribed procedures rather than for creating innovative solutions to organizational problems. Other organizations or units seem to correspond more closely to the human relations and resources ideal. Why, one might ask, do these differences exist? Or in systems theory terms, what internal and external pressures lead to the emergence of traditional and human relations and resources patterns of organizing?

One of the earliest answers to this question was proposed by Thomas Burns and G. M. Stalker. Their extensive interviews with the managers of twenty British manufacturing firms led them to conclude that the kind of organization depicted in the traditional model (their label for this type of organization was "mechanistic") worked well for organizations whose environments were stable. When an organization's markets changed frequently and the scientific and production technology that it used advanced rapidly, it could cope more effectively if it fit the human relations and resources ideal (which they called an "organic" organization). Six years later Paul Lawrence and Jay Lorsch published a more extensive series of studies which confirmed Burns and Stalker's findings.[3]

Lawrence and Lorsch argued that organizations which exist in rapidly changing, turbulent environments are effective when their internal work and communication structures allow a free, open, and rapid flow of information. These organizations often face complicated problems unlike any they have faced in the past. Open communication structures (like those envisioned in the human relations and resources model) allow information about sudden environmental changes to be diffused throughout the organization quite rapidly. In addition they allow any employees who have information or expertise relevant to the new situation or problem to be involved in deliberations about it. For example, firms which manufacture plastics products (this is one of Lawrence and Lorsch's examples) face rapidly changing environments. Sources of raw materials (petroleum) are not particularly stable or predictable, as American plastics firms learned repeatedly during the 1970s. Production technology and research advances almost daily, and customers' preferences and market demands change even more rapidly. What would you do with a warehouse full of hula hoops, for instance? In a sense turbulent environments "require" an organization to adopt highly differentiated (flat) structures and to develop complex and open communication networks. Environmental changes create confusing and ambiguous situations; the free and rapid exchange of information and expertise allows an organization to manage that ambiguity.

Stable environments place less-extensive demands on the *ambiguity-management function* of communication. Problems can be anticipated and situations understood rather easily because there almost always have been precedents in the past; solutions generally are available in tried-and-true ways of doing things. Expertise, decision making, and authority can be centralized; communication can be restricted to the chain of command; and so on. When information is needed, it usually can be obtained through formal channels; biases can be checked out; distortions can be discovered and offset; and effective decisions can be made. In stable environments, traditional organizations cope quite well with the limited amount of uncertainty that they face. Of course, all organizations do have a degree of latitude available within which they can adjust.[4] But according to this version of contingency theory, each organization's environment imposes some kind of strategic requirement; that is, the environment requires the organization to develop a kind of task and communicative structure which allows it to manage the level of change and ambiguity that it faces. To the extent that organizations develop appropriate structures, their potential effectiveness is increased. To the degree that they fail to do so, the chances of their being successful are reduced.

In general, research since these pioneering studies has supported the relationships among environmental turbulence, communication, and organizational structure initially discovered. Environments do place demands on organizations, and organizational effectiveness does seem to be related to the extent to which structure allows the ambiguity-management function of communication to be fulfilled.[5] The most recent relevant research has taken a more specific perspective, focusing on the ways in which environmental pressures effect the different people who work within particular organizations. Environmental pressures do not impinge on every member of an organization in the same way or to the same degree. Some employees are more completely buffered by boundary spanners than others are. Some employees perform tasks which place them closer to the source of an organizations' uncertainties. For example, if the turbulent part of an environment involves its raw materials (plastics firms facing the political turmoil of the Middle East), employees whose job is to obtain raw materials will face more extensive and more sudden changes than will employees whose tasks involve packaging completed products. If the turbulence involves output (competing products or market trends) or throughput (technological innovations), different employees will feel the effects of environmental changes.

Employees' tasks influence their vulnerability to environmental change in two additional ways. First, some tasks are more complex and involve more unexpected events than others. Complex tasks can be disrupted by many different kinds of environmental changes. Second, some tasks provide employees with only a small number of possible responses to changing events. Other tasks offer a wide range of options from which an employee must select the best course of action. When few options are available, solutions can be identified by clear, straight forward techniques. A light bulb fails to come on for one or more of a small number of known and identifiable reasons. The range of possible causes can be narrowed by a simple procedure—checking the light bulb, then the circuit in the lamp, then the wiring to the lamp, the the wiring to the outlet, and so on. Many other tasks involve events and problems which cannot be analyzed in any straight forward way. People who do these tasks face a high degree of uncertainty about how to respond to situations. Consider modern automobile mechanics who often complain that today's complex, computerized vehicles are unrepairable. Their task once required a great degree of skill but involved a number of relatively straight forward analytical steps. But fuel-efficient and pollution-reducing technologies have created engines in which the many subsystems are so highly interrelated that there no longer is any direct way to diagnose a problem. As a result mechanics now have to rely on computerized machines to analyze the malfunctions of other computerized machines. The mechanics' task has become highly ambiguous, complex, and time-consuming almost wholly because environmental factors have forced changes upon them.

In summary, because of the relationship between tasks and an organization's environment, some employees face greater communication-related burdens than others. In the long run they may find that the increased power they obtain because of their roles may compensate for this burden, but in the short term they must adapt to it.[6] When each employee develops communicative strategies appropriate to the information needs imposed by the organization's environment, that person can be most effective. When organizations adapt to the information and ambiguity-management needs of their employees, they are more effective than when they do not.

Contingency Theory 2: Production Technology and Communication

Unlike the first group of contingency theories, which focused on the relationship between suprasystems (environments) and systems (organizations), the second group of models has concentrated on the pressures created within organizations by their component subsystems. One of the earliest of these models examined the relationship between the production "technology" of organizations and the effectiveness of different organizational designs and communicative structures. In a series of studies of English manufacturing firms, Joan Woodward classified task systems according to their technologies: *small-batch technologies*, in which relatively independent work groups produced a "batch" of goods in response to consumers' orders; *large-batch technologies*, as in assembly lines; and *process production technologies*, where highly interdependent units collaborated in a continuous process to produce chemicals, pharmaceuticals, or similar products. Woodward found that human relations and resources communicative structures had emerged in the first and third groups, and more traditional communicative patterns had emerged in the assembly-line organizations. In addition, her research indicated that effective organizations of all three types tended to have communicative structures which fit the information-processing needs of their technologies.[7]

A recent extension of Woodward's work has taken a somewhat more specific focus. Late in her career Woodward concluded that it was virtually impossible to define the concept of technology so that it could be measured in any reliable way. She still believed that technology was important to an organization, not so much because it requires particular kinds of communication structures as because it influences the means of control that supervisors should use. Her revised theory has been developed in some detail by James Thompson and by William Ouchi.[8] Organizations control the actions of their members by monitoring, evaluating, and rewarding them for behaving in certain ways or for producing certain things. Some organizations have technologies and tasks which allow them to rely on *behavior controls;* others can rely on *outcome controls;* others can rely on both; some can rely on neither. Traditional, or mechanistic, organizations (for example, automobile, tin can, or typewriter plants) can use either form of control, at least until they become so large that their employees cannot be observed closely by supervisors. Other organizations, like life insurance firms or clothing boutiques, cannot standardize employees' behaviors but can measure and assign responsibility for outcomes. These organizations can use output but not behavioral controls. Still other organizations can create neither clear rules of behavior nor unambiguous measures of output. Such organizations, like research laboratories, universities, or the foreign service, have to rely on means of control that do not use systems of reward and punishment.

In addition to being adapted to an organization's technology, control systems must be adapted to its goals. Sometimes goals are not internally consistent. Department stores may have the dual goals of maximizing sales volume and presenting a "neat and clean" image to the public. A reward system of commissions on sales (an output control) would encourage employees to spend all their time and effort selling products and little or no effort straightening shelves, controlling inventories, ordering new stock, and so on. Consequently, organizations must often use peculiar mixtures of control systems to fit their unique mixtures of technologies and goals. The success of any particular system of controlling employees is *contingent* on achieving an appropriate match among all these factors.

A large number of researchers have continued the line of thought that Woodward initiated. Unfortunately, differences in their methods and theoretical orientations make it quite difficult to draw any overall conclusions from their work.[9] However, there does seem to be consistent evidence that organizations with nonroutine technologies need to adopt less-formal communication networks, less-centralized decision making, more-equal distribution of power, and less-traditional means of control than organizations with more-routine technologies. When communicative and decision-making structures are appropriate to an organization's technology, work is structured more efficiently and job satisfaction is increased.

Contingency Theory 3: Motivation and Performance

Even a brief glance at a modern textbook on organizational theory leaves the impression that there are almost as many contingency theories of leadership as there are taxicabs in New York City. Because there are so many models and because many of these were summarized in Chapter 5, this section will review only those which are related most directly to communicative structures.[10] One of the earliest and still perhaps the best known was developed by Fred Fiedler and his associates. Fiedler's main assumption was the same as in other contingency models: The achievement of a good fit between system pressures and leadership strategies will contribute to work group effectiveness. The factors included in Fiedler's model are summarized in Figure 6.2. Two system pressures, "good" versus "bad" leader and group member relationships, and "strong" versus "weak" formal power of the leader, are self-explanatory. The third factor, one Fiedler labeled *task structure,* is a bit more complicated. It has four dimensions: (1) the clarity of the group's goals; (2) "path multiplicity," the number of courses of action potentially available; (3) the "effect verifiability" of the group's decisions (the extent to which group members have access to tangible or other unambiguous information about the effects of their decisions; and (4) the specificity of the decisions that they must make. "Structured" tasks involve clear goals, low path multiplicity, high verifiability, and specific decisions. "Unstructured" tasks have the opposite characteristics. Fiedler's model includes eight possible combinations of these three system pressures. In his research, highly performing work groups in four of these combinations had task-oriented leaders who presumably concentrated on command-related communication, and effective groups in three of the other conditions had relationship-oriented leaders.

Similar, but more successfully replicated models have been developed by

FIGURE 6.2   Fiedler's Contingency Model

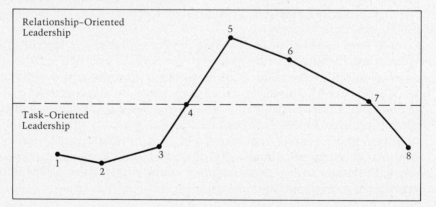

Leader–Member Relation	Good	Good	Good	Good	Poor	Poor	Poor	Poor
Task Structure	Structured		Unstructured		Structured		Unstructured	
Formal Leader–Position Power	Strong	Weak	Strong	Weak	Strong	Weak	Strong	Weak
Combinations:	1	2	3	4	5	6	7	8

Robert House and by Lyman Porter.[11] House's "path-goal" theory of leadership asserts that (1) the degree of satisfaction which employees gain from performing their tasks (their "intrinsic" as opposed to their "extrinsic" rewards), (2) the ambiguity and complexity of their jobs, and (3) the communication strategies adopted by their supervisors will combine to influence their overall job satisfaction and/or performance. In highly complex, intrinsically satisfying jobs, supervisors who provide direction and structure will help their employees clarify the confusing situations they face, make it easier for them to do their jobs well, and therefore increase both their satisfaction and performance.[12] Being considerate will have little or no effect on either the satisfaction or performance of these employees because the intrinsic satisfaction they gain from doing their tasks well is so great that they do not need the additional satisfaction gained from warm relationships with their supervisors. Conversely, in low-level, unsatisfying jobs, consideration will increase workers' satisfaction because it can help offset the frustrations created by boring and repetitive tasks. However, it will not substantially influence workers' performance. If supervisors are directive and attempt to provide structure in this situation, their efforts will be perceived as attempts to force their subordinates to concentrate on their dissatisfying jobs and thus will create anger, decrease satisfaction, and increase grievances and turnover. But they probably will increase performance (see Figure 6.3). In effective work groups, supervisor and subordinate communication patterns appropriate to the tasks being performed by employees will emerge. In ineffective groups, less appropriate patterns will exist.

Porter, working with Edward Lawler and J. Richard Hackman, proposed a model which includes elements of all three kinds of contingency theories discussed so far in this chapter.[13] One factor is the extent to which organizations are mechanistic or organic, using Burns and Stalker's terms. The other factors are the complexity of each employee's tasks and the strength of his or her needs for personal and professional growth. Their research found that (1) the highest levels of job satisfaction and performance existed in the two extreme "congruent" conditions: organic organizations plus complex jobs plus high need for growth and mechanistic organizations plus simple jobs plus low need for growth, and (2) the lowest levels of satisfaction and performance occur in the least congruent combinations of conditions. Subsequent research has supported this model while indicating that task complexity is the most important of the three factors.

In summary, the search for the precise combination of factors to maximize employees' performance in different kinds of organizational situations still is taking place. The models developed by Fiedler, House, Porter, and their associates are important pioneering efforts to sort out a maze of simultaneously interacting factors. In a sense they represent the goals of contingency theory in their clearest terms; they seek viable predictions of outcomes based on the systematic interrelationships among a number of system pressures. But, as the quotation at the beginning of this chapter suggests, contingency theories

FIGURE 6.3   House's "Path-Goal" Model

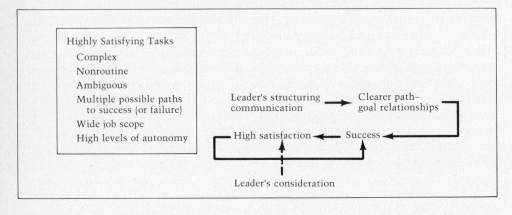

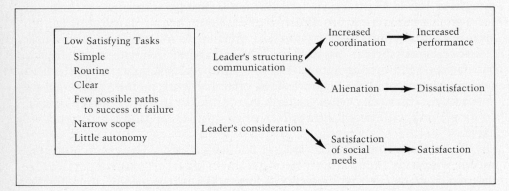

seem to dominate modern organizational theory. Based on the complex inter-relationships included in general systems theory, these models have supported the conclusion that individual satisfaction and performance and organizational effectiveness depend more on an appropriate fit among a plethora of situational, technological, environmental, and personal variables than on the use of any single approach. Although different contingency theories focus on different aspects of these interrelationships, they share a concern with the processes through which employees use communication to manage the ambiguities, un-certainties, and complexities that they face.

The systems-contingency ideal is more difficult to evaluate than either the traditional or human relations and resources models. The most recent critiques argue that existing models provide important insights but tend to take too narrow a focus. None of the models that has been discussed in this chapter explains a large proportion of variations in employees' satisfaction or per-formance, which suggests that each model includes a number of important factors but none includes all the important factors. For instance, most of these models have separated relationships of environment and structure from those of work group and communication. Consequently, they over simplify the complex nature of organizational systems.[14] Only when contingency models simultaneously consider the external pressures which stem from an organization's relationship to its environment *and* the internal pressures created by its subsystems can they begin to explain why different types of organizations are sometimes effective and sometimes not. Of course, this is neither a fatal nor an insoluable flaw. It is clear that existing contingency theories begin by taking slices out of organizational theories. In doing so they deemphasize some factors and over emphasize others. But it is equally clear that contingency theorists realize that their slices are incomplete, and they are moving steadily toward the development of more comprehensive models.

COMMUNICATION AND THE MANAGEMENT OF AMBIGUITY

The systems-contingency theorists have painted a picture of organizations and organizational communication quite different than the one sketched by either Frederick Taylor or Elton Mayo. They have indicated that many of the "truths" accepted by earlier theorists need to be examined carefully and critically. Contingency theories have led us to understand that there may be no one best way to design organizations, manage employees, or communicate with people. And they have indicated that the most important characteristic of human beings is not that we react in predictable ways to simple internal drives—economic, social or self-actualizing—but that we actively perceive, process, and respond in often unpredictable ways to the situations we face. Because both the situations and human choice-making processes are complicated, organizations function best when they adapt to complex contingencies.

The second cornerstone of the earlier universalistic theories also recently has been challenged: Organizations and the people in them are "rational actors." Traditionally it has been assumed that employees encounter problems or challenges at work; systematically seek out the information and expertise needed to choose among alternative courses of action; and make objective, reasoned decisions based on the available information. Organizations function in a similar way. Rational employees collaborate in making rational decisions for their organizations (see Figure 6.4). Both employees and organizations sometimes make unwise decisions, but these errors result from a lack of adequate information, perversities of group pressures, momentary slips in thinking, or some other aberration. Even when bad decisions are made, the decision-making process still is seen as an essentially rational and objective enterprise.

Recently, analyses of organizational decision making have offered a different perspective, one that argues that "rational" processes may be present in some situations, less important in others, and virtually absent from others. This perspective also suggests that "rationality" sometimes may not even be desirable either for employees or organizations.

FIGURE 6.4   The Rational Actor Model of Organizational Decision Making

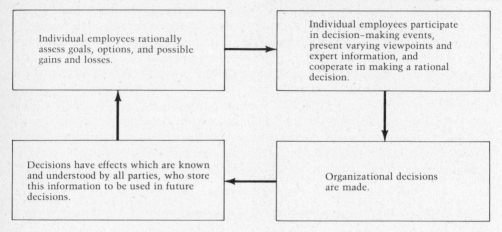

The remainder of this chapter will summarize the most important elements of this alternative perspective. Many of the ideas that will be presented, particularly those about nonrational organizational decision making, are so new that they must be thought of as tentative, sometimes even speculative, explanations of people's actions in organizations. The contingency theories presented earlier in this chapter are based on the results of a lengthy series of studies of employee actions in a variety of organizations. In contrast, the model of organizational nonrationality that will follow is grounded in theoretical arguments, case studies of individual organizations, and the results of research conducted outside of organizations. This does not mean that the perspective is inadequate; it only suggests that it is only now being developed and thus is more likely to be modified by the results of future research than the other contingency theories.

Even with this limitation, however, the perspective is important for two reasons. First, it is an effort to describe and explain how choices *are* made in organizations rather than an attempt to prescribe how choices *ought to be* made. For this reason it can potentially provide employees with a more reliable way of making sense out of organizational life than the earlier models. Second, it stresses the role that communication plays in the creation and maintenance of different kinds of organizational cultures. The view stresses the fact that what people *do* in work situations molds those situations and thereby guides and constrains what they can do in future situations.

The statements that neither people nor organizations are rational and that rationality may not always be desirable are a radical departure from our "common sense" notions about how people and organizations operate. They may be very difficult to accept because the concept of successful nonrationality attacks many of the most fundamental assumptions on which Western civilization is based. In a provocative article aptly entitled "The Technology of

Foolishness," James March explains that our society embraces three primary articles of faith:

    1. The Preexistence of Purpose: We begin with goals, make choices based on these goals, and can offer adequate explanations of our actions only in terms of our goals.

    2. The Necessity of Consistency: We choose to act in ways consistent with our beliefs and with our roles in our social groups (families, oganizations, communities, and so on).

    3. The Primacy of Rationality: We make decisions by carefully projecting the probable effects of different courses of action, *not* by intuition (which means that we act without fully understanding why we do what we do) or by tradition or faith (which mean that we do things because they always have been done that way).[15]

A major part of our acculturation involves learning these three commandments. We learn that children act impulsively, irrationally, and playfully. Adults act calmly and rationally, making decisions based on careful consideration of a number of complicated factors, and are spontaneous only when they have rationally decided to be spontaneous. Because our individual identities are linked to our beliefs that human beings and their creations are rational, the assertion that we may not be wholly so is at least mildly upsetting.

    The idea that people and organizations sometimes function nonrationally suggests that communication also sometimes functions nonrationally. The picture of human beings as rational actors includes a depiction of communication as a process through which people obtain information in order to *reduce* the ambiguity and confusion that they face and make reasoned decisions. The alternative perspective views ambiguity as an inevitable and unresolvable part of human action and communication as a process through which people *manage*, rather than reduce, confusion and ambiguity.[16] People face nonsensical situations and act in response to them. In acting they change those situations. These changes create confusion and ambiguity for other members of their organizations, and probably for themselves as well. Their actions also lead others to act in ways which change the situation. In time these cycles of acting and interacting transform the situation, creating new ambiguities and confusion, and so on in a continuous cycle of acting, confusing, and coping (see Figure 6.5). The situation never really becomes clear; ambiguity never really is eliminated or reduced. It is merely modified. As a result, problems that employees thought they had solved long ago crop up over and over again. Like the mythical Sisyphus, pushing a rock up a hill only to have it roll back down over and over again throughout eternity, members of organizations find themselves communicating with others in efforts to make sense out of their confusing and ambiguous surroundings. Fortunately the ever-present ambiguity does not paralyze them. Eventually they develop processes of communicating and acting which allow them to manage their surrounding and to act in relatively successful ways. But learning to *manage* ambiguity begins with

FIGURE 6.5   Acting, Coping, and the Continuation of Ambiguity

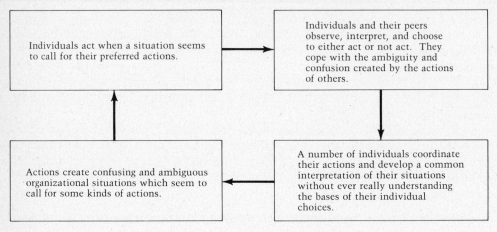

unlearning, with the realization that the myths of rationality that underlie our culture are just that—mythic statements which tell us more about what we want to believe about ourselves and our institutions than what they are really like.

Communication and the Myths of Individual Rationality

Our culture supports and is supported by a "rational actor" model of individual decision making.[17] Rational actors choose among all the available courses of action in a particular situation by comparing the probable outcomes of each alternative and opting for the one which promises the greatest return. For example, in choosing among three proposals of marriage (made by possible mates X, Y, and Z), a person will determine the possible effects of marriage in terms of a group of criteria (for the purposes of this example, on the prospective mate's wealth, passion, excitement, and permanence of the relationship), the values attached to each criterion, and the probability that each effect will occur with each option. The person then multiplies each value by its associated probability, adds the products, and chooses a mate (see Table 6.1). But in order to use this system successfully, the person must have (1) a complete list of potential options (mates) and valued outcomes; (2) accurate and complete information about the expected outcomes and probabilities; (3) knowledge of all options, outcomes, and probabilities at the same time and/or the ability to use the same estimates during each of a series of decisions; and (4) sufficient time and computational skill. Studies of individual's actions during decision-making situations indicate both that humans *cannot* act in accordance with this model and that they do not do so.[18] At most they appear to act in ways that are consistent with the model.

TABLE 6.1   A Marriage Decision: A Rational Model

Career of lover	Wealth		Permanence/Stability		Passion		Excitement		Total
X (Surgeon)	.9(7)	+	.8(2)	+	.1(9)	+	.2(11)	=	8.3
Y (Professor)	.1(7)	+	.5(2)	+	.1(9)	+	.1(11)	=	5.5
Z (Baseball shortstop)	.4(7)	+	.1(2)	+	.3(9)	+	.9(11)	=	9.1

In this example, the person values excitement a lot (11), passion a bit less (9), wealth a bit less (7), and permanence/stability very little (2). He or she estimates that the probability of a surgeon mate being wealthy is quite high, of a shortstop moderate (the shortstop evidently wants to stay in Minneapolis for an entire career), and a professor quite low. The person also believes that short-stops are exciting both during and between seasons and passionate at least during the off-season; professors and surgeons are too tired or preoccupied to be either exciting or passionate at any time, and so on.

Why Humans Cannot be Rational Actors   People cannot be rational actors for two reasons: We lack the necessary intellectual capacities and the needed self-discipline. The former limitation reflects the boundaries of our rationality; the latter is concerned with the "intransitivity" of our choices. Human rationality is bounded because our capacity to obtain and process the information we need in order to make the predictions that are built into the rational actor model is severely limited. We may never have *complete* information about our options, values, and probabilities in real situations, or possess unlimited computational time or ability. We rarely even have *sufficient* information and analytical skills available. In short, we lack the foresight, knowledge, and capacity to make effective choices through the processes envisioned in this model. Instead, we make decisions which meet minimum criteria of acceptability. We "get by," making choices of a satisfactory degree of quality. We search through a haystack of complicated options looking for a needle that we can sew with, not for the sharpest needle available.[19] Although the rationality of some people seems to be more tightly "bounded" than others, and although some situations are more complex than others, choice making in real situations cannot rely on the rational actor model.

   Our rationality also is bounded by our inability to separate the value we attach to an event from the probability of its occurrence. Like Pollyanna, we overestimate the likelihood of "good" outcomes and underestimate the probability of "bad" ones. For example, no matter how much information students are given about past patterns of grading in a course and about their own academic records, they invariably seem to overestimate their chances of receiving A's and B's and underestimate their chances of getting D's or F's.

   We also tend to make different choices in different situations, partly because of our tendency to change our preferences, values, and probability estimates between decisions. If our mythical decision maker had received the marriage proposals in a sequence, or even two at a time, that person probably would have arrived at different scores for each proposal than when they were received all at once. The outcomes, values, and probabilities would have changed.

The goals that we have in different situations also vary.[20] Even in the marriage example, the relative salience of the goals of wealth, security or stability, passion, and excitement would change over time. Passion may be exceptionally salient for decision makers aged thirteen to twenty-nine, but less salient for other age groups. As external circumstances change, the salience of various goals also changes. Finally, the degree to which people are emotionally involved in decision making also varies. When decisions are important to people and they have high levels of energy available for decision making, they will tend to be very much involved in the process. They will search actively for information; utilize their information-processing abilities to the greatest extent possible; and consider as wide a range of outcomes, values, and probabilities as they can. But when the decision is less salient or they have less energy, their choice making will deviate from the rational actor model even more than is usual. If X's, Y's, and Z's marriage proposals are the fifteenth, sixteenth, and seventeenth received, and our decision-maker is trying to choose her or his thirteenth mate, both the perceived significance of the decision and the energy the person has left for marital decision making (or anything else for that matter) could be quite low. Decision making in this situation would be even less "rational" than usual.

For a variety of reasons, then, individuals *cannot* behave as "rational actors." But people still have to make choices. To do so they have to make the decisions that they face manageable. They can do so largely because they are able to communicate. Once two of my students (an engaged couple) sought advice about purchasing a new automobile. Their espoused goal was a noble one, to shift from their old "gas guzzler" to a fuel-efficient model in order to do their part to forestall a worldwide energy crisis. I suggested that this goal would be best achieved if they kept their old car, arguing that the amount of fuel they would save during the lifetime of their new car would be far less than the amount of energy and nonrenewable minerals that would be used in the manufacture of their new car. Besides, there was no guarantee that the person who purchased their old car would use it to replace an even less fuel-efficient vehicle. Thus the net effect of their buying a new car, regardless of how fuel-efficient it might be, would be to increase the depletion of nonrenewable resources, bringing the world even closer to ecocatastrophe. Now, according to the rational actor model, they would respond to my argument by seeking out information about the resources used in fabricating new automobiles, the means of controlling the energy use of potential purchasers of their old car, the relative scarcity of petroleum compared to the scarcity of the other resources used in the fabrication of cars, and a host of other topics. The model does not predict that they would discover that I was correct. It just predicts that they would use their communicative and intellectual skills to obtain the information needed to find out whether I was right or not.

However, they chose a somewhat different course. A lengthy discussion between them produced the following modifications of their position: (1) We are only going to be concerned about gasoline (ignoring all other resources), (2) we are going to ignore the effects that our decision has on anyone else's energy use, and (3) we're going to buy a new fuel-efficient car because it will *symbolize* our commitment to conservation whether it has that effect or not. In retrospect our discussion did not lead to a rational decision, at least not as the rational actor model defines that term. But it did allow them to redefine the decision they faced in a way that made it manageable. They were, in the end, able to make a decision and to make it with conviction. Often it is the making of decisions rather than the making of "rational" decisions that is facilitated by communication.[21]

Varieties of Nonrational Decision Making   The rational actor model presumes that we determine desired outcomes, values, and decision-making processes and seek out needed information *before* we make decisions. Observations of human decision making, including organizational decision making, suggest that often we reverse the sequence, *first* making choices and acting on them and *then* seeking out the information and beliefs which will support them. We discover, for instance, that we have married a shortstop and *then* determine that we value excitement and passion more than security. We make a decision that seems to be a correct one and *then* construct a picture of our decision-making process that makes us seem to be rational. This kind of "backward thinking" seems to occur in almost all kinds of human decision making. It has been observed as the key process through which people acquire their beliefs and as a procedure sometimes used by researchers to build their theories.

Psychologist Daryl Bem developed a "self-perception" theory which concludes that people first observe their actions and then discover that they hold the beliefs and values which would make their actions seem rational. If we find ourselves marching against the proliferation of nuclear weapons, we begin to belive that control of nuclear weaponry is good and that this belief is what led us to march. This process allows us to perceive ourselves as "rational adults" and to persuade other people that that is what we are.[22]

Philosopher Abraham Kaplan argues that researchers often "think backwards," beginning their work by choosing a particular course of action (a research method in which they have been well trained, for example), then searching for a research problem to which they can apply their favored course of action, and finally searching for information which suggests that their choice of research method was appropriate after all. Kaplan labels this process the "drunkard's search," after a vaudeville joke in which the following discussion takes place:

A PASSERBY TO A DRUNK WHO IS CRAWLING AROUND UNDER A STREET LAMP: "What are you looking for?"

THE DRUNK: "A quarter that I dropped coming out of that bar" (pointing down the street).

PASSERBY: "Why aren't you looking for it over there?"

DRUNK: "Because the light's better over here."

There is a growing realization that the decision-making processes of employees sometimes are more like the drunkard's search than the rational actor's deliberations. Actions and the beliefs, values, and information which support them are not responses to organizational problems. Instead, actions are responses in search of situations in which they can be carried out.[23]

Employees' "nonrational" decision-making processes involve a number of steps. First, through the experiences that they have at work, employees learn (1) what their capacities and limitations are, (2) what kinds of "solutions" require the organization to rely on their unique talents and abilities and therefore give them opportunities to demonstrate their skills and value to their organization, and (3) what kinds of situations are appropriate to their preferred solutions. Day-by-day events give them a stream of problems which they can either step into or avoid. At some points they will decide that everything seems "right" for them to suggest their preferred solutions, and they will actively intervene in the decision-making process. They act, observe their actions, and then construct a plausible explanation for why they acted as they did and why their action was appropriate to the problem.

Karl Weick has described this kind of "nonrational" process in a model which uses the key terms *enactment* (acting), *selection* (observing one's actions) and *retention* (constructing an explanation of one's actions). See Figure 6.6. People use this "backwards" decision-making process primarily because it allows them to redefine complex, ever-changing, frustrating situations into manageable simplicities. They can remember a list of past actions which they believe were successful and the most important features of those situations. This list gives them guidelines about when not to act and how and when to act. Unfortunately, these guidelines may lead them to make two different kinds of errors. They may overlook important lessons from their past actions or ignore elements of their current situation which makes it quite different from the precedents. They become unable to adapt to new organizational situations because they have adapted so successfully in the past. In effect they become trapped in their simplifying interpretations of current circumstances.[24] But when the event is over they will have acted, and in acting they will have changed the situation.

FIGURE 6.6   Weick's Model of Organizational "Learning"

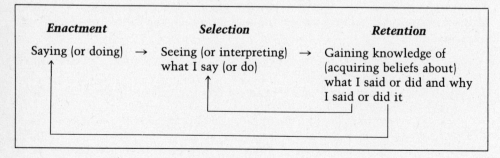

Communication and the Myths of Organizational Rationality

When it is applied to organizations, the rational actor model depicts decision making as a systematic process: (1) An employee recognizes that a problem exists and that it is caused by some unexpected or as-yet-untreated change in the organization's environment or by the actions of some of its members; (2) each member of the organization, who because of his or her formal position, expertise, or available information, has an interest in the problem, is told about it and invited to join in efforts to solve it; (3) alternative courses of action are compared through open, problem-solving communication, using some form of the "standard agenda" of decision making developed by the American educator John Dewey; (4) the optimal solution is chosen and implemented; and (5) its impact is monitored and information about its effects is gathered and stored for use in similar situations in the future. Through feedback the rational decision process is able to correct itself. That organizations always do solve problems in this way is, of course, an illusion. But it is a persistent illusion, one supported by three important cultural myths.

The Myth of Understanding According to "nonrationality" models, organizations are to some degree self-monitoring anarchies. They are composed of people who have a number of different goals, which constantly are undergoing change, generally are inconsistent with one another, and often are not clear to anyone who is involved. Employees discover their goals and those of their peers by observing one another's actions. The "intelligence" of an organization is more a loose and transient collection of ideas than a systematic and logical group of tightly interlocked preferences and procedures. Each employee possesses a set of preferred "solutions" and is looking for problems to which they can be applied; an organization is a collection of choices looking "for problems, issues and feelings looking for decision situations in which they might be aired and decision-makers looking for work."[25] In spite of these deviations from "rationality," organizations continue to operate successfully. They prosper primarily because their employees are incredibly capable of learning by trial and error and because their creativity often overcomes their nonrationality.

Organizational decisions are made, and once they are made, the participants begin to construct, share, and publicize a "rational" explanation and justification. Often decision makers search more actively for information relevant to the problems they face *after* they make decisions than before they do so. Even when their searches for information come before their decisions, they sometimes use information as much because it is easily available as because it is accurate or relevant to the problem. This phenomenon occurs because of the costs involved in searching for information. It takes time and effort to obtain relevant information, especially in large and complex organizations or when it is necessary to follow the chain of command. In addition, seeking information always involves admitting one's ignorance, and in organizations in which appearing to be knowledgeable is rewarded, easily accessible information may be preferred over information that may be more reliable but cannot be obtained without a public admission that it is needed.[26]

By selectively perceiving available information (ignoring or distorting negative information and accenting positive information), decision makers are able "rationally" to conclude that they have made the best possible decision. By arguing in favor of their choice, they provide one another with evidence which supports it and maintains their images as rational decision makers. By artificially reducing the range of options to those with which they are most familiar and comfortable, they are able to conclude that they have made the only choice which realistically was available. Then they can gather even more information, all of which can readily be perceived as legitimizing their choice and providing evidence that they indeed are rational decision makers.[27]

Although these nonrational processes may seem to be downright bizarre, they often serve a very effective and important function. They create sensible, shared, and manageable interpretations of the situations decision makers face. As illogical as they might seem to be, they often lead to decisions which fulfill at least the minimum requirements for satisfactory organizational performance. Of course, they can become counterproductive if they lead decision makers to persist in failing policies long after they should be abandoned. An excellent example of such failing policies has been provided by American utility companies. Suddenly in the early 1980s utility planners admitted that they had maintained a commitment to constructing nuclear power plants far beyond the point at which abundant evidence indicated that the plants would not in the foreseeable future be cost effective. The specter of partially completed, mothballed fission reactors, which already have cost customers billions of dollars, sitting idle across the countryside may offer a permanent momunent to the myth of rational organizational decision making.

The Myth of *Solving* Problems   The rational actor model also presumes that the focus of decision-making activities is on *solving problems*. Observations indicate, however, that their focus sometimes is on *taking action*. Organizational problems may be solved in the process, but that is not the primary function of decision-making activities.

Decisions can be made through any of three different "styles": (1) *Oversight* is making quick choices when it appears that waiting may allow the problems to become more complicated. Once the decision makers act they no longer are responsible for the problem; they will have completed their assigned responsibility. (2) In *flight* a choice is delayed until the problem becomes less complex because other people have acted. Since complicated organizational problems usually involve a number of people, all of whom feel pressure to act, delaying a decision may both simplify the problem and allow the decision maker to shift responsibility for errors to others. For example, an employee may leave town on the day before a crisis erupts. If other people handle the situation well at that time, the problem may almost be solved when the person returns. Then the person can intervene in the process, make the choices which still need to be made, and claim credit for resolving the crisis. If the others perform poorly while the person is away, he or she can return and make decisions which appear to "pick up the pieces." In either case, delaying action will have served the person's purposes. (3) *Resolution* is working through problems in a way which approximates the rational actor model.

All three of these styles make complex problems more manageable. But in some organizations, decisions seem to be made through resolution only when it is impossible to use the other approaches. Since oversight and flight do little to solve the underlying causes of problems, the same problems recur over and over again, providing decision makers with continuous opportunities to act (make decisions) and to legitimize their rightful roles as decision makers. The *focus* of choice making is not so much on solving problems as on being visibly involved in choice-making activities. The *function* of decision making often is symbolic rather than practical. Like initiation rites in fraternities, sororities, and other primitive cultures, decision-making events are *rituals* through which members of organizations demonstrate their competence, power, and commitment to the organization by *participating* in the ritual. Of course, these events are a very special kind of ritual. Not only do they support the images of decision makers, thereby increasing employees' confidence in the rationality of their leaders, but also they often generate satisfactory decisions. Many complex problems should be avoided; many situations can be improved in important ways by making minor changes. But to an outside observer, especially one who believes that decision making ought to be "rational," it will seem that "nothing ever gets done" in these decision-making events. If one is an anthropologist or sociologist, one soon will realize that what "gets done" is the "doing," the act of making choices. If the observer is a recently hired college graduate who has been trained in strategic decision making, it may take years to realize that what goes on in meetings is meeting. When former students return to their alma maters and complain to their mentors that "I'm always going to meetings where nothing ever gets decided" (as they invariably seem to do), they provide testimony to the ritualized nature of organizational decision making.

Viewing decision-making events as rituals also helps explain the otherwise mystifying processes through which employees decide when and how to become involved in decision making. Employees have a variety of personal goals, favored actions, and "pet" plans. They move along during the day-to-day activities of their organizations until they discover a decision-making event which is relevant to one of their preexisting concerns. They then choose to participate in that event. Other members choose to participate in the same event for different reasons. If they eventually do agree on a course of action, their consensus may be based on a long list of individual and often inconsistent goals. One supervisor may support a building plan because it will give subordinates more overtime; a department head may support it because of the attendant opportunity to transfer two troublesome workers to another section; and other employees may agree because it will divert upper management's attention away from the large equipment purchases they plan to make next week. Of course, it is quite improbable that any of these "real" motives will be expressed openly during the decision-making episodes. Instead, the participants will search for a rationale for the building project which is acceptable to everyone concerned and can be stated in public. Communication thus functions to obscure the participants' real motivations rather than to reveal them. But in the process it also allows them to make a "rational" decision. When an agreement is reached in an organization, it sometimes is an agreement over *decisions and public justifications of them*, not over the reasons or goals which lie behind the choice (see Figure 6.7).

March and his associates have captured the essence of ritualized decision-making processes in their description of such events as "garbage cans."[28] When a number of employees decide to become involved in an event, they use it like a garbage can, dumping into the discussion a plethora of concerns, only some

FIGURE 6.7   Coping with Multiple Aims and Multiple Decision Events*

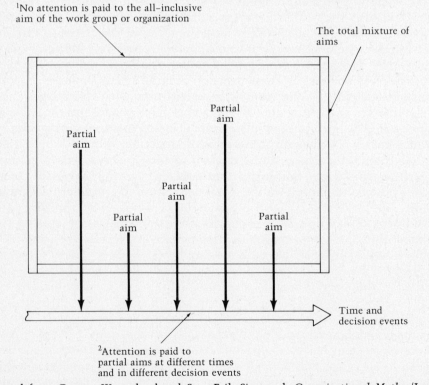

[1]No attention is paid to the all–inclusive aim of the work group or organization

The total mixture of aims

Partial aim

Partial aim

Partial aim

Partial aim

Partial aim

Time and decision events

[2]Attention is paid to partial aims at different times and in different decision events

*Adapted from Gunnar Westerlund and Sven-Erik Sjostrand, *Organizational Myths* (London: Harper and Row, 1979).

of which are "logically" related to the problems discussed. Although some organizations generate more garbage-can decisions than others, all of them have some problems that rarely are "solved." A very small proportion of the input dumped into decision-making sessions, March, et al. argue, is oriented toward actually *solving* a problem.

The goal of the preceding pages has been to suggest that people often do not act in ways which conform to the "rational actor" model, either in everyday decision making or during organizational decision-making episodes. This is not to suggest that humans never act rationally or that they make decisions in wholly nonrational ways. Instead, contingency theories indicate that for a number of understandable reasons people act in ways which violate the myths of rationality embedded in our culture. In some cases individual and organizational decision making deviates only slightly from the rational actor ideal; in other cases the deviations are quite large. Consequently, organizations can be categorized by the degree of "nonrationality" which characterizes their usual decision-making processes. Like the aspects of organizational action discussed in Chapters 1 through 5, the appropriateness of different kinds of decision-making processes seems to be contingent on a number of factors.

Although researchers have only recently started to define these factors, a preliminary categorization is possible. Varieties of decision making can be arrayed along two continua. At one pole of the first continuum are simple problems where the information needed to made the decision is finite, only a limited number of options are available, communication networks are small, necessary information readily available, and the effects of different courses of action can be quantified. At the other pole are situations so ambiguous, problems so complex, and information so inaccessible that rational decision making is almost impossible (see Figure 6.8).

FIGURE 6.8   A Continuum of Forms of Decision-Making

"Rational Decision making" *–Both Possible and Preferable*	*"Rational Decision-making"—Either* *Impossible or Inappropriate*
quantifiable outcomes	ambiguous outcomes
clear decision-effect links	ambiguous decision-effect links
"finite" communication	unknown or ill-defined parameters
redundant sources available	"infinite" communication
defined information needs	unknown or indefinite information needs
limited communication networks	diverse or undefined communication networks
minimal organizational and environmental change	constant organizational and/or environmental change
precedented and/or simple problems	unprecedented and/or complex problems

The second continuum reflects Ouchi's argument that organizations differ from one another in terms of the kind of control systems they have.[29] In some organizations traditional (behavior and/or outcome) forms of control are appropriate and possible. But in others, the products produced by the organization, the processes used to create them, and the factors which influence employees' performance are so complicated and ambiguous that traditional control cannot work effectively. These organizations must rely on the abstract, symbolic strategies societies always have used to limit and direct the actions of their members—rituals, rites, myths, and stories about what constitutes good and evil. For instance, universities would find it quite difficult to regulate professors' actions through rules of behavior. Few people know what universities produce; fewer still claim to be able to measure objectively and unambiguously professors' performances. Quality of teaching, research, and service simply are not easily quantifiable outcomes. In these organizations, control is achieved through subtle processes of acculturation, establishing barriers to entry, requiring symbols of professionalism, and so on, not through overt processes of reward and punishment. These symbolic strategies succeed because they allow employees to fulfill nontangible needs for status, self-esteem, and so on.

An organization's control mechanisms and mode of decision making are interrelated in complicated ways. The features that make a particular form of control appropriate also influence the kinds of decision making that are possible. Because the outcomes of professors' activities are ambiguous and intangible and the factors that influence their performance are so varied and abstract, symbolic forms of control are most appropriate. Similarly, because the "products" of professors' actions are intangible and ambiguous, it is next-to-impossible to objectively or reliably assess the effects of key organizational decisions. Because the professors within an academic department or division of the university work independent of one another and thus have different self-interests, it is improbable that they would arrive at a consensus about the rationale behind a decision through open discussion, although it is quite possible for them to agree to support a particular proposal for their own idiosyncratic, private, and possibly contradictory reasons. In this kind of situation, both symbolic control and nonrational decision making are appropriate and likely. In other kinds of organizations, different combinations of control systems and modes of decision making will be appropriate. (see Figure 6.9). For example, paper plants generally face stable environments, their members are involved in simple decisions and have finite information needs (thus allowing them to make decisions rationally), and they can rely on systems of output control (reward systems) and behavioral control (rules). Restaurants can prescribe behaviors and measure employees' performances, but they face complex decisions and changing environments. Advertising agencies may be able to employ rational decision-making processes but find it difficult to measure outputs or control behaviors, and so on.[30]

Now, none of the comments made in this chapter are intended to disparage organizations or their members. Instead their goal is to suggest that our

FIGURE 6.9   **Continua of Organizational Decision Situations**

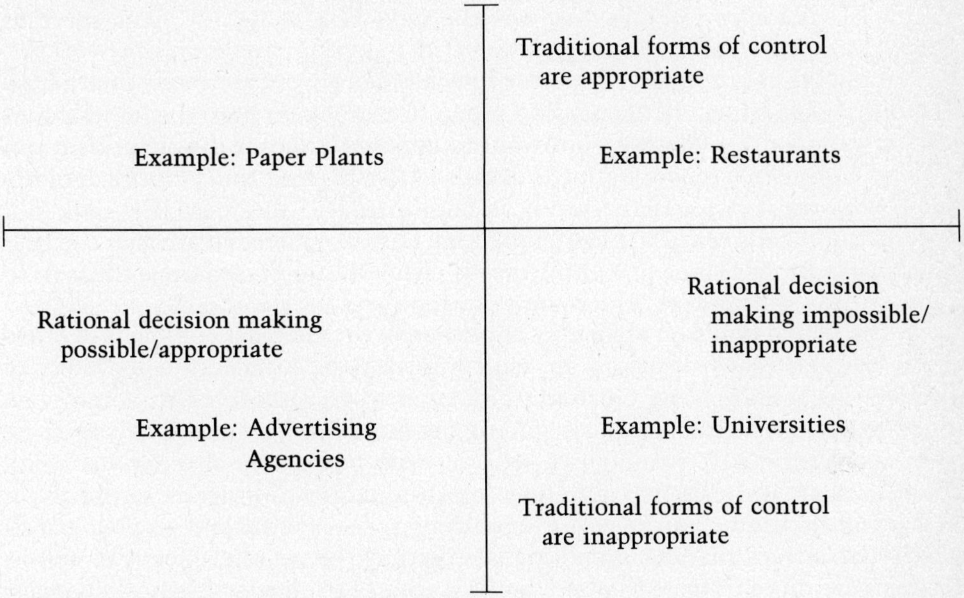

Traditional forms of control
are appropriate

Example: Paper Plants   Example: Restaurants

Rational decision making
possible/appropriate

Rational decision
making impossible/
inappropriate

Example: Advertising
Agencies

Example: Universities

Traditional forms of control
are inappropriate

cultural ideal of rational decision making is a bit unrealistic. Human choice making is a complicated activity which is influenced by a myriad of concerns, ranging from a desire to use one's talents to solve problems to the need to participate in organizational rituals. Fulfilling all these needs is an important function of organizational communication and decision making. Johann Olson observed that Norweigian villages still hold active and well-attended town meetings, even though the real decision-making power shifted long ago to the town council.[31] The town meetings allow citizens to be involved in a democratic ritual and fulfill their need to feel involved in their communities and to have some control over them. Organizational rituals and ritualized decision making meet important needs, both for the organizations and their members. In some cases they are the only forms of action which can meet those needs. Traditional theories focus on the information and expertise which participants communicate to one another during decision-making events. Contemporary models suggest that an equally important dimension is what is communicated by the act of participation itself.

The Myth of Plans as Solutions   Karl Weick, citing Cohen and March, suggested that "plans are important in organizations, but not for the reasons people think.[32] The first four of these reasons are related directly to organizational communication: (1) Plans serve as *symbols*—signals to outsiders that the organization really does know what it is doing. For example, when small Japanese-built automobiles began to take more than 20 percent of the

American market, it would have been helpful for American manufacturers to unveil a new line of competitive cars. But since no cars were available, unveiling *plans* for competing cars was the next best thing. (2) Plans serve as *advertisements*—tools with which to attract investors or mobilize workers. (3) Plans serve as *games*—ways to see how serious people are about their ideas. Planning takes time and energy. If a group of employees presents an idea that a supervisor dislikes but does not want to oppose in public, the supervisor can create a committee to work out the details of the proposal and place each of the employees on it. Unless the group is committed to the idea, they will not expend the effort needed to plan. In the long term employees learn that the best way to stay off of planning committees is either to not present new ideas or to support only those ideas which are very good and very workable.

The fourth function of plans is to allow the eventual development of other plans. Because many decisions are too complex to be sorted out completely in a single decision-making episode, they need to be simplified in some way. Complexity can be managed by reducing the number of courses of action being considered seriously. Amibiguity will be even less if the alternatives being considered are only slightly different from the policy or program currently in effect. Information about existing conditions is more reliable than predictions about the effects of new proposals. Predictions about the effects of minor changes are more reliable than predictions about the effects of radical changes. So if decision makers limit their considerations to a small number of relatively conservative changes, they can manage complex situations. They do not eliminate the sources of ambiguity, but they do simplify their task. Once one of these conservative options is chosen and put into effect, the situation is changed, allowing further consideration of a progressively more limited range of minor changes.

In a provocative series of publications, Charles Lindblom argued that governmental organizations make choices through this procedure of "successive limited comparisons." Organizations "muddle through" (Lindblom's phrase) problems, making decisions and taking actions which help them simplify complex situations. Plans help decision makers make sense out of complicated problems and convince others that they really do understand those problems.

SUMMARY: COMMUNICATION, CONTINGENCIES, AND THE MANAGEMENT OF AMBIGUITY

Analyzing these three myths—*understanding, focus on solutions, and plans as solutions*—reveals processes of organizational choice making quite different than those depicted in the rational actor models. The analysis tells us two very important things about the function of communication in organizations. First, it indicates that both the *processes* and the *products* of communication (decisions, plans, deals, and so on) allow members of organizations to manage ambiguous and confusing situations. If one embraces the cultural ideal of rational decision making without questioning it, or if one accepts the assumptions of the traditional and human relations and resources models, the ambiguity-management function of communication will seem to be inefficient and perhaps a little bit perverse. But blending rational and nonrational elements of decision making together in the same decision-making episodes may be neither strange nor ineffective.

In a six-year study of how hospitals make decisions about purchasing CAT scanners and other equipment costing millions of dollars, Alan Meyer uncovered a recurring decision-making process which combined rational and nonrational processes in a complicated maze.[33] In general, the decision-making episodes began with careful considerations of program needs, equipment costs, projected payoff periods, and other objective factors. Necessary information was gathered before decisions were made, important people were involved in the process, and so on. In short, the decision-making process approximated the rational actor model. But eventually, in many of the episodes, the process started to deviate from the rational model. Communication among participants became more vague and imprecise and started to focus on abstract and intangible topics, like the parties' shared beliefs, values, goals for the hospital, and vision of its future. Later the decision makers began to restructure and redefine what actually had taken place during the deliberations so that they seemed to fit the myths of rational decision making.

The later, nonrational phase of the process served two important purposes for the hospitals' personnel. First, it allowed them to emerge from what often had been highly competitive, heated discussions with a revised image of themselves as tough but cooperative members of a functioning team. Second, the symbolic strategies allowed them to gain a sense of psychological closure on the process—to *feel* that the decision has been made, the battle was over, and their attention now needed to turn toward using the new equipment effectively. In effect these groups had used the communication strategies which bind societies together—myths, rituals, and ceremonies—to reunify themselves into a cohesive mini-society. In hospitals where the decision makers used rational communication strategies throughout the process, the groups seldom reunified. Dissension continued, debates proliferated, and in some cases key staff members resigned and expensive new equipment was left sitting in the basement unused or underused. Meyer's research suggests that rational communication strategies are neither superior nor inferior to less narrowly rational processes. Instead, they are forms of communication which serve organizational decision makers in different ways. It is their appropriateness to the particular type of decision and phase of decision making that is important, not their conformity to social myths about how people "ought" to act or how organizational decisions "ought" to be made.

Second, the analysis indicates that human beings do seem to be able to find ways to cope successfully with the situations they face. They simplify overly complex problems, redefine potentially divisive issues, and unify diverse groups. They find ways of fulfilling their own muddled, idiosyncratic and inconsistent goals while collaborating with one another in ways that allow their organizations to function rather successfully. Their ways of coping may not be at all like those which organizational theorists expect or would like to have employees develop. But they often seem to work just the same.

However, these comments imply neither that more rational prescriptions about organizations are incorrect nor that members of organizations will succeed if they just "do what comes naturally." In all organizations relatively successful *patterns of communications* eventually do *emerge*. They do so naturally and inevitably. But these patterns can become unproductive and harmful if they lead employees to act in one of two ways. If they attempt inappropriately or too suddenly to *impose* idealized communicative processes, constraints, or rules on one another, they can short-circuit the natural coping processes. It matters little whether the "ideal" being imposed is traditional, human relations, human resources, or contingency. Attempts to force employees to adopt power sharing or participation—or any other major change—may upset the relationships they have formed to make their worlds stable and predictable.[34] Conversely, attempting to limit communication to formal channels may short-circuit valuable informal communication networks. In both cases the problem does not lie with the ideal model of communication itself. It lies with the attempt to impose it in a situation in which it does not belong. In the end this is the essence of the systems-contingency model. Idealized strategies will succeed only where they are appropriate to the complex patterns of action which have emerged in a particular organization, and only when they are introduced in a way that respects and adjusts to those patterns.

The second potentially harmful response occurs when employees become "trapped" in successful patterns of communication. Because naturally emerging communicative patterns seem to employees to meet their needs so well, they may become static and inflexible. Stability is, of course, the greatest virtue of these natural patterns. Even when individual employees leave an organization and different people take their places, the patterns continue. Newcomers step into these existing patterns and have a head start on making sense out of their new organization. But as Weick has noted, the development of communication patterns adapted to the needs of an organization may themselves prevent the organization from adapting to new needs and demands. Adaptation may prevent adaptability.

In order to avoid both these problems—inappropriately imposing models of communication and becoming trapped in successful patterns of communication—employees must constantly monitor their communication and the communication patterns of their organizations, searching for strategies which can improve their ability to adapt. Employees must be able to ask themselves, "does strategy X work? Should I use it?" rather than asserting "I know X works. We should use it." They must be able to obtain and process information accurately which casts doubts on their perceptions, beliefs, and interpretations. And they must be able to suspend temporarily their views of the "realities" of their organizations in order to understand how they can best respond to new situations.

Conclusion to Unit I

This unit began with comments about communication that were hundreds, even thousands, of years old. The unit was organized around Weber's theory of ideal types, a concept developed more than a half-century ago. It concluded with ideas about how organizations differ from one another that are so recent and changing so rapidly that each draft of Chapter 6 was radically different than drafts written only weeks before. But in a sense the systems-contingency perspective has taken us back to the key ideas of the earlier theorists. This circle is illustrated most clearly in one of the most popular new contingency theories—Ouchi's "Theory Z."[35]

Like Weber, Ouchi argued that in order to succeed, organizations must be adapted appropriately to the key characteristics of the culture from which they recruit their employees. He labels one ideal type of organization "type J"; another, "Type A." The two types differ in terms of seven defining characteristics (see Table 6.2). Type J firms are appropriate to cultures like Japan's because the Japanese long have been taught to value group membership and collective activity. Cultural norms place loyalty to groups (and thus to organizations) above individual achievement. The structure of Type J organizations creates a broad understanding of how the organization functions and makes frequent performance evaluations and promotions inappropriate. Each dimension interacts with each other dimension to (1) support norms of collective action and (2) prevent employees from acquiring the specialized skills which would allow them to move to another firm. The culture and organizational structure combine to *reduce employees' incentives* to abandon their work group in pursuit of individual advancement and to *reduce their ability* to do so. In a culture where individuality is valued highly, this combination of necessary features would be inappropriate, as unsuccessful attempts to use Type J organizational designs with American workers have illustrated.

Type A firms are appropriate in cultures which value individuality more

TABLE 6.2   Ouchi's Organizational Types*

Type A (American)	*Type J (Japanese)*
Short-term employment	Lifetime employment
Individual decision making	Consensual decision making
Individual responsibility	Collective responsibility
Rapid evaluation and promotion	Slow evaluation and promotion
Explicit, formalized control	Implicit, informal control
Specialized career path	Nonspecialized career paths
Segmented concerns	Holistic concerns

*Taken from Ouchi and Jaeger "Type Z", p. 308.

than group membership and which provide people with opportunities to fulfill their social needs through involvement in nonwork organizations—churches, community groups, and neighborhoods. This kind of culture existed in Weber's Germany and until recently it existed in the United States. It was no accident that Type A organizations evolved in Western, capitalist, individualistic cultures. The combination of dimensions which make up Type A organizations are appropriate to the perceptions, values, and patterns of action of the people who became their employees. However, Ouchi argues, although our culture still values individual achievement, factors like urbanization, increased geographical mobility and so on have reduced the ability of nonwork organizations to meet our social needs. No longer is the Type A organization appropriate to our culture, but neither is the Type J organization. Type Z organizations, which retain individual achievement and advancement but also provide a sense of community at work, now are an appropriate option.

However, even Type Z organizations will not be appropriate in all situations. U.S. culture is not homogeneous—there are many subcultures which value community more than individuality, and there are some areas in which nonwork organizations still fulfill employees' higher-order needs. In these areas, Type A organizations are still appropriate, and attempts to impose a Type Z organization on employees would be resisted. Ouchi's point is essentially like those made by Weber and Barnard years earlier. Part of an organization's environment is the set of beliefs, values, and patterns of action supported by its employees' culture. Organizations will function best when they are adapted to their environments. But Ouchi's ideal type (as well as those proposed by the other contingency theorists) differs from the earlier ideals in two important ways. First, it is more comprehensive, including more dimensions of organizational systems, subsystems, and suprasystems and their interrelationships. Second, it depicts employees and organizations as flexible, adaptive organisms. Implicit in the earlier models were a number of constants: People were assumed to have stable, preset needs, values, or drives; organizations were assumed to have stable characteristics. But the only constant in the systems-contingency models is the constancy of change. Employees are continually monitoring, interpreting, and responding to the organizational situations they face. Organizations are continually adapting to the internal and external pressures they encounter. Through constant adaptation, both employees and organizations create new situations, new contingencies, and new solutions. In a constant process, action creates the need for additional action.

The focus of this unit has been on *differences*—among types of organizations and the functions of communication in each. However, organizational situations are rarely unique; there are *recurring patterns* of problems, situations, and strategies. The goal of Unit II is to examine a number of these recurring situations and to suggest communicative strategies that employees can use to cope with them. Like this unit, it will be organized around a single core concept—not Weber's theory of ideal types but Kenneth Burke's ideas about comic and tragic frames of reference.

The Graduation Case

As I have suggested throughout this book, educational institutions are complex, bureaucratic structures and often can be understood only as such. Each year hundreds of thousands of people come together in stadiums under the blazing sun or in overheated gymnasiums or auditoriums to wear strange, rented costumes, perspire profusely, and celebrate the graduation of the Class of 19__. What function, one might ask, do these exercises fulfill for the organization? No decisions are made. A high school secretary or a university registrar already has decided who will graduate and who will not. In most institutions, even those few who will not are allowed to participate in the exercise and are handed empty diploma holders while marching alongside their more successful peers. Few lives are changed by the ceremony. Even the most inspirational commencement address falls on the ears of graduates whose minds are clouded by thoughts of planned postcommencement activities and/or whose precommencement celebrations have left only minimally capable of being challenged to a lifetime of virtue.

What happens in these organizational exercises is the exercise. Graduations, I believe, serve three important purposes for educational organizations. The first is ritual bonding. Parents generally have made major sacrifices to see that their children arrive at this point and need to believe those sacrifices have not been in vain. Faculty members need to believe that their contributions to their students and thus to society are far more valuable than their salaries would suggest. And students need to believe both that parents and faculty members are concerned about them and willing to help them make the transition from the "ivory tower" to the "real world" and that all their work has been worth the effort. Graduation exercises allow the three groups to join together in a ritual act which fulfills each of their needs. In one brief shining moment the academic community can act as if it is just that—a disparate group of individuals united by a common concern and a shared experience.

Graduation also serves a public relations function. It allows large, bureaucratic, and often impersonal organizations to present themselves to outsiders as intimate, individualized, caring service agencies. Perhaps more important, it allows the same organizations to present themselves to their caring, concerned employees as the kind of institution in which the humanitarian values of these employees are actualized. The extent to which the image corresponds to objective reality is of little importance. It is the belief that the image is accurate that creates commitment to the organization. Because high morale is such an important determinant of performance in complex, abstract jobs like teaching and research, this belief and the ritualized symbolic acts which support it enhance the performance and productivity of the organization's members.

Finally, graduation functions as advertisement. I have yet to attend a university graduation exercise in which the fund-raising activities of the alumni association or scholarship program are not prominently displayed. Sometimes these hints to contribute are as subtle as a wedding (that is, gift) invitation from a casual acquaintance. Usually they are more tactful. In essence the message is that this ritual and the community that it represents exist because of outside financial support which must continue if the community is to continue. All organizations have important rituals and all rituals, if they succeed, fulfill the functions of bonding, commitment-building and advertisement.

Notes

1. Like Max Weber and Thorstein Veblen, von Bertalanfy rarely is read by U.S. students. This unfortunate state of affairs results, I think, from the kindness of professors who seem to realize that the original works of philosophers and many social scientists are almost unreadable for most students. Of course, they can be read and understood, but only with great pain. As a result they are assigned to graduate students, since there also seems to be a belief among professors that experiencing and mastering pain is an important part of graduate school. For readers who wish to have this experience, the bibliography at the end of this book contains a number of appropriate citations.

2. See J. Stacy Adams, "The Structure and Dynamics of Behavior in Organizational Boundary Roles," in *Handbook of Industrial and Organizational Psychology*, ed. Marvin Dunnette (Chicago: Rand-McNally, 1976), pp. 1,175–1,199; Michael Tushman, "Impacts of Perceived Environmental Variability on Patterns of Work-Related Communication," *Academy of Management Journal*, 22 (1979), 482–500; and Howard Aldrich and D. Herker, "Boundary Spanning Roles and Organizational Structures," *Academy of Management Review* 2 (1977), 217–230.

3. Tom Burns and G. M. Stalker, *The Management of Innovation* (London: Tavistock, 1961); Paul Lawrence and Jay Lorsch, *Organizations and Environment* (Boston: Harvard Business School, 1967).

4. H. Mintzberg, *The Nature of Managerial Work* (Englewood Cliffs, N. J.: Prentice-Hall, 1980); R. Miles, A. Meyer, and H. Coleman, "Organizational Strategy, Structure and Process," *Academy of Management Review*, 3 (1978), 546–562.

5. L. L. Cummings, "Organizational Behavior," *Annual Review of Psychology*, 33 (1982), 541–579; Jay Galbraith, *Designing Complex Organizations* (Reading, Mass.: Addison-Wesley, 1973); C. Perrow, *Organizational Analysis* (Belmont, Calif.: Wadsworth, 1970); J. Pfeffer and G. Salancik, *The External Control of Organizations* (New York: Harper & Row, 1978).

6. R. Daft and N. Macintosh, "A Tentative Exploration Into the Amount and Equivocality of Information Processing in Organizational Work Units," *Administrative Science Quarterly*, 26 (1981) 207–224; D. Hambrick, "Environment, Strategy and Power Within Top Management," *Administrative Science Quarterly*, 26 (1981), 253–271; M. Tushman and D. Nadler, "Information Processing as an Integrating Concept in Organizational Design," *Academy of Management Review*, 3 (1978), 613–624; Aldrich and Herker, "Boundary Spanning Roles." Chapter 7 will examine the concepts of organizational power and politics in detail.

7. Joan Woodward, *Industrial Organization: Theory and Practice* (London: Oxford University Press, 1965). Follow-up studies are summarized in Daniel Katz and Robert Kahn, *The Social Psychology of Organizations*, 2nd ed. (New York: John Wiley, 1978).

8. For a summary of Thompson's work see Katz and Kahn. Also see W. Ouchi, "Markets, Bureaucracies and Clans," *Administrative Science Quarterly*, 25 (1980), 129–141, and "A Conceptual Framework for the Design of Organizational Control Mechanisms," *Management Science*, 25 (1979), 833–848; S. Kerr and J. Slocum, Jr., "Controlling the Performances of People in Organizations," in *Handbook of Organizational Design*, ed. P. Nystrom and W. Starbuck, (New York: Oxford University Press, 1979),Vol.2, pp. 116–134.

9. C. Berger and L. L. Cummings, "Organizational Structure, Attitudes and Behavior," in *Research in Organizational Behavior*, ed. B. Staw (Greenwich, Conn.: JAI Press, 1979), vol. 1, pp. 169–208; D. Dalton, W. Todor, M. Spendolini, G. Fielding, and L. Porter, "Organizations, Structure and Peformance: A Cricital Review," *Academy of Management Review*, 5 (1980), 49–64; D. Rousseau, "An Assessment of Technology in Organizations," *Academy of Management Review*, 4 (1979), 531–542.

10. See H. Mintzberg, *Structuring in Fives* (Englewood Cliffs, N.J.: Prentice-Hall, 1983).

11. See, for example, Robert Dewar and James Werbel, "Universalistic and Contingency Predictions of Employee Satisfaction and Conflict," *Administrative Science Quarterly*, 24 (1979), 426–447; C. Schriesheim and M. A. von Glinow, "The Path-Goal Theory of Leadership," *Academy of Management Journal* 20 (1977), 398–405; Robert Vecchio, "An Empirical Examination of the Validity of Fiedler's Model of Leadership Effectiveness," *Organizational Behavior and Human Performance*, 19 (1977), 180–206.

12. House uses the terminology of the Ohio State Leadership Studies: "A Path-Goal Theory of Leadership Effectiveness," *Administrative Science Quarterly*, 16 (1971), 321–339.

13. J. Pierce, R. Dunham, and R. Blackburn, "Social Systems Structure, Job Design and Growth Need Strength," *Academy of Management Journal*, 22 (1979) 223–240.

14. Aldrich and Herker, "Boundary Spanning Roles"; Rousseau, "Assessment of Technology."

15. James March, "The Technology of Foolishness," in *Ambiguity and Choice in Organizations*, ed. James March and Johann Olson (Bergen: Universitetsforlaget, 1970), pp. 69–81.

16. Karl Weick, *The Social Psychology of Organizing* (Reading, Mass.: Addison-Wesley, 1969). Detailed studies of how people manage ambiguity have been completed by Charles Bantz and David H. Smith, "A Critique and Experimental Test of Weick's Model of Organizing," *Communication Monographs*, 44 (1977), 171–184; Gary Kreps, "A Field Experimental Test of Weick's Model of Organizing," in *Communication Yearbook 4*, ed. Dan Nimmo (New Brunswick, N. J.: Transaction, 1980); Linda Putnam and Ritch Sorenson, "Equivocal Messages in Organizations," *Human Communication Research*, 8 (1982), 114–132.

17. See the articles summarized in Paul Slovic, Baruch Fischhoff, and Sarah Lichtenstein, "Behavioral Decision Theory," *Annual Review of Psychology*, 28 (1977), 1–39. The model was proposed by John von Neumann and Oskar Morganstern, *Theory of Games and Economic Behavior* (New York: John Wiley, 1947). This is another painful book which only graduate students are asked to read.

18. See J. Robert Cox, "Symbolic Action and Satisfactory Choices" (paper presented at the Speech Communication Association Convention, New York, 1980); Leonard Hawes and David H. Smith, "A Critique of the Assumptions Underlying the Study of Communication in Conflict," *Quarterly Journal of Speech*, 59 (1973), 423–435; David H. Smith, "Theoretical and Research Problems with the Concept of Utility" (paper presented at the International Communication Association Convention, Acapulco, 1980). The distinction between *cannot* and *do not* is important; the rational actor model has been defended on the grounds that although people do not consciously use the system, they behave as if they do. Ward Edwards, "Subjective Probabilities Inferred from Decisions," *Psychological Review*, 69 (1962), 109–135, and "Utility, Subjective Probability, their Interaction and Variance Preferences," *Journal of Conflict Resolution*, 6 (1962), 42–50.

19. James March and Herbert Simon, "The Concept of Rationality," in *Human Behavior and International Politics*, ed. David Singer (Chicago: Rand-McNally, 1965), p. 343.

20. Kenneth May, "Intransitivity, Utility and Aggregation of Preference Patterns," *Econometrica*, 22 (1954), 1–36; T. Dolbear and L. Lave, "Inconsistent Behavior in Lottery Choice Experiments," *Behavioral Science*, 12 (1967), 14–23.

21. Also communication allows us to pretend that we are rational and thus confirms our culture's myths of rationality.

22. Daryl Bem, *Beliefs, Attitudes and Human Affairs* (Belmont, Calif.: Brooks-Cole, 1972).

23. Weick, *Social Psychology of Organizing*; March and Olson, eds., *Ambiguity and Choice*; G. Westerlund and S. Sjostrand, *Organizational Myths* (New York: Harper & Row, 1979). These three works are important sources for the ideas presented in the remainder of this chapter.

24. Kenneth Burke, *Attitudes Toward History* (Boston: Beacon Press, 1937), has called this process "adopting a tragic frame." This idea will be developed in detail in Unit II.

25. M. Cohen, J. March, and J. Olson, "A Garbage-Can Model of Organizational Choice," *Administrative Science Quarterly.* 17 (1972), 2.

26. C. O'Reilly, "Variations in Decision Makers' Use of Information Sources," *Academy of Management Journal,* 25 (1982), 756–771.

27. J. March and M. Feldman, "Information in Organizations as Signal and Symbol," *Administrative Science Quarterly,* 26 (1981), 171–186; D. Caldwell and C. O'Reilly, "Responses to Failure," *Academy of Management Journal,* 25 (1962), 121–136; B. Staw, "Knee Deep in the Big Muddy," *Organizational Behavior and Human Performance,* 16 (1976) 27–44; B. Staw and J. Ross, "Commitment to a Policy Decision," *Administrative Science Quarterly,* 23 (1978), 40–52; F. Fox and B. Staw, "The Trapped Administrator," *Administrative Science Quarterly,* 24 (1979), 449–456.

28. Cohen, March, and Olsen, "Garbage Can."

29. W. Ouchi and A. Jaeger, "Type Z Organization," *Academy of Management Review,* 3 (1978), 305–314; also see W. Ouchi, *Theory Z* (Reading, Mass.: Addison-Wesley, 1981).

30. It is not accidental that the majority of the research on nonrational decision making that has been reviewed in this chapter takes place in academic organizations.

31. Johann Olson, "Local Budgeting, Decision-Making or Ritual Act," *Scandinavian Political Studies,* 5 (1970), 85–118.

32. Weick, *Social Psychology of Organizing,* p. 10. The first four of these functions are discussed by Weick; the fifth is drawn from C. Lindblom, "The Science of Muddling Through," *Public Administration Review,* 19 (1959), 1–21.

33. Of course, my brief summary oversimplifies Meyer's research. See "Mingling Decision Making Metaphors," *Academy of Managament Review,* 9 (1984), 6–17.

34. A friend of mine once told me of an instance in which he inadvertently upset these processes. After attending a "human relations" training program he decided that it was inappropriate for him to park his car in his plant manager's space when he had workers who were in much poorer health than he was and who were forced to walk far longer distances to and from their cars. After a brief period of parking in the employees' lot and inviting them to park in the manager's space, his workers informed him that managers were supposed to have privileges like parking spaces and that they expected him to accept them.

35. Ouchi and Jaeger, "Type Z"; Ouchi, "Theory Z."

UNIT
11

Coping With Organizational Situations

INTRODUCTION

In 1970 rhetorical theorist Lloyd Bitzer published an article which has become one of the best known and most often cited works in the field of speech communication. Bitzer's "The Rhetorical Situation" proposed that "rhetoric" is a kind of purposeful communication which takes place in a particular kind of setting, or "situation." *Rhetoric* is communication in which people try to change the conditions they perceive exist around them. It is different than communication designed to *express* a person's beliefs or feelings and it is different than communication designed to present *information* to others solely for the sake of doing so.

A *rhetorical situation* is defined by three characteristics—an exigence, an audience, and a set of constraints. An *exigence* is a condition which calls for rhetorical communication. It is a problem, obstacle, or event about which a person believes that communication is necessary for change and that his or her actions can affect the condition. A rhetorical *audience* is a person or group of people who are capable of being influenced by the speaker's communication and who have the capacity to help implement the changes that the speaker advocates. *Constraints* are all of those factors—beliefs, attitudes, communication skills, power relationships, and so on—which limit the range of communication strategies available to a communicator, restrict his or her ability to affect change, or influence the audience's willingness or ability to respond favorably to the speaker's communication. When combined, person's perceptions of the *exigences, audiences*, and *constraints* in a particular situation form the parameters within which they must make choices about when and how to communicate.[1]

Although there is no evidence that Bitzer ever intended his model to be applied to communication in formal organizations, it does provide a useful starting point for understanding the most important communicative situations people face at work. In essence, communication in organizations is rhetorical communication. It takes place within situations which call for actions of certain types, is limited by a complex matrix of constraints, and is addressed to people who may be able to change the organization and the situations faced by its members. It is communication which has an *instrumental* purpose, which involves a variety of goals in addition to the sheer need to express emotions or provide information. It may involve objectives as personal as creating a desired image of oneself in the minds of others or as broad as improving the firm's market share. Of course, employees sometimes do engage in communication which primarily serves to express their emotions or disseminate information. They may lock themselves in restrooms and scream just for the thrill of it all. Or they may mechanically pass information on to other employees solely for the sake of doing so.[2] But it is *rhetorical communication* which allows organizations and their members to succeed and which helps them to fail. Effective organizational communication depends on the rhetorical skills of employees. The purpose of Unit II of this book is to discuss the rhetorical situations people often face at work and explain how workers can choose communicative strategies appropriate to those situations.

ORGANIZATIONAL CONSTRAINTS AND EXIGENCES

Unit I provided an extended summary of the factors which make up the situations employees face (see Figure II.1). Each of these factors is present to some degree in every organization and every situation. The *relative* importance of the factors does vary, however. They combine in groupings which "call on" employees to act in certain ways and which constrain their options. Sometimes the combination of exigences and constraints gives employees clear and workable guidelines about how they should act. It is clear that acting in some ways is "required" and that acting in other ways is prohibited. In these cases, choosing an appropriate course is not terribly difficult.

In other cases, however, choosing an appropriate response is more difficult. In some cases it even may be impossible. Complex situations sometimes *paralyze* employees. One kind of paralysis occurs when the exigences of a situation are clear to an individual but the constraints are unclear or unknown. If it seems to employees that they can respond to a situation in any conceivable way, they have no guidelines for acting. Like some families, some organizations give their members very little structure, guidelines, or con-

FIGURE II.1 Constraints and Exigences in Organizations

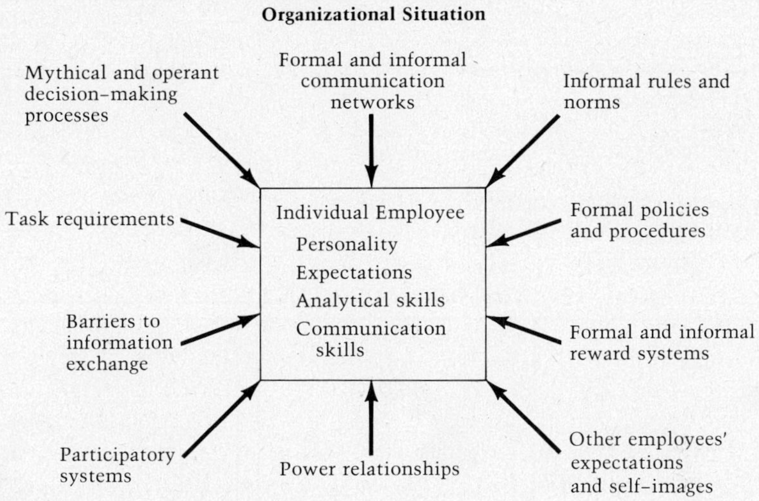

Organizational Situation

straints. For example, telling therapists to "do good work" or hospital administrators to "cut costs," or elementary schoolteachers to "stimulate all the childrens' interests" provides so few guidelines that employees cannot make meaningful choices about how to proceed. Unless employees are given some sense of what directions to pursue, they must rely wholly on their own devices to make sense out of their situations. They are paralyzed, at least momentarily, while they construct what seem to be viable guidelines for acting. As Chapters 8 and 11 will explain, this kind of paralyzing situation is one of the greatest problems new employees face and one of the most common sources of organizational stress.

Another form of paralysis occurs when action is called for but existing constraints leave an employee with no productive way to respond. Like Lucy in the cartoon in Figure II.2, members of an organization sometimes communicate messages which leave other members with little realistic opportunity for choice. Presumably, Linus' purpose is to gain the childlike fun that comes from a friendly snowball fight. But Lucy's comments leave him with both a command to act (since dropping the snowball is an act) and no productive way to achieve his purpose. Throwing the snowball will fail; so will not throwing it. Lucy has taken the fun out of snowball fights and has robbed Linus of any opportunity for meaningful choice. Organizations sometimes place their employees in analogous situations. They create exigences which require action and constraints which leave them with no productive course(s) of action. Between the two extremes of exigences with no constraints and exigences with no choice are the kinds of situations employees typically face—those that allow a range of potential actions, which can serve both their purposes and the purposes of their organization.

A particular employee's ability to cope with a range of situations depends

©1976 United Features Syndicate, Inc.

on a number of personal factors—*expectations, analytical skills* and *message-creating skills.* Each of these characteristics may either give the employee a wide range of potential coping strategies or reduce the available options. High levels of analytical skills may allow people to discover constraints which others would overlook, thereby giving them guidelines for actions in unstructured situations. Or in other situations, their skills may allow them to discover response options that others fail to detect and thereby free them from excessive constraints. Expectations and message-creating and -sending skills have similar effects on employees' abilities to cope with organizational situations.

Consequently, it is the combination of organizational factors and personal characteristics which makes the lives of employees complicated (see Figure II.1).

In Unit I a number of different dimensions of the various types of organizations were described. Those which parallel the traditional ideal impose many distinctive guidelines and constraints on their employees. Communication is to flow only through certain channels and in certain forms; tasks are to be completed only in prescribed ways; specific responsibilities are assigned and reinforced. Other organizations impose different guidelines and constraints, with different problems and effects. In all organizations these exigences and constraints evolve and change over time and with new circumstances. Eventually, successful employees learn to cope with complicated situations because they develop two kinds of communicative skills. The first of these is the ability to *examine critically* the situations they face to understand how the personal and organizational factors limit their freedom of action. Successful employees are able to see their organizational situations for what they are—matrices of communicative processes, exigences, constraints, and audiences. The second necessary skill involves the ability to understand messages and create *strategically appropriate messages* in response.

Chapter 7 will discuss the key element of organizational situations—power and power relationships. Chapter 8 will examine the processes and problems involved in analyzing organizational situations and apply these principles to the experiences of newly hired personnel. Chater 9 will discuss message management. The final three chapters will analyze three kinds of problematic situations faced by employees of modern organizations—those which involve conflict, stress, and sex roles.

Notes

1. *Philosophy and Rhetoric,* 1 (1968), 1–14. During the decade or so since the publication of Bitzer's article, a lengthy and sometimes heated debate has taken place about his ideas. This interchange led him to modify his original model. Coincidentally, many of the examples that he has used in these later articles involve organizations and organizational communication. See, for

example, "Functional Communication: A Situational Perspective," in *Rhetoric In Transition*, ed. Eugene White (University Park, Pa.: Pennsylvania State University Press, 1980), especially pp. 27, 36–37. The ideas presented in Unit II of this book draw on his concepts of exigence, constraints, and audience but are not intended to reproduce them exactly as they have been offered.

    2. Frankly, I do not believe that nonrhetorical communication exists. But since it would take a great deal of time and space to explain why, I have used the traditional distinctions.

7

Communication, Power, and Politics in Organizations

THE BASES OF ORGANIZATIONAL POWER
Gaining Power Through Personal Characteristics
Gaining Power Through the Control of Key Resources

THE FACES OF POWER

THE EXERCISE OF POWER
Communication, Power, and the Myths of Rationality
Communication, Power, and the Management of Interpersonal
  Relationships

CONCLUSION

POSTSCRIPT: THE MYTH OF MERITOCRACY

Whatever else organizations may be . . . they are political structures. This means that organizations operate by distributing authority and setting a stage for the exercise of power.
                                               —Abraham Zalzenik

Insofar as knowledge is power, communication systems are power systems.
                                               —David Barber. [1]

The words *power* and *politics* are part of almost every adult's normal vocabulary. The concepts of power and powerlessness often are used in everyday conversations to explain a variety of human actions. Consumers complain about their powerlessness in the face of big business; students explain that they are victimized by arbitrary professors and administrators and can do nothing in response; subordinates vow to change their organizations for the better as soon as they advance to positions of power. Because these topics are ever-present parts of people's common knowledge about how organizations and societies operate, it is surprising that they rarely have been examined in works about organizational communication.

On second glance this oversight can be understood. It is explained in part by the prominence of the myths of rationality that were discussed in Chapter 6. Because our culture values rationality and objectivity so strongly, it is difficult for us to admit—even to ourselves—that people and their institutions are influenced by nonrational factors like power and politics. Since managers perceive themselves as adult, objective, and rational people, it is threatening to admit that they are influenced by such factors. Another explanation involves the dominance of the human relations movement in business and education during the last twenty years. When power was included in the human relations model, it was treated as a necessary evil which needed to be controlled by giving relatively equal amounts of it to every member of an organization. For the human relationists, the very word *power* conjured up images of Machievelli advising his employer about the best ways to assassinate rivals. *Power* was an obscene word and was not to be uttered in research, theory, or other public places.

But recent changes in the focus of research—toward the nonrational dimensions of decision making discussed in Chapter 6 and the concept of organizational cultures examined throughout this book, for example—have led theorists to concentrate on the factors which influence employees' actions in real organizational situations. Perhaps the most important of these factors is the power relationships employees believe exist in their organization. Peoples' beliefs about who has power influences their choices about which audiences to address (and which to avoid) and how to approach them. Political considerations lead to conclusions about what actions must be taken (exigences) and what activities and emotions should be suppressed (constraints). Consequently, analyzing organizational situations and constructing strategic messages (the primary concerns of Chapters 8 and 9) both depend on an employee's sensititivity to power relationships. Understanding organizational power requires a consideration of its three elements; the *bases* of power, the *faces* of power, and the *dynamics* of exercising power.

THE BASES OF ORGANIZATIONAL POWER

Power is in the eye of the beholder.[2] It is the belief by some members of an organization that they should obey the requests or commands and seek the favor and support of other members. Powerful employees are perceived by others as capable of having their wishes fulfilled. Obtaining and keeping power—that is, creating and sustaining these perceptions—is important to every member of an organization. But having power is particularly important for people who can do their jobs only if other people cooperate with them. The more an employee's performance or success *depends* on the performance of others, the more important it is for him or her to be able to influence and control others' actions—to have power over them. If managers depend on a large number of people or are exceptionally dependent on a smaller number of people, obtaining power over these people is a necessary and crucial element of their ability to succeed. If an employee is relatively autonomous and independent, creating and maintaining the perception of power is less important. But only in the very rare instance when a worker is completely self-sufficient is power not important. Because organizations are composed of people who are involved in interdependent roles, power relationships are an important determinant of their success or failure.

The early models of organizations (traditional and human relations and resources) assumed that power and power relationships could be formalized and imposed. Max Weber assumed that superiors could draw on cultural norms and gain influence over their subordinates because of their formal positions. Frederick Taylor presumed that selection, training, and formal reward systems would lead subordinates to believe that they should comply with their supervisors' instructions. The human relations theorists believed that formalized systems of power sharing could maintain workers' self-esteem, reduce their resistance to commands, and create the cooperative climates necessary for the success of interdependent relationships. But formal power relationships rarely provide employees with sufficient power to overcome their dependency on others. This is perhaps most clear when employees have high levels of job security. A few years ago an employee of the U.S. Government Printing Office in Pueblo, Colorado, was suspected of destroying, rather than processing, citizens' requests for booklets. His supervisors devised an ingenious scheme for gaining evidence of his malfeasance. They secretly marked a number of order forms and then searched the employee's wastebasket at the end of the day. Soon they located a large number of discarded requests, which they could prove were the employee's responsibility. The employee was dismissed, but an appeals board reinstated him on the grounds that he had been unfairly "entrapped" by the supervisors. As a result of the board's decision, the supervisors were left with virtually no formal power to discipline the employee, even for as unambiguous an action as refusing to do his job. In order to influence his—or any other employee's—actions in the future, they had no choice but to rely on nonformal sources of power. Of course, this is an atypical example. But there are gaps in all formal systems of power. If there were not, employees would not act in unanticipated and undesirable ways. Employees soon learn that they must compensate for these gaps by acquiring power on their own, independently of the formal power relationships sanctioned by their organizations.

Employees can gain this supplemental power by creating the impression that they possess one or more valued *personal characteristics* and/or that they occupy a *position* in the organization from which they can control the distribution of *resources* valued by other people. But characteristics and resources cannot be transformed into power unless they are *scarce* (in limited supply and not readily available through other sources), *significant* (necessary for the performance of the organizaiton or its members) *and irreplaceable* (depleted but not easily replaced). The impressions that an individual possesses characteristics and occupies resource-controlling positions are the primary *bases* of power in organizations.

Gaining Power Through Personal Characteristics

Two kinds of personal characteristics give people power: expertise and their ability to form and maintain successful *interpersonal relationships.* Expertise has at least three dimensions. First, it includes a person's *actual knowledge* of a job. Managers who know how to manage, accountants who know how to "count," salespersons who know how to sell—all have the *potential* for gaining power. But an individual's job-related expertise can provide him or her with power only if it is shown to be scarce, significant, and irreplaceable. If everyone in a freight-handling company can repair broken machinery, mechanics will have little power. If only one person can do so, that person will have exceptional power. Almost everyone recognizes this fact of organizational life at some level. It explains why people sometimes do not want to hire (or promote) the most competent applicant. If the newcomer has the kind of expertise that an existing employee has used to obtain power, the newcomer will be quite threatening. People realize that when you're the only person who can operate the computer system, you have almost complete power. When you're one of two people who know, you have almost no power. And it explains why employees sometimes develop equipment or procedures which only they understand. Secretaries who devise filing systems that only they understand may well be irreplaceable.

Communication is also necessary to transform expertise into power. If powerful members of an organization are aware of, understand the importance of, and respect an individual's expertise, potential for advancement will be enhanced. Sometimes, however, power holders are not aware of the skills and contributions of individual employees. At other times the power holders may lack the background to understand why a particular employee is important to the organization. This seems to be one of the reasons why it generally is more difficult for staff personnel to obtain power than for line personnel to do so. The upper management of chemical firms often are chemists, not human resource specialists. Engineering firms usually are controlled by engineers, not former directors of personnel. They can understand easily why new chemical formulas or equipment are important to their organizations. They may find it more difficult to see why developing a new appraisal system is important. Having a high level of expertise makes it easier to create the images necessary for expertise to become a base of power. But the expertise itself does not give a person power. The perceptions of it do that.

The second dimension of expertise is an individual's ability to *articulate* positions effectively, to argue successfully in favor of preferred courses of action. Unit I presented a number of different views of how decisions are made, all of which involved important communicative processes. If, as the traditional and human relations and resources ideals suggested, organizations are made up of capable people who can and do make fair, rational, and objective decisions, the ability to advocate a particular course of action is crucial. Without these skills, employees cannot bring their expertise to bear on important problems.

They will become frustrated by their inability to influence decisions, they will be perceived by their associates as being less competent than they really are, and their organizations will suffer because their expertise is not being used. If, as was suggested in Chapter 6, organizations make decisions and then search for justifications and rationalizations for them, the ability to argue positions effectively is even more important. As Peter Drucker observed, any normally functioning adult can find facts and arguments to support a position on complex issues. It takes far more skill to marshall arguments in favor of decisions already made. But an employee will be perceived as being expert (and as understanding "how things work") only to the extent that that person can discover and articulate plausible explanations for decisions already made. Regardless of whether reasons precede or follow decisions, it is a person's ability to draw on expertise to advocate and justify actions, not the expertise itself, that creates *perceptions* of competence. Through the effective use of argument and advocacy, expertise can become personal power.

The third dimension of expertise is the ability to assess power relationships and adapt appropriately to them. Being an expert in a particular area often allows a person to determine which course of action the organization should follow. Presenting that option and a vast array of facts and arguments in support of it can create the impression that the individual is very competent. But if the individual makes a presentation that is rejected, that impression will be marred. Repeated losses eventually weaken credibility. It will matter little that the individual was "right" on each occasion in an objective sense. The person will be viewed as a failure, not as an expert, and power will be reduced. Good proposals often are rejected solely because they violate existing power relationships. They may involve scuttling a powerful member's pet (but failing) project. They may involve shifting the staff and budget of a powerful department to a less powerful one. Or if very well conceived and articulated, they may even provide evidence that a subordinate is more expert in a field that the supervisor. In any of these cases, the proposal will be threatening to powerful interests and may be resisted and, ultimately, rejected.

To summarize, people can create the perception that they are expert (powerful) by advocating measures which are cogent and accepted. Creating this perception depends both on one's technical expertise and on one's ability to understand and adapt to existing power relationships. In what may seem to be a kind of perverse logic, expert people are those whose ideas are accepted, and people whose ideas are accepted are perceived as expert people.

The second primary base of personal power is the creation of valuable interpersonal relationships. People comply most readily with the wishes of people with whom they have good relationships for two reasons. First, they value a relationship for its own sake. If they perceive that refusing to comply with a friend's request may threaten the relationship, they may comply with it. For instance, there is some evidence that supervisors can occasionally be autocratic toward subordinates with whom they have warm, positive relationships without creating hostility or resistance. They cannot be autocratic with other subordinates without creating opposition. Second, people comply more readily with messages from friends because they have a ready rationalization for doing so; for example, "I wouldn't do this for anyone else, but I'll back Judy up because she is my friend."

Maintaining effective interpersonal relationships also increases a person's power in less direct ways. People tend to view those with whom they have good relationships as being more expert, more powerful, and more trustworthy than others. They also communicate more freely with friends than with nonfriends, giving their friends information that can be used to their advantage. An employee who is a friend to a number of people eventually comes to know more about what is going on in the organization and can use that information to create an impression of expertise and power. Since we are attracted to expert, powerful people, we tend to form friendships and share information with them. Our sharing in turn provides them with additional information and apparent expertise. In a complex cycle, creating and sustaining interpersonal relationships also enhances an individual's access to other bases of power.

Friendships also may have the opposite effect. One of the most interesting term papers I ever have received was an analysis of a student's trials as a pool manager. For years he had worked as a lifeguard alongside a number of his friends. Recently he was promoted to pool manager, a position which required him to supervise both old friends and new lifeguards. Initially he had no problems with the newcomers—they accepted his role as supervisor (position power) and granted him the right to make schedules, establish and enforce rules, and so on. From the outset his friends made his life miserable. They viewed him as a peer, making it impossible for him to rely on position, expertise or legitimate power. His supervisors required him to pay everyone the same wages and often intervened when the oldtimers complained about having to work undesirable shifts (thus denying him access to rewards and coercive power). Eventually the newcomers complained that they were being treated unfairly because only they had to work bad shifts, or work at all for that matter. When he responded to their complaints by "cracking down" on his friends, they interpreted his actions as personal attacks, robbing him of the ability to influence their actions through referent power. In his organizational situation, the lack of formal power combined with his interpersonal relationships in ways which left him virtually powerless. The bases of power operate in ways which mutually influence one another.

The final base of personal power is obtaining access to the symbols of power. In all organizations certain tangible materials symbolize rank, power, and prestige: large offices, large desks, royal blue carpets, the keys to the executive washroom, invitations to social events which include powerful people, and even office windows. Jeffrey Pfeffer argued that an outsider can tell how much power the departments in a large West Coast university have by noting how far down the hill their buildings are from the main administration building.[3] Symbols create the impression that the person who possesses them should be honored and obeyed. They take on meaning and importance completely disproportionate to their "real" value. When they are the only evidence of power, they become even more important. Some of the most intense and humorous battles ever observed in an organization involved an office with a large window and office space which neither combatant really needed. While I was an undergraduate, I worked in a metal-processing foundry. The key symbol of power there was a protective hardhat—peons had none, foremen had blue ones, supervisors white ones. One day one of my friends and I started wearing yellow, plastic, nonprotective hardhats that we had borrowed from one of my neighbor's children. For two weeks the foremen and supervisors puzzled over what to do about our toy hats. From the outset they agreed that *something* had to be done about them. Since there was no official rule about wearing toy hardhats we were violating no policy, but we were upsetting the power relationship by violating (and making fun of) its most important symbol. Finally, after a one-hour high-level meeting, a new policy was enacted which forbade the wearing of "unapproved" hats, "because they provided no added safety for workers," of course. Possessing symbols of power creates the perception of power, but only if powerless people are denied access to them.

In summary, personal power is in the eye of the beholder. It is gained and retained through the use of communication strategies which create the image of expertise, maintain effective interpersonal relationships, and link a person to the organization's symbols of power. Individuals gain power by creating the perception that they possess these valued characteristics. They are able to use their power most advantageously if they focus their efforts on gaining power over those people on whom they are most dependent. And as the final section of this chapter will explain, they will be able to retain their power only if they learn to exercise it in appropriate ways and within certain limits.

Gaining Power Through The Control of Key Resources

Resources are controlled by people who occupy one of three powerful positions in organizations: (1) People who are *key communicators* or *gatekeepers* in *communication networks* are able to control one of the most important resources in any organization—*information*. (2) Employees who occupy formal positions from which they can distribute legitimate *rewards* and *punishments* have access to power. (3) People who are *members* of a large number of effective *coalitions* may be able to control the distribution of resources.

Central Positions in Communication Networks.[4]   Knowledge can be a potent source of power. It allows people to anticipate organizational problems and either prevent them or be ready with solutions to them when they do occur. It enables employees to assess the needs and biases of other employees and to act in ways which meet these needs and do not upset these biases. It helps them locate and exploit the weaknesses of their adversaries and to discover other employees with whom they have common interests. But knowledge can be acquired only from other employees. Although students can learn general principles about how people act in organizations from a number of sources, they can learn about the intricacies of their own organizations only from other employees. Since the most important information is often sensitive or secret, it usually is obtained through informal communication channels. Employees who occupy a central role in communication networks—the key communicators described in Chapter 5—have access to more information than people who occupy more peripheral roles.

Being a key communicator and possessing great amounts of information tend to reinforce one another. A person who has information attracts information from others. People need to feel that they understand what is going on around them, and they meet that need by seeking out people who are reputed to be "in the know." In conversations, usually the seeker tells the key communicator that "I have observed such and such" and "I think it means. . . ." These messages provide the key communicator both with information about what is going on and with insight into the values, biases, and thought processes of the seeker. As long as the key communicator reinforces the seeker by providing additional information or merely by listening or comfirming interpretations, the communication link will continue to exist. The key communicator will gain even more information, which will attract others, and will solidify a central position in the informal communication network.

Key communicators send as well as receive information, often withholding it when it is strategically wise to do so and revealing it only at the optimal time and to the right people. Information is a significant resource in all organizations. But it gives people power only if it is scarce. If it is available to everyone, it gives no one the ability to influence others. If it is disseminated carefully and selectively, it can enhance an individual's image as an expert and increase the ability to act in strategically appropriate ways. In a fine study of how an organization chose between two different computer systems, Andrew Pettigrew explained the strategies a middle manager used to make sure that his preference was purchased. He gathered information about both systems from his subordinates, passed little information about the system he opposed on to his supervisors (unless that information was negative), and sought out and sent on favorable information about the system that he favored. Since he was in as central position in the formal communication network and was able to enforce norms which limited communication to the chain of command, he was able to control the upward flow of information.[5] This control gave him influence. Of course, in organizations with active informal communication networks, controlling information is a more difficult task. But since key communicators in informal networks also tend to be in central positions in formal networks, it is not impossible.

Formal Control of Rewards and Punishments   Some positions in the formal hierarchy of an organization involve officially sanctioned control of scarce resources. The television show "M*A*S*H." featured a number of episodes in which the plot revolved around a supply sergeant withholding necessary equipment from the doctors. Secretaries in universities have enormous power because they control professors' access to stamps, stationery, paper, typewriter ribbons, and long-distance telephone connections—resources vital to everyday activities. In both cases, the official duties of the employee involve the control and distribution of scarce, valuable, and irreplaceable tangible resources.

Resource control gives people power in two ways. First, it enables them to reward or punish (promise gains or threaten losses) other employees. As long as they threaten subtlely or promise tactfully, they will be able to exercise power effectively. Second, it allows employees to persuade others to provide them with some of the resources at their disposal. Our culture has deeply ingrained norms of reciprocity. When people give us something, and especially if we believe that they gave it to us voluntarily, we feel pressure to reciprocate. The cult of suburban housewives who have subscribed to Marabel Morgan's "total woman" approach to marital relationships is a superb example of the power of this norm. Being totally dependent—giving their husbands everything that they could possibly want in Saran-wrapped packages—pays off solely because the husbands will feel pressure to reciprocate.

Although any scarce resource can be used successfully to threaten or promise, the most important one is money. Individuals and committees which control funds invariably are the most powerful parts of an organization. Money is a particularly potent source of power because an individual need not control all of it. In all organizations a substantial proportion of the budget is fixed. The allocation of the remainder (usually less than 10 percent) is flexible and can be distributed among the members of the organization. Once this 10 percent is distributed, the units or people who have recieved it begin to depend on it. They start payments on new capital equipment, hire new staff, or expand sales territories. But if the discretionary funds suddenly are withdrawn, the person or unit will face very serious problems. Payments will not be met, new staff will have to be fired, and new clients will have to be abandoned. Consequently, control of the distribution of discretionary funds (the 10 percent) is a very potent source of power. It provides an exceptionally strong basis for making threats, promises, or bribes. It's a new golden rule: "One who has the discretionary gold makes the rules."

Roles in Coalitions[6] People can also gain power by forming alliances with others. Coalitions are particularly important for employees or units of organizations which lack power. Alliances are based on common interests— policies that each party wants to see enacted, threats that each party has received but cannot overcome alone, resources that each party wants to obtain and is willing to share with others. Coalitions are flexible and ever changing. When the factors that created the common interests change, the coalition either becomes temporarily inactive or dissolves. Like informal communication links, coalitions are sometimes active and often quiet. They will be available when their members need them only if they are sustained over time by activities which maintain communication ties. It takes time to form coalitions and they can be created only if each potential member is aware of the needs and interests of each other potential member. The need for time explains why less powerful members of an organization often can be observed trying to delay decisions. They hope that they will be able to build a winning coalition before any final choice is made. It also explains why powerful members, who understand the formation of coalitions quite well, try to force decisions. What may seem to be innocuous motions to refer an issue to a committee or take a straw vote may be symbols of important underlying struggles for power. Because of the dynamics of coalitions, relatively powerless employees suddenly may find that they have substantial influence because of being wooed by a number of different and competing coalitions. Especially in organizations which make decisions by majority rule, unimportant persons suddenly may become powerful solely because they have the tie-breaking vote. After the vote is taken, they will just as suddenly return to their powerless status unless they are wise enough to use their temporary power to extract important concessions from powerful people. Coalitions are inherently unstable, both because issues and interests change and because each member of a coalition always has the option of defecting and joining a different alliance.

Coalitions are also unstable because of the dynamics of size, which are influenced by two pressures. Alliances are based on the expectation that some form of "spoils" will be divided up if the coalition is victorious. Each member's rewards will be increased and obligations to the other members decreased if the alliance is of the "smallest winning size." But employees also must think about the future and the need to implement the decision once it is made. Implementation usually requires the support of a large number of people. These people will support the policy most actively if they are part of the alliance that got it passed. So in order to gain the alliegance of these people, the members of the coalition will have to give up some of their potential rewards to people who are not necessary for winning the battle but who *may be* necessary in the future. Each member of the coalition thus will be ambivalent about the presence of each other member. Existing research and theory make it difficult to predict which of these pressures will be dominant in a particular situation. However, it does rather clearly indicate that coalitions are inherently unstable. But for some members, they are the only available base of power.

To summarize, power is in the eye of the beholder. Individual members of organizations can create the perception that they are powerful by developing a particular kind of personal image and/or the impression that they hold and will use information, an important place in potent coalitions, or control of resources and rewards. Although these bases have been discussed as if they were independent of one another, in real situations they are interrelated in complicated ways. People who occupy central places also tend to be perceived as having substantial expertise and generally are involved in a large number of interpersonal relationships at work. Individuals who are supposed to have powerful allies often are seen as being more expert and having better access to information than other people. Our perceptions of others are not separate and discrete. They merge together and overlap in complicated ways. The communication strategies people can use to establish one base of power also influence other bases of power. Individuals or units of organizations are seen as being powerful or powerless depending on the *composite image* that their communicative acts establish in the minds of other members of their organization.[7]

THE FACES OF POWER

One of the most common errors made by new employees is assuming that power always is exercised overtly and openly.[8] It is, of course, true that power often is exercised overtly, sometimes quite bluntly. Threats and promises are made, deals are negotiated, and coalitions are proposed and solidified in discussions which are open but usually private. But overt actions form only one of the faces of power. There is a second, more subtle and more potent, face.

David Mechanic once observed that theories about organizational power usually focus on the rare occasions when relatively powerless employees refuse to obey more powerful employees or speak out against them. The common, normal, everyday pattern—in which less powerful people carry out instructions and seek the support of more powerful people—has largely been ignored. The second, hidden face of power is present when power relationships quietly and covertly influence the normal, everyday, obedient actions of employees.

The second face of power works in two ways. First, it forms the parameters within which employees make decisions about when and how to challenge more powerful members. An important part of the socialization process that new employees undergo is learning the power relationships which exist in their organization. "Older" employees recount stories about what has happened to employees in the past when they chose to fight for certain changes. They also provide newcomers with advice about how to "get ahead" in their organization, and they explain that some actions are expected of new employees and that other actions are forbidden. Armed with this knowledge, the sensitive new employee begins to adopt some patterns of action and to avoid others.

Still other processes are even more subtle. Within all cultures people learn to explain events and actions in certain ways and to see some behaviors as natural and morally right. Formal organizations, as the chapters in Unit I indicated, are mini-cultures. Their members develop certain ways of perceiving and explaining events, certain categories for good, bad, natural, and unnatural behaviors.[9] Part of these cultural frames of reference are power relationships. It is perceived as natural and morally correct for students to defer to professors, for workers to stay out of the executive dining room, for production personnel to get Christmas turkeys, and managers to get holiday stock bonuses. In all organizations people adopt characteristic recurring patterns of acting and not acting, patterns which seem to be the only "normal" way of interpreting and responding to events.[10] Employees' actions are limited and directed not through overt processes but through the employees' way of perceiving their organizational world. If these ideas seem to be abstract and esoteric, ask yourself this:

Why do you wait for a stoplight to change when there is no traffic and no police officers around?

Why do you avoid parking in spaces reserved for the disabled (or park in them) when the chance of being arrested for doing so is minimal?

Why do you stand quietly in line while another customer unfairly harasses a salesclerk, interrupting your shopping?

The second face of power also works by regulating public and private issues. Newcomers soon learn that some issues are not to be discussed in public, some potential solutions are not to be considered openly, and some arguments are not to be made. Open discussions are limited to "safe" topics (those which powerful employees are willing to have discussed in public), acceptable alternatives, and unofficially sanctioned premises for making decisions. Consensus in open discussions is the rule, not the exception. When disagreements do occur, they tend to be over minor issues and serve the purpose of perpetuating the myth that open, rational, and objective decision making exists in the organization. If individuals violate these constraints, they will either be ignored or attacked by the rest of the group. If they persist they will be "educated" by an unofficial tutor. If they cannot be educated, they will be removed.

Luckily most newcomers are educable. A young, highly competent accountant was hired by a populous county to manage its multimillion dollar budget. An audit of the past two years revealed that an expensive program for assaultive teenagers (AT) had enrolled a tiny and steadily declining number of clients. Further research revealed that the use rate had declined because the population base of the county had become older, leaving very few teenagers within its borders. During the same time, the Retired Citizens' Rehabilitation Center (RCRC) had become seriously overloaded and understaffed. Since population projections indicated that the shift would continue at least through the year 2000, the young accountant devised a plan to shift resources from the first program to the second. A detailed, twelve-point presentation, complete with slide-tape and video-tape aids, was created to support the accountant's arguments that (1) the needs of the residents would best be served by the shift, (2) the county would save a great deal of money because the licensed psychologists and attorneys then on retainer as consultants for the AT could be dismissed, and (3) the funds could be used more efficiently because the success rate of the RCRC was almost four times as great as that of the AT. Before going to the county board of commissioners with the proposal, however, the young accountant asked the county manager to sit in on a rehearsal of her presentation.

Fortunately, the manager saw himself as a supportive mentor for the junior accountant. After the rehearsal he congratulated her for the quality of the presentation, but suggested that there were some details of which she might not be aware: (1) one of the board members had two children in the AT program and had saved thousands of dollars in psychotherapy expenses because it was available, (2) another commissioner's spouse was a consultant for the AT program, (3) two others had been reelected primarily because they claimed to have done a great deal for the county's retired citizens (which suggested to the accountant that the comparison of funding levels included in the slide presentation almost certainly would embarrass them), and (4) in the past the commission had voted in favor of money-saving recommendations only in odd-numbered years when a majority of them were up for reelection.

The young accountant was perceptive enough to understand that these were invaluable hints. She revised her presentation, making three major changes. First, instead of arguing that the county was inadequately meeting its obligations to retired citizens, she argued that the major growth in the use-rate of the RCRC demonstrated how effective the existing programs had been under the leadership of the current board and suggested that their programs warranted continuation and expansion. Second, she argued that the plummeting use-rate of the AT program demonstrated the success of professionally designed and led treatment, and proposed that the staff be professionalized further in a two-stage process. As nonsupervisory personnel resigned (something which happens quite often in programs with assaultive adolescents), their salaries would be frozen until a sufficiently large sum was available to hire the most senior consulting psychologist (who coincidentally was the commissioner's spouse) on a full-time basis. Since the AT staff's professional skills would be increased by the completion of step 1, the remaining consulting contracts could be shifted to the RCRC and the remaining nonsupervisory personnel could be transferred to that agency. Finally, the accountant arranged to have the county manager present the proposal at the February, 1985 commission meeting, which she would attend in order to provide "technical support." Thus, she was able to adapt to the existing power relationships, and to do so without the knowledge of anyone save her supportive, and quite satisfied, supervisor.

The normal mode of exercising power in organizations is through the second, hidden face. Assumptions about power relationships so constrain the actions of employees that instances of open, overt disagreement or open, overt exercise of power are really quite rare. In a sense, when employees openly challenge powerful people, power has failed. It can be reinstituted, but only through some overt exercise of power and at some cost to the more powerful members of the organization.

THE EXERCISE OF POWER

Power begets power. Actions create the perceptions on which power relationships are based. But power is most effective if, when it has to be exercised, it is exercised tacitly and tactfully through appropriate communication strategies. The first of these already has been mentioned briefly—acculturating new employees. The second and third means are more complex. One involves the use of communicative strategies which maintain the myth of rationality (discussed in Chapter 6). The other involves organizational "politics," the creation and management of coalitions.

Communication, Power, and the Myths of Rationality[11]

It was in explained in Chapter 6 that for a number of reasons, neither individual members of organizations nor organizations as a whole are always capable of making rational decisions about complex problems based on careful assessments of objective information. When decisions are not made on this basis, on what basis are they made? An increasing array of evidence indicates that employees' assessments of power relationships significantly influence their decision making. When problems are simple and unambiguous, objective criteria and reliable information do seem to influence choices to a substantial degree. In this kind of situation, power seems to have only a limited impact on decision making, partly because simple decisions are within the information-gathering and -processing capacities of employees and partly because powerful members of organizations rarely are interested in simple problems. But as problems become more complex and information becomes more incomplete and ambiguous, rational decision making becomes less possible and powerful people become more involved. In these situations, decisions are influenced in important ways by power relationships. However, in all decisions people need to maintain an image of rationality. Employees' self-images are based in part on their rationality, and the self-esteem of employees who lose battles can be protected only if they can explain the decision to themselves and to others with objective and reasoned considerations. For everyone's sake, then, the myths of rational decision making need to be maintained.

In short, the role of power in decision making and the need to sustain an image of rationality combine in ways which complicate emloyees' attempts to exercise power. If they openly present information and arguments which support policies that violate existing power relationships, their efforts will fail and their reputations as powerful (capable and knowledgeable) people will suffer. On the other hand, if they openly admit that they are acting on the basis of their assessments of power relationships rather than suporting the most "logical" course of action, they appear to others to be acting irrationally, and their power also will be reduced. Power can beget power, but *only* if it is exercised within the constraints imposed by the Scylla of power relationships and the Charybdis of the myth of rationality.

Employees can manage this complicated problem if they adopt appropriate communication strategies. To do so they first must obtain information about when they should become involved assertively in discussions of an issue, when they should be present but inactive during open deliberations, and when they should avoid the issue. If the issue is related to expertise or information that an employee possesses, it does provide an opportunity to demonstrate an ability to solve organizational problems. But if the issue is so politically hot that even discussing it may alienate one or more powerful people, avoiding it is the best course of action. Unfortunately for them, fools sometimes do rush in where angels fear to tread. Of course, these processes mean that important organizational problems may never be addressed. They also suggest that when problems are resolved it often is more because powerful people want them to be solved than because someone suddenly had a new insight. There are far more logical solutions to organizational problems than there are politically viable solutions. The first step in adapting to the paradox of power and rationality is determining when and how to act and which solutions can safely be proposed.

The second step is determining which bases of power employees have available. If they are perceived as having certain kinds of expertise, they can reveal that expertise in appropriate circumstances and thereby have influence. If they have not created that perception or have done so only for a limited range of topics, merely presenting information is an ineffective way to exercise power. If, on the other hand, their power is based on their membership in important coalitions, they can exercise power by asserting that other people will be willing to support some proposals and unwilling to support others. Persons who control valued resources can reveal that those resources may be available to "friendly" people for some projects and not to others for other purposes. People who lack these bases of power cannot exercise them, and they can reduce their credibility by trying to do so.

The final step is determining which of the many possible justifications one might propose has the best chance of being accepted. In all discussions there are a large number of available facts and arguments.[12] When they assess their own bases of power they will find that some of these are not available to them. Of the remaining ideas, facts, and arguments, some will be acceptable to powerful members of the organization; others will be perceived by powerful people as being nonsense. For example, in some organizations arguments about morality, equality, and social responsibility are acceptable justifications for acting. In others they are perceived as silly, unresolvable, academic matters which ought not to be allowed to cloud serious decision making. In still others they are viewed as appropriate rationalizations to be presented to people outside the decision-making group but not as appropriate topics to be discussed within the group. When employees articulate reasons for making a decision which are acceptable to the powerholders in their organization, they enhance their own influence and even may be able to see their preferences put into action. But when they advocate policies or actions on unacceptable grounds, they doom their proposal, reduce their power, and thereby decrease their ability to succeed in the future. The worst enemies of good ideas are not their opponents but their well-meaning but naive friends.[13]

Employees can obtain and exercise power by adopting communicative strategies appropriate to organizational power relationships. This concept does not require an employee to act either irrationally or unethically. Instead, it means that employees' actions are bounded—directed and constrained—by their power and by the power of others. Anyone over the age of twenty one can marshall facts and arguments to support their ideas. But it takes a substantial level of analytical and communicative skill to assess the power-related constraints that an individual faces and still be able to develop arguments that appear to be objective and rational and also have some chance of being accepted.

Communication, Power, and the Management of Interpersonal Relationships

The second primary means of exercising power is through the management of effective relationships with other employees. Since the means of doing this will be examined in detail in Chapters 8 and 9, this section will describe briefly three attitudes which enable employees to use relational strategies successfully. The first of these attitudes is realizing that working relationships have both personal and professional dimensions. The age-old adage that "you shouldn't do business with friends" suggests that it always has been difficult and important to keep these dimensions separate. Complete separation is, of course, impossible. But unless an adequate distinction is maintained, employees may begin to interpret other employees' business decisions as a comment on their relationship and may make unwise business decisions because of personal considerations. It is because it is so difficult to maintain an appropriate separation that many firms try to discourage romances between employees and adopt antinepotism policies (which prevent spouses or family members from working together). In short, employees must be able not to mix the business and pleasure sides of their working relationships.

Second, employees must be sensitive to the norms of their organization and must be able to determine what their associates expect of them. Relationships at work are based on trust and mutual self-interests. Research on trust in all kinds of relationships indicates that a person can destroy the trust of others by acting in ways which either hurt them or are unexpected. It takes far more time and successful communication to build trust than to destroy it. Being predictable, and thus seeming to be trustworthy, is instrumental to the development and maintenance of effective working relationships.[14]

Finally, employees need to understand that it may take a long time to develop working relationships which are mutually and equitably rewarding. As explained in Chapter 2, successful relationships are characterized by balanced and reciprocal exchanges of intrinsic and extrinsic rewards. All employees face a number of organizational constraints on their actions. As a result, it may take them some time to reciprocate with other employees. And even when they are able to reciprocate, they may not be able to do so with equivalent kinds of rewards. Neither delay nor the inevitability of differences in the items exchanged doom working relationships. They simply suggest that unlike "natural" relationships in which exchanges can be immediate and identical, working relationships operate under a different set of limitations. Unless employees recognize this and adopt a realistic time frame for calculating cost-reward ratios, they will find that their working relationships are unstable, unsatisfying, and unrewarding.

In summary, for working relationships to provide employees with power, they must be stable, predictable, and mutually rewarding. If they lack these characteristics they can neither form the basis for long-term, stable coalitions nor provide the kind of visibility and personal support that underlie relational power. Although working relationships depend on each party's possessing a certain set of communicative skills, the effective use of these skills depends on the acceptance of a congruent set of attitudes.

CONCLUSION

Chapter 1 of this book introduced the ancient concept of *kairos*, of people adapting communication to situations. Subsequent chapters explained that managers and theorists have developed a number of ideal types of organizations and have attempted to put their ideas into practice in a number of real organizations. The effect of these efforts consistently has been to impose certain kinds of constraints on the actions and communication of employees. In traditional organizations limits are imposed on workers' decisions about who to communicate with, what to communicate about, and when to communicate. The primary means of regulating their activities required effective communication of *rules, norms,* and *reward systems.* The human relations and resources ideal attempted to influence the choices of employees through communication strategies which focused on *openness, supportiveness,* and *participation.*

The early contingency models provided an even more-complex set of exigences and constraints by training employees to adapt their communication to a complicated set of situational factors. Contemporary research has started to investigate the ways in which social and organizational myths and power relationships guide and constrain the actions and communication of employees. The hidden assumption underlying each of these models is that teaching potential employees to recognize, assess, and evaluate the constraints they face is a necessary first step in teaching them to adapt to the situations at work. Only through understanding the processes and problems of communication in different types of organizations can employees begin to select and use the strategies that might contribute to their success and to the effectiveness of their organizations.

The remaining chapters in Unit II are designed to indicate how the concept of adapting to different kinds of situations can be used to understand some common types of difficult problems. The next two chapters will present two additional concepts—becoming rhetorically sensitive and managing images. The final three chapters will draw on many of the concepts discussed so far to explain why conflicts, stress, and problems related to sex roles arise in organizations and to indicate how employees can confront these problems productively. At no time will these chapters attempt to present cookbook formulas for handling complex organizational situations. Generalized step-by-step rules of acting will work only when people face simple problems and are asked to engage in simple activities, like baking cookies. When problems are as complex as those found in organizations, step-by-step instructions tend to obscure the specific characteristics of the situation. They often lead people to act in inappropriate ways, and worse still, make them believe that it is their fault when the simplistic solutions fail. The goal of the rest of this book is to provide guidelines which employees and prospective employees can use to make sense out of their unique situations and begin to choose from among the available responses.

Postscript: The Myth of Meritocracy[15]

Perhaps the most pervasive myth about organizations is that advancement is influenced more by competence and performance than by any other factor. Educational institutions go to great lengths to persuade students that success is a function of merit, diligence, and hard work. Organizations establish elaborate appraisal systems which presumably are designed to ensure that performance and advancement are correlated closely. More-elaborate state and federal rules, regulations, and laws are designed to have the same effect. These systems support the *image* that advancement is based on merit, regardless of their actual impact.

In some cases, the image is consistent with reality. In jobs in which both the quantity and quality of an individual's performance can be determined through objective measures, demonstrations of competence seem to be rather strongly related to success. But for careers which involve more complex and intangible tasks—the kinds of career to which most college students aspire—the relationships among competence, merit, and success is much less pronounced. Both quantitative studies and reports from members of organizations suggest that a number of factors only indirectly related to performance substantially influence advancement in complex jobs.

The first of these factors is the extent to which an individual is perceived by powerful members of the organization as being similar to themselves. People of the same race, gender, ethnic and socioeconomic background, citizenship, residence (even in terms of the same suburban subdivision), and education (degree, major, and school) as powerful employees tend to rise more readily than do people who are different.

The process of ensuring that people who are similar to those who occupy upper-level positions has a number of advantages for organizations. People who have complex jobs, and especially those who have complex managerial positions, live in confusing, stressful, and unpredictable worlds. They often have to make rapid decisions in crises. The higher they are in the hierarchy, the larger is the number of people whose actions or inactions can complicate their lives. The potential confusion, uncertainty, and ambiguity can be reduced if powerful employees are able to surround themselves with predictable people. Since people who are like them are the most predictable and seem to be the most stable, trustworthy, and loyal, the powerful employees understandably prefer to see similar individuals promoted through the ranks of the organization.

In addition, it is easier to communicate effectively with people who are like us. When we encounter unexpected and complex problems we can rely on them to provide clear, understandable, trustworthy information and to do so rapidly and efficiently. When supervisors and subordinates are homophilous, communication breakdowns occur less frequently than when they are heterophilous. Since one of the requirements for advancement to managerial positions is effective communication, similar subordinates will seem to be more deserving of promotions than dissimilar subordinates. Natural perception and communication processes tend to support preferences for promoting similar subordinates.

Second, the relationship between merit and promotion is influenced by the dynamics of power relationships. Power holders may gain an important advantage by promoting people who have marginal or inadequate performance records. Once promoted, these employees will owe their positions to the power holder. Their job security and their opportunity for further mobility depends on their ability to maintain the good favor of the power holder. Employees with strong performance records can use their demonstration of competence to justify their promotion and thus are not as dependent. Because the employees with weaker records are wholly dependent, they dare not act in ways that offend. Thus, by promoting marginal employees, the power holder can expect to always be surrounded by supportive, cooperative, and easily controlled people.

Power holders face important risks, however, if they *do* promote capable people. Competent subordinates invariably are a threat to supervisors. They are the people who have the greatest access to nonrelational bases of power. If they are promoted, it is likely that their power will expand and they will become even more of a threat to the power holder. Less competent subordinates have less access to these bases of power, and thus provide little threat. If they are promoted, their potential power base increases little, and, if the promotion makes them more visible or places them in positions that they cannot handle adequately, it may even reduce their power. For both of these reasons, power holders will be most secure in their positions if they reward dependent subordinates and overlook meritorious ones.

Finally, promotions to positions which involve substantial responsibilities and complicated tasks are also influenced by interpersonal relationships. Alliances are one base of power, and power is related strongly to advancement. In addition, alliances allow individuals to demonstrate their competence. In all but the simplest jobs it is very difficult to determine which factors separate "good" and "bad" performers. It generally is assumed that performance in complex jobs is influenced by a person's ability to work successfully with other members of the organization. These characteristics are a function of the ability to form and maintain effective relationships. For example, appraisal instruments for managers generally include items like "is loyal," "is an effective leader," "has a high level of peer acceptance," and "works well with upper management." These intangible definitions of managerial "performance" are directly related to interpersonal relationships and only indirectly related to performance of tasks. Thus, because so much of management involves interpersonal relationships, it should be no surprise that "it ain't what you know, it's who you know."

Relationships are linked to perceived competence in other ways. Even when performance can be measured objectively, it will lead to promotions only if the people who make personnel decisions are aware of individuals' success and are persuaded that it provides evidence that they can perform capably in a higher-level position. Employees can take steps on their own to communicate this information—by seeking out and taking on highly visible assignments, by becoming involved in projects which allow them to report directly to powerful individuals, and by taking credit for their successes, abandoning the false modesty that children often learn. But more important, employees can cultivate relationships with people who can and will communicate favorable evaluations of their performance and abilities to powerful members of the organization.

Although for different reasons, maintaining effective relational ties is important for people both in complex, middle- and upper-level positions and in lower-level jobs. In the former success can be attributed to a number of different factors, only one of which is the employee's competence. If powerful people believe that an employee's success is the result of luck; the general economic situation; or co-workers, subordinates, or supervisors, effective performance will not lead to advancement. In simpler jobs, success often is attributed to an employee's competence in *that particular organizational role.* Since upper-level positions require a different set of skills and abilities than lower-level positions, success in the latter may not be perceived as evidence that an employee can succeed in an upper-level position. Thus, lower-level employees face a "Catch 22" situation. If they concentrate on doing their current jobs well, they may not create the impression that they have the different skills and abilities needed in upper-level jobs. And they may become so proficient in their current jobs that the organization cannot afford to promote them. On the other hand, if they do not concentrate sufficiently on their current jobs to succeed in them, they will create the impression that they cannot handle even simple positions and their promotion potential will be reduced to zero.

Subordinates can escape this paradox only if they (1) know which skills are thought to be necessary for the positions which the might someday be promoted, (2) obtain assignments which allow them to demonstrate that they possess these skills, and (3) have advocates who will tell powerful people that they are both effective in their current jobs and have the necessary skills to succeed in upper-level positions. All three of these factors depend on the employees' being able to form and maintain effective relationships with people who have the necessary information, can make the appropriate assignments, and "have the ears" of powerful people.

The final effect of interpersonal relationships on upward mobility involves the role recommendations play in promotions. Because organizations tend to be structured like pyramids, the number of available positions shrinks very rapidly above the level of middle manager. Since promotion processes tend to move people up who are very similar to the organization's power holders, the employees who reach the middle-manager level usually are very much like one another. Consequently, decisions about further promotions can rarely be based on "objective" differences among the candidates. As jobs become less and less tangible, recommendations from other members of the organization become more and more important. The people who are promoted thus tend to be the ones with the largest number of strong recommendations from powerful employees. Unless employees have formed effective relationships with the right people, they will not have the strongest set of recommendations. And unless their performance has been significant and visible, their sponsors will have no evidence available on which to justify their recommendation. It is at this level that performance does influence advancement. The myths of organizational rationality demand that personnel decisions be rationalized in objective, performance-related terms. If an employee's performance has been excellent, the employee provides the data his supporters need to rationalize their recommendation and denies opponents the data they need to oppose it. If it has been poor, the situation is reversed.

Now, the purpose of this section is not to suggest that merit is wholly unrelated to advancement. Neither is it intended to produce hoards of depressed readers. It is designed to suggest that for a large number of reasons, performance alone rarely leads directly to advancement. Like any other organizational decision, personnel decisions are based on the perceptions held by powerful persons. Creating the kinds of impressions which enhance an individual's potential for promotion requires both merit and effective communication of one's skills and contributions. Of course, just as professors overtly argue that only performance influences grades, members of organizations overtly assert that only merit influences promotions—the myths of rationality and meritocracy must be maintained carefully. But fortunately for those who catch on, the myths fool only some of the people some of the time.

Notes

1. Abraham Zalzenik, "Power and Politics in Organizational Life," *Harvard Business Review* (May-June 1970), 47–60; David Barber, *Power in Committees* (Chicago: Rand-McNally, 1966), p. 65. The literature on social and organizational power is almost overwhelmingly extensive, so much so that it would be impossible to list here even a small proportion of the important works. Instead, I will cite a number of sources which summarize the main ideas presented in the chapter. More complete listings are available in Charles Conrad, "Organizational Power: Faces and Symbolic Forms," in *Communication and Organizations*, ed. Linda Putnam and Michael Pacanowsky (Beverly Hills, Calif.: Sage, 1983), pp. 173–194; Charles Conrad and Mary Ryan, "Power, Praxis and Person in Social and Organizational Theory," in *Organizational Communication Research and Theory*, ed. Phillip Tompkins and Robert McPhee (Beverly Hills, Calif.: Sage, in press).

2. William Gamson, *Power and Discontent* (Homewood, Ill.: Dorsey, 1968). Many of the ideas developed in this chapter are grounded in the research summarized by Jeffrey Pfeffer, *Power in Organizations* (Marshfield, Mass.: Pitman Publishing, 1981); Samuel Bacharach and Edward Lawler, *Power and Politics in Organizations* (San Francisco: Jossey-Bass, 1980); John Kotter, *Power in Management* (New York: AMACOM, 1979). Research on the bases of power can be traced to a seminal article by J. R. P. French and Bertram Raven, "The Bases of Social Power," in *Studies in Social Power*, ed. Dorwin Cartwright, (Ann Arbor: University of Michigan Press, 1959).

3. Pfeffer, *Power in Organizations*.

4. See, for instance, Edward Lawler and John Rhodes, *Information and Control in Organizations* (Pacific Palisades, Calif.: Goodyear, 1976); Andrew Pettigrew, "Information Control as a Power Resource," *Sociology*, 6 (1972), 187–204. The most important sources on communication networks are those by Farace, Monge, Richards, and their associates cited in Chapters 4 and 5. Richard M. Emerson, "Power-Dependence Relations," *American Sociological Review*, 27 (1962), 31–41, provides a classic discussion of how interdependencies influence power. Pfeffer, *Power in Organizations*, suggested many of the examples used in this section.

5. Pettigrew, "Information Control."

6. A fine summary of power and coalitions is Bacharach and Lawler, *Power and Politics*.

7. Bertram Raven and Arie Kruglanski, "Power and Conflict," in *The Structure of Conflict*, ed. Paul Swingle (New York: Academic Press, 1970).

8. An extended version of the ideas presented in this section is available in Conrad, "Organizational Power." Also see David Mechanic, "Sources of Power of Lower Participants in Complex Organizations," *Administrative Science Quarterly*, 7 (1962), 349–364; Peter Bacharach and Morton Baratz, "Two Faces of Power," *American Political Science Review*, 56 (1962), 947–952.

9. Excellent summaries of contemporary ideas about organizational cultures are available in the December 1983 *Administrative Science Quarterly* and in Michael Pacanowsky and Nick O'Donnell-Trujillio, "Organizational Communication as Cultural Performance," *Communication Monographs*, 50 (1983), 126–147. Also see Conrad and Ryan, "Power Praxis and Person."

10. Acculturation processes will be discussed in more detail in Chapter 9.

11. Many of the ideas in this section are drawn from the sources listed in the Notes to Chapter 6. Readers who are interested in more complete summaries should consult Jeffrey Pfeffer, *Organizations and Organization Theory* (Marshfield, Mass.: Pitman Publishing, 1982), and "The Bases and Uses of Power in Organizational Decision-Making," *Administrative Science Quarterly*, 19 (1974), 453–473; Richard Cyert and James March, *A Behavioral Theory of the Firm* (Englewood Cliffs, N.J.: Prentice-Hall, 1963).

12. Communication theorists long ago labeled these *topoi*, following the lead provided by the ancient scholars mentioned in Chapter 1, primarily Gorgias and Aristotle. The processes of selecting topoi appropriately will be examined in greater detail in Chapter 9.

13. Gamson, *Power and Discontent*.

14. Relevant research on organizations and trust is summarized in W. Charles Redding, *Communication Within the Organization* (New York: Industrial Communication Council, 1972).

15. See Pfeffer, *Power in Organizations*.

8

Analyzing Organizational Situations

EVALUATING ORGANIZATIONAL SITUATIONS
Analyzing Audiences
Analyzing Perspectives: Adopting a Comic Frame of Reference

ENTERING ORGANIZATIONS: STAGES, PRESSURES, AND COPING
   PROCESSES
Stage 1: Anticipation
Stage 2: Encounter

CONCLUSION

Throughout the previous chapters of this book there have been suggestions that organizations can be productively thought of as small "cultures," small societies. The members of a culture develop distinctive ways of perceiving, interpreting, and explaining the events and actions that they observe around them. Although every member of a culture perceives the world around him or her in somewhat different ways, their world views are similar in many ways—more like each other than like those of people from other cultures. Regardless of whether they are composed of isolated New Guinea tribal members or modern bureaucrats, cultures are *communicative* and *historical* creations. It is through communication that members of cultures (and thus of organizations) learn who they are, what their roles are, and what kinds of actions are expected of them. Through communicating they demonstrate that they are part of the culture, that they act in appropriate and predictable ways and will continue to do so in the future.[1]

Cultures also are *historical*. They emerge and develop over time, adapting to changes in their membership, functions, problems, and purposes. The *legacy* of past events, people, and patterns of communicating continues to be reflected in the ways in which people perceive their organizational situation. Similarly, the *expectation* that the culture will continue to exist influences the ways in which people perceive their organization and one another and thus effects the way they act toward and communicate with one another.[2] The historical aspect of a culture is reflected in its characteristic patterns of communicating. The events that led to the development of a particular way of communicating may be long forgotten, although the patterns that were established in the past persist. Organizations continue to enact rituals which reflect some situation or problem buried in their pasts. Academic departments may gather together each morning for coffee or hold weekly faculty meetings or social events at Christmas. Once there may have been a purely functional reason for these rituals—all the professors taught the same course and needed to coordinate their activities each morning, or the department once used wholly participatory decision-making systems which required weekly meetings or had a large number of graduate students who could not go home for the holidays and needed to feel like they had a surrogate family at school. Rituals and ritualized communication continue to endure long after the functional reasons for their existence have disappeared. Their function becomes one of maintaining the culture of the organization. Participation in them symbolizes one's membership in and commitment to the culture and its other members. Refusal to participate signals one's disenchantment with the organization or lack of sensitivity to its culture. In a sense ritualized communication contains the history of an organization and reflects the constraints that history imposes on its members.

EVALUATING ORGANIZATIONAL SITUATIONS

The culture of an organization provides the background in which specific situations arise. It establishes broad parameters for acting—general exigences and constraints which are present to some degree in every communicative situation. Each situation also contains more specific guidelines for and limitations on action. Organizational communication is addressed to an *audience*, whose beliefs, biases, goals, and perceptions of the communicators impose constraints on their actions. Communicative situations also include at least one communicator whose flexibility and adaptability is limited by his or her own beliefs, biases, goals, and most important, *frame of reference*. The remainder of this chapter will explain how audiences and frames of reference contribute to exigences and constraints. It also will indicate how the concepts of organizational culture, audience, and frame of reference can explain many of the problems typically faced by new employees.

Analyzing Audiences

Communication is addressed to an audience. Sometimes the audience is the speaker alone. Sometimes it is an unidentified group of people who are not even present when the message is created. In the communicative situations most common in formal organizations, at least part of the audience is definable and accessible. To some extent the speakers and audiences are like one another. The dynamics of organizational cultures ensure that each member has somewhat similar ways of perceiving, interpreting, and responding to events and persons. But employees also differ from one another. Appropriately adapting to communicative situations requires both an analysis of exigences and constraints and an investigation of audiences.

To understand the role that audiences play employees must understand three deceptively simple ideas. The most important is that audiences are composed of people who have their own beliefs, ideas, self-interests, perceptual biases and capacities, and information-processing abilities. In complicated and covert ways, each of these characteristics may lead members of an audience to resist or oppose other employees and their ideas. Naive actors often assume that good ideas—realistic, feasible solutions to recurring and important problems—have a persuasive power all their own. If presented effectively in a "free and open marketplace of ideas," truth will be recognized and accepted and the spokespersons of what is right will be rewarded. A more realistic view is that ideas gain power from their appropriateness to the audience to which they are proposed. That is, their "truth" comes from their congurence with the perceptual processes, beliefs, and self-interests of the audience. Because audiences differ from one another, the power of any particular message and the impact of any individual employee will vary.

The second simple idea is that audiences also differ in their "rhetorical-ness," to distort Bitzer's language only a little. Some organizational audiences are capable of effecting the changes desired by an employee. Others are not. Members of organizations can adapt their communication strategically only if they recognize this distinction. All employees sometimes engage in "gripe sessions" in which a small group of employees expresses complaints or ideas shared and supported by the other members of the group. Rarely, however, are any of the participants capable of doing anything to alter the situation being discussed. This does not imply that this kind of communicative episode is worthless. Quite the contrary, such sessions can serve an important *cathartic* (tension-releasing) function for the participants. But they are engaging in *expressive*, not *rhetorical*, communication. It cannot effect desired change, and in fact, may prevent change. Groups of relatively powerless employees may join together and engage in expressive communication, which eventually leads them to accept the situations that they face. Their groups become "failure support groups," which (1) rob them of the incentive to engage in rhetorical communication precisely because of the power of catharsis, and (2) keep them from being able to engage in effective rhetorical communication because they often become isolated from employees who are valuable sources of information and power.

People also lose the ability to use organizational communication strategically when they confuse rhetorical and nonrhetorical audiences. They may engage in expressive communication with rhetorical audiences, with counterproductive results. At most their efforts will allow auditors to understand the depth of the speaker's emotional responses to the issue or condition being discussed. When the audience has no vested interest in the topic, knows of no organizational barriers to implementing the changes being demanded, and has reason to believe that issues which generate emotional responses among employees should be addressed, expressive communication eventually may generate some desired changes. But in all other cases, expressive communication only serves to persuade powerful auditors that the employee is expressive and emotional. Since our culture values the image of calm, controlled rationality (especially among managers and other professionals), inappropriate expressiveness may only reduce the credibility of the employee and reduce his or her ability to effect needed changes in the future. At best it leads auditors to respond (as one of my friends often does), "I'm sorry, but you must be confusing me with someone who gives a damn."

Conversely, engaging in strategic persuasive communication with non-rhetorical audiences also may be counterproductive. It cannot succeed in effecting change because the audience is incapable of influencing the situation. It can alienate the speaker from the audience because it destroys the cathartic effect of the gripe session. Whenever members of an audience respond to an employee by asking themselves "Why is this person telling *us* all of this?" or "I don't care about the facts; my mind's made up," they begin to become suspicious of the speaker. Becoming alienated from the group, the speaker loses access to the information the group reveals during their expressive exercises. Eventually the speaker may lose a place in the group, and without the information the group provides, will be less capable of engaging in strategic rhetorical communication. Without a safe group with whom to share emotional reactions, that person is more prone to engage in expressive communication with rhetorical audiences, again reducing the ability to influence the organization, and as Chapter 11 will explain, becoming more prone to stress.

Employees err when they engage in the right kind of communication with the wrong kind of audience. They also err when they play the role of communicator when they should be playing the role of auditor. It takes time, patience, and a vast amount of information to understand the complex exigences and constraints that make up organizational situations. When employees are playing the role of message sender, they reduce their access to valuable information. By taking positions on issues, they encourage people who do not share their conclusions to withhold or distort information. They also encourage others to give them information which serves to confirm their possibly incorrect perceptions. As explained in Chapter 7, possessing information allows people to obtain more information. It is listening, not taking positions on issues, that gives employees access to information-based power. But because employees (especially new ones) need to feel part of organizational decision-making and need to demonstrate their expertise and problem-solving abilities, they often tend to be speakers when they ought to be listeners. Put in very unsophisticated terms, one of the most important lessons to learn about organizations is that sometimes the best communication strategy is to be very quiet.

Finally, employees need to recognize that their audiences always are larger than the group of people sitting in front of them. Informal communication networks guarantee that other people will learn of the content and tone of comments made in even the most private settings. "Hidden" audiences exist for a number of reasons, some subtle, some blatant. Perhaps the most subtle reason is that each employee is involved in a number of different networks. Information obtained through one network often will be transmitted to others, usually with the provision that it must be kept completely confidential. Particularly interesting tidbits of information eventually will be known by almost everyone in the organization, all of whom will pretend that the information is private and secret. The point is that organizational "secrets" abound, but they are not secrets unless someone outside the immediate audience to which the information initially was revealed knows about it.

Hidden audiences are also present in less subtle ways. Powerful employees often have representatives in even the most private, off-the-record discussions. Sometimes the representative is "officially" designated and announced to the group ("I'm here because George wanted me to sit in and 'help' in any way that I could.") In other cases, the representative role is not openly revealed. In still other cases, the representative operates with all the secrecy expected of spies. Although it would not be fair to suggest that formal organizations have members like George Orwell's Big Brother, it is true that members of firms do use electronic devices to spy on other firms and on their associates and subordinates. A less technologically sophisticated example was provided by the secretary in the movie *9 to 5* who often hid in one of the stalls of the women's restroom, in order to overhear conversations and report them to her boss. Of course, both these examples are extreme and thus atypical. But they do suggest that audiences often have members who are not seen but who do hear.

To summarize, organizational situations are composed of three dimensions—*exigences*, *constraints*, and *audiences*. Coping successfully with these situations involves understanding the communicative processes through which they are created and the communicative strategies through which they can be understood. The focus of this chapter has been on the ways in which situational factors direct and limit the actions of members of organizations. The central concept is the idea that people often become trapped in the situations they create. Perhaps the most important aspect of strategic communication is recognizing that situations are situations—complex combinations of factors which reduce employees' capacities to choose among available courses of action.

Analyzing Perspectives: Adopting a Comic Frame of Reference

Organizations are able to function successfully only because they can limit and direct the actions of their members. This was the goal of the models discussed in Unit I of this book and the focus of the discussion of power relationships in Chapter 7. Through processes of communication, members establish the exigences and constraints within which they will make choices. In some cases these parameters are communicated to employees in overt, often blunt, ways. Like Moses, someone comes down from an organizational mountaintop with a list of "thou shalts" and "thou shalt nots," carves them in stone, and sets them before everyone to be obeyed. These commandments form part of a behavioral contract which anyone who wishes to remain a part of the organizational culture must obey. But in most instances the parameters are communicated more subtlely, more indirectly. Employees learn to perceive their situations in ways which fit the frame of reference of their organization. They learn to pay attention to some events and ignore others, to believe that some actions are natural, appropriate, and strategically wise and others are aberrent and foolish. Becoming part of the organizational culture involves becoming enmeshed in a particular mode of perception.

Sometimes acceptance of the dominant framework for interpreting and acting will cause employees to be productive and successful members of the organization. But sometimes, in trying to adapt to the demands of their organizational culture, people can become trapped in nonproductive ways of communicating. They adopt what symbolic theorist Kenneth Burke called *tragic frames of reference.* Burke argued that people are capable of adopting two distinctively different ways of viewing their surroundings.[3] Tragic frames of reference are perspectives which people do not realize are perspectives. Employees who have adopted them accept the picture of reality expressed by their organization's culture as if it was reality itself. They have lost sight of the fact that their way—and their organizational culture's way—of viewing the world is only one of an infinite number of different perspectives. They base their actions and communication on a particular set of assumptions about "how things work." Eventually they accept certain kinds of explanations uncritically, without realizing that those explanations are the product of the beliefs of their culture. They become trapped in their view of events and become incapable of interpreting their own actions or the actions of others in any other way.

Tragic frames of reference lead to two specific kinds of errors in interpretation. On the one hand, they lead people to oversimplify the complex factors involved in peoples' actions. They judge the goodness or badness of actions, events, and other employees without being able to sort out the factors which led to the events. Although they may realize that situational factors guide and constrain their choices, they forget that other employees also face pressures that limit their freedom of action. Since their frames of reference tell them what and who is good and evil, they are able to make decisions by a simple process of opposing the forces of evil and championing the forces of good. Organizational life becomes a *Star Wars* saga, where everyone knows the players, the plot, and (unless they are awfully dense) how the drama will end. Analysis of the complex details of their situations is unnecessary and distracting because the truth is already known.

On the other hand, tragic frames cause people to exaggerate the role of human agents. Heroes and villains make everything happen. Because people develop exaggerated notions of the power of others, they may resign themselves to conditions as they currently exist or exaggerate their capacities for effecting change, underestimating the power of constraints. In both cases, they lose sight of the situations that surround them because they view the world in a way which obscures its most important features.

In contrast, *comic frames of reference* allow people to anlayze the situations. They are based on people's ability to "step outside of" their usual interpretations of people and events and consider other ways of perceiving the "reality" around them. They allow people to see others, not as heroes and villains, but as actors like themselves who are making choices within ever-changing and complicated situations. Comic frames allow people continually to realize that the interpretations they develop and share with the people around them are just that, arbitrary decisions about how to perceive and respond to their situations.

Comic frames are difficult to construct and frustrating to maintain. They require people continually to question their assumptions, perceptions, and interpretations. They keep people from creating clear and simple explanations of events. Tragic frames, in contrast, have the dual virtues of stability and consistency. In organizations they allow people to "know" the right and wrong ways to act. Once the lines have been drawn, every event and every problem can be explained. Tragic frames provide easy answers to difficult questions. Problems exist because some people are greedy, stupid, power mad, ineffective communicators, inhumane, and so on (the list can go on forever). Successes occur because the good guys are temporarily able to overcome the forces of evil. Unfortunately, these simple explanations have two tragic features: (1) They often are wrong, and (2) they almost always lead people to act in ways which make their interpretations seem to be correct. Once members of organizations are labeled heroes and villains and events are attributed to their virtues and vices, every member of the organization knows how to act, who to communicate with, who to withhold information from, who to cooperate with, and who to challenge. In recurring cycles of acting and explaining, the labels become progressively more "correct" and the frame of reference becomes more constraining. Soon employees lose sight of the fact that it is their definition of the situation that is leading them to act in particular ways. They become trapped in their sense-making processes and lose the capacity to analyze their situations and respond productively to them. Adopting comic frames, and avoiding tragic ones, is the one necessary ingredient for effective strategic communication.

The remaining chapters of this book are designed to illustrate how these rather abstract ideas influence employees' communication in different kinds of situations. They will suggest, for example, that conflicts often become unmanageable because employees become immersed in tragic frames, that normal and moderate stress is transformed into unmanageable pressures by tragic perspectives, and that many of the problems related to sex roles in organizations result from the intransigence of cultural and organizational frames of reference. The following section of this chapter begins to make the abstract concepts of exigences, constraints, audiences, and perspectives more concrete. The topic for this first case study is the "entry experience," the processes and problems that arise during the first few months of a new job. The case study does not suggest that analyzing communication situations is important only during the early stages of a new job; employees need continually to analyze the situations they face throughout their careers and tenure in an organization.

But it does admit that processes of analysis are especially important for newly hired employees. Newcomers who succeed during the initial months seem to continue to succeed. They become assertive and confident, accept and master important and difficult challenges, form effective working relationships, and are readily accepted and often assisted by other employees. Newcomers who initially fail become progressively more unsure of themselves, less satisfied with their jobs, and less capable of handling added responsibilities. They tend to withdraw from their tasks and from their associates, making it progressively harder for them to develop the skills they need, to obtain the information they could use to advance, or to learn about the biases, preferences, and personalities of powerful members of the organization. In the same way that early success seems to breed success, early failure increases the chances of continued difficulty. Because the communicative processes involved in analyzing organizational situations are particularly important to newcomers, the entry experience provides a valuable illustration of those processes.

ENTERING ORGANIZATIONS: STAGES, PRESSURES, AND COPING PROCESSES[4]

The experiences of new employees during their first few months on the job can be understood most easily if they are viewed as characteristics of three overlapping stages (see Figure 8.1). Each of these stages demands that the new

FIGURE 8.1   **Stages of the Entry Experience**

Arrival

Encounter

Coping with surprise
Choosing appropriate roles
Obtaining task-related skills

Anticipation

Implicit contracts and expectations
Self-concept
Letting go of the familiar

employee manage a different group of cognitive, perceptual, and communicative skills with at least an adequate degree of success.

Stage 1: Anticipation

Once individuals have accepted a new position, whether in their current organization or in a new firm, they begin to anticipate what the new job will be like and to develop expectations about the new situation. For some people these expectations will be quite accurate. They will have sufficient information about the new organization, their role in it, and their tasks to meet with few surprises. In other cases prospective employees will receive less-detailed or less-accurate information. In all cases, the expectations that new employees develop before beginning a new job will have important effects on their ability to cope.

Employees' expectations are translated into *implicit contracts* with their organizations. New employees believe they will be treated in certain ways by their supervisors, be given certain amounts of autonomy in their jobs, be assigned some kinds of tasks and allowed to avoid others, and experience certain rates of advancement. Sometimes these expectations are spelled out in detail, and the "contract" between the newcomer and the organization is made explicit. Written job descriptions, formal employement agreements, and union contracts provide at least a general statement of contractual arrangements. But even in these cases, some dimensions of the contract are vague and implicit. The employees will have developed tacit expectations which they believe will be fulfilled but which never are overtly communicated to any other member of the organization.

Existing members of the organization also develop tacit expectations about their newly hired colleagues. They expect the newcomers to be capable, competent, and able to fit in to behave in predictable and appropriate ways. They also may expect the newcomers to solve problems that they have as yet been unable to eliminate. Frequently, both the newcomers' and the old-timers' expectations are violated. Rarely are newcomers exactly what people expected them to be; even less often is a new job exactly like it was supposed to be. When either set of expectations is violated, people feel betrayed, their trust in the other parties is reduced, and they begin to perceive that the others are less reliable than they had previously thought them to be. As explained in Chapter 3, low levels of trust impede both the amount and accuracy of communication between employees. As the quality of communication between newcomers and old-timers is reduced, it becomes progressively more difficult for either employee or organization to understand each other's messages and/or perceptual processes. New expectations and implicit contracts are formed. Because they are based on small amounts of potentially inaccurate information, these new contracts do not accurately predict the actions of either party, and thus are easily violated. As employees become less predicable to one another, they tend to withdraw, making it even more difficult for them to communicate effectively. Their expectations become even less realistic, their orientations toward one another less trusting, less open, and less cooperative. Their access to the information they need to perform their assigned tasks effectively is reduced.

Fortunately, this cycle of unfulfilled expectations, reduced trust, and isolation is not an inevitable part of the anticipation stage. Organizations can prevent it to some degree by attempting to create accurate expectations among new employees and old-timers. Its effects can be reduced if new employees understand that their anticipation of a new job distorts their perceptions and if they adopt communication strategies which help them cope with the cycle. In any event, coping with the expectations-contracts-isolation cycle is a key element of the anticipation stage.

The second important process is managing conflicts between one's generalized self-concept and one's organization-specific self-concept. Every person has a general view of oneself before entering an organization. From childhood on people develop images of themselves through communication with others. They acquire complicated sets of beliefs about who they are, how they act toward others, and how others should act toward them. Three components of people's generalized self-concepts are directly relevant to their roles in organizations: (1) their perceptions of their *competencies*, (2) their preferences for *independence* and *autonomy*, and (3) their sense of *self-respect*. When people enter new organizational roles they receive messages from others which will, to one degree or another, confirm or deny these components. They develop organization-specific self-concepts which may or may not be congruent with their general self-concepts.

People are assigned tasks which require a certain level of competence. In some cases these tasks will exceed new employees' perceptions of their ability. In other cases the tasks will be so simple that they are insulting. In either case, people will feel frustration and alienation. Their generalized perceptions of their self-competence are not consistent with the messages they receive from the tasks given them by their organization. In similar ways new employees' preferences for *autonomy* and *independence* and their senses of *self-respect* may be either frustrated or confirmed by their new organizational roles. It is for this reason that systems of job enrichment and job enlargement are satisfying only to the extent that they are appropriate to the characteristics of specific employees (see Chapter 5).

However, when inconsistencies exist, it usually is the new employee who must adjust. As indicated in Chapter 6, members of organizations develop stable patterns of communicating and acting. They become accustomed to having certain people play certain task, communication, and interpersonal roles. Newly hired employees enter into a preestablished set of expectations and responsibilities. The roles that the old-timers expect them to play will sometimes conflict with their general self-concepts. But the old-timers will be comfortable with newcomers only to the extent that they adapt to expectations about how they will act. If new people refuse to accept these constraints, they will upset the patterns of action which the old-timers have developed in an attempt to make their working relationships stable and predictable. Through some subtle and other not-so-subtle means, "older" employees will pressure new employees into conforming to their "assigned" roles. Since it is natural (and also strategically wise) for newcomers to want to fit in with their associates, it is difficult to resist these pressures. But since it also is difficult to accept a role which violates a person's general self-concept, trying to fit in can be very frustrating.

The final element of the anticipation stage is the process of letting go of past experiences. Managing one's expectations and self-concepts are aspects of coping with a *new* situation, of changing *to* fit a new environment. But new employees also must change *from* their old situations. Humans develop complex means of effectively perceiving, analyzing, and coping with their environments. To some extent the coping processes which work well in one situation will not work in other situations. But because they have worked so well in the past, employees rely on them to provide a bit of stability in the chaotic world of their new organizations. People attempt to hold on to accustomed ways of perceiving, acting, and communicating. Unfortunately, the old ways of making sense out of a situation may keep new employees from adapting appropriately to their new situations. If their old and new situations are alike in some ways, people will tend to perceive that they are alike in other ways, overlooking important differences between the two situations. Then, when unexpected things happen, they become confused and even hostile because the unanticipated events do not "make sense," at least not within their old perceptual sets. On the other hand, if the two situations are very different, newcomers may become overwhelmed with the new conditions. They will tend to hold on to their old ways of perceiving and acting because they provide some degree of stability in a wholly unpredictable world. Newcomers impose a comfortable world view on their new situation and begin to see it inaccurately and respond to it inappropriately. The third key process of the anticipation stage, then, is adjusting the ways of perceiving and acting so that they are appropriate to a new environment.

Stage 2: Encounter

Soon after their first days on a new job, newcomers move from anticipating the new world to confronting it. The shift from the first to second stages is neither sudden nor clearly defined; stages often blend together. The expectations that developed during anticipation begin to be tested and revised. Some aspects of the new job are quite as expected; others are quite surprising. With surprises comes questioning, expecially about why new and "foreign" people act as they do. With questioning comes attempts to make sense out of the new situation and the perplexing actions of the new people. If the expectations and perceptual frameworks that developed during the anticipation stage are appropriate to the new situation, making sense out of the new organization is relatively simple.

If they are not appropriate, making sense is more difficult, more traumatic, and more exhausting.

Meryl Reis Louis identified a number of different kinds of surprises that newcomers often meet. The first kind occurs when newcomers discover that some of their expectations are either not met or are met inadequately. The procedures through which people are selected and hired often help create expectations which will never be met adequately. Interviews give both applicants and hiring agents opportunities to create the most favorable (as opposed to the most accurate) images of themselves and their organizations. Negotiations over terms of employment also may create inaccurate expectations. For example, representatives of an organization have strong incentives to hire their top-ranked applicants. A certain amount of status accompanies success in these negotiations, and there are a number of practical reasons for wanting to hire the best available personnel. Conversely, applicants have a number of incentives for making the firm believe that hiring them is a "victory" over competitors. Both the firm and the applicant typically engage in communication which is very much like romantic courtship, with each party striving to present the best possible image of itself. But as in many marriages, the realities of the first six months may be quite different from the courtship.[5] This is not to imply that either party intentionally misleads the other (although either of them sometimes may do so). It is to suggest that the selection process itself can generate expectations which may not be fully met. The nature of most jobs also may create the feeling that expectations have been violated. Even the "richest," most complex jobs have some mundane but necessary dimensions. During anticipation, people focus on the more interesting dimensions and ignore the mundane elements. When they encounter their new tasks, it is no longer possible to ignore the boring and revel in the challenging and stimulating. Task-related expectations will be unmet or undermet.

New employees also may surprise themselves. They may have chosen a position, or even a career, because they thought they wanted certain outcomes from their work—achievement, independence, a sense of contribution to social justice, or whatever. Once they are given an opportunity to achieve that goal, they discover that it was not what they wanted after all. Most of the college students of my generation thought they wanted to "make the world a better place to live." Many of them have discovered that what they really want is to be able to afford a house.

Surprise also occurs when employees take things for granted and find that they should not have done so. When they are hired as professors, graduate students often assume without really thinking about it that they will have an office, telephone, stamps, stationery, and the automatic respect of hordes of adoring undergraduates. When they encounter their new role they may be surprised to find that none of these tacit assumptions was accurate. Finally, surprise also occurs when newcomers find that the *experience* itself is not what they thought it would be. Medical students know at a cognitive, intellectual level, that they will work sixty to eighty hours a week while in residency; mental health professionals know that they will be overloaded with complicated cases and buried in administrative red tape. But, they do not—indeed they cannot—know what it will *feel* like to have these experiences until they actually do so. Making sense out of a new situation requires a person to cope with both cognitive and feeling dimensions of *surprise*. Even if new employees have absolutely accurate and complete *information* about their new situation before they enter it, and even if they are able to adopt a completely appropriate frame of reference when they encounter it, they *still* will feel affective surprise and still will need to find ways of coping with it.

Coping successfully with the surprises of the encounter stage depends largely on the processes discussed in the first section of this chapter. The first step involves *learning the culture* of the organization *and recognizing* that it is a culture, a symbolically constructed way of interpreting situations, making choices about how to act, and making sense out of the actions and messages of others. Cultures are human creations. However, sometimes creations which are productive for the group as a whole may not be productive for all of its members. Accepting the old-timers' interpretive frameworks may cause newcomers to draw conclusions which are damaging to them. For example, learning that manager X is hostile to everyone in their unit, newcomers may then interpret communication from that manager so that that impression is confirmed. As a result, they may become involved in unnecessary conflicts with manager X or may fail to build an alliance with the manager which could have been valuable later on. Or newcomers may learn that a certain component of their task is unimportant and expendable. They may learn too late that there are powerful people in other parts of the organization who depend on them to fulfill the "unimportant" parts of their jobs. The newcomers' new perceptions may lead them to act in ways which indicate to the powerful that they do not understand their role in the organization. Organizational cultures and the frames of reference that go along with them allow citizens to create stable and predictable perceptual worlds. But they also may lead them to adopt tragic perspectives.

The second key process of the encounter stage is *assessing exigences and constraints* and determining their implications. Almost all newcomers eventually learn the parameters of their organizational culture. Through informal communication and trial and error, they learn that they are expected to act in ways appropriate to their organization and formal position in it. Even though they are never given an official script, employees learn to play their parts. Managers learn never to say anything negative about their firm or its products in public; officers (supervisors) learn that they do not fraternize with enlisted personnel (subordinates); employees learn to maintain the public images of their roles and their firms. They use its products, live in its neighborhoods, and subscribe to its dress code.

In fact, one of the few tangible indications of the power of an organizational culture is its effect on the dress of its members. For example, on weekdays an airport near my home has three kinds of clients—government employees; professors from three major universities; and executives from three large, rather conservative, manufacturers of business machines and computers. I am convinced that anyone can look at any line at any ticket counter or gate in this airport and predict with at least 80 percent accuracy the group to which each traveler belongs simply by looking at the attire. The executives are wearing well-tailored, expensive gray or blue suits with average-width lapels, average-width ties, and expensive leather briefcases. The government employees are wearing nontailored, relatively inexpensive gray, blue, or brown suits with average-width lapels and ties (and perhaps a pastel shirt) and carry pretend-leather briefcases. The professors are wearing everything else (except, of course, business school professors and other consultants who often appear to be part of the executive group). Homogeneity is achieved, not because employees are issued matching uniforms, but because people learn that part of their role in their organization is to fulfill expectations about dress.

There are, of course, other behavioral expectations to be learned which are less tangible, more subtle, and more important. Some of these involve tasks and responsibilities. Most job descriptions present only a broad, ill-defined picture of an employee's responsibilities. They exclude some responsibilities which are mandatory and include others which are forbidden. For example, job descriptions for executive secretaries rarely include making coffee for the bosses, buying presents for their relatives, or lying to their spouses about their location or activities. But these "tasks" are often informally defined as the responsibility of the employee. Other positions involve other kinds of unofficial duties which are not included in official job descriptions. Other responsibilities are included in official descriptions of duties and benefits but are effectively excluded from the role. For example, few professional positions provide formal monetary reimbursement for working "overtime." Instead they include provisions which allow professionals to accumulate "compensatory time" which can be turned into extra "vacation" time during periods of light workloads. But in contrast to these "official" systems, it also is made quite clear to new professionals that they are expected *not* to use any of their accumulated time. Or, as Lou Grant once told Mary Richards, "You're a professional. You don't punch a time clock. You can even work through your lunch if you want to." Or employees may have accepted a position in part because its official description includes some desirable "perk"—representing the firm at trade conventions, for example,—only to find that their supervisors prefer to perform that particular task themselves.

Newcomers also learn to adapt to power relationships. They discover that they are expected to defer superiors on any significant issues; remain quiet when their supervisors accept credit for their work; and invite superior-grade personnel to dinner parties, show concern for their spouses and families, note their birthdays and anniversaries, and so on. New employees move into an existing set of formal and informal hierarchical relationships. They are expected to behave in ways which, at least on the surface, support and perpetuate that hierarchy.

Finally, employees are expected to behave as if they have cooperative, friendly, and professional relationships with their associates. "Team spirit" is demanded by amost all organizations, and acting like a member of the "team" is expected of every employee. In many cases these expectations will be easy to fulfill. Newcomers soon will feel that they actually are part of a team. In other cases they will have to pretend that they do. And because fulfilling expectations is important, the most successful new employees often are the most consummate pretenders.

To successfully complete the encounter stage newcomers must manage a wide variety of exigences and constraints effectively. They can respond to these parameters in one of three general ways.[6] They can become *custodians* of their assigned roles, choosing to interpret their situation precisely as old-timers say they should and acting only in ways prescribed by the organization. They can be *innovators*, conforming the broad, general, and sacrosanct expectations but acting in some novel and unexpected ways, usually in response to minor or noncontroversial events. Or they can be *radicals* who violate both general and specific expectations and constraints. Each of these responses is strategically appropriate in some situations and wholly inappropriate in others. What is important is that the newcomers carefully *choose* among the three kinds of responses, basing their choices on a careful analysis of how productive each option will be for them.

The first step in choosing the appropriate role is recognizing that the one most productive for the newcomers may not be the response desired by their organization or associates. First, consider the *custodial* reponse. For the organization and for the old-timers, this may be the most desirable response for new employees to take. When newcomers conform to established ways of perceiving their environment, they help maintain the stability and predictability of the culture. In some cases, this response may be productive for everyone concerned. If the organization is coping successfully with its tasks and if the employees have discovered and implemented patterns of communicating and acting which provide everyone in the organization with acceptable rewards, it is wise to maintain those patterns. In these cases conformity also can be productive for newcomers because it allows them to become part of the successful pattern. Very soon they will be seen by others as predictable and trustworthy, and they will rapidly become part of a productive team which shares its success and rewards with each of its members. As long as the existing patterns of action are productive for everyone involved in them, *custodianship* is an appropriate response.

In other cases the only productive strategy is to take on the role of a *radical*. In the introduction to this unit two extreme kinds of organizational situations were explained—those in which there are exigences but no constraints and those in which there are significant constraints but no guidelines for acting. In neither of these extremes is it productive to accept the situation as it is or modify it only in minor ways. Unfortunately, the processes by which people encounter their organizations make it highly improbable that they will adopt a radical role. And since newcomers rarely have sufficient power to overcome the combined power of the people who create the exigences and constraints, it is also highly improbable that they could succeed as radicals.

Between the two extremes of perfectly productive and pathological situations are a wide range of different combinations of productive and paralyzing factors. In these more typical situations, newcomers cope most effectively by playing the role of an *innovator*. To do so they must learn the expectations that others have for them and carefully assess the degree to which fulfilling each of those expectations will contribute to their own success and effectiveness. Managing the encounter stage depends on newcomers' ability to analyze, to think critically about (1) the *patterns of communication* they observe and what those patterns imply about their role in the organization;[7] (2) *their own interpretations* and frames of reference, that is, what their perspective allows them to see clearly and accurately and what it obscures, and (3) what *actions they must take and must avoid* in particular situations in order to attain their own goals and the legitimate goals and objectives of the organization.

Coping with the encounter stage involves *learning the culture* of the organization, *assessing behavioral expectations*, and finally, *developing task-related skills*. Almost all organizations place newcomers in some kind of training program, which may be lengthy, extensive, and expensive. Budding managers may spend their first one to three years in relatively brief (six months seems to be common) stints in each of an organization's different offices, learning a variety of skills from a number of different tutors. Other programs are brief, almost pro forma. For a day or two someone reads company policies and procedures to the newcomers, "walks them through" a typical day, and concludes the session by giving them an official company notebook which tells them precisely what they have just heard (often in exactly the same words.). Regardless of how extensive a firm's training program is, its newcomers will have to manage two processes successfully before they can become adept at performing their new tasks.

The first process is *becoming initiated* to the new job. Newcomers must learn what actions their tasks involve, what skills they require, and what level of "success" can realistically be expected. Newcomers enter jobs with a general set of skills and abilities. Sometimes they are not wholly aware of which skills they possess and which skills they lack. In other cases they may have a relatively accurate picture of their own skills but only a vague notion of what specific ones are required for their new jobs. In order to adjust to demands, newcomers must determine which necessary skills they lack and then take carefully designed steps to remedy those deficiencies. Of course, the more accurate newcomers' perceptions of their own skills and the requirements of the job, the easier it is to discover and acquire necessary abilities. Newcomers can sharpen some skills while maintaining others, eventually achieving a match between their abilities and the skills required.

The second process is *developing the skills required for movement into upper-level positions* in the employee's career path. As suggested in the postscript to Chapter 7, upward mobility depends on employees' ability to master both the skills for the current job and the skills necessary to perform successfully in the position to which they eventually may be promoted. The first step in developing long-term skills is to determine the career paths available. Sometimes these paths are formally explained in written policies and procedures. Unit managers must once have been section chiefs, who must once have been supervisors and so on. When one inquires into the backgrounds of the people currently in upper-level positions, one finds that with the possible exception of relatives of the owner, these career paths actually have been operating as they are formally defined. In some cases it is more difficult to determine which positions are a newcomer's most probable next step. In other cases there may be no next step, at least not within the organization itself. Whatever the situation, newcomers must determine what career paths are available, and the most reliable indicators are the careers of people who previously occupied their position. Newcomers, then, must find out where their predecessors are today—in which firms and in which positions in them—what steps they took to get there, and what amount of time they spent in each position along the way.

The second step in developing advancement-related skills is to learn the skills necessary in the probable next steps. Newcomers can either obtain the education, experience, and skills necessary in the paths potentially open to them or they can attempt to arrange a transfer into a entry-level position in a path that corresponds more closely to their existing skills and abilities. Finally, newcomers must make it clear to powerful members of their organization that they do possess the skills that make them promotable. They may seek out and accept assignments which allow them to develop and demonstrate their mastery of those skills and avoid assignments which prevent them from doing so. They must capitalize on opportunities to make their skills visible to those employees who have influence over promotions. Of course, newcomers also must be careful to demonstrate that they can successfully perform their existing jobs and maintain effective relationships with their peers and subordinates.

This seems to be a difficult lesson for many newcomers to learn. Students often seem to visit campuses within a few months of starting their careers and announce, with a great deal of pride, that their associates are happier with them than they were with their predecessors because they are "more serious" about their jobs and "spend less time brown-nosing" with upper management. When asked "What happened to your predecessor?" they often respond that "He's my supervisor" or "She is assistant manager of the Oakland plant" or something else which suggests that their predecessors are moving up through a clearly defined career path. There are two morals to these stories. One is that employees cannot be so concerned with creating visible evidence of their promotability that they alienate their peers and subordinates. After all, peers may become supervisors, and managers will be perceived as competent only to the extent that they can maintain cooperative relationships with their subordinates. The second moral (one that seems to escape former students) is that "brown-nosers" who leave a position often do so in order to move up. And there may be a third moral: "Brown nosers" are people who are blatant and successful in their efforts to demonstrate their promotability; "upwardly mobile professionals" are "brown-nosers" who are subtle and successful in creating that image.

CONCLUSION

Organizations develop distinctive ways of perceiving, interpreting, and acting, creating their own mini-cultures. The characteristics of organizational cultures provide the broad background in which specific communicative situations arise. Generalized cultures and specific situations interact in ways which demand communication of an appropriate type (exigences), limit communication in a number of ways (constraints), and define specific groups of people as audiences. Strategic communication begins with a careful and systematic analysis of these features.

Notes

1. People often believe that when others communicate appropriately those people also understand their organizational culture. Although it sometimes is true that employees' actions reveal a conscious awareness of the characteristics of their culture, this is not always the case. We often act in certain ways without being aware of it or without consciously recognizing that our actions are consistent with and guided by the expectations of our culture.

Important contributions to the idea of organizational cultures have been made by Andrew Pettigrew, "On Studying Organizational Cultures," *Administrative Science Quarterly*, 24 (1979), 570–581; Peter Berger and Thomas Luckman, *The Social Construction of Reality* (New York: Anchor Books, 1966); Karl Weick, *The Social Psychology of Organizing* (Reading, Mass.: Addison-Wesley, 1967); Michael Pacanowsky and Nick O'Donnell-Trujillio, "Organizational Communication as Cultural Performance," *Communication Monographs*, 50 (1983) 126–147.

2. Richard C. Palmer, *Hermeneutics* (Evanston, Ill.: Northwestern University Press, 1969).

3. This concept is developed most completely in *Attitudes Toward History* (Boston: Beacon Press, 1961). It is presented in some form in Burke's *Permanence and Change* (New York: Bobbs-Merrill, 1965) and *A Grammer of Motives* (Berkeley: University of California Press, 1945).

4. The entry experience is one of those areas of organizational research in which theoretical explanations have advanced more rapidly than empirical research. Consequently, some of the ideas developed in this section are based more on scholars' extensions of related research than on work dealing specifically with organizational entry. Although I will not attempt to list the relevant sources, comprehensive summaries can be found in the research on which this section is based: Meryl Reis Louis, "Surprise and Sense-Making in Organizations," *Administrative Science Quarterly*, 25 (1980), 226–251; John van Maanen and Edgar Schein, "Toward a Theory of Socialization," in *Research in Organizational Behavior*, ed. Barry Staw, (Greenwich, Conn.: JAI Press, 1979), vol. I; Daniel Feldman, "The Multiple Socialization of Organization Members," *The Academy of Management Review*," 6 (1981), 309–318.

5. The courtship process may be just as misleading for average as for excellent applicants. If, for example, the firm has interviewed four finalists and has been turned down by the top three, it has even more incentive to hire the fourth candidate than it had to hire the first. If it fails to land

that person, it will be forced to expend extra time and energy conducting another search. If a unit of an organization fails to hire the fourth candidate, it risks losing the position to other units of the organization. However, because the candidate is fourth, the firm has little incentive to make actual changes in the autonomy granted the newcomer or the "richness" of the job. But since the person has been courted so vigorously by the firm, he or she may have come to expect a substantial degree of freedom, responsibility, and so on.

6. Adapted from John van Maanen and Edgar Schein, "Occupational Socialization in the Professions," *Journal of Psychiatric Research*, 8 (1971), 521–530.

7. Louis, "Surprise and Sense-Making," p. 243. Also see Bernard Weiner, *Achievement Motivation and Attribution Theory* (Morristown, N.J.: General Learning Process, 1974).

9
Adapting to Organizational Situations

The goal of this chapter is to provide guidelines for readers to use in developing their strategic communication skills. I shall discuss three general kinds of personal characteristics, each of which is important for organizational communicators: (1) adopting *strategically appropriate attitudes* about communication, (2) developing *image-management* skills, and (3) developing *message-management* skills. The guidelines are not designed to substitute for in-depth training and interpersonal and public communication. In fact, readers who have completed courses in these related areas will be better able to use the guidelines. However, the chapter is designed to provide all readers with an understanding of how related communication skills can improve their ability to cope with situations at work.

ADOPTING STRATEGICALLY APPROPRIATE ATTITUDES: BECOMING RHETORICALLY SENSITIVE

In early 1972 communication theorists Roderick Hart and Don Burks introduced the concept of "rhetorical sensitivity." It was based on a distinction between "expressive" and "instrumental" (or "rhetorical") communication, one which is very much like the distinction presented in the introduction to this unit. Hart and Burks started with the observation that expressive communication is very attractive to people because it involves the virtues of frankness, honesty, open-heartedness, nonpossessive warmth, and nonmanipulative intentions toward others. But as attractive as expressive communication is, it rarely provides people with effective means of creating and sustaining mutually beneficial relationships. Communication is most effective and relationships most stable and rewarding if people are rhetorically sensitive and communicate in ways which reflect that sensitivity.[1]

Rhetorical Sensitives, Noble Selves, and Rhetorical Reflectors

What is a rhetorically sensitive person? What kind of communication reflects rhetorical sensitivity? In a later study Hart and his associates described a rhetorically sensitive person through a comparison to two other types of people. *Noble selves* are people who perceive that they should not adapt to other people or to situations in any way which violates their beliefs, values, or normal activities. Doing so would be both hypocritical and unproductive. For them communication is a means of informing others of the truths that they have learned. At the other extreme are *rhetorical reflectors*, people who communicate as if they have no beliefs, values, or normal actions to call their own. They present a different picture of themselves to every person and in every situation, *reflecting* the image they think others want them to present. In contrast to both of these extremes are *rhetorical sensitives*, people whose attitudes about communication include five basic beliefs: (1) People are complex beings who are capable of taking on a large number of different roles, each of which represents part of their identity. For example, people who define themselves as parents can legitimately and ethically communicate in ways which are nurturing, demanding, structuring, supporting, or disciplining in response to different circumstances and still be true to their identities as parents. (2) People should avoid rigid patterns of communicating. They should be flexible, adjusting their communication appropriately to different circumstances, even if doing so sometimes violates social norms or conventions. (3) People should be conscious of the needs of other people, but they should not sacrifice their own ideas and feelings to placate others. (4) People should appreciate that ideas and feelings should be expressed only when it is appropriate to do so. Some situations involve personal and interpersonal risks that are so great that not communicating is the only appropriate response, whereas in other situations expressing one's feelings can only harm the relationship or worsen the situation. (5) People should be tolerant of the need to search for the best way to communicate ideas and feelings. Rhetorical sensitives allow others to try one way of communicating and then to revise their communciation when it is necessary to do so. They also allow themselves the same right.

Of course, all people play each of these three roles to some degree, but most people are closer to one of the three types than to the others. Each profile reflects tendencies that have been encouraged or discouraged in varying degrees by the backgrounds, training, and experiences of each person. They are not permanent orientations toward communication but attitudes that can be revised if and when a person finds it wise to do so. The attitudes associated with rhetorical sensitivity are important to employees for a number of reasons. First, the other perspectives involve beliefs which prevent employees from employing strategically appropriate communication. Rhetorical reflectors focus their attention so completely on the actions and purposes of others that they lose sight of their own goals, ends, needs, and roles in their organizations. They risk becoming so totally immersed in the frames of reference of their associates that they no longer can act in productive ways. There are instances in which organizations profit from disagreement. Rhetorical reflectors acquiesce in these situations and fail to make their expertise and insight available. Their actions tend to support the status quo, regardless of its inherent merit.

Similarly, noble selves risk becoming so enmeshed in their own frames of reference that they no longer can act in productive ways. In their efforts to "correct" the errors of others they may become so alienated and isolated that they can have little impact. Their attempts to improve flawed situations make them incapable of playing an effective corrective role. In both cases the employees' orientations toward communication place barriers between them and their ability to act in strategic productive ways.

Second, the orientations of the noble self and rhetorical reflector can reduce employees' abilities to listen effectively to the messages they receive. Effective "listening" has three dimensions: listening for *multiple levels of meaning*, listening for the *organizational implications* of messages, and listening for the *personal implications* of messages. Each involves the kind of flexibility characteristic only of the rhetorically sensitive orientation.

Developing Strategic Listening Skills

Every message, every utterance, is polysemous.[2] That is, it has different levels of meaning. Messages have "meaning" on a cognitive level—they convey bits of information. It is this level that people attend to most closely. They listen for and record (physically or mentally) the information overtly expressed. But messages also include meanings at emotional and relational levels. It is relatively easy to detect a speaker's emotional tone and intensity during face-to-face communication. People know when they are involved in emotionally charged conversations. They can "feel the tension" (or concern or love or other emotion) in the air. They can observe a speaker's nonverbal cues—pace and loudness of speech, level of physical movement, pupil dilation, facial expressions, and so on. And they can observe the content of messages, knowing that even when statements about ethical principles or personal affronts are delivered in calm and measured tones they have clear and important emotional components. But in many other situations, emotional tone is more difficult to detect. Emotional meanings are also lost when messages are communicated in writing—which is one of the reasons why there are more good memowriters than fine playwrites. Even during face-to-face conversations, communicators often attempt to hide the emotional tone of their remarks. In formal organizations where calm rationality is valued and emotionality is denigrated, people learn to cover the level of emotional involvement in what they are saying. In time they become quite adept at suppressing emotional displays. But other employees can accurately understand their messages only if they are able to detect underlying emotions. Unless people consciously and continually listen for the emotional level of meaning, they will not fully understand what others are trying to communicate.

Finally, messages have meanings on a "relational" level.[3] They say something about the sender's interpersonal relationship with the receivers, with other members of the organization, and with the organization itself. Messages reveal individuals' perceptions about their role in the organization: what they believe they can contribute, what actions are appropriate for them, and what they feel are legitimate demands that they can make on others and others can make on them. Messages also reveal people's perceptions of who their allies are, who has power over them, who they should defer to, who should defer to them, and who is worthy of respect and who is not. Rarely, however, is the relational dimension of meaning revealed explicitly in the content of a message. The norms of team spirit, cooperation, and objectivity usually are so strong that employees rarely label others as friends, enemies, powerful, powerless, competent, or incompetent in public. These perceptions are revealed by the timing of the message, the audiences that are selected or avoided, and the arguments that are proposed or suppressed. All messages contain a relational dimension of meaning. But because this dimension is so subtle, it can be detected only when employees actively "listen" for it.

Simultaneously listening for cognitive, emotional, and relational dimensions of meaning is important for two reasons. First, it gives employees more accurate and more complete information about the purposes which underlie communication from others. For example, when an old-timer tells a newcomer that "that's a pretty good idea, for a rookie," the comment may reflect a variety of purposes. It could be intended to focus attention on a good idea (primarily a content-related purpose), to express a tutor's pride in the accomplishments of the mentoree (an "emotional" purpose), to establish that the newcomer is a subordinate ("rookie," a relational purpose), or any combination of the three. The rookie can accurately understand the comment and its purposes only by thinking "what does it mean at content, emotional, and relational levels?" Listening for multiple levels of meaning also gives employees a sense of what responses are appropriate to different messages. For example, the effects of the rookie's responding, "Yep. . . . Gee I'm smart, aren't I" will depend on the old-timer's purpose(s). If it was one of content, the response would have little impact. But if the purpose was either the emotional or relational one, the response could have unfortunate effects. It would deny the old-timer's right to feel pride in the mentoree or it would challenge the hierarchical relationship that exists between the two people. In either case the response would alienate the old-timer. Responding appropriately to messages depends on understanding the many purposes and levels of meaning that are part of communication.

Just as employees must listen for multiple levels of meaning, they also must listen for the *organizational implications* that messages contain. Three kinds of implications are present in almost all messages. The first involves the *function* of the message in the operation of the organization. Chapters 6 and 8 explained that what often *seem* to be decision-making situations really are organizational rituals. Some messages are decision-making messages. They are important in direct proportion to the importance of the problem(s) to which they are related. They call for responses which focus on the problem(s) and potential solutions. Responses which express disagreement, for example, are appropriate to these messages, providing that the responses are objective, problem- or solution-oriented, and so on. Other messages only *seem* to be part of a decision-making process. For example, when upper-level personnel resign or retire, messages like "What can we ever do to replace Alice" abound. They do so regardless of how important or irreplaceable Alice was. Although these messages sound like a call for decision making, interpreting them in this way would miss the point. More important, treating them as decision-making messages by responding "Well, Fred, Judy, or Stanley could easily move up and do quite well" or "Ah, come on . . . any idiot could handle Alice's job" would be wholly inappropriate (and quite foolish). Messages have different kinds of functions. Interpreting them and responding appropriately requires listening for their implications.

The second implication of messages involves the *negotiation of organizational roles.* Often messages serve as invitations for others to affirm that they understand and accept their roles in the hierarchies of the organization. "Don't you agree, Julie?" often means "Don't you agree that managerial trainees are supposed to agree?" The implication of the message is that organizations are allowed to enforce hierarchical roles. Members who do not hear that implication may respond in ways which inadvertently challenge the hierarchy.

Finally, messages contain *personal implications.* Whenever employees make a statement, they comment on the content being discussed, the emotions they feel, and their relationships with other members of the organization. In addition, each and every message carries certain risks for employees' "public" image and for their private conception of themselves. The optimal response is one which promises the greatest potential for achieving one's personal, relational, and organizational goals while providing the least risk. The need to balance these considerations is illustrated very clearly by the situation faced by "whistle blowers," people who report illegal activities within their firms to the appropriate authorities. The risks to an employee's advancement, relationships with co-workers, and personal safety often are quite large and the gains quite small. But the personal costs of not reporting the actions—reduced self-esteem, guilt, and fear that someone else will report it, leaving the employee in the role of an accomplice—also may be quite large. In this case deciding whether to communicate or not is in itself a very complicated problem. In general, responses which promise equivalent gains and risks are only marginally satisfactory; those which involve substantial risks with little opportunity for gain are unwise.

Selecting among available responses is complicated further by the fact that there are situations in which all three goals cannot be met simultaneously. Opportunities to gain personal objectives may involve significant risks to valued relationships (recall the case study in Chapter 1). Although it is impossible to calculate exact estimates of potential gains and risks, rhetorically sensitive people at least attempt to consider each before deciding on a course of action. Life is simpler for noble selves and rhetorical reflectors. But it usually is less productive and much less fun.

As the preceding paragraphs suggest, strategic listening is neither a simple nor an easy process. It requires employees to consider simultaneously three different levels of meaning and expend much energy in efforts to analyze situations and choose appropriate communicative strategies. Strategic listen-

FIGURE 9.1   Guidelines for Listening

Productive Attitudes about Listening

Listening is a difficult, demanding activity.
You must listen for and respond to multiple levels of meaning.
Listening is a skill, and like any skill, requires training and practice.
Other employees generally have something worthwhile to say.
Meanings depend on both verbal and nonverbal cues.
Messages contain a large number of items of information which vary in
   importance.

Productive Listening Activities

Prepare yourself to listen.
Remove or control physical distractions (choose a quiet setting; stop phone calls
   or other interruptions).
Control psychological distractions.
   Be aware of your own predispositions and biases.
   Be aware of any topics or words to which you respond emotionally.
   Delay drawing conclusions about or evaluating what the other person is saying.
Consciously try to take the other person's point of view.
Paraphrase and check perception ("I understand your point to be . . . ") when it is
appropriate and not awkward.

---

ing can be enhanced when employees accept a number of relatively simple ideas about the listening process and become proficient at a number of different listening skills (see Figure 9.1). However, unless they also strive to be rhetorically sensitive, even the most highly developed listening skills will not be translated into strategically appropriate responses.

ADOPTING APPROPRIATE IMAGE-MANAGING STRATEGIES

For milennia communication scholars have recognized the impact of a communicator's image on the impact of his or her communication. In the first comprehensive analysis of rhetorical communication, Aristotle observed around 330 B.C. that the images speakers create of themselves are the strongest persuasive tool that they have. If speakers create the impression that they embody the values of the culture from which their audience is drawn, an audience will be more prone to make the choices they want it to make. Aristotle listed the three most valued characteristics of speakers by Athenian audiences—*knowledge* or *expertise,* trustworthiness, and *orientation toward the audiences* (that is, the extent to which the speaker was concerned with their interests and well-being). Of course, the strength of Aristotle's concept of ethos (image) does not stem from this list. Its enduring value—and its relevance to communication in formal organizations—arises from two additional dimensions.

The most important dimension of ethos is the idea that images are created through communication. Although listeners often have formed impressions about communicators before any particular message is presented, those images are not permanent. They were created through communication, through previous messages presented by the speaker or about the speaker, and they can be altered by subsequent communication. The second dimension is that a communicator's *image* and the *content* of the message mutually influence one another. The conclusions that communicators offer, the justifications they provide, and the values they espouse, all will affect their image. Conversely, the image they create and have created will affect their audience's evaluation of their comments.

Two modern rhetorical theorists, Chaim Perelman and L. Olbrechts-Tyteca, have extended Aristotle's concept of the interrelationships between image and content in their discussion of *presence.*[4] They argue that communicative situations are complex and ambiguous. When communicators construct messages they can choose to stress some aspects of those situations and to deemphasize others. If their audience perceives that what they have chosen to emphasize is sensible, given the existing time, place, relationships, and purposes, they will enhance both their image and the acceptability of what they say. Their interpretations will influence others' interpretations of the situation and thus will increase the speakers' credibility. By adopting communicative strategies appropriate to the situation, communicators can establish and/or exploit their image.

To summarize, the concepts of *ethos* and *presence* are particularly important for members of organizations. In the long term, communicators can modify the interpretations of "reality" which exist in their organizations. They can alter *exigences* and *constraints* by adapting to parts of them while attempting to change other parts. In the short term, employees can use these concepts when they seek to create the kinds of personal images they desire. Members of organizational cultures share certain values and interpretations of reality. Employees who are able to *create and maintain images* which suggest that they *embody these values* will have more impact than employees who do not. And since organizations promote and reward individuals based on their *personae*, on the images they communicate to other employees, image-managing communication is related strongly to organizational success.

Managing Organizationally Appropriate Images There are two kinds of people in organizations, those who are promotable and those who are not. More precisely, there are two kinds of personae. The term *persona* refers to the audience's perceptions of the characters portrayed in a play. Actors present a carefully designed and enacted image of their roles. What the audience sees is not the *person* of the actor but a contrived image. Audiences respond to the persona, not to the person. The success of employees depends on the personae they create and the extent to which those images are appropriate to their organizational stage.[5] For example, hiring decisions are based largely on selection agents' conclusions about the extent to which different candidates seem to fit their images of the kind of person needed for a particular position. Promotions are granted and withheld primarily on the basis of how well an employee's image conforms to decision makers' impressions of what characteristics are required for effective performance in higher-level positions. Persons, the realities of what people are, never can be known to others except through the personae they create.

Occasional news reports of successful Engineers or Ph.D.s who have falsified their credentials indicate that a very small number of people spend much of their lifetimes creating wholly false personae. Studies of distortions and factual inaccuracies on résumés and in selection interviews suggest that a large proportion of candidates occasionally attempt to project inaccurate but favorable images of their backgrounds and experiences.[6] Students who once worked the cash register at a local hamburger emporium report "substantial financial and budgetary experience"; people report having A− averages, knowing full well that the average grade given at their university is an A−; and so on.

Employees inevitably create images of themselves. Everything they say or do or fail to say or do (or are reputed to have said or done) will contribute to these impressions. Employees cannot choose between creating a persona and not creating one. They live in fishbowls (or given the size of most organizations, in aquariums) in which they are constantly observed and their actions analyzed and interpreted. Employees can choose between creating a persona by chance or doing so by design. If they do choose to manage the impressions they create, they can do so without being misleading. Every person has a number of abilities, traits, and personality characteristics. Impression management means choosing to communicate in ways which make other people more aware of some of those characteristics and less cognizant of others. It involves putting on one's "best face" but not putting on a false face. Erving Goffman, a sociologist whose research provides the most thorough analysis of image management explained that "instead of allowing an impression of their activity to arise as an incidental byproduct of their activity, they [people] can re-orient their frame-of-reference and devote their efforts to creation of desired impressions."[7] Productive impression management involves two processes: (1) creating an organizationally appropriate persona and (2) sustaining that persona.

Steps in Image Creation   The first step in creating a productive image is determining what kind of image is advisable. Earlier chapters of this book suggested that promotable people seem to have the characteristics and engage in the communicative patterns summarized in Figure 9.2. In addition, every organization has its own particular definition of a promotable employee. These organization-specific images are relatively easy to discover. One simply col-

FIGURE 9.2   Impressions and Related Communication

Impression	*Communication Which Creates This Image*
1. Is rational	Limits and controls emotional responses. Provides justifications for comments which are organized, relevant, acceptable to others (especially more powerful employees), and based on seemingly objective data. Says things others expect and wish person to say (are predictable).
2. Is professional	Expresses values and perceptions appropriate to role and rank in organization. Forms interpersonal relationships with people of parallel or superior rank and specialization and remains more distant from subordinates. Adopts the in-group language of unit or profession.
3. Is loyal	While in public communicates only positive impressions of co-workers, job, firm, and its products. Expresses a willingness to sacrifice time and commitment to other relationships in order to fulfill organizational role.

lects the impressions other employees have of the people who have been successful in the organization and those who have not. The features common to the personae of the first group indicate those that make one promotable. The features which emerge from the second group indicate those that keep people from being promoted. Features common to all the members of the unsuccessful group should not be communicated. Features true of only one or two of the nonpromotable people should be examined further. Some of them will not be relevant. Some nonpromotables may have alienated a powerful employee who is no longer with the firm; others may be members of religious or ethnic groups excluded from the upper levels of the firm; still others may have come from the "wrong" colleges. But some of these relatively idiosyncratic nonpromotability factors may be relevant (one may be from the "wrong" college, for example) and must be compensated for. Eventually one will be able to construct a composite persona of a promotable employee and learn that communicative strategies were used by promoted employees to create their personae.

Once employees have constructed this promotable persona, they need only to adopt patterns of communication which make them seem to fit that image. Adopting image-creating patterns is made difficult, however, by two factors. The first is the degree of discrepancy between the persona required by the organization and the pattern of communication typically employed by the employee. If the gap is too great, the employee will be required to engage in a great degree of playacting. Acting is exhausting work. If actors are playing intensely unnatural roles, they will expend great amounts of energy maintaining it and often will slip out of it and communicate in ways which destroy their personae. As time goes by it becomes easier to play new roles. Being a "lady" was difficult for Eliza (in *My Fair Lady*) at first, but she adapted very quickly; playing the role of a prince initially was impossible for Mark Twain's pauper, but it became much easier as time went by. However, in some cases the gap will be too great. In these instances, employees can adjust in one of two ways. They can abandon their aspirations or move to an organization or career where the appropriate persona is more like their natural patterns of communication. Professors who enjoy performing in the spotlight should gravitate toward institutions which value undergraduate teaching; those who are most comfortable working alone or with small groups are more effective in major graduate research universities.

Creating an appropriate image also is made more difficult by the dynamics of nonverbal communication. In general, and for most people, it is more difficult to control nonverbal than verbal cues. It is easier to say "I respect my boss and all of my associates" than to look like you do while you say it. Since people tend to believe nonverbal cues when there are discrepancies between the two, employees must monitor and adjust both verbal and nonverbal cues in order to create a consistent and believeable persona.

"Presenting an appropriate self" (as Goffman labels the image-maintenance process) is made easier by two factors. The first is that people usually cooperate with one another in maintaining their images. Especially in formal organizations, where part of the image of promotability is cooperating and understanding what's going on, there are pressures to help others maintain their chosen images. People establish working agreements to support one another's faces. If any participants violate the agreement they risk having others retaliate by "unmasking" them.

Image creation is also aided by the availability of "front stages" and "backstages." Personae are created and maintained in public, on "front stage," where actions can be observed by an audience. Even in organizational fishbowls there are times and places in which people can rehearse and perfect the communication patterns they are trying to establish. This is one of the reasons employees have resisted "open office" arrangements: Walls and doors create backstages. Removing these physical barriers to communication robs employees of the vital process of rehearsing their persona.[8] Part of organizational loyalty is the willingness to accept others' right to a backstage, to occasionally practice their *personae* in private.

However, even with the advantages provided by (1) being able to adapt to a persona, (2) working agreements, and (3) backstage action, it is inevitable that employees' personae will sometimes break down. They may fail to act in ways consistent with the images they have created, or others may communicate in ways which violate the groups' working agreements. When these breakdowns occur the parties must take steps to restore their images and their agreements. Goffman calls the process of maintaining personae "face work" or "face management." Researchers from a variety of academic disciplines have discovered a relatively small number of communication strategies used to maintain personae.

Image Maintenance   One of the best illustrations is Bernard Berk's study of the "single's dance."[9] These events have a long history, both in time and in each person's experience. They start sometime during grammar or junior high school. Some well-meaning but incredibly cruel adult(s)—usually schoolteachers, PTA officers, or officials in church groups—decide that the children in their charge "lack social graces." So they design a "mixer," an event where all the children are herded into the same room and given an opportunity to demonstrate convincingly that the adults are right (that the children have no social graces, that is). Their mere presence at the event damages their egos, since in itself it provides evidence that someone believes they are socially inept. But to make matters worse there inevitably are one or two perverse couples who dance, joke, and generally act in a socially "ept" way while the rest of the children stand around in the corners of the gym telling groups of their same-sex friends just how miserable they are. I am convinced that with the possible exception of the socially "ept" couples, "mixers" are more responsible than any other single factor (save perhaps acne) for the misery that accompanies adolescence. The fact that these painful and degrading rituals continue at least through the first year of college is ample testimony to the sponsors' essential sadism or warped memories of what adolescence was really like (choose one).

However, these ordeals are important experiences. They teach us to endure excruciating psychological pain and embarrassment and they communicate the importance of being able to "save face." Berk's analysis of adults' mixers (singles' dances) revealed eight typical face-saving communication strategies.

> DENIAL: "I'm not really here" or "I'm a sociologist doing research."
> REDEFINITION: "This really isn't so bad after all. I like lime sherbert punch."
> IMAGE ENHANCEMENT. TYPE A: "I came here with my friend Jimmy. He broke up with his girlfriend and needed to get out" or "I had six dates for tonight but decided to come give these poor folks a break." TYPE B: "I had to come (my parents/teacher/boss/minister made me")" or "I was kidnapped and forced to come" or "I'm lost, where am I?" or "I'm just leaving" or "I just got here, what's it like?"
> WITHDRAWING: "I'm above all this."
> ONE-DOWNING OTHERS: "These people are all ____" (fill in the blank with your favorite insulting adjective)."
> INTERNALIZATION: "Yep, I'm socially inept and I need this. Kick me, please."
> ALLIANCES: "How did *we* get into a place like this?"
> REVISING ONE'S SELF-CONCEPT: "I thought I needed this, but now I *know* I don't" or "Well, I'm socially adept now."[10]

The value of each of these strategies is that it allows people to rationalize and cope with undesirable circumstances created by their actions. In organizations, face-saving strategies allow employees to accept situations that violate their identities. If upwardly mobile employees find that they are "stuck" in dead-end jobs, they can manage their frustrations by *redefining* their current jobs as stimulating and rewarding, *withdrawing* from their work and concentrating on other aspects of their lives, *"one-downing"* other employees, and so on. These face-saving strategies allow people to adapt their images of themselves to the realities of their situations. But, unfortunately, they also may needlessly accept unproductive organizational roles.

Face-saving strategies can also be used to maintain or defend the image an employee has created in the minds of others. B. L. Ware and Wil Linkugel studied the strategies public figures use to respond to attacks made on their credibility, honesty, or integrity when they cannot ignore the charges lest they lose their carefully cultivated public images. Their responses often are presented as apologies but are designed to maintain their public images more than to apologize. There are four common ways to maintain one's image, each of which parallels some of Berk's face-saving strategies. People can use *denial*, by which they attempt to separate themselves from the action which led to the attack. They deny doing anything wrong, assert that they did not intend to make the error or to act improperly, or argue that they were the innocent victims of circumstances or other people. The second strategy is *bolstering*, in which the accused accepts the charges but attempts to overcome them by linking themselves to relationships, concepts, or objects that their audience values. An employee who states that "regardless of what you may think about this one mistake, you know that I've always been a loyal supervisor who has your best interests at heart" adopts a bolstering strategy.

In *differentiation* and *transcendence*, the accused persons attempt to give their audience a way of viewing the event which absolves them of blame. The new perspective may involve a change in time: "Wait to judge me until the quarterly reports are in" or "You have to understand that happened back in 1980 in order to realize that my decision was a good one." Or the new perspective may involve a different viewpoint: "Walk a mile in my shoes," or "I have to take a organizationwide (or very narrow) viewpoint when I make these decisions. You don't."[11]

These four strategies can be used by employees to maintain their images in the face of adverse events or errors. Shifting responsibility and changing perspectives allow employees to maintain their image of rationality, expertise, and competence in the face of the errors they inevitably will make. Bolstering can distract attention from specific, tangible events and perhaps even improve one's image. But all face-saving strategies involve presenting information to others which alters their interpretations of events. To maintain their images employees must have access to and control of valuable information, and they must understand the strategies that can be used to save face. It is inevitable that employees develop personae. The decison they must make is whether they should allow their image to emerge through accident or as the result of careful strategic communication.

DEVELOPING MESSAGE-CREATING AND MESSAGE-SENDING SKILLS

Becoming *rhetorically sensitive*, developing *strategic listening skills,* and *managing images* are important aspects of strategic communication. Each approach allows employees to analyze situations and present themselves to others in appropriate ways. But they are important for an additional reason. They provide employees with the information and insight that are necessary prerequisites for constructing strategically appropriate messages. Situational anaysis provides guidelines about what to say and how to say it. One's persona influences what one can say and still be influential and how one can say it. Messages are inextricably linked to their sources in the minds of listeners. The credibility of a message affects the ethos of its author, just as the persona of the author affects listeners' interpretations of the credibility of the message. This interplay can be as blatant as the tendency for people to discount even obviously true statements when they are made by untrustworthy supervisors. Or it can be as subtle as the tendency to believe some parts of a message because it is consistent with the hearer's image of the speaker and discount other parts because "it's not like so-and-so to say this." Messages are credible and effective in direct proportion to the (1) propriety of the *topoi* of which they are composed; (2) their internal characteristics; and (3) the relationships among the topoi, the internal characteristics, and the persona.

What is a Topos and Why Would I Want One?

Rhetorical communication, and thus organizational communication, involves the giving of reasons. Employees inevitably need to explain their recommendations, proposals, and positions on issues and actions. Explanations come in two forms, *justifications* (which are presented in public before an action is taken, a policy is implemented, or an issue is resolved) and *rationalizations* (which are presented after a decision has been made or an act has taken place). Both forms of explanation are essentially the same. They are presented by a persona to an audience through some medium of communication and consist of reasons arranged in some kind of order. In the best of times employees carefully choose the reasons, structure, medium, and persona. In the worst of times they do not. Explanations have the most favorable impact, on both the proposals being advocated and the persona of the person who presents them, when they include the kinds of reasons the audience will find acceptable.

The construction of messages begins with a search for acceptable reasons. In his *Rhetoric*, Aristotle observed that there are two kinds of places in which acceptable reasons can be found.[12] The first place is in the assumptions that people hold about all of life, the beliefs common to all areas of thought, for example, anything that has a beginning has an end; if excellent examples of something exist, so do mediocre examples; if the less probable of two events has taken place, the more probable also has taken place; or if certain predictable events followed a person's actions, then the person must have intended those results. The second place (really a group of places) is in the assumptions which characterize a specific area of thought. If a speaker plans to discuss tariff policies, the speaker can discover the kinds of reasons which generally are used to justify actions taken on matters of trade and commerce. Whenever people begin to plan a message, their ability to discover acceptable reasons will depend in part on their knowledge of where those reasons can be found. The terms Aristotle used for these places was *topoi*.

In this century Perelman and Olbrechts-Tyteca tried to update Aristotle's concept. Like Aristotle they observed that there are two different kinds of starting points for the discovery of acceptable reasons. The first group contains the assumptions acceptable to all people, the reasons which concern those things believed to be real and true (facts, values, and unquestioned beliefs). The myths of organizational rationality that were discussed in Chapter 6 are examples of this kind of reason. That decision making should be "rational" is a presumption universally accepted, at least in Western culture and Western organizations. The second group of reasons involve that which is preferred by a particular group of people. Some reasons are superior to others because they are perceived as being normal, precedented, and/or acceptable within a particular culture. The argument "that's what Susan believed when she founded this company and it's what we've believed ever since" is an instance of this kind of reason. Employees can discover the reasons that can be used effectively in their organizations by paying attention to and categorizing the justifications expressed by other employees.[13]

Compiling a list of acceptable reasons is a very straightforward process. Employees merely listen to reason-giving communication and take note of what arguments are proposed and what potentially available arguments are avoided. If they notice that rationalizations often are based on statistical data of a certain type, they can hypothesize that this kind of statistical data is a place from which they can draw reasons for other policies or actions. Conversely, if they find that statistical data *never* are offered as a reason or that when they are used they rarely have any impact on decisions, employees can hypothesize that this is not a viable place from which to draw reasons. For example, there sometimes is a mistrust of statistical data among members of "humanities" departments of educational organizations. Even when the nature of a decision makes statistical reasoning logically acceptable (for instance, basing course offerings on assessments of past student enrollment), the beliefs of the decision makers make it an unacceptable kind of justification. Although employees can point to enrollment patterns as a reason in these situations, to be effective they must be able to define enrollment patterns in nonquantitative terms. By cataloging acceptable and unacceptable reasons, employees eventually can develop a *hypothetical* typology of possible and impossible justifications for their organizations.

Now, *hypothetical* is the key word in the previous sentence. At first glance one would assume that when employees start constructing their own messages, they would choose from the list of possible (successful) reasons and avoid using reasons from the unacceptable list. However, for three different reasons the selection process is not that simple. First, the items in the first list may not be salient in all situations. Perceptive employees will notice that some of the acceptable reasons are used in some kinds of situations and that others are used in other situations. They may, for example, notice that moral concerns regarding fairness, equity, and honesty have been used successfully in personnel decisions but not in budget decisions. Although fairness-related justifications might not be rejected if offered during discussions of budgets, they will not have any force, any impact. In other cases, the situation may require some temporary adjustments in the lists. It was indicated in Chapter 6 that organizations sometimes make decisions and then frantically search for rationalizations for them. Sometimes they will find that none of the reasons in their "acceptable" list can be used to justify the decision. They then must turn to the usually unacceptable reasons, choose one, and create some plausible explanation of why it is acceptable *in this case and only in this case,* for example, "We *never* want to eliminate American jobs, but in this case union greed has forced us to move our operation to Taiwan. But we'll never do it again and wouldn't have done it this time except that. . . ." The point is that (1) the actions of employees in organizations determine which reasons are acceptable and which are unacceptable, (2) they sometimes change their minds, and (3) naive employees can get caught in the middle of the shift if they are not careful.

Second, the items in the acceptable list may not be logically consistent with one another. "We must hold our market share" and "we must not overextend our production capacity" both may be acceptable reasons for an action. But one probably ought not to include both of them in the same message, at least not in the same sentence. "Logical consistency" is a universal value in Western culture and appeals to it can be used to discredit almost any seemingly inconsistent message.

Finally, employees need to express some kinds of reasons even when they know that doing so will have little or no impact. Their persona may require them to do so; the myths which define their organizational culture may require *someone* to do so; universal values of representation or participation may dictate that a particular reason must be considered. For example, decision-making episodes in educational organizations almost always seem to include the argument that "we must consider the needs of the students" whether the decision makers intend to consider those needs or not. For symbolic reasons *someone* (usually those who have created the image of being "student-oriented") has to say this, even if no one intends to pay any attention to it.

The entire matrix of factors which comprise a rhetorical situation determines which items on a hypothetical list of justifications can be employed successfully. At times employees' personae require them to use some reasons while preventing them from using others. At other times the history of the organization necessitates very narrow constraints; at still other times these precedents will be irrelevant. Arguments and reasons are neither good nor bad based on some a priori criteria. They either have force in a particular situation or they do not. Naive employees often respond to reasons given by others by thinking "My God, they're stupid." (Exceptionally naive ones may even say so in public.) Strategically sensitive employees respond to these "stupid" reasons by asking themselves

1. How do others respond to this reason?
2. Why does it succeed or fail in this situation?
3. Why was it presented and what impact might it have had in other situations?
4. When, if ever, might I be able to use it effectively?

Choosing Among Message Characteristics

One of the truisms of modern communication theory is that the form of a message and its content mutually influence one another. For example, research on persuasive communication has indicated that (1) audiences generally value and respond more favorably to messages which they believe are "rational," and (2) in general they are unable to differentiate "rational" arguments from well-organized, clearly presented arguments.[14] Any good public speaking book (or course) will summarize general guidelines for constructing messages.[15]

1. Messages should be expressed in language which is clear, accurate, precise, concise, and concrete (with the level of each factor determined by the topic and the capacities of the audience).

2. Messages should be organized so that main ideas (topics or key themes) are easily identifiable, and supporting or component ideas are presented, explained, and linked to the main ideas.

3. Messages should be arranged in a format which (a) is familiar to and easily understood by the audience (in our culture, chronological, problem-solution, spatial, and topical formats are most readily understood), (b) emphasizes important ideas and deemphasizes other ideas, and (c) provides smooth and clear transistions between ideas.

Messages presented in organizational situations should also (a) support the image of the organization and its members, (b) be appropriately ambiguous, and (c) be presented in an appropriate mode.

Sometimes it is difficult to maintain a positive image of an organization, although employees usually are creative enough to do so. After contracts are signed, even the most bitter labor-management negotiations are depicted as difficult struggles between cooperative negotiators whose common goal was reaching a mutually beneficial outcome. Boards of directors make unanimous recommendations to stockholders; personnel committees always seem to arrive at a consensus; and so on. One of the greatest challenges facing employees is constructing messages which both advocate the positions they prefer (and which meet their own interests) and perpetuate their organization's image. It can be done, but only with a great deal of care.

One way to manage the advocacy-image conflict is by creating and sending messages which are appropriately ambiguous. The archetype of a strategically ambiguous message is one which says, in effect, "making a good decision on this issue is more important to this organization than pretending that we all agree and get along" but does so in a way that will keep anyone other than insiders from knowing that that is what has been said. One of the marvelous features of communication is that people can communicate a great deal of information without saying anything explicit. Items that are omitted often say more than items that are included. Messages can *imply* many things without ever saying them. Consider a quasi-organizational example of ambiguity, the letter of recommendation (see Figure 9.3). Strategic ambiguity provides people

FIGURE 9.3   Stated and Implied Meanings in Fictional Recommendation Letters

Statement	*Implied Meaning*
He is particularly well suited for people-related jobs like tending bar or being a steward or social director on a cruise ship.	He is flighty, irresponsible, and has spent most of his career partying.
Objective measures suggest that she is capable of mastering and retaining substantial amounts of information.	She does well on the Mickey Mouse objective tests that I give because she can memorize and then forget vast amounts of trivia. But ask her to think, and, well. . . .
He will bring a dimension of thoughtfulness to your deliberations.	He is a real pain in the neck, and disagrees with everything regardless of its merit.
She is punctual, has excellent penmanship, and completes assignments on time.	Honest, I don't remember this person (or do remember her and couldn't think of anything to say).

with the ability to violate images and expectations without overtly doing so. But it works only when both the sender and receiver are willing to tolerate ambiguity and when both of them understand its value and use.

Another way to manage the advocacy-image conflict is by the selective use of different modes of communication. The relative features of written and oral communication were discussed in Chapter 1. One of those differences involves the permanence of the message. Because written messages are more permanent, people respond differently to them. Written messages also allow employees to document their actions, providing a permanent justification. Put in typical (but blunt) organizational terms, written messages allow people to "cover their asses." Politically sensitive situations or actions can be made manageable by requesting written interpretations from others. Then, if one's actions are ever questioned a document can be produced which will shift the blame to someone else. But the strategic use of documents is possible only if employees remember four facts of organizational life:

1. Documents can be used by anyone, supervisor and subordinate alike.

2. They destroy the ambiguity which is often needed to make organizations function smoothly and which gives employees adequate discretion and freedom of action.

3. Their existence must be kept as secret as possible and their use must be solely under the employee's control (if you're going to make White House tapes you'd better be darned sure that no one else gets their hands on them).

4. They can often be mistaken for strategies of job enlargement or job enrichment (when people tell you that they're enlarging your *responsibilities,*

a word that means both "duties" and "blame," they may be telling you the truth).

Messages need to be constructed so that they perpetuate the images of the organization and its members and the persona of the communicator. They should be appropriately ambiguous and communciated through the proper mode. And they must be sent to the right people at the right time. Many of the communication breakdowns examined in Chapter 3 resulted from information being needlessly distorted, delayed, and misrouted. Employees have to understand the roles other employees play in the organization well enough to be able to anticipate and meet their communication needs. This is especially true of people who are more powerful than they are. Supervisors want their subordinates to keep them informed, help them anticipate and prevent problems, give them important information, and spare them from trivial details.[16] Fulfilling these demands forces subordinates to (1) filter information in a way that corresponds to their supervisors' needs and (2) highlight significant items while deemphasizing less important details. The primary criterion for determining which items of information should be transmitted and highlighted is the supervisors', not the subordinates', role in the organization.

CONCLUSION

The objective of Chapters 8 and 9 was to outline briefly the processes, problems, and strategies of employees in their efforts to make sense out of and respond appropriately to their situations at work. Hopefully, these chapters have created the impression that there are no simple techniques, no cookbook recipes, for successfully managing organizational situations. Although some general guidelines do seem to hold true in most situations, their *exigences*, *constraints* and *audiences* are so complicated and so different that the only sensible advice that can be given to employees is (1) look for indicators of certain recurring problems and (2) analyze the situations you face in certain ways before choosing to adopt any particular strategy.

The most important concept discussed in these chapters was the principle of the *comic* and *tragic frames of reference.* Through communication, members of organizations create situations, develop interpretations, and confront limitations. Their ways of making sense out of their environments can either provide them with productive, stable guidelines for acting or trap them in outworn patterns of communication. Much as Max Weber's theory of ideal types was the organizing principle for Unit I of this book, the concepts of situational adaptation and comic versus tragic frames of reference will be the central organizing principles for the remaining chapters Unit II. Employees are able to cope with conflict, stress, and problems related to sex-role stereotypes largely to the extent that they can adapt strategically to organizational situations and avoid becoming enmeshed in tragic patterns of communication.

Notes

1. Roderick Hart and Don Burks, "Rhetorical Sensitivity and Social Interaction," *Speech Monographs*, 39 (1972), 75–91; Roderick Hart, Robert Carlson, and William Eadie, "Attitudes Toward Communication and the Assessment of Rhetorical Sensitivity," *Communication Monographs*, 47 (1980), 1–22.

2. Northrop Frye, *Anatomy of Criticism* (Princeton, N.J.: Princeton University Press, 1957).

3. Paul Watzlawick, Janet Beavin, and Don Jackson, *Pragmatics of Human Communication* (New York: W. W. Norton, 1967).

4. Chaim Perelman and L. Olbrechts-Tyteca, *New Rhetoric* (Notre Dame, Ind.: Notre Dame University Press, 1970); Chaim Perelman, *The Idea of Justice and the Problem of Argument* (London: Routledge and Kegan Paul, 1963).

5. Victor Thompson, *Modern Organizations* (New York: Knopf, 1963).

6. E. Mayfield, "The Selection Interview—A Reevaluation of Published Research" *Personal Psychology*, 17 (1964), 240–246; E. Mayfield, "Summary of Research on the Selection Interview Since 1964," *Personnel Psychology*, 22 (1969), 391–413.

7. Irving Goffman, *The Presentation of Self in Everyday Life* (New York: Doubleday, 1959); Thompson, *Modern Organizations*.

8. Jeffrey Pfeffer, *Organizations and Organization Theory* (Marshfield, Mass.: Pitman Publishing, 1983.

9. These ideas were introduced by Goffman in "On Face Work," *Psychiatry*, 18 (1955), 213–231. Also see Bernard Berk, "Face Saving at the Singles' Dance," *Social Problems*, 24 (1977), 530–544.

10. Ibid. The categories are Berk's; some of the examples are mine.

11. B. L. Ware and W. A. Linkugel, "They Spoke in Defense of Themselves," *The Quarterly Journal of Speech*, 59 (1973), 273–283.

12. See Aristotle's *Rhetoric*, especially in Book II, and Perelman and Olbrechts-Tyteca, *New Rhetoric*.

13. This brief description is imprecise at one point. When Perelman and Olbrechts-Tyteca discuss loci which are universally acceptable they do not really mean to everyone. The "universal audience" is a fictional entity, not the summation of every living human. It is a speaker's perception of what "everybody knows to be true," and in that sense reflects his or her internalization of the values of the culture.

14. Judee Burgoon and Michael Burgoon, "Message Strategies in Influence Attempts," in *Communication and Behavior*, ed. G. Hanneman and W. McEwen (Reading, Mass.: Addison-Wesley, 1975).

15. A standard source is Edward Rogge and James Ching, *Advanced Public Speaking* (New York: Holt, Rinehart and Winston, 1966).

16. Cal Downs and Charles Conrad, "Effective Subordinancy," *Journal of Business Communication* 19 (1982), 27–38.

10

Communication and the Management of Organizational Conflict

THE PHASES AND BASES OF ORGANIZATIONAL CONFLICT

COMMUNICATION STRATEGIES: THE DYNAMICS OF OVERT
  CONFLICT

ESCALATION AND TRAGIC CONFLICTS
Forms of Escalation
Bases of Escalation

CONFLICT: AFTERMATH

One of the unspoken goals of this book is to suggest that there are very few constant and unchanging "truths" about human action, organizations, or organizational communication. When "truths" have been proposed, they generally have been so abstract that they are only indirectly linked to practical guidelines about handling everyday situations. Knowing, or to be more precise, "believing" that humans are choice-making beings who actively create, interpret, and respond to their perceptions of the "realities" they face does not give one step-by-step formulas for making it through a rainy Monday morning. Understanding that organizational decision making is rarely "rational" does little to help people cope with repeated errors on their credit card bills. Knowing that bureaucratic organizations inherently rely on written communication provides little solace while one is in the process of completing, in quadruplicate, a request for a postage stamp.

However, some more practical "truths" have been discovered and explained. Distortion of communication does occur and can be anticipated and compensated for. Participation in decision making has predictable effects on employees' attitudes and actions and can be employed in ways which minimize its negative side effects. This chapter will examine another practical reality of organizations: Disagreement and conflict are inevitable aspects of working relationships, and the need to manage conflicts is always with each of us.

For many years researchers and theorists viewed organizational conflict as inherent evil. Conflicts revealed a weakness in the organization, a flaw in its design, operation, or communicative processes.[1] Conflicts needed to be "resolved"; that is, their sources had to be discovered and eliminated and peace and stability had to be returned to the organization. Like its close relative *power*, the word *conflict* conjured up images of otherwise equitable societies and rational organizations "gone bad."

However, like modern theories of organizational power, contemporary views of conflict present a quite different view. Organizational conflicts are inevitable. Conflicts are neither inherently good nor intrinsically bad, although they do vary in their *productiveness* and *destructiveness*. Conflicts which are relatively productive for the organization as a whole may be highly destructive for some of the individuals who are involved and highly productive for other participants. Similarly, episodes which are disruptive and damaging to the organization may be productive for many of the participants. Organizational conflicts are "good" or "bad" depending on three considerations: (1) the *bases* of the conflict, (2) the *dynamics* of their development, and (3) their *outcomes*.

THE PHASES AND BASES OF ORGANIZATIONAL CONFLICT

Typically when people hear the term *organizational conflict* they imagine executives shouting at one another in a boardroom, giant oligopolies making bids to purchase a majority share of a competitor's stock, or for the more fanciful of us, secret meetings on foggy nights where technological secrets are exchanged for chalets on the Riviera. Although such overt and sometimes hostile confrontations are part of organizational conflict, they are only one part. Whether in friendships, marriages, or organizations, conflicts are *based* on one or more of a recognizable group of perceptions which change as the conflict progresses through its different phases.

Theorist Louis Pondy has developed one of a number of quite similar depictions of the phases and bases of organizational conflict. Phase 1 is *latent* conflict, in which two or more parties must both cooperate with one another and compete for certain desired rewards. Almost anything can be a desired reward: tangible objects like awards and bonuses; or intangible factors like status, respect, autonomy, and self-esteem. People may fight battles over the ability to control rewards or resources or over any of the bases of power discussed in Chapter 7. In fact, anything employees could want or need can be the source of a latent conflict, providing that one party perceives that competition with the other(s) is necessary in order to obtain it.

Grounds for conflict exist whenever people are involved in *interdependent* and *interactive* relationships. When employees' roles are interdependent, there are many topics over which conflicts can arise. When people rarely interact with one another, they have few opportunities to fight. However, the objective features of conflicts, the dependencies and potential areas of friction that an outside observer might see in a given working relationship, may be very different from the employees' perceptions of them. Of course, this distinction between perceptions and "reality" is not a new concept. Much of this book has argued that even through the "objective reality" of organizational situations may provide the parameters within which employees act, the perceived reality that employees create through their communication with each other influences their choices.

Stage 2 in Pondy's model is *perceived* conflict. This stage exists when one or more parties believes that their situation has the characteristics of *interdependence* and *incompatibility*. Perceived conflict can exist when latent conflict does not, as when siblings fight over a serving of rapidly melting ice-cream which is so large that they could not possibly consume all of it. There is no objective reason for conflict in this situation, although they believe that their interests are incompatible. Also, latent conflict can exist without perceived conflict, as when siblings are given a seemingly but not actually uncomsumable mound of ice-cream. This distinction becomes important when the role of communication in conflict is considered. In the former situation, "improved communication" would help the childen understand one another's needs and goals, making the conflict more manageable (as in "I can't possibly eat half of this. Can you?") In the latter situation, improved communication would transform what is at least a temporally cooperative situation into a competitive, conflictful one (as in "I'm gonna' want more than half of this. Are you?") In organizations, perceived conflict exists without latent conflict if employees believe that someone else is an "enemy" when their interests really do coincide. Latent conflict exists without perceived conflict if people choose to ignore or overlook minor day-to-day frictions of if they decide to concentrate so completely on routine or easily resolved disagreements that they suppress major problems.

Perhaps more than any other single factor, employees' perceptions influence what happens during conflicts and what effects conflicts have on organizations. Figure 10.1 summarizes a number of different ways in which employees may perceive conflict. If they define a situation as "all or nothing," see only a small range of alternatives as acceptable solutions, or believe that the difference of opinion has a strong moral or ethical dimension, they will tend to impose their wills on others, perceive others as hostile and untrustworthy, and adopt a narrow and inflexible course of action during any overt conflicts.[2]

In addition to perceiving conflicts in different ways, employees also differ in their perceptions of how conflicts ought to be managed. Kenneth Thomas developed a model of five "typical" *orientations* to conflict, although he recognized that an infinite number of possible orientations exists (see Figure 10.2).

FIGURE 10.1 Defining Conflict

Definitions Which Make Conflicts Easier to Manage Productively	*Definitions Which Make Conflicts Difficult to Manage Productively*
1. "Mixed motive" (or non-zero-sum) definitions: All parties perceive that they can obtain desired outcomes without the other losing the same amount of reward.	1. Zero-sum: Parties perceive that whatever one gains the other loses. The outcome will either grant them complete success or complete failure.
2. Empathic definition of the issue: Parties perceive the issue from both their own and the other parties' perspectives.	2. Egocentric definition of the issue: Parties perceive the issue only from their own frame of reference.
3. Broad contextualization of the issue: Parties search for underlying concerns which places the overt issue in a broad, organizational context.	3. Narrow focus on a single issue and its immediate effects.
4. "Commercial" issue: The issue is defined as problem-centered.	4. "Ideological" issue: The conflict is defined as a moral struggle between forces of good and evil.
5. Large number of possible solutions are available.	5. Small number of alternatives are available.

FIGURE 10.2 Orientations to Conflict: Continuum

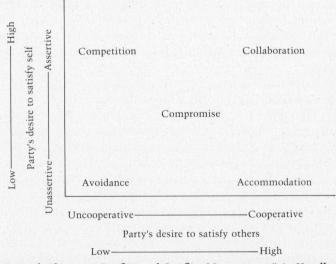

Adapted from Kenneth Thomas, "Conflict and Conflict Management", in *Handbook of Industrial and Organizational Psychology*, ed. Marvin Dunnette (Chicago: Rand-McNally, 1976).

AVOIDANCE: Believing that unassertive and uncooperative behavior is the best approach, either because the issues are not worth fighting about, the potential costs of open confrontation are greater than the potential gains, or the issue will "go away" if it is left alone. Requires little communication.

ACCOMMODATION: Acquiescing to the perceived goals of the other(s). Requires little communication.

COMPROMISE: Searching for a resolution which satisfies both parties in part. In our society compromise generally means "splitting the difference" on a fifty-fifty basis. Requires some degree of willingness to sacrifice goals, some communication, and some degree of assertiveness.

COMPETITION: Seeking to dominate others and impose one's preferences on them. Involves some communication, though usually not as much as compromise.

COLLABORATION: All parties believing that they should actively and assertively seek a mutually acceptable solution and being willing to spend large amounts of time and energy to reach such an outcome.[3]

The orientation an employee takes depends on a number of factors, the most important of which seems to be the desire or tolerance for communicating with others. As Chapter 11 will explain in detail, both the anticipation of communication and the act of communicating are stressful, especially for some people. For them, the less assertive orientations—avoidance, accommodation, and compromise—are the most attractive because they promise to minimize prolonged or tense communication. The quality of the interpersonal relationship between parties—the legacy of past interactions, current feelings toward one another, and anticipation of future interactions—also seems to influence their orientations.[4] These interpersonal factors may operate implicitly, as when one party accommodates a co-worker without even telling that person, who is also a friend. Or they may be quite explicit, as when one party decides to support the other on a current issue to make it easier to gain that person's support for a more important issue that will come up at a later date.

The orientations taken by employees are important because they influence the ease with which conflicts can be managed. When the parties are oriented in complementary ways conflicts tend to be more productive. For instance, if two parties have misunderstood one another's communication or goals and have good reasons to cooperate, and both prefer collaborative approaches, their conflicts can be managed productively. They will discover mutual, important goals; learn to understand each other better; and resolve their differences. But if they really do have incompatible goals, or if one prefers a competitive orientation, face-to-face, open conflicts will tend to degenerate into power struggles or escalate into intense moral confrontations. If two parties have accommodative orientations and real differences, they will tend repeatedly to ignore the problems and over time may build up a large reservoir of unexpressed hostility, which will make it difficult to manage conflicts in the future.

In addition, some orientations are appropriate in some situations and inappropriate in others. And each orientation has characteristic strengths and weaknesses (see Table 10.1). Because the potential effectiveness of different orientations depends so much on the characteristics of specific situations, the most recent focus of research has been on developing contingency theories of conflict management.[5]

Phase 3 is *felt conflict,* the point at which the parties begin to personalize perceived conflict. Differences of opinion and interests, which once were only vaguely perceived, begin to be focused on and defined, and parties start to see their situation as "me against them." Internal tensions and frustrations begin to crystallize around specific, defined issues, which take on exaggerated importance because they symbolize the parties' feelings about their relationship with each other. During this phase, employees start to make choices about how they will *define* the conflict, how they will *orient* themselves toward it, what *communication strategies* they will use to confront it, and what *range of possible solutions* they will be willing to accept. In short, they establish the plot lines within which the conflict will be played out. These plot lines have three important characteristics: (1) They are *constraining,* making it harder for employees to maintain a degree of flexibility and rhetorical sensitivity. (2) They are *private* and can only be inferred by other parties. As in a poker game, in which no one *knows* what choices the other players have made, only educated guesses can be made. Often these guesses are incorrect and thus make it even more difficult to manage conflicts productively. (3) Plot lines are capable of being *altered without loss of face.* Because the parties' choices have not yet been communicated openly to one another, no one has taken positions to which they must remain committed. This is the last point before patterns of communication begin to influence conflicts and decision making, and it is often the final opportunity for the parties to use potentially productive communication strategies.

The felt conflict phase also is the point at which the different faces of organizational power are most important. In Chapter 7 it was explained why overt, open conflicts reveal only part of the power relationship. The most potent face of power is composed of the hidden processes through which employees make choices about who to challenge openly and when, where, and over what issues. This choice-making process is the key characteristic of the felt conflict phase. Employees first choose between openly confronting others and accepting the situation as it is. These decisions are influenced by their general orientations to conflict and the quality of the relationships they have with the other people who might become involved. But the choices also depend on the power relationship perceived by the employees. Open confrontation is a very risky choice. It can alienate powerful people and, if the employees lose the battle, may reduce their status in the eyes of others. Both of these effects reduce their organizational power. But confrontation also may have productive results. Winning battles or arguing positions effectively can enhance employees' power and self-esteem, lead the organization to make decisions which can benefit both the organization and their standing in it, and dissipate destructive emotions and pent-up hostilities. But provoking or participating in open confrontations is wise only when the potential gains outweigh the probable risks.

TABLE 10.1 Orientations to Conflict: Characteristics

Orientation	Definition	Strengths	Weaknesses
Collaboration (also known as *problem solving*)	Seeking resolution through face-to-face confrontation to find a mutually acceptable definition of and solution to the problem; most appropriate when there are common goals which cannot be achieved without the cooperation of all parties	Effective when the conflict stems from communication breakdowns or misunderstanding; when used repeatedly establishes norms which support collaborative problem solving	Time-consuming and inappropriate when there are legitimate differences among the parties or when they have different goals or values
Avoidance	Includes withdrawal and suppression; sometimes can be coupled with expansion of the rewards available	Natural, simple response to conflict; avoids labeling parties as winner and loser, thus reducing the negative legacy that sometimes accompanies conflicts	Usually provides no productive resolution of differences; a temporary expedient, even when combined with expansion of available rewards
Accommodation (also known as *smoothing*)	Plays down differences while emphasizing common features; responds to emotions which accompany conflicts while ignoring the base; includes compromise	Exploits cooperative elements which exist in all conflicts	Temporary expedient; leaves legacy of unresolved issues, unmanaged emotions; outcome depends more on relative power of the parties than on the legitimacy of their complaints or wisdom of the solution
Competition (also called *forcing* or *autocratic*)	Solution imposed by most powerful party	Effective when members recognize and accept power relationship; time efficient	Fails to treat base of conflict; temporary, with residue of unmanaged emotions; fails to address real problems

245

Accepting a situation is a viable response when the risks of confrontation are far greater than the potential benefits and when the employees have not so completely personalized the issue that acquiescing will damage their self-esteem.

Employees make two more specific decisions during the felt conflict phase: They adopt objectives for the conflict (decide on the range of outcomes they are willing to accept) and make preliminary decisions about the communicative strategies they will employ. Both choices are important because they guide and constrain subsequent choices. If the employee chooses to accept only total victory or to be aggressive from the outset of the episode, the probability that the conflict will escalate is increased. For example, historians' analyses of U.S. strategy during World War II indicate that once President Roosevelt announced we would accept only the complete surrender of Japan, we were committed to use every weapon at our disposal to obtain that outcome. Consequently, once the atomic bomb was developed, it was almost inevitable that it would be used against the Japanese.

To summarize, the three preliminary stages of organizational conflicts are important because they establish the plot lines within which the conflict will be played out. *Definitions, orientations, and choices* influence the course the conflict will take, the communicative strategies that should be used to manage it, and eventually, the degree to which the conflict is productive or destructive.

COMMUNICATION STRATEGIES: THE DYNAMICS OF OVERT CONFLICTS

Sometimes all the potential parties to a conflict choose to accept the situation as it is and never raise the issue in public. When these choices are made, communication will have little immediate effect. Its role in these conflicts stems from its impact on employees' perceptions that a certain set of risks, potential gains, and power relationships exist. When one or more parties choose to express openly their felt conflict, communication becomes crucial. The purpose of this section is to survey research and suggest guidelines for managing overt conflicts through strategic communication.

The study of conflict in general and organizational conflict in particular has had a long and detailed history, but a relatively small proportion of this research has examined the communication strategies participants use during overt conflicts. This gap is somewhat surprising because it long has been recognized that episodes of conflict must be understood as communicative processes. Orientations, definitions, and choices are significant because they create the parameters which limit and guide communication during open conflicts. But conflicts are made up of completed cycles of response and counter response. Once they begin, their development and outcomes are not within the control of any one participant.[6] And, a conflict cycle tends to have a momentum all its own. Participants begin to make choices about how they will respond (communicate), based in part on the communication strategies used by the other parties. They base predictions about how the others will react to the different strategies they might use on their interpretation of the communication of other parties. The most important aspect of conflict *interactions* is their tendency to develop into self-perpetuating and self-reinforcing cycles of response and counter response which escalate beyond the participants' control. Conflict cycles are made up of communication strategies, and understanding these strategies and the dynamics of communication in conflict is an important first step in being able to adapt appropriately to conflict interactions.

Table 10.2 summarizes the communication strategies that most often have been observed in interpersonal, marital, group and organizational conflicts.[7] The first group of strategies allows parties to *avoid* a divisive issue and to manage a potentially escalating conflict. Delaying or procrastinating can be overt ("I don't have time to talk about it now") or more subtle. Employees can manipulate procedural rules to delay or avoid sustained confrontations. For instance, they can refer an issue to a committee or manipulate agendas so that it is excluded or considered so late in a session that time constraints force a superficial judgment. Or they can focus the discussion so completely on establishing proper rules of interaction that the issue itself is never addressed. American and Vietnamese negotiators argued for months about the shape of the bargaining table, proper display of flags, and rules for speaking times and turns. Although these topics were important for symbolic reasons (round tables symbolize the equal status of the participants; rectangular tables do not), discussion of them served to delay the consideration of key differences. Often one or more parties refuse to admit that there is an issue between them, either through statements like "I really think we basically are in agreement on this" or transcendence to a level where agreement does exist: "I know we both have the welfare of the students at heart." Sometimes parties regress to childlike tactics or quietly make commitments to "let this one go by but get the bastard in the end." Some of these regressive tactics are relatively rare in organizations, but others are quite typical. Commitments to get revenge, silent obsession about felt conflicts, and pouting all seem to be far too common among adults and children alike.

Just as an avoidant orientation is sometimes appropriate, avoidant strategies can be quite productive. If issues really are trivial, potential parties lack the communication skills necessary to prevent destructive escalations, circumstances surrounding the issue are likely to change, potential losses from an open conflict outweigh possible gains, or there is insufficient time to work through the issue adequately, avoidance may be the best response. However, avoidant strategies merely delay confrontations; they do not resolve differences. The employees who chose to raise the issue openly are frustrated by people who respond with avoidant strategies. They have taken risks without an opportunity to realize any gains. Consequently, avoidant strategies may only generate hostilities which will come out in conflicts over other issues, thus making it more difficult to manage them productively.

TABLE 10.2 Communication Strategies in Conflicts

Structuring Strategies	Confrontive Strategies	Avoidant Strategies
1. Definition of Issue Initiating focal or new issues Focusing issues through repitition or clarification Modifying the scope of the issue (enlarging, narrowing, or fog-ging) Attaching emotional labels to the conflict or to the positions taken 2. Establishment of Evaluative Criteria Overt Exclusion of alternative criteria 3. Manipulation of Relationships Bribery Altercasting Predicting self-feelings Altruism Appeals to guilt	1. Coercion: Overt Displays of Power Formal rank Coalitions Expertise 2. Coercion: Threats or Promises 3. Personalization Moral accusations Ad homineum Revelation of secrets 4. Toughness Pure form Reformed sinner	1. Delay/Procrastination Manipulating procedures "Putting off" communication Focusing on rules of interaction 2. Regression 3. Commitments to Revenge 4. Refusing to Admit Existence of Conflict

The second group of strategies serves to structure conflicts.[8] Because conflict situations are so ambiguous and complicated and because people often become uncertain about how to act in stressful situations, employees may become defensive and begin to communicate in ways which lead to escalation. Consequently, communication which helps structure a conflict and reduce its ambiguity can help the parties move toward a productive solution and avoid a destructive escalation. There are three forms of structuring strategies. First, some of them *define* the issues that will be discussed. By initiating discussions of some issues and not others, by focusing the group's attention on a particular issue by repeating or clarifying it, or by fogging an issue (commenting on part of a complex issue in order to divert attention away from other parts), parties give structure to the conflict. Each structuring strategy is potentially available to every party. They are strategic because they limit the range of responses that the other participants perceive as being legitimate and appropriate and thereby affect their choices.

However, as suggested in Chapters 6 and 8, structuring strategies are used most successfully by powerful employees. The extra credibility given to powerful people affords them with an exceptional opportunity to define and redefine conflicts. People *listen* to powerful people and generally act as if they perceive situations in the same ways.[9] When situations are complex and ambiguous, as is the case in almost all organizational conflicts, it is very difficult to provide a "rational" reason for rejecting a powerful person's use of a clarifying strategy.

Power is related to structuring strategies in a second way. If a party adopts structuring strategies congruent with that person's sources or bases of power, the likelihood that the strategy will succeed is enhanced. People whose power is based on their financial expertise can define issues in financial terms; participants with high levels of "position power" can broaden issues by taking an organizationwide perspective or narrow them by asserting that "this is a purchasing problem"; and so on. It is probable that the rest of the participants will accept that structuring and discuss the issue on grounds which favor the parties with the greatest influence. Financial issues are examined on financial grounds, allowing financial experts to dominate the deliberations legitimately because of their expertise.[10]

Power also is related to the second kind of structuring strategy, *establishing evaluative criteria*. Criteria for decisions are not imposed on a conflict; they emerge through the use of structuring strategies. Consider a promotion decision: Subordinate X has an excellent record. Supervisors Y, Z, and Q like her and want to see her promoted. But Supervisor B, with whom X would work most closely if promoted, although recognizing that she is quite capable, is threatened by her and wants to block the promotion. B must find a way to get the group to base its decision on criteria which will reduce X's chance of being promoted. To do so, he must eliminate past performance as a criterion because X's record is good. This can be done rather easily, either by highlighting X's few errors, and defining the new position as one which *absolutely* demands the attribute(s) that X's errors indicate she lacks, or by arguing that the new position is so fundamentally different from X's current position that her past record is irrelevant. But B still needs to create a reason for rejecting X. Since "personality" criteria generally are seen as legitimate for all upper-level positions, they may give B the key that he needs. But since X, Y, and Q like X, not just any personality characteristic will do. So B decides to argue that being "a team player" is the most important characteristic for this particular position. Since "being a team player" is a legitimate criterion, since B has a more legitimate reason to be concerned about it than do the other supervisors (because X would be joining B's "team"), and since the concept is almost impossible to define, B can argue that X does not meet this most important criterion. To support his argument, all he has to do is recount an instance or two when X disagreed with some other employee. Once the criterion is presented and the example is produced, Y, Z, and Q have few responses available. If they disagree with any of B's arguments, *they* violate the team player criterion in the most offensive way—by trying to force B to accept someone on his team that he does not want. The point of this not-entirely-mythical example is that structuring strategies *work* because they leave opponents no legitimate, overt response. They may not lead to optimal outcomes, but they often do lead to the outcomes preferred by powerful employees.

The third and final group of structuring strategies involves *redefining relationships*. Bribery, "altercasting" (asserting that "good" or "wise" or "evil" or "stupid" people would agree or disagree with me on this issue), predicting others' responses to certain actions ("you'll feel good, or guilty, or will respect yourself in the morning"), or appealing to interpersonal relationships ("remember, this is *me, friend,* talking") all serve to define a conflict in personal and relational rather than issue-oriented terms.

If neither avoidant nor structuring strategies are available, parties in conflicts can resort to direct *confrontative* strategies. Probably personalization and coercion are best known, more because they are so often used than because they are the strategically wisest or most productive. Attacking the *person* of one's opponent(s), especially when the attack (1) impugns morals, (2) reveals secrets known to the attacker, or (3) makes accusations of assorted "isms" (racism, sexism, facism, communism, and so on), denies that person any response save counterattack or acquiescence.[11] *Coercion* comes in at least two forms. One is the overt display of formal, expert-based, or coalition-based power. These elicit compliance only when all parties grant the attacker this kind of power and see their use of it as legitimate. If they do not, the strategy will fail and their power will be reduced.

The second form of coercion involves threats or promises.[12] These function in essentially the same way, depend on the same conditions for their success, and are, in effect, two sides of the same coin. Three conditions must be present for threats and promises to succeed. First, the sources must be credible. They must be perceived as being capable of controlling the reward or punishment they threaten or promise to provide and being willing to carry out their statement. Creating these perceptions is particularly important when the parties have a competitive interpersonal relationship. If their relationship is cooperative, promises also depend on the target's perceiving that the promiser is trustworthy, knows what is best for both of them, and has good intentions. Second, the threat or promise must be communicated in a way which makes the desired responses clear and specific and the consequences of compliance or noncompliance "vivid." Both "I'm gonna' cover you with honey and tie you to a hill of biting red ants in a glaring Arizona sun" or "I'm gonna' cover you with whipped cream and . . ." are vivid threats and/or promises. Third, the consequence must be perceived as being fair, equitable, and appropriate to the magnitude of the action that is requested. Consequences that are either trivial or horrendous compared to the request will not be taken seriously.

The difficulty with using threats and promises is that peoples' perceptions about what is credible, equitable, fair, and appropriate differ quite widely. Making predictions about another person's perception is a risky proposition, especially because the *act* of threatening or promising may influence those perceptions in idiosyncratic ways. The tendency to misestimate perceptions is lower when the parties are homophilous or have observed one another's responses to threats and promises in the past. To complicate their use further, threats and promises tend to provoke counterthreats and promises, creating a sometimes comical ("my mommy will beat up your daddy") and rarely productive cycle of escalation.

A final competitive strategy is "taking a tough stance." In its pure form, where everyone initially refuses to concede their positions, taking a tough stance generally can lead to productive results. Since no party appears to be willing to acquiesce or be intimidated, all parties are eventually forced to search for a mutually acceptable resolution of their differences. In a variant of this strategy, often called "playing the reformed sinner," one or both parties take a tough stance, until it appears to the other that no mutual solution is possible, and then makes a significant concession. Often, it seems, the others reciprocate, and a pattern of cooperation is established. Productive outcomes follow.[13]

This rather lengthy summary of communication strategies used in conflicts has been provided primarily to indicate that a very wide range of strategies is available. This observation is very important. Conflicts are not made up of one party employing one strategy. They are made up of interactions, of patterns of communication and response and counter response. In productive conflicts these patterns consist of a number of brief episodes during which the parties adopt a wide range of strategies. Coercion, threats, promises, redefinition, relational comments, digressions, joking, relaxing, and so on are intermixed in a variety of different proportions. No single strategy takes over: no sustained cycle of threat and counter threat, coercion and regression, is present to distort participants' perceptions or cloud their analysis of the situation. In destructive conflicts a narrow range of communication strategies are used. Escalating cycles of threat, coercion, expansion of issues, and personalization lock parties into competitive, zero-sum patterns of interaction. Sometimes—perhaps often—destructive cycles are accidentally initiated by the more powerful members of the group. They misperceive less powerful people as jealous, resentful, or hostile and overreact, adopting confrontive, competitive strategies when other approaches might have been more appropriate. Or they inadvertently place weaker people in positions where they feel that they must either fight or be humiliated.[14] But conflict cycles are never under any one members' control. Sometimes they escalate until they are out of everyone's control. It is the participants' ability to manage and control these tendencies for escalation that determines whether a conflict will be productive or destructive.

One final note: Rarely are any of these communication strategies used alone. More often, each employee uses a complicated combination of strategies. For example, in a time-honored approach to negotiating for real estate and used cars, the potential buyer expands the scope of the issue by nitpicking about the age of the object, small dents in the fenders, color of wallpaper, or whatever, so that the buyer will be able to make a large concession (the re-formed sinner strategy) in the hope of eliciting a reciprocal concession from the potential seller on a different issue (for instance, price). An almost infinite number of possible combinations of strategies exists. The effects of each depends on an even larger number of relational factors and on the combination of strategies adopted by the other parties. An adequate summary of these combinations would take an additional book (at least) and a significant amount of careful research that has not yet been completed.[15] But the common thread running through most analyses is the importance of not becoming trapped in escalating (or to use Kenneth Burke's term, "tragic") cycles of interaction.

ESCALATION AND TRAGIC CONFLICTS

Forms of Escalation

Escalation can take three forms—*expansion of issues, involvement of self and face*, and *dominance of emotion and symbol*.[16] The first is self-explanatory. When episodes of conflict begin they revolve around a small number of issues that immediately concern the participants. Sometimes the nature of these issues leads the groups to a consideration of other, more basic issues. In fact, a number of models of conflict management recommend careful, systematic broadening of the issue being discussed. As long as the group continues to focus on the central problem, uses the "broadening" to take new and different perspectives on that problem, and eventually considers a wider range of potential solutions, expansion of issues can be productive. For instance, an academic department is faced with a need to keep its enrollment high despite reductions in the size of its faculty. This problem has within it the seeds of a highly destructive escalating conflict—angry arguments over the fairness and equity of current teaching loads, possible alienation among faculty because of differences in rank and power, attacks based on subjective judgments about educational philosophy and quality of teaching. But the group could also develop the following kind of sequence:

The problem is defined and its importance agreed upon.

Faculty member 1 asserts that the key question is how to maintain or improve the quality of the education provided by the department.

Faculty member 2 argues that the existing undergraduate internship program causes part of the problem because it exhausts so much faculty time for so few students.

Faculty member 3 argues that using graduate students as teaching assistants in large lecture courses causes part of the problem because faculty members still must spend time lecturing and training the assistants.

Faculty member 4 suggests that since most of the department's interns are looking toward careers in training and development, some of them could be used as teaching assistants in lecture courses, thus releasing graduate students to teach their own classes. Discussion continues, focused on the optimal ways of using the three of resources available to the department. As this episode continues, the issues expand, but so do the range of available solutions.

However, issues in conflicts often expand in a very different way. The archetypal example of destructive escalation is a standard fare of television sitcoms. The cycle begins when the husband complains about a burned pot roast. The wife responds that if he doesn't like it he can get off his butt and cook it himself. Before the interchange ends with one of the two storming out of the room (usually after he walks into a closet by mistake), they will have discussed both spouse's parents (who also are lazy, bad cooks, or whatever), stereotypical sex roles, housecleaning and repair needs, their relative incomes, and their sex lives. In these conflicts the expansion of issues obscures the initial problem, reveals no possible solutions, and redefines the problem in ways which make it impossible to arrive at any productive resolution of the initial (pot roast) disagreement.

Conflicts also escalate when they begin to involve the *self-esteem* or *self-images* (faces) of the participants. Had any of the professors in the previous example said "We wouldn't have this problem if all of us were good enough teachers that our courses were filled with students," the issue would suddenly have become a personal one, not a substantive one. People typically respond to a particular communicative strategy with a similar one.[17] In addition, as explained in Chapter 9, personalizing strategies create a need for others to defend themselves, to save face. Typically they do so by adopting their own personalizing strategies ("I have low enrollments because I make demands of my students" or "You have high enrollments because you give away A's"), which create pressures for others to save face, and an escalating cycle of personalization begins.

A final form of escalation involves breakdowns in rhetorical sensitivity— the balanced consideration of situations, self-interests, and others' interests.

Once episodes start they create their own situation. Participants often begin to base choices only on the immediate conflictful situation—on the communication that is taking place during the episode. Dimensions of the larger organizational situation—the parties' roles in the organization, the importance of the issue and reaching a productive solution to it, the need to maintain effective working relationships—may become lost in the more immediate conflict. In other words, the *conflict* takes on a *symbolic* importance that transcends the other dimensions of the situation. Winning the battle becomes the only concern. In trying to win, actors lose sight of their desires to arrive at a satisfactory solution.[18] For example, a number of researchers have argued that this kind of escalation explains why women tend to become more competitive during episodes of conflict than men. Because of their acculturation, women are more sensitive to immediate patterns of communication and less responsive to broader goals. Once one party in a conflict adopts a competitive strategy, women reciprocate, responding to the pattern of interaction, and the conflict escalates. Men, who are less sensitive to immediate patterns of communication and more responsive to potential payoffs, can continue to take a broader view.[19]

Although these three forms of escalation differ in some respects, they are similar in two important ways. First, they tend to go unnoticed by the participants. Escalation occurs without anyone realizing it. Communication strategies generate counter strategies in a seemingly natural and appropriate sequence. Conflicts become tragic; parties make choices about how to communicate without realizing where their choices are taking them, and they become trapped in escalating cycles. They perceive that their increasingly hostile actions are merely responses; that if anyone is responsible for the escalation, it is someone else. Paul Watzlawick, and his colleagues call this process *punctuation*. The parties each choose a different "starting point" for the sequence of communication and response. By perceiving that someone else "started it," they can blame the conflict on others and justify their own contributions to the escalation as just and proper. They begin to employ nonproductive avoidant or aggressive strategies and ignore potentially productive collaborative approaches. They may withold or distort information relevant to the issue being discussed.[20] Communication becomes a weapon with which they can win the battle, not a process through which differences can be managed productively.

Second, the three different forms of escalation can be recognized by the same cues, the most important of which are:

1. Parties argue emotionally for their preferred outcome rather than explain it and its implications calmly.

2. Parties use individual or coalition-related pronouns rather than group-oriented ones [I want; *you* should; *we* (coalition) think; and so on].

3. The time and emotional energy devoted to a topic is disproportionately greater than its importance (parties may begin to ask themselves, "Why is this so important?" and not be able to produce a sensible answer).

4. Parties cannot (or can only vaguely) remember the issue that started the discussion or the links between it and the topic currently being debated.

5. Parties find themselves thinking more about persons, positions, and strategies than about problems and solutions.

When any of these cues are present, participants should conceptually "step back" from the interaction and consciously search for and use appropriate deescalating strategies. Sometimes this withdrawal may be physical, as when "cooling off" periods are imposed on labor-management negotiations. At other times the withdrawal may be purely cognitive. But unless the parties are able to separate themselves from the cycle of communication in some way, the escalation will continue.

Bases of Escalation

Unfortunately, the previous comments about processes of escalation make them sound aberrant, almost perverse. But the situation is quite the opposite. The potential for escalation exists in all conflicts for easily understandable reasons. Some of these bases of escalation are related to the nature of organizations. In our culture people are conditioned to compete and achieve, and the cultures that develop in formal organizations often accent these aspects. In addition, every organizational conflict carries with it a legacy of past conflicts and the anticipation of future conflicts. The perfect organizational conflict—where every participant and the organization find a solution and relationships are strengthened by the interaction—is quite rare. In fact, it may never have happened. Each conflict leaves its own legacy. When organizations adopt norms which suppress or repress overt conflicts, or when parties inappropriately use avoidant orientations or strategies, this legacy of hidden dissatisfaction is very intense. When overt conflicts do occur, the legacy provides impetus to "win this one because I may never get another chance" or "I lost the last one."

Escalation is also supported by the two faces of organizational power. Conflicts are fought in the open when some members of the organization choose to confront existing power relationships. Whatever risks are involved in doing so are incurred at the moment the conflict becomes overt. These risks can be offset only if the employees gain power or rewards from its outcome. For this reason they have an absolute incentive to push the conflict to a point where they "win." Similarly, for the more powerful members, the existence of an open conflict threatens them and their position in the power structure. Once the conflict opens up, the hidden face of power is being attacked. Since it is the hidden face which allows power holders to maintain their dominance, it must be defended. "Winning" the conflict will allow them to reestablish their superior position. Losing the battle, or compromising on the issues, diminishes their power. The interrelationships between conflict and power relationships establish a motive for employees to adopt a win-lose orientation, increasing the potential for escalation.

Still another base of escalation is the nature of human communication. Chapter 8 explained that all messages have both a content and a relational dimension. If the participants in a conflict focus on the relational dimension of one another's communication, the conflict will be personalized and escalation becomes probable. Perceptual processes also contribute to escalation. If an interaction is tense, as conflicts are, parties focus their attention on the "evidence" of hostility and competition present in the communication of others. It has been shown that people in business, as well as other subjects, perceive their opponents in conflicts as more competitive than they really are and themselves as more cooperative than they really have been.[21] As conflicts escalate, parties begin to perceive opponents and their ideas as wholly evil and begin to see themselves, their allies, and their ideas as wholly good. Trust begins to dissolve, and participants begin to listen less and advocate more. Eventually communication breaks down, little information is exchanged, more information is distorted, and hostility and distrust grow. Parties begin to narrow the range of their communication strategies and the outcomes they will accept. Escalation continues. When combined, *cultural, organizational*, and *communicational* factors make escalation an inevitable problem in overt conflicts.

CONFLICT: AFTERMATH

This Chapter began with a summary of Pondy's three preliminary phases of conflict—latent, perceived, and felt conflict. The fourth phase in his model, *manifest* conflict, and the role of communication in it, has been examined in some detail. The final phase in Pondy's model is the *aftermath* of conflict. Two aspects of conflicts are important for evaluating their short-term effects—the quality of the final decision that is made and the effect the conflict has on working relationships. If a sensible solution is found, which meets the needs of every party and/or is supported by a legitimate consensus, the short-term effects on the organization and its members will be positive. However, such integrative solutions are infrequent, and consensus is an elusive state. The more probable modes of terminating conflicts—compromise, majority vote, or acquiescence by one or more parties—leave residual frustrations, which will provoke future conflicts and complicate their management. Similarly, the dynamics of the episodes may leave behind changed perceptions of each party, unmanaged emotions, and commitments to get revenge, which will influence the working relationships between the parties and the potential for future conflicts. If they are repeated often, escalating conflicts may lead employees to define their relationship as competitive rather than cooperative. Since their tasks are interdependent, competitive relationships may undermine the participants' performance and the organization's success.

This potential for long-term negative effects on working relationships has caused many organizations to employ formal procedures and make structural changes in order to minimize the impact of unproductive conflicts. Some have attempted to reduce unit or employee interdependence, in an attempt both to minimize the number of issues over which differences might occur and to decrease the effects of long-term relational problems. But interdependence cannot be reduced beyond a certain point, and when it is reduced, the parties' incentives to cooperate with one another also are reduced.[22] Other organizations create formal "conflict managers" or formal procedures for handling disagreements. Third-party interventions *can* prevent escalation, providing the third party is skilled in conflict management and given sufficient formal "position" power.[23] Formal rules and procedures can structure conflicts in ways which reduce ambiguity and prevent the use of the kinds of communicative strategies that prompt escalation. Although there are limits to the effectiveness of structural changes, their use accents the need to evaluate the productiveness of each episode within the long-term perspective of the organization's operation.

Conflicts can be valuable and productive both for organizations and for their members. For the organizations, conflict can stimulate creative problem solving, generate or publicize superior ideas, and adjust perceived power relationships to better fit the skills and abilities of their employees. For the individuals, conflict can provide opportunities to test, expand, and demonstrate their skills; better understand their organizations; and develop their self-esteem and confidence. If conflicts are limited and controlled and if satisfactory solutions to problems can be found, the total impact of each conflict can be positive. If not, conflicts will be destructive. Two implications emerge from this comment. First, conflicts in organizations must be evaluated in terms of many considerations. Open conflicts invariably are disruptive and often leave behind negative legacies. But their impact on the long-term effectiveness of the organization may on balance be favorable. Often attempting to suppress or repress conflict damages an organization more than allowing them to surface and be managed. Second, controlling processes of escalation is the key to productive conflict management. The aftermath of organizational conflicts depends on maintaining patterns of communication during episodes which allow people to demonstrate their competencies and analyze and solve problems. Escalation robs the participants of these opportunities and establishes the bases of nonproductive legacies. The strategic use of communication is the key to productive conflict management.

Notes

1. This section is based primarily on four sources: Louis Pondy, "Organizational Conflict: Concepts and Models," *Administrative Science Quarterly*, 12 (1967), 296–320; Morton Deutsch, "Conflicts: Productive or Destructive," *Journal of Social Issues*, 25 (1969), 7–41, and *The Resolu-*

tion of Conflict (New Haven, Conn.: Yale University Press, 1973); Stephen Robbins, "Conflict Management and Conflict Resolution Are Not Synonymous Terms," *California Management Review*, 21 (1978), 67–75. There is an almost infinite number of other important citations. They are summarized effectively by Kenneth Thomas in "Conflict and Conflict Management," in *Handbook of Industrial and Organizational Psychology*, ed. Marvin Dunnette, (Chicago: Rand-McNally, 1976).

2. Harold Guetzkow and James Gyr, "An Analysis of Decision-Making Groups," *Human Relations*, 7 (1954), 367–381.

3. Thomas, "Conflict and Conflict Management."

4. Charles Conrad, "Power, Performance and Supervisors' Choices of Strategies of Conflict Management," *Western Journal of Speech Communication*, 47 (1983), 218–228.

5. See the special issue of *California Management Review* (Winter 1978).

6. L. Kriegsberg, *The Sociology of Social Conflicts* (Englewood Cliffs, N. J.: Prentice-Hall, 1973). An excellent summary of research on communication in conflict is Joseph Folger and M. Scott Poole, *Working Through Conflict* (Chicago: Scott, Foresman, 1983).

7. This summary is based on a number of sources. The most important are Alan Sillars, "Stranger and Spouse as Target Persons for Compliance-Gaining Strategies," *Human Communication Research*, 6 (1980), 265–279; Richard Walton, *Interpersonal Peacemaking* (Reading, Mass.: Addison-Wesley, 1969); George Marwell and D. Schmidt, "Dimensions of Compliance-Gaining Behavior," *Sociometry*, 30 (1967), 350–364; Steven Lukes, *Power: a Radical View* (London: MacMillan, 1974); Peter Bacharach and Morton Baratz, "Two Faces of Power," *American Political Science Review*, 56 (1962), 947–952; Morton Baratz, *Power and Poverty* (New York: Oxford University Press, 1970); Bertram Raven and Arie Kruglanski, "Power and Conflict," in *The Structure of Conflict*, ed. Paul Swingle, (New York: Academic Press, 1970).

8. Charles Smart and I. Vertinsky, "Designs for Crisis Decision Units," *Administrative Science Quarterly*, 22 (1977), 640–657.

9. Elizabeth Janeway, *Powers of the Weak* (New York: Morrow-Quill, 1980). Power is both an advantage and a constraint. Our society negatively values coercion. This value makes it difficult for powerful people overtly to impose their wills on less powerful people, unless of course, others perceive that the powerful have been provoked. But the hidden face of power usually leads less powerful employees to act in ways which do not provoke the powerful. Thus, if they are to achieve their goals they must be able to exercise their power subtlely. They can do so, as Bacharach and Baratz argued, by using communicative strategies which structure conflict.

10. H. Meyers, E. Kay, and J. R. P. French, "Split Roles in Performance Appraisals," *Harvard Business Review* (1965), 21–29.

11. Julia Wood and Barnett Pearce, "Sexists, Racists and Other Classes of Classifiers," *Quarterly Journal of Speech*, 66 (1980), 239–250.

12. See Parke Burgess, "Crisis Rhetoric" *The Quarterly Journal of Speech*, 59 (1973), 61–73; James Tedeschi, "Threats and Promises," in *The Structure of Conflict*, ed. Paul Swingle.

13. O. J. Bartos, "Determinants and Consequences of Toughness," in *The Structure of Conflict*, ed. Paul Swingle.

14. Raven and Kruglanski, "Power and Conflict"; S. S. Komorita, "Negotiating from Strength and the Concept of Bargaining", *Journal of the Theory of Social Behavior*, 7 (1977), 56–79.

15. Of course, a number of such books have been written. See especially Folger and Poole, *Working Through Conflict*; Samuel Bacharach and Edward Lawler, *Negotiation* (San Francisco: Jossey-Bass, 1980); Daniel Druckman, ed., *Negotiation* (Beverly Hills, Calif.: Sage, 1977); Max Bazerman and Roy Lewicki, *Negotiating in Organizations* (Beverly Hills, Calif.: Sage, 1983).

16. Morton Deutsch and Robert Krauss, "Studies in Interpersonal Bargaining," *Journal of Conflict Resolution*, 61 (1962), 52–76; Folger and Poole, *Working Through Conflict*.

17. Timothy Leary, *Interpersonal Diagnosis of Personality* (New York: Ronald, 1957); Kenneth Thomas and Richard Walton, *Conflict-Handling Behavior in Interdepartmental Relations* (Los Angeles: UCLA Graduate School of Business Administration, 1971).

18. Alan Tegar, *Too Much Invested to Quit* (New York: Pergamon, 1980); Smart and Vertinsky, "Designs for Crisis Decision Units"; Guetzkow and Gyr, "Analysis of Decision-Making Groups." Also see Chapter 5 of this book.

19. Anatol Rapoport, Melvin Guyer, and David Gordon, *The 2 × 2 Game* (Ann Arbor: University of Michigan Press, 1976); James Ruben and R. Brown, *The Social Psychology of Bargaining and Negotiation* (New York: Academic Press, 1975).

20. Paul Watzlawick, Janet Beavin, and Don Jackson, *Pragmatics of Human Communication* (New York: W. W. Norton, 1967); Linda Putnam and Charmaine Wilson, "Development of an Organizational Conflict Instrument" (paper presented at the International Communication Association convention, 1982); Sillars, "Stranger and Spouse."

21. Deutsch, "Conflicts"; Robert Stagner and H. Rosen, *Psychology of Union-Management Relationships* (Belmont, Calif.: Brooks/Cole, 1965).

22. E. Rhenman, L. Stromberg, and G. Westerlund, *Conflict and Cooperation in Business Organizations* (New York: John Wiley, 1970).

23. Paul Lawrence and Jay Lorsch, *Organizations and Environment* (Homewood, Ill.: Richard D. Irwin, 1969).

11

Communication and Managing Organizational Stress

Stress suddenly has become one of the "in" terms of the 1980s. The fact that publications as different as the *American Journal of Orthopsychiatry* and the *National Enquirer* have featured articles on stress and stress management suggests that a great many people are concerned about the stresses of life. In fact, by 1980 more than 150,000 books and articles about stress had been published. The reasons for this interest are quite clear. Everyone experiences stress to some extent; millions of people have illnesses related to unmanaged stress; thousands die from stress-related illnesses; and organizations lose somewhere between $20 and $30 billion each year because of stress-related absenteeism, illness, and premature turnover.[1] A large but indeterminable number of additional millions of dollars are lost through the inefficiencies, conflicts, and poor decision making that results from unmanaged or improperly managed stress.

Of course, human beings have experienced high levels of stress since the beginning of the species. For millenia life's stresses were imposed on us primarily by nonhuman factors—the constant pressures of survival. And still for many millions of human beings, it is the constant daily struggle for adequate nutrition, housing, and medical care that creates stress. But in the industrialized world, humans face a group of different, humanly created stressors. Many of them stem from the characteristics of the organizations in which people work. The impact of work-imposed stress is increased by the stressful nature of modern society. Many of the activities and resources which humans traditionally have used to manage the negative effects of stress have virtually disappeared. The social and emotional support once received from members of extended families and tightly knit communities; the moderate pace of life and opportunities for occasional creative relaxation that accompanied rural life; and the regular, vigorous exercise that once was part of "work" all have been victims of economic growth and technological change. Family members are separated by thousands of miles, employees are transferred in and out of housing areas before they ever become communities. Life moves by so rapidly that time itself has become a source of stress. "Relaxation" has come to mean planned, performance-oriented activities, which often worsen rather than reduce stress. Most employees move little that is heavier than a pencil. No longer do our normal activities help us manage the stressors we encounter. Conscious, careful efforts to manage stress have become a necessary part of coping with organizational life.

In 1964 Robert Kahn and his associates published the first extensive study of the dimensions of organizational stress.[2] Research since then has led to the realization that the dynamics and effects of organizational stress depend on a complicated and not-yet-fully-understood interaction between an employee, the organization, relationships with other employees, and resources for managing stress. One of the most consistent findings in this research has been that communication and communicative processes are both sources of and important solutions to stress. In some ways organizational communication causes or reduces stress (it is a "stressor"), in others it influences the impact other stressors have on employees (it is a "moderator"), and in still others it increases or reduces employees' abilities to manage stress. The following sections of this chapter will explain the dynamics of organizational stress and the role of communication. Later sections explain how organizations and employees can alter their communication in order to help them manage stress.

THE DYNAMICS OF ORGANIZATIONAL STRESS

Perhaps the single most important aspect of stress is that its effects depend largely on the employee's personality and perceptions. At least forty dimensions of organizations and work environments have been identified as potential sources of stress (factors which will be called *stressors*.) For some people some of these factors are stimulating and enjoyable parts of their jobs. For others these same factors are annoying, offensive, and stressful. For example, some people find rules about punctuality to be a constant source of annoyance. For them this stressor generates *stress*—a group of *feelings* (frustration, anger, inadequacy, or helplessness) and *physiological changes* that can stem from any number of sources. For others, rules encourage them to structure their morning, to get started when they would have difficulty doing so themselves. "Stressors" are not stressors unless and until individuals perceive them as such. Perhaps more than any other single factor discussed in this book, stress depends on the "realities" that employees create.

Individual perceptions determine the relationship between potential stressors and felt stress in another way. Almost everyone seems to be able to tolerate a certain degree of every potential stressor. But when a particular pressure reaches a certain level of intensity, it becomes stressful. For example, being interrupted occasionally by coworkers is acceptable. But there is a threshold beyond which interruptions become annoying. These threshold levels are different for each person, and each person's threshold for one potential stressor is different than it is for other stressors.[3] As a result, a situation especially pleasant for one person can be maddening for another. Two people will respond to the same situation differently, and they may not be able to understand one another's responses. More than any other single factor, individuals' perceptions influence the dynamics of organizational stress.

However, there are a number of features of stress and of responses to it that hold true for most people most of the time. Figure 11.1 depicts the general relationships among stressors, moderating factors, felt stress, and responses to stress. Potential stressors generate felt stress. Certain features of organizational communication and of individual employees can either buffer an employee from stressors (reducing the amount of stress felt) or exacerbate the stress that results. When people feel stress they may respond in many different ways, some of which are constructive adaptations and some of which are mal-

FIGURE 11.1   General Relationships Among Stressors, Stress, and Responses

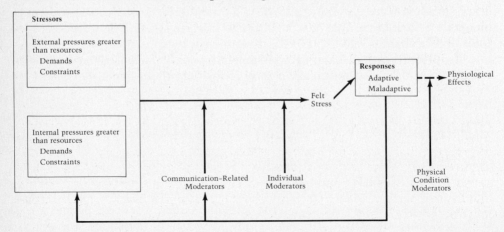

adaptive. One of the first steps in learning to manage stress constructively is to recognize that stress is normal and inevitable and that some reactions to it are natural and predictable.[4]

The Stressor-Stress Relationship

When people feel *pressures which exceed* the *resources* they have to cope with them, they may feel stress. These pressures may either be imposed by conditions and persons other than the individual or they may be self-imposed. *External pressures* come in two forms: *demands for action* made by other people, or *constraints* on one's activities imposed by outside forces. Demands can create stress if the individual perceives them as legitimate and believes that they cannot be met. Constraints generate stress if they are perceived as being enforceable.

External Pressures   Three groups of demands have been identified as potentially stressful:[5] (1) characteristics of the *tasks*, (2) work and communication *loads*, and (3) physical *working conditions*. Perhaps the most important are the characteristics of assigned *tasks*. In general, tasks that are "rich" (see Chapters 4 and 5) are more stressful than those that are not. Supervising people is more stressful than supervising "things." Jobs which involve substantial amounts of communication create more stress than those which demand less communication. This description fits the tasks typically assigned to managers almost perfectly. Estimates of the proportion of time managers spend communicating range from 60 to 85 percent. The act of communicating produces anxiety to some degree for almost everyone.[6] When communication interrupts other activities, as when people receive telephone calls or visitors, it is even more stressful. When the communication networks in which an employee is involved include a large number of people, or when these people have varied interests and needs, communication is even more demanding. And if a manager is expected to serve as a liason between different units of the organization or between the organization and outsiders (the boundary-spanning role discussed in Chapter 6), communication becomes an even greater part of the job and an even more potent source of stress.

   A number of noncommunication factors impose stress on employees. Making decisions, especially ones that require a high degree of creativity; excessive travel; coping with frequent changes at work or at home; and handling the effects of mistakes all create stress.[7] If a manager is located in the middle of the organization's hierarchy the list of stressors is even greater. Middle managers feel "pay compression" (where the starting salaries of new recruits get closer and closer to their own); job insecurity, because of the threat of forced early retirement and replacement by younger personnel; the lack of power but substantial responsibility; and frustrated aspirations. In addition, middle managers are generally involved in extensive and diverse communication networks and have only limited ability to control interrupting phone calls or visits from their supervisors and subordinates. Since a substantial number of a middle manager's tasks involve controlling the flow of information, communication is a very potent stressor.[8]

Just as *what* people must do may be stressful, the *amount* of work they are asked to do can be a stressor. At one point researchers believed that both *overloading*—giving workers more tasks or information than they can process effectively—and *underloading* can be stressful. There is evidence that for employees whose self-concepts are linked closely to their jobs or who feel guilt when they are less than fully challenged, work underload is a stressor. Similarly, if people feel isolated or alienated from their co-workers because they have too few opportunities to communicate (underload), they may feel stress. And in monotonous, repetitive jobs, a strange combination of underload and overload is created. Few skills are required of workers in these jobs, but the ones that are used are overloaded. Sawmill operators, for example, must be able to concentrate on and control their physical movements for hours on end. These two skills are overloaded, all others are underloaded, and stress results. However, it does seem that most people are able to cope quite well with underload. They may rationalize the situation as someone else's responsibility or resort to time-filling, stimulating activities like daydreaming, socializing, focusing on nonwork activities, or psychologically disengaging from work.[9] Usually it is work and/or communication *overload* that generates stress.

Overload comes in a number of forms. It may be *quantitative,* where workers are required to work too many hours or produce too much output. It may be *qualitative,* where they are asked to perform tasks that require skills and abilities they lack. They also may be overloaded when they are asked to perform tasks incompatible with one another. This type of *role conflict* (a different type will be discussed later in this chapter) occurs when used automobile salespersons are told to "clean up their reputation" and "sell something to every customer," when teachers are challenged to "maintain classroom discipline" and "keep students excited every moment," when supervisors are ordered to "be management" and "stay in touch with the union," or when professors are required to focus on both research and teaching.[10]

Communication overload also produces stress. It may involve too many communication events in a given period of time or too much information to process. Communication overload also may be qualitative. Messages may be too complex to handle, or the combination of messages an employee receives at one time may create a communication situation so complicated that there seems to be no productive response.

Finally, a number of physical *working conditions* create pressures. Poor visibility (insufficient light, glare, or flickering lights), annoying noise, excessive vibration, heat, cold or wind, exposure to chemicals, radiation or atmospheric pollutants, and changing hours of work are all potential stressors.

To summarize, although forty or more external demands have been identified as potential stressors, it is possible to group them into three major categories—*tasks*, work and communication *load*, and physical *working con-*

ditions. Demands become stressors when they are perceived as legitimate and when they exceed the resources for coping with them that are available to each *individual* employee. Their impact is increased when employees also face any of three kinds of external *constraints.*

Task and load pressures become exceptionally stressful when employees face frequent and unmanageable *deadlines* and perceive that failing to meet those deadlines will have serious consequences. Role conflict is most stressful when inconsistent demands are made by people who the employee believes has substantial organizational power, especially over the employee's promotion or tenure.[11] Deadlines, performance demands, and penalties are stressful because they limit an employee's freedom of action. As has been suggested throughout this book, organizations employ a variety of mechanisms to limit employees' choices so that they will act in specific and unnatural ways. Each of these mechanisms—rules, regulations, reward systems, group or organizational norms, interpersonal pressures—constrains employees. If they are linked to salient penalties—fines, dismissal, ostracization, reduced self-esteem, or whatever—they are potential stressors. But in order to function, organizations must limit and direct the activities of their employees. If control systems are to succeed, they must restrict employees' actions. Consequently, constraint-related stressors are present and inevitable in all organizations at all times. Both *demands* and *constraints* are necessary and inevitable features of organizational life *and* are potential stressors.

Internal Pressures Sometimes stressors are imposed on people. Sometimes people create their own. For any number of reasons employees may impose demands on themselves which either cannot be met or cannot simultaneously be met. For example, women who started careers during the 1960s and 1970s often demanded of themselves superhuman behavior—devoting extraordinary time and effort to their careers, husbands, and children. Fortunately, there recently has been an increasing realization that it is physically impossible to play all three roles as effectively as do people who play only one.[12] Often internal pressures stem from cognitive factors. Individuals have beliefs and values about how they should act and how well they should perform which are either unrealistic in general or impossible to implement in their particular jobs. Cary Cherniss observed that human service professionals (social service workers, mental health clinicians, teachers, and so on) typically are dedicated to a set of humanitarian values which are impossible to implement in their bureaucratic organizations. They cannot treat clients as individuals because rules and regulations prevent them from doing so; they cannot empathize fully with their patients because their excessive caseloads rob them of the psychological energy necessary to be empathic; and they cannot establish supportive and caring relationships with co-workers because they are able to communicate with them only through memos or in brief conversations in the hallway.[13] Their values conflict with the realities of their work, creating stress which eventually may lead to burnout.

Internal pressures also may involve employees' emotions. In our culture people are taught to withold or control emotional responses, particularly in public or at work. The nature of the emotion matters little—anger, joy, anxiety and pleasure, all are supposed to be suppressed (or to be more precise, repressed). Both the feelings and the act of repressing them create internal pressures and thus are potential stressors. Beliefs about how one ought to act toward others also can create stress. Employees' backgrounds and training often lead them to expect that they will be treated in certain ways by their colleagues and that they themselves will exhibit certain kinds of behaviors in their dealings with associates. Myths of meritocracy, rational decision making, and participation in decision making are fostered by our culture and educational systems. When employees believe they are treated inequitably (and the complications of reward systems that were discussed in Chapters 3 and 4 suggest that they inevitably will) or are not allowed to participate in decision making to the degree they desire, they feel stress.[14] Employees' beliefs, values, and assumptions about how members of organizations should act may either create stress directly or make certain kinds of external stressors very salient.

Factors That Moderate the Stressor-Stress Relationship

Sometimes pressures which exceed the resources an employee has available produce stress; sometimes they do not. Part of the reason for this difference already has been mentioned—different people have different thresholds for different stressors. If pressures exceed resources to a degree that is below employees' threshold levels, they will not feel stress. If the pressures employees face are those which they find enjoyable and challenging, the potential stressors may even reduce stress. In short, if the environment includes pressures which fit employees' preferences and thresholds, felt stress will be minimized. If not, the lack of fit will generate stress.[15]

Stress also occurs when people feel vulnerable, alone, or powerless. If they have received insufficient or confusing information about what their work *goals* should be, what their *colleagues expect* of them, or what their *role* in the organization as a whole is, they may feel vulnerable. This *role ambiguity* exacerbates the effects of other stressors. For example, it is more difficult to manage work overload when one does not understand what one is responsible for or which task is most important to colleagues and supervisors. It is harder to sort out conflicting or overloading information when employees are unsure of their work goals. It is easier to choose strategies for communicating with others when employees understand their role in the organization, and so on.

Inappropriate feedback also may create stress. When supervisors give their subordinates fair, relevant, and helpful feedback about their performance, the employees gain a sense of direction and support and thus can manage pressures more effectively. However, if employees receive too little feedback, they may begin to feel vulnerable and lost. If the feedback they do receive is either all positive or all negative, they are robbed of a sense of direction and support and may feel stress. Of if they are given direct advice ("do it this way" or "watch me do it") rather than communication which helps them discover their own solutions, their self-esteem and sense of accomplishment may be reduced. In any of these cases, performance-related communication may both create stress and increase the effects of other stressors.[16]

The final and most important communication-related moderator is supportive communication from other people.[17] As used here, the term *supportive* has a very specific meaning. It does not mean mere interpersonal communication. Rather, it means communication from other people which expresses concern for and emotional attachment to employees, allows them to express their feelings, affirms their self-concept and self-worth, and provides aid in overcoming their problems or stressors.[18] Employees can gain support from members of their extended families, spouses, co-workers, or supervisors. If supportive communication is not available from these people, either because they are absent from the scene, isolated from the employee by various communication barriers, have weak interpersonal communication skills, or lack consideration for others, the employee will feel stress. Social support serves as a buffer, allowing employees to manage higher levels of stressors without feeling stress. Also, supportive communication often provides information which reduces role ambiguity, provides performance feedback, clarifies peer expectations, gives employees opportunities to separate themselves constructively from their work, and helps them avoid blaming their experiences on their own shortcomings. When old-timers tell newcomers that "no one cares about when you get your paperwork done" or "everybody fills those forms out incorrectly at first," they provide both emotional support and information, each of which helps reduce stress. Support directly and indirectly reduces the stress people feel in stressful situations.

The second group of moderating factors involves five key personality characteristics—tolerance for ambiguity, need for structure, chronic anxiety, self-esteem, and susceptibility to Type A behavior. Some of these moderators are stressor-specific; that is, they affect some stressors but not others. For example, high tolerance for ambiguity reduces the effects of role ambiguity and excessive job richness, has less impact on work overload, no effect on noise, and may even reduce people's ability to manage excessively constraining rules and regulations. Other personality factors seem to be specific to organizational roles. For example, J. R. P. French and his associates found that qualitative work overload caused stress for professors and reduced their self-esteem, which created additional stress. But qualitative overload had no impact on the self-esteem of college administrators and thus did not moderate the stressor-stress relationship.[19] Still other factors seem to have a generalized effect; for instance, chronically anxious people are influenced more by all stressors than are people who normally are less anxious.

The final personality factor, susceptiblity to Type A behavior, needs to be explained in more detail. During the 1960s Meyer Friedman and Ray Rosenman found that men who had a high incidence of coronary heart disease (CHD) tended to exhibit a pattern of behavior different from that of men with a low incidence of CHD. These Type A men were more competitive, aggressive, restless, impatient, and hyperalert than their Type B counterparts. They also were so involved and committed to their work that they neglected their outside lives, continually felt they were working under time pressures and faced major responsibilities, and exhibited a particular type of speech—tense expressions and rapid, explosive speech patterns. Subsequent studies which improved Friedman and Rosenman's research methods linked Type A behavior to a number of important risk factors in CHD (high serum cholesterol and high triglycerides) and to CHD itself. It now appears that Type A behavior is both a response to continual stress and reflects a personality-related propensity to

FIGURE 11.2   Characteristics of Persons with a Significantly Related Risk of Stress-Linked Cardiovascular Illness

Note: It is important to recognize that the physiological effects of Type A behavior may be offset through a number of stress-reduction techniques. As a result many Type A individuals are able to minimize risks.

Type A Behavior

1. Chronic and severe sense of time urgency.
2. Persistent desire for recognition and advancement.
3. Neglect of all aspects of life except career.
4. Persistent involvement in multiple functions subject to deadlines.
5. Habitual propensity to accelerate pace of living and working (rushing through traffic, etc.).
6. Excessive competitive drive.
7. Feelings that "only I can do the job."
8. Explosiveness of speech.
9. Excessively frequent extraneous body movements.
10. Tendency to rush the pace of ordinary conversation (mentally or overtly finishing others' sentences for them).

Suggestions for Changing Type A Behavior

1. Plan some idleness each day (for relaxation or stress-reduction exercises).
2. Discontinue polyphasic thinking (mind off somewhere else).
3. Listen without interrupting.
4. Read books that demand concentration.
5. Learn to savor food.
6. Have a retreat (place and time) at home.
7. Avoid irritating competitive people whenever possible.
8. Restructure trips and vacations.
9. Live by the calendar, not the watch.
10. Consider any day lost that does not contain something of memory value.

Adapted from R. H. Rosenman and M. Friedman, *Type A Behavior and Your Heart.*

respond to stressors in a certain way. In other words, although everyone may sometimes exhibit Type A behavior, some people are more prone to do so than others.[20]

One of the most perplexing aspects of organizational stress is that some people find some situations intolerably stressful, others find the same situations acceptable, and still others find them enjoyable. However, the stressor-stress relationship is even more complex than the preceeding paragraphs have suggested. Each moderator influences the level of some of the stressors present in an employee's "environment." Social support requires time, effort, and close interpersonal contact. It simultaneously can reduce role ambiguity and feelings of powerlessness and increase communication overload, chronic anxiety, and role conflict (by increasing the amount of contact between the employee and the people causing the conflict). It also can exacerbate individual employees' propensities to engage in Type A behavior. Supportive work groups are cohesive work groups. Sometimes this cohesiveness can lead members to concentrate more and more on their jobs. Eventually the entire group may begin to engage in a kind of group Type A behavior.

In a similar way, intolerable amounts of one stressor can influence the effects of others. Rules and regulations (external constraints) can provide direction and structure, raising an employee's tolerance for complex and ambiguous tasks while at the same time frustrating the need to participate in decision making. Interestingly, the negative effects of adverse physical working conditions is increased when employees also face internal stressors and stressors that are not related to work.[21] Communication-related and individual moderators also seem to influence one another. What emerges from a careful description of organizational stress is a complex maze of interrelated and mutually influential stressors and moderators which combine in an almost infinite variety of ways to create different levels of felt stress (see Figure 11.3). There is thus no simple formula for reducing organizational stressors or the stress that employees feel. Discovering an effective means of managing stress is almost necessarily an individual project. Organizations can take steps to reduce common stressors, but almost any organizationwide change will increase felt stress for some employees while it decreases it for others.

The Stress-Response Relationship

Human beings seem to respond to felt stress in a characteristic pattern, labeled the "stress response syndrome," and with a limited number of strategies.[22] The strategies can be grouped into two categories, usually adaptive and maladaptive.

There are two kinds of reactions to felt stress. Certain patterns of *specific physiological* responses seem to follow events that are perceived as stressful. The sympathetic nervous system becomes very active; the endocrine glands release hormones (primarily adrenalin and cortisone) which heighten pulse and respiration rates, elevate blood sugar, increase perspiration and blood flow to

FIGURE 11.3   Stressor-Moderator-Stress Relationships

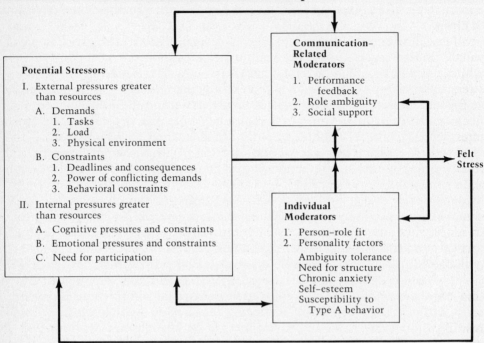

the skeletal muscles, and lead to a general tightening of the muscles. People become more alert, their senses sharpen, and they become more sensitive to their surroundings. If the stress continues over a long period of time their store of adaptive energy is depleted and they are no longer able to resist the stressor(s) effectively. When exhaustion occurs serious physical symptoms—migraine headaches, hypertension, ulcers, colitis, insomnia, and impotence—may develop. Hans Selye, who has directed the most extensive program of research on stress, labels these three stages the "general adaptation syndrome" (G.A.S.) and argues that it is a specific and predictable combination of physiological responses (a *syndrome*) to felt stress. It is important to note that G.A.S. results from any number of potential stressors (it is a *specific* response to a *nonspecific* set of stressors), some of which may be "favorable" and some "unfavorable." Selye notes that either "a passionate kiss or the crack of a whip" may start the process.

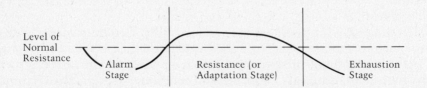

A second kind of response involves patterns of *behaviors*. People may choose to *fight* stress, either by attempting to identify and reduce the stressors or changing communication-related and individual moderators. Fighting may involve overt, direct actions or changes in an individual's attitudes, beliefs, or values. Social service workers may push for changes in their organization which make it less bureaucratic, or they may abandon their values regarding client care. Richard Lazarus and Raymond Launier described two major forms of fighting, seeking information and taking direct action, and two forms of fleeing. *Flight* may involve an "inhibition" of action (withdrawing from a stressful situation, avoiding stressors, or refusing to do anything until the stressors are removed) or "intrapsychic defenses," like changing one's perceptions so that stress is repressed or adopting an "I don't care" attitude.[23] In general, people seem to fight stress when the stressor is role ambiguity, overload, or some other form of threat. They flee role conflict, interpersonal conflict, or internal pressures. Neither fight nor flight is, in itself, good or bad. In some situations and for some people fighting is the appropriate adaptation; in other situations and for other people, fleeing is adaptive and fighting is maladaptive.

Table 11.1 summarizes what seem to be the most frequently used behavioral responses to felt stress. It also indicates which of these responses *usually* are adaptive and which are less adaptive. For example, because stress so often results from ineffective communication or from work and communication overload, seeking additional information or increasing one's efficiency in handling information or tasks may be productive.[24] *Strategic withdrawal*, in which employees draw clear boundaries around their work and nonwork lives and strives to keep one set of stressors from spilling over into the other realm, or productively use opportunities to get away physically from work pressures through brief holidays or vacations, can be adaptive ways of fleeing overload or communication-related stressors. The responses farther to the right on the continuum in Table 11.1 are the frequently used behavioral responses which usually are less productive, that is, more maladaptive. Increased level of activity (without increased efficiency) may be adaptive in some cases but usually is not. If, for example, the stressor is a temporary increase in work load, increased activity may be appropriate. However, increased activity alone normally is not very productive. In fact, one of the key distinctions between Type A and Type B behavior is that Type A's work harder (more activity) and Type B's "work smarter" (more efficient activity). Switching from task to task is an analogous fleeing response. It may allow employees to keep a number of different stressors all below their individual threshold levels, but it also may reduce efficiency and increase frustrations because none of the tasks ever gets finished. Being less innovative may reduce the complexity of a job, but it also may cause employees to act in ways which perpetuate the problems that gave them stress in the first place.

At the far right of the continuum are responses which almost always are maladaptive. Pathological withdrawal—becoming sullen, reclusive, and iso-

TABLE 11.1 Fighting and Fleeing Stress

	Adaptive Responses			Maladaptive Responses		
Fighting	Increasing work efficiency; Increasing information seeking	Seeking social support	Increasing activity level	Projecting hostility onto peers or family; interfering with others' work	Causing accidents	Attacking others or property
Fleeing	Withdrawing strategically (compartmentalizing work and non-work activities or physical withdrawal)	Switching from task to task	Reducing innovativeness	Passively resisting change	Having accidents	Withdrawing destructively; Being paralyzed; Using intrapsychic defenses

lated—rarely helps reduce stress, although in some extreme cases of role conflict it may do so. Attacking other workers, causing others to have accidents or make errors, and destroying property almost never are productive responses. Overt attacks are of course rare in organizations, but adopting an "attacking" communication style seems to be a frequent response to stress. Loyd Pettegrew and his associates observed that physicians and managers in medical organizations often react to common stressors by becoming more argumentative and quarrelsome; more precise and defensive in their communication; and less open, relaxed, and friendly.[25] When people are under stress, they begin to engage in precisely those kinds of communication which create defensive work climates, reduce group social support, and foster suppression and distortion of information. Interpersonal conflicts increase; role conflict, ambiguity, and overload become more intense; anxieties grow; and Type A behavior becomes more probable. Stress leads to maladaptive responses, which increase stressors, and so on in an escalating and tragic cycle.

In summary, from the analysis presented in this chapter, a complex stress-response cycle emerges. External and internal pressures begin to exceed available mental, physical, and material resources. Individual and communication-related factors may either increase the stress people feel or provide buffers which allow employees to continue to function effectively in a stressful environment. Felt stress generates a wide range of responses, some of which may actually reduce key stressors below a person's threshold *level* or alter moderators. For instance, seeking information may either fulfill an employee's need for participation in decision making (a direct effect) or reduce role ambiguity (a moderator effect). Other responses may increase stressors and/or the effects of moderators. Type A behavior, for example, often reduces work efficiency, accents role conflict, leads to isolation and reduced social support, and reduces self-esteem. Each of these results normally will increase felt stress. Stressors, moderators, felt stress, and responses are interrelated in ways which form closed, reinforcing cycles. The key to managing these cycles successfully is to find productive ways of breaking into the dynamic, of short-circuiting the process.

MANAGING STRESS

Both organizations and individual employees can take a number of steps to reduce stressors. In most cases effective programs of stress management incorporate both organizational and personal change.

Organizational Stress Management[26]

In an important way, most of the approaches to organizational design discussed in Unit I of this book can be used to reduce stress or its adverse effects. Three types of strategies are potentially most valuable. First, organizations can attempt to be *more flexible* in the demands and constraints they impose on employees. If stress results from a number of nearly simultaneous deadlines, as often is the case at the end of a calendar, fiscal, or school year, steps can be taken to separate them in time. Some deadlines cannot easily be changed. For example, accountants cannot begin to prepare tax reports until after the year ends, and they must have them completed on time. But other deadlines can be moved ahead or back with no reduction in efficiency. Sometimes stress results from inefficiencies in time utilization that are imbedded in the way a firm operates. Keypunchers arrive at 8:00 A.M. and wait until 10:00 A.M. for their work to arrive from the coding department. As a result they have to work exceptionally hard during the afternoon in order to catch up. Staggering arrival and leaving times for the two departments or changing deadlines for less pressing projects to the next day could both improve efficiency and reduce stress.

Often stress results from organizational procedures and policies that have become antiquated or inefficient. For example, "flexitime" schedules, at virtually no cost to the firms, can reduce life stresses for employees who must arrange for child care or must commute long distances in heavy traffic. Organizations can establish formal systems which encourage employees to use the adaptive coping strategies described in the previous section. For instance, productive withdrawal can be facilitated in a number of ways. Workers who face peak load periods during the year can be encouraged to take their vacations during the week immediately after the peak periods end. In fact, many of the reward systems discussed in Chapters 3, 4, and 5 can be used to reduce stress. Or if some tasks assigned to a unit are more stressful than others, task rotation or systems which encourage employees to engage in "task switching" can be productive. If organizations are willing to abandon precedents when it is appropriate to do so, they not only profit from reduced stress but also gain from improved efficiency. Just as recurring conflicts sometimes signal the need to make changes, persistent or severe organizational stress may provide an indication of where and how needed changes should be made. But productive change will occur only if organizations take stress-induced losses seriously, systematically assess stressors, and are flexible enough to make realistic changes.

Second, organizations can use education and training to reduce stress. Job previews and entry-level training programs can prepare employees for the particular stressors their jobs involve while giving them information about how to cope. Opportunities for advanced or continuing education can help employees cope with the qualitative overload that accompanies technological change or promotions. Also, training in personal stress management can be valuable if it is adapted to the specific needs of different groups of employees, and especially if it is used in conjunction with other changes.

Finally, organizations can concentrate on improving their internal communication. Although reducing all types of communication breakdowns will help alleviate stress, two improvements are most important. The first involves systems of goal-setting and performance appraisal. Each of the characteristics of effective appraisal systems discussed in Chapter 5 helps reduce organizational stress. When subordinates openly negotiate goals and ways to measure their attainment, they feel more in control of their lives. When supervisors use appraisal processes to give their subordinates clear and explicit guidelines for completing complex tasks (while still granting them a degree of autonomy), role ambiguity and overload can be reduced.

The second improvement involves support systems. Organizations can encourage employees to give one another social and informational support. In some professions the tasks people perform force them to be isolated from their peers. Many times this isolation will persist unless and until the organization acts specifically to overcome it. Sometimes the action required may be as simple as creating an open lounge area near the center of natural traffic patterns and encouraging people to use it. In other cases, meetings may be scheduled for the specific and expressed purpose of exchanging information, clarifying expectations and goals, and providing emotional and social support. Although some valuable rituals develop naturally in most organizational cultures (having morning coffee together, for example), in many cases their development needs to be encouraged by management. The importance of these meetings is that they are not perceived as meetings—required, task-related, decision-making sessions. As James March observed (see Chapter 6), the purpose of these meetings may be meeting, although in this case, for very productive reasons. Also, through close consultation between supervisors and subordinates, jobs can be designed so that their richness and degree of participation in decision making better match the desires and personalities of employees.

Many of these changes will not be possible or appropriate in a particular organization. In some cases they will be resisted for good reasons: They may reduce stress for a few employees and increase it for many others or be so expensive to implement compared to potential gains that they are not a wise investment. In other cases the values operating in an organizational culture may not allow it to address some stressors directly. Changing an employee's values, need for achievement, tolerance for ambiguity, and so on may be beyond the capacities of the organization. Or the upper managers of the organization may believe that they have neither the right nor the responsibility to do so. In still other cases changes which reduce stress and improve organizational efficiency may be resisted because they violate entrenched precedents. For all these reasons, almost all employees will need to develop their own means of managing felt stress.

Individual Stress Management: Adopting a Comic Frame

The common theme running through each of the chapters of this unit is that employees often communicate in ways which trap them in tragic frames of reference. They interpret and respond to situations through communication strategies which perpetuate and strengthen constraints and exigences. This concept explains why new employees sometimes fall into nonproductive patterns of acting during their first few months on the job and why managers often find themselves trapped within unproductive and escalating conflicts. But the concept may be even more relative to the stress response cycle.

Tragic perspectives generate two different kinds of cycles. In one employees blame themselves for their problems. They may be unable to complete all their assigned tasks, for example, and they attribute this situation to their own failings, lack of ability, or lack of training. Their self-esteem falls, the level of activity or hostility increases, and contact with other people is reduced. When they withdraw from others into their work, task-related information and social support become more and more scarce and felt stress increases. Becoming isolated also makes it progressively more difficult to step back from stress-producing events and search for more productive explanations of them. Through a process of *mortification*, of blaming oneself for one's situation, employees may become trapped within a maladaptive cycle of stress, response, and increased stress.

A second tragic pattern of action involves *victimage*. It begins when individuals blame someone else for their situation. Once a potential scapegoat is identified, the stressed individuals change their communication with the scapegoat, becoming more confrontive and less supportive, cooperative, and helpful. Alienation leads to isolation and distorted communication, the scapegoat begins to withhold and distort information, and the process continues. If the blamed person responds to the increased stress with either mortification or victimage, the process of stress, withdrawal, and communication breakdown continues. Once the mutually reinforcing cycles begin, neither party can accomplish tasks as effectively or efficiently as before, new stressors are added, and the cycle is strengthened.

Stress is in the perceptions of the employee. No external or internal pressure automatically and invariably creates felt stress. Stressors become stress only when they are perceived in very specific ways. If employees decide that the stressors they face are *someone's fault* they may become trapped in tragic patterns of action. But if they consistently view stressors as natural and inevitable aspects of work which can be managed strategically, they may be able to avoid becoming trapped. *Comic* frames exist when employees consciously and continuously step outside stressful situations, evaluate the factors producing their stress, and examine the stress-related effects of their own communicative behavior. Perhaps the most important individual stress-management strategy is adopting a comic frame of reference.

Individual Stress Management: Preparation

Two general types of stress management strategies are available to individuals. The first involves preparing for stressors and their effects. *Preparation* may include changing one's attitudes or values when they seem to be constant sources of stress. Career aspirations may need to be adjusted so that they fit the realities of one's situation. This is especially true of people who have reached middle management because the numerical realities of pyramidal organizations mean that relatively few of them will move up through the hierarchy of the organization. Recognizing that one's values are idealistic or that one's chosen career is inconsistent with them can reduce self-imposed stress. This does not mean that employees should abandon their ideals and values. Rather, they must realize that a myriad of factors present in all organizations delay or prevent the implementation of those ideals. Managing stress may be as simple as accepting the fact that although there are a near infinite number of things that should be changed in every organization (an almost infinite number of ways in which organizations can be made to be more efficient and satisfying), employees will have the greatest positive effect if they spend their time and energy changing those things that can most readily be changed. As Selye expresses this idea, "fight for the highest attainable gain but never put up resistance in vain."

Preparation also should involve a systematic assessment of stress by each employee for two reasons:[27] (1) Since stress depends on individual perceptions, only the employee can accurately evaluate his or her environment and responses to it, and (2) the act of performing a stress assessment gives a sense of control and thus can reduce a person's felt stress. In a stress assessment four questions should be answered:

1. What stressors does one face, both constantly and at different times of the day, week, or year? When and under what circumstances are those stressors greatest?

2. What symptoms does one exhibit when one feels stressed?

3. What thresholds does one have for each of the stressors typically faced?

4. What responses and coping strategies does one typically employ? What effect(s) do these responses have on stressors, felt stress, and other employees?

The first question provides information which may allow an employee to *confront* stressors *productively*. Some recurring stressors can be reduced through direct action. Subordinates can request regular performance feedback, ask for clarification of ambiguous role demands, and seek out official descriptions of who they are responsible to for the different parts of their jobs. If an assessment reveals that some stressors vary in intensity at different times, people can plan ahead for these episodes. Other tasks can be completed early or delayed until after the peak period, allowing the employees to focus all their resources on the stressful demand. Vacations or other forms of relaxation can be planned for the days immediately after these peak times occur in order to provide a constructive withdrawal. A stress assessment also will reveal stressors which cannot be confronted directly, pressures beyond the employee's control. Realizing that some stressors *are* beyond their control helps employees avoid falling into tragic patterns of response. It also helps them expend their energy changing conditions which can be changed and accepting those which cannot be.

Answering the second question (individual symptoms of stress) allows one to determine a "base line" to indicate when stress is becoming serious enough to warrant extra attention. People sometimes fail to recognize that they are feeling high levels of stress until after it is too late to use many of the productive responses that are available. As the stress response syndrome suggests, when stressors increase there is a momentary exhilaration from the added challenge, excitement, and activity. By the time the excitement turns into exhaustion, it often is too late to plan variations in work load, develop more efficient ways of performing tasks, gain clarification of duties and responsibilities, or cultivate social support networks. There is evidence that executives who report physiological effects of stress (ulcers, cardiovascular problems, and so on) have no greater stressors than those who do not, but they delay their efforts to cope with stress longer. Every person exhibits certain early warning signs of stress. For example, one person alters communication when he is under stress—it becomes more rapid; almost wholly task-oriented; and almost devoid of social niceties, attempts to provide or obtain social support, and relationship-oriented communication. Another responds by starting to question the quality of her decision making. But these signals are distinctive to each person and only that person can differentiate his or her normal patterns of thinking and communicating from the stress-induced patterns. Once warning signals and a base line are determined, an employee can recognize and respond to stress early enough to adopt productive coping strategies.

Coupled with early warning signs is a self-assessment of thresholds for different stressors. If employees know which stressors they cannot tolerate, they can be sensitive to the kinds of environmental changes likely to cause stress. One faculty member, for example, has a very low tolerance level for attending meetings (five minutes once a month is the threshold). But he also has a very high threshold for talking with graduate students. Knowing this, he can plan ahead to cope with meeting-induced stress by finishing pressing projects just before the meetings begin, thus reducing his feeling that he *must* have something better to do with his time, and planning to exercise after the meeting ends. Exercise seems to release pent-up tensions and provides a socially accepted opportunity to scream, moan, and swear, each of which must be repressed during the meetings. He also can plan to hold office hours with graduate students when he needs to get away from other stressors. But he can plan ahead only because he has conducted a number of careful stress assessments.

The final step in performing a stress assessment is to determine which responses one typically uses and gauge their effects. Employees who have only one or two different ways to cope with stress generally manage it less effectively than those who use many strategies. If employees find that their repertory does not include some potentially productive responses or only contains usually unproductive responses, they consciously can attempt to adjust appropriately.

A third form of preparing to manage stress concerns the relationship between stress and its physiological effects. Good health habits—regular aerobic exercise; adequate diet, including a normal daily intake of vitamins and minerals; and the avoidance of stress-related activities like smoking, excessive drinking, overeating, and irregular sleep patterns—all seem to reduce the physiological effects of stress. These steps also may influence the stressor-stress relationship, allowing people to develop higher tolerance levels.[28] Staying in good physical condition will not eliminate stress, but it can reduce its adverse physiological effects.

Individual Stress Management: Intervention Strategies

Although American employees now seem to value leisure more than ever before, there is growing evidence that their life-styles rarely give them opportunities for productive, stress-reducing relaxation. Presumably this was once not the case. In the nostalgic past workers led a slower, less hectic pace of life; they took time out to sit around the fire, sharing memories, and to gather together on the front porch to relax, swing and sing, and so on. This picture of life probably is more myth than reality. After all, only a relatively small proportion of our population has even owned a front porch, and the sixty-hour work week, common until the middle of this century, left little time to sit and swing. In addition, it is clear that stress still is a significant problem for rural families. But although there may never be a real Mayberry or Walton's Mountain, it is true that contemporary life-styles do not automatically build in significant time for relaxation. Employees often need to develop consciously time for and effective means of relaxing.

Recently a plethora of relaxation programs were devised and implemented by consulting firms and organizations. In fact, it seems that some form of structured relaxation is available for every person and preference. Biofeedback allows people who like machines to relax with them; systematic desensitization allows people to curl up with their tape recorders and imaginations; yoga provides metaphysicians with release, and relaxation exercises for muscular tension help sensorial people feel themselves relaxing. At base, each of these programs "works" because (and only if) they (1) allow people constructively to escape stressors and reenergize themselves and (2) can be used *during* stressful times and in stress-producing settings.[29] What works depends on each individual employee. Yoga and muscle relaxation may strike some people as unnatural. For them either activity may become a stressor in itself. Because biofeedback machines allow managers to chart their physiological responses, they may become part of a Type A pattern of behavior. In addition, it may not be possible to use a favored technique while people are at work or under stress. One of the problems with all programs of stress management is that employees tend to abandon them at precisely those times when they are needed most. Relaxation takes time, and when employees are overloaded they may not be willing to use their available time for managing stress. Developing an effective *personal* stress-management program involves *experimenting* with different techniques until effective ones are discovered and *becoming adept* at using those approaches in stressful situations.

CONCLUSION

Organizational stress is becoming a much-discussed and examined phenomenon. Although stress is a complex response to any number of possible sources, it is influenced by the communication processes of organizations and the communicative skills of individual employees. Both communication breakdowns and the act of communicating may generate stress. Involvement in supportive informal communication networks may help reduce felt stress or help employees manage the stress they feel. But involvement in communication networks may generate nonproductive responses. Stress can be managed effectively only when organizations and their employees understand the dynamics of stress and act in ways appropriate to the situation.

Spouses, Families, and Stress

This chapter implied that the only relationships that influence an employee's ability to manage stress are those formed at work. Although most of the existing research on organizational stress takes this perspective, it is, of course, quite unrealistic.[30] All employees are simultaneously "partially included" in a number of different relationships and different social structures. Their experiences and actions—including those related to stress—depend on the combination of different pressures in all these relationships. The most important nonwork relationships employees have are with their spouses and families.

Figure 11.4 depicts the multiple interrelationships among organizational stressors, family stressors, sources of social support, and responses to stress. *Work stress generates responses* which influence employees' relationships with their families. For example, when employees are overloaded at work they often tend to express negative emotions (being moody, short-tempered, and so on) at home. Their spouses begin to feel extra life stresses and worries, have more frequent stressful events, and often develop reduced feelings of security and well-being. In time both spouses begin to be less satisfied with their marriages, especially when the employees respond to work stresses with Type

FIGURE 11.4   Work and Family Stress Interrelationships

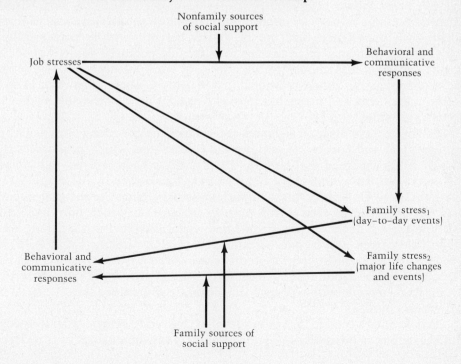

A behavior. In addition, some kinds of jobs lead directly to family stress. Frequent traveling, frequent moves from one location to another, and irregular work hours upset families, their normal activities, and their comfortable patterns of communication.[31] Unemployment also influences family stress directly. Rosabeth Moss Kanter grouped the features of jobs which affect family stress into five major categories:

1.   The degree to which the job demands *actions* from other family members, for example, attending or hosting social events for colleagues or requiring children and spouses to maintain relationships with children or spouses of co-workers

2.   Job demands which rob the family of the employee's time or upset the timing of family activities

3.   Rewards and resources, or the lack of them, provided by employment

4.   The values and attitudes demanded by the job and their relationship to the family's values

5.   Emotional spillover from work events[32]

Family and life stresses also influence job stress. Major life changes (see Table 11.2) may result in nonproductive attitudes, like reduced intrinsic motivation and lowered psychological involvement in the job, and/or maladaptive behaviors, like increased absenteeism and tardiness and nonproductive withdrawal from co-workers.[33] Family demands also may inhibit an employee's ability to respond productively to stresses at work.[34] Although family stresses have not been shown consistently to have a direct impact on work stress, nonwork stressors do have an important influence on the total amount of stress an employee experiences and on the ability to cope with it successfully.[35] Nonwork interpersonal relationships also provide potential sources of social support and thus may moderate the effects of work stressors. The buffering effects of supportive family relationships probably is not as important as supportive supervisors and peers, but in many cases it may be the only source of support available.[36]

So far we have discussed general interrelationships among dimensions of organizational and family stress. Like the research on which it is based, the discussion has assumed that families are traditionally structured—a husband who works full time outside the home, a wife who does not, and a number of minor children. One of the most important social changes of the past twenty years has been the growth in the number of families which do not fit this traditional mold. Because they are not traditional patterns, single parent, dual earner, dual career, and couples without children face unique stressors. Most of the institutions and support systems of our society are adapted to meet the needs of only the rapidly disappearing traditional family.[37] Particularly important to the people who will read this book are the unique stresses faced by dual-career couples.

People have a certain maximum level of time and energy available to cope with the demands imposed on them by all the many dimensions of their lives.

TABLE 11.2   Life Changes and Stress Potential

Life Event	Value
1. Death of spouse	100
2. Divorce	73
3. Marital separation	65
4. Jail term	63
5. Death of a close family member	63
6. Personal injury or illness	53
7. Marriage	50
8. Being fired from work	47
9. Marital reconciliation	45
10. Retirement	45
11. Change in health of a family member	44
12. Pregnancy	40
13. Sex difficulties	39
14. Gaining a new family member	39
15. Change in financial status	38
16. Death of a close friend	37
17. Change to a different line of work	36
18. Change in number of arguments with spouse	35
19. Mortgage of over $10,000 (20,000)	31
20. Foreclosure of mortgage or loan	30
21. Change in responsibilities at work	29
22. Son or daughter leaves home	29
23. Trouble with in-laws	29
24. Outstanding personal achievement	28
25. Wife/husband beginning or stopping work	26
26. Beginning or ending school	26
27. Revision of personal habits	24
28. Trouble with supervisor	23
29. Change in work hours or conditions	20
30. Change in residence	20
31. Change in schools	20
32. Change in recreation	19
33. Change in social activities	18
34. Mortgage of less than $10,000 ($20,000)	17
35. Change in sleeping habits	16
36. Change in number of family "get-togethers"	15
37. Change in eating habits	15
38. Vacation	13
39. Minor violations of the law	11

80% of people who had total points of more than 300 during one year had significant stress-related problems.
53% of people with totals between 150 and 300 had such problems.
33% of people with scores less than 150 had stress-related problems.

Adapted from T. Holmes and R. Rahe, "The Social Readjustment Rating Scale," *Journal of Psychosomatic Research*, 11 (1967), 213–218; and B. Dohrenwend and B. Dohrenwend, *Stressful Life Events* (New York: John Wiley, 1974).

Traditionally, couples have coped with these many pressures by dividing them up along the lines suggested by traditional sex roles—the husband is responsible for handling work-related pressures and making major decisions; the wife is responsible for managing family pressures and providing the husband with social and emotional support. For most traditional couples, life is sufficiently complex that the vast majority of both partners' time and energy is exhausted by these demands. When the wife enters the work force, the total number of demands placed on the couple increases while the total amount of available time and energy either stays the same or is reduced. The brunt of this increased demand is borne by the wife, whose job pressures generally are added on top of her same nonjob pressures. In fact, the total number of nonleisure hours (work plus home) demanded of husbands is greatest in traditional couples, less in couples where the wife works part time, and least in dual-earner or dual-career couples. Evidently the wife's income allows the husband to quit working overtime and taking on extra jobs. He has more leisure time because, typically, husbands of working wives spend no more time on home-related demands than do husbands whose wives play more traditional roles. In contrast, the total number of nonleisure hours demanded of the wife increases markedly when she enters the work force. Thus a modern Currier and Ives picture of the "typical" couple might show a wife writing year-end reports and cleaning the family's bathroom while the husband drinks beer, relaxes, and if recent studies of life satisfaction are accurate, complains that his wife no longer spends any leisure time with him.

Dual career couples can respond to these added demands in a number of different ways. Francine Hall and Douglas Hall described four patterns of response and indicated the relative degree of stress associated with each (see Table 11.3).[38] Dual-career couples have three kinds of work and home stress: *overload* from too many demands; *conflict* from difficulty coordinating time demands, like vacation schedules or expectations about how the two will act toward one another; and *change* imposed by career transitions or relocation. *Acrobatic* couples feel the most stress, *adversaries* the next most, *allies* the next most, and *accommodators*, who are the most like traditional couples, the least. Whatever their philosophical orientation, dual-career couples who cope best with stress seem to be those who develop a "protean" pattern of acting. They develop their own, unique, and flexible styles of living. They refuse to conform to traditional social pressures or to timetables and career demands imposed on them by their organizations. They openly negotiate a life-style which fits both of their needs and which stresses their mutual development and self-fulfillment. Often this alternative involves delaying, limiting the number of, or choosing not to have children. But in rebelling against traditional social pressures, protean couples face additional stressors.

Robert Rapoport and Rhona Rapoport identified four stressors particularly pressing for dual career couples:

1. *Normative dilemmas*—couples have daily confrontations and conflicts with people or institutions because they act in nontraditional ways. For

TABLE 11.3 Dual-Career Types and Stress

Type	Work Involvement	Home Involvement	Level of Stress and Reasons
I. Accomodators	Spouse A high and Spouse B low or Spouse B high and Spouse A low	Spouse B high and Spouse A low or Spouse A high and Spouse B low	Relatively low; normal work stressors; little additional stress; pattern approximates traditional family
II. Adversaries	Both high	Both low (but both value a well-ordered home)	Second highest; normal work stressors or both; high total overload and conflict; constant need to negotiate and renegotiate
III. Allies	Both low or both high	Both high or both low (with low value for well-ordered home)	Second lowest; normal work stresses and agreement on relative importance of work and home realms, and if high in one realm and low in other, time available for relationship itself
IV. Acrobats	Both high	Both high	Highest; normal work stresses, abnormal life stresses; insufficient reserves of energy to manage change-induced stress

Adapted from Francine Hall and Douglas Hall, *The Two-Career Couple* (Reading, Mass.: Addison-Wesley, 1979), and "Stress and the Two-Career Couple," in *Current Concerns in Occupational Stress*, ed. Cary Cooper and Roy Payne (New York: John Wiley, 1980).

instance, try to start a checking account when you and your spouse are at work from 9:00 A.M. to 5:30 P.M., or explain to your parents that you and you spouse have decided not to have children because of your mutual career goals.

2. *Identity dilemmas*—part of one's identity is linked to traditional values and sex-role stereotypes. For instance, try to tell yourself that you have decided to forego having children when you have been taught that reproducing is the only thing that proves you are fully a man or a woman.

3. *Social network dilemmas*—time and energy must be found to form and maintain social ties.

4. *Role-cycling dilemmas*—organizational demands out of phase with the situation of the other spouse must be managed. For instance, rarely do dual-career couples find that their career development paths require or allow them *both* to *move at the same time.*[39]

The paradox faced by dual-career couples really is quite simple: to cope with "traditional" stressors they must develop nontraditional relationships and life-styles. But acting in nontraditional ways creates new and different stresses. It may be that the dual demands impose a set of stressors on dual-career couples from which there is no escape, a pattern of action which is a complete tragic frame.

Notes

1. O. Niehouse and K. Massoni, "Stress—An Inevitable Part of Change," *S.A.M. Advanced Management Journal* (Spring 1979), 17–25.

2. R. Kahn, D. Wolfe, R. Quinn, J. Snoeck, and R. Rosenthal, *Organizational Stress* (New York: John Wiley, 1964).

3. These threshold points depend in part on the individual employee and in part on the total amount of stressors faced. When total pressure is greater, the threshold levels for each stressor are lower. Gary Cherniss, *Staff Burnout* (Beverley Hills, Calif.: Sage, 1980).

4. R. Lazarus and R. Launier, "Stress-Related Transactions Between Person and Environment," in *Perspectives in Interactional Psychology,* ed. L. Pervin and M. Lewis (New York: Plenum, 1980); Hans Selye, *The Stress of Life* (New York: McGraw-Hill, 1956). Unfootnoted quotations from Selye are from his presentation at Pfeiffer College, Misenheimer, N.C., November 9, 1979.

5. R. Payne, "Epistemology and the Study of Stress at Work," in *Stress at Work,* ed. C. Cooper and R. Payne (New York: John Wiley, 1978). Particularly good summaries of external sources of stress are this book and Cherniss, *Staff Burnout.* In his famous "executive monkey" studies, D. Rioche found that even non-human subjects feel stress when placed in the kinds of work situations that managers face; cited in Daniel Katz and Robert Kahn, *The Social Psychology of Organizations,* 2nd ed. (New York: John Wiley, 1978).

6. Phillip Zimbardo, *Shyness* (Reading, Mass.: Addison-Wesley, 1977).

7. C. Sofer, *Men in Mid-Career* (Cambridge, Eng.: Cambridge University Press, 1970); J. Kearns, *Stress in Industry* (London: Priory, 1973).

8. E. Kay, "Middle Management," in *Work and the Quality of Life,* ed. J. O'Toole (Cambridge, Mass.: M.I.T. Press, 1974); Rosabeth Moss Kanter, *Men and Women of the Corporation* (New York: Basic Books, 1977).

9. B. Gardell, "Alienation and Mental Health in the Modern Industrial Environment," in *Society, Stress and Disease*, ed. L. Levi (London: Oxford University Press, 1971), Vol. I, 146–166. See Chapter 5 of this book for a discussion on the limits of job-enrichment programs.

10. There is an ongoing debate among academic personnel about whether the research-teaching conflict is an example of task incompatibility (developing the skills needed to be a researcher reduces one's mastery of needed teaching skills) or "temporal" conflict (just too little time is available to concentrate fully on both tasks).

11. R. Payne, "Stress in Task-Focused Groups," *Small Group Behavior*, 12 (1981), 253–268.

12. Kahn et al., *Organizational Stress*; Robert Kahn, "Conflict, Ambiguity and Overload" in *Occupational Stress*, ed. A. McLean (Springfield, Ill.: Chas. C. Thomas, 1974), pp. 47–61. Of course, the pressures are "internal" in the sense that unrealistic societal expectations have been internalized; that is, they are not the "fault" of the individual. These and related issues will be examined at length in Chapter 2.

13. Cherniss, *Staff Burnout*.

14. James Segovis and Rabi Bhagat, "Participation Revisited," *Small Group Behavior*, 12 (1981), 299–328.

15. J. R. P. French and R. D. Caplan, "Organizational Stress and Individual Strain," in *The Failure of Success*, ed. A. Marrow (New York: AMACOM, 1972), pp. 30–66; Cary Cooper and Judi Marshall, "An Audit of Manager (Di)Stress," *Journal of Enterprise Management*, 1 (1978), 185–196. This seems to be particularly true when the employees' aspirations do not fit their situation (ibid., p. 190).

16. Cherniss, *Staff Burnout*, p. 116.

17. Terry Beehr, "Perceived Situational Moderators of the Relationship Between Subjective Role Ambiguity and Role Strain," *Journal of Applied Psychology*, 61 (1976), 35–40; Terrance Albrecht, R. Irey, and A. Mundy, "Integration in Communication Networks as a Mediator of Stress," *Social Work*, 27 (1982) 118–129; T. Albrecht, "Coping with Organizational Stress" (paper presented at the International Communication Association Convention, 1982).

18. R. Burke and P. Bradshaw, "Occupational and Life Stress and the Family," *Small Group Behavior*, 12 (1981), 329–375; Payne, "Epistemology"; French and Caplan, "Organizational Stress"; L. Pettegrew, R. Thomas, J. Ford, and D. Costello, "The Effect of Job-Related Stress on Medical Center Employee Communicator Style," *Journal of Applied Psychology*, 66 (1981).

19. In Katz and Kahn, *Social Psychology*; M. Mallinger, "Effective Coping," *Small Group Behavior*, 12 (1981), 269–284; J. House and J. Wells, "Occupational Stress, Social Support and Health" in *Reducing Occupational Stress*, ed. A. McLean, G. Black, and M. Colligan (Washington, D.C.: U.S. Government Printing Office, 1978); Kahn, "Conflict, Ambiguity and Overload."

20. M. Friedman and R. Rosenman, *Type A Behavior and Your Heart* (New York: Knopf, 1974); House and Wells, "Occupational Stress."

21. Cherniss, *Staff Burnout*; E. Christopher Poulton, "Blue Collar Stressors" in *Stress at Work*, ed. Cooper and Payne, pp. 51–80.

22. This section is our extension and integration of the models presented by H. Selye and Mardi Horowitz, *The Stress Response Syndrome* (New York: Jason Aronson, 1976).

23. Lazarus and Launier, "Stress-Related Transactions."

24. One of the more productive ways to increase work efficiency is through improved management of time. For an introductory treatment of time management see J. Ferner, *Successful Time Management* (New York: John Wiley, 1980).

25. Pettegrew et al., "Effect of Job-Related Stress." Also see Chapter 3 of this book.

26. A fine introduction to organizational strategies is provided by A. Pines, E. Aronson, and D. Kafry, *Burnout* (New York: The Free Press, 1981).

27. Personal strategies are summarized in D. Norfolk, *The Stress Factor* (New York: Simon & Schuster, 1977).

28. There still is substantial debate about the effects of exercise on stress.

29. Herbert Benson, *The Relaxation Response* (New York: Avon Books, 1975).

30. Payne, "Stress in Task-Focused Groups."

31. Burke and Bradshaw, "Occupational and Life Stress."

32. Rosabeth Moss Kanter, *Work and Family in the United States* (New York: Russell Sage, 1977); R. Seidenberg, *Corporate Wives—Corporate Casualties?* (New York: AMACOM, 1973); D. Dooly and R. Catalano, "Economic Change as a Cause of Behavioral Disorders," *Psychological Bulletin,* 87 (1980), 450–468.

33. Rabi Bhagat, "Effects of Personal Life Stress on Individual Performance and Work Adjustment" (paper presented at the American Psychological Association Convention, Montreal, 1980).

34. T. Holmes and R. Rayhe, "The Social Readjustment Rating Scale," *Journal of Psychosomatic Research,* 11 (1967), 213–218; B. Dohrenwend and B. Dohrenwend, *Stressful Life Events* (New York: John Wiley, 1974).

35. P. Evans and F. Bartolome, "The Relationship Between Professional Life and Private Life," cited in Burke and Bradshaw, "Occupational and Life Stress."

36. J. LaRocco, J. House, and R. French, "Social Support, Occupational Stress and Health," *Journal of Health and Social Behavior,* 21 (1980), 202–218.

37. Ralph Smith, ed., *The Subtle Revolution* (Washington, D.C.: The Urban Institute, 1979), examines the particular problems faced by single-parent, childless, and dual-earner couples.

38. D. Hall and F. Hall, *The Two-Career Couple* (Reading, Mass.: Addison-Wesley, 1979), and "Stress and the Two-Career Couple," in *Current Concerns in Occupational Stress,* ed. Cary Cooper and Roy Payne (New York: John Wiley, 1980).

39. R. Rapoport and R. Rapoport, *Dual Career Families Revisited* (New York: Harper & Row, 1976).

12
Communication, Sex Roles, and Organizations

THE STATUS OF WOMEN

ACCULTURATION, SEX ROLES, AND EMPLOYEES' ACTIONS

SEX ROLES AND ORGANIZATIONAL SUCCESS
Determinant of Organizational Success 1: Power
Determinant of Organizational Success 2: Mobility

ORGANIZATIONAL COMMUNICATION AND SEX ROLES

CONCLUSION

We are undergoing a revolution—at times obvious, at times only dimly perceived. . . . In less than a generation the size of the female labor force has more than doubled and now includes the majority of working age women. . . . Between now and 1990 an additional one million women will enter the labor force each year.
—Ralph Smith

The most important part of the experience of our generation—a group sometimes called the "baby boomers"—has been the need to cope with the major changes that have taken place during our lifetimes. Perhaps the most far-reaching of these changes involves societal attitudes toward the appropriate roles and behaviors of women and men. As the Urban Institute's 1979 study clearly suggests, paid work outside the home is now a central part of the lives of most women.[1] As women continue to move into traditionally male occupations and organizational ranks, sex roles are becoming an increasingly important aspect of organizational communication. This chapter is designed to summarize the complicated relationships among the characteristics of formal organizations, our society's conceptions of appropriate sex roles, and employees' communication. Our intent is to provide insights about managing these complicated interrelationships that will be useful to both male and female employees. However, we recognize that the strategic use of communication to manage sex roles is of primary importance to female professionals.

THE STATUS OF WOMEN

In 1961 the President's Commission on the Status of Women reported that women and men were treated in substantially different ways regarding career opportunities and income. In the economy as a whole, women's incomes for each hour worked was approximately half that of men. After rising above 60 percent, today that percentage has fallen slightly to approximately 59 percent. Although the size of this gap varies in different industries, age groups, educational backgrounds, and occupations, very few women today can realistically expect to earn more than 75% of the income of their male counterparts at any point during their lifetimes (see Figure 12.1).[2] There are a number of expla-

FIGURE 12.1   Life Cycle Earnings Potentials by Gender

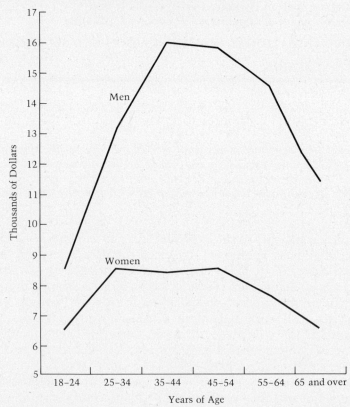

See Ralph Smith, ed., *The Subtle Revolution* (Washington, D.C.: The Urban Institute, 1979).

nations offered for these differences, some accurate in part and some wholly unsupported. Among the unsupported explanations are these:

1. Women are less well-educated than men.
2. Women interrupt their careers to bear and raise children.
3. Women are less committed to their careers and spend less time and energy on career development and advancement.

Although the first and second observations are accurate to some degree, they do not explain differences in income or advancement. Figure 12.2 depicts the effect education has on lifetime earnings of men and women; for both groups education enhances earnings, but to very different degrees. Even highly educated women can expect to earn less than men with substantially less education. Similarly, although women do have more frequent and longer career interruptions than men, these interruptions are not significantly related to differences in earnings. Even when the effect of career interruptions is held constant, women with bachelor's degrees can expect roughly the same lifetime earnings as men without high school diplomas. There is also evidence that

FIGURE 12.2   Life Cycle Earnings by Gender and Education

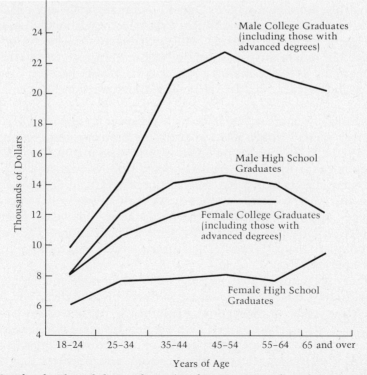

See Ralph Smith, ed., *The Subtle Revolution* (Washington, D.C.: The Urban Institute, 1979).

supports the third observation, but the factors involved are so complex and the available data so confusing that differences in potential cannot be linked directly to commitment or to "energy." In fact, if there is a relationship between these factors, it seems to be in the opposite direction—when women realize that their options are limited and incomes discriminatory, they sometimes become less committed to their careers.

There are other, more accurate explanations for differences in earnings. First, women are paid less than men for identical and/or comparable work. In spite of the existence of affirmative action programs, wide gaps in salaries within occupations are the norm rather than the exception. Second, women are disproportionately concentrated in careers having lower earning potentials. Women tend to opt for educational programs and career tracks that place them in what have been called "pink collar" occupations—clerical and service work and retail sales—or careers which involve "nurturing" others—education, social work, nursing. Even within high income occupations, such as medicine, a disproportionate number of women specialize in psychiatry or pediatrics, whereas very few concentrate on surgery or gynecology. The group of "women's specialties" has lower salaries than the group of "male" concentrations, even though they require comparable education, training, and skills. The reasons for differential career choices are varied, ranging from overt, open discrimination by employers and labor unions in traditionally male occupations to more subtle acculturation processes which limit the range of occupations that women consider. Overall, approximately one-quarter of career income differences can be attributed to this factor, although it is a far more important factor for white, married college graduates. And, to complicate the situation further, when large numbers of women begin to enter traditionally male occupations, average salaries begin to fall, in part because of overt discrimination and in part because of increased competition for available positions.

Unfortunately, there seems to be little prospect for change. Differences in career choices seem to have changed very little during the "revolutionary" 1960s and 1970s. A 1978 survey of 5,000 women who planned to work outside the home found that about 80 percent of noncollege women and 75 percent of college women anticipated being in traditionally female occupations at age thirty-five. Current projections suggest that the adverse effects of different career choices will *increase* during the next twenty-five years, as increasing numbers of women enter traditionally female occupations. This will cause increased competition for available positions, which will tend to drive down wages and salaries.[3]

Another explanation involves the promotion of male and female employees. Although there has been an increase in the number of firms which employ women in supervisory or managerial positions, *very few* women have moved past the middle management level. This phenomenon cannot be explained by differences in education, experience, behavior, or seniority.[4] Since it is related directly to the characteristics of organizations and organizational communication, it will be the primary focus of the remainder of this chapter.

ACCULTURATION, SEX ROLES, AND EMPLOYEES' ACTIONS

Understanding the effects that sex roles, organizational structures, and communication have on one another begins with an investigation of the nature and impact of traditional acculturation processes. Recall Max Weber's observation that the ways in which employees perceive, process, interpret, and respond to situations at work are influenced by the expectations and perceptual frameworks that society accepts and perpetuates. This concept is perhaps best illustrated by the impact of traditional sex-role assumptions on the actions of male and female employees.

Careful observers of human societies have recognized for millenia that cultures remain stable largely because their members share a set of social "myths."[5] Unfortunately, the common use of the term *myth* equates the concept with childhood foolishness—mythical beliefs in the tooth fairy, Easter Bunny, and Santa Claus which serve as adequate explanations of certain events for children, but are abandoned by adults. However, in analyses of social myth the term is defined in a very different way. Cultures are based on a group of assumptions about human beings and their relationships to one another and to the world around them. These assumptions cannot be empirically proven or denied. The beliefs that "honesty is virtuous and dishonesty evil," "thou shalt not steal," and "life is sacred" cannot be confirmed by scientific experiment. But if societies are to function in any cooperative or stable way, their members must share some core beliefs about how they should act. Since people cannot learn these assumptions solely by observations or personal experiences, they must be taught indirectly. To teach these lessons, societies develop a complex group of stories and myths which indirectly communicate the assumptions that define and stabilize the culture. For example, Washington's cherry tree and Lincoln's walk to return a customer's change are stories which perpetuate the belief that "honesty is the best policy." Through these and similar myths citizens learn what actions are normal, are expected of them, and are morally good. Social mythologies provide people with stable and predictable social worlds—they tell us how to act, predict how others will act, and make sense of social events.

Mythologies stabilize societies. Unfortunately, the specific myths that define a particular culture often stabilize it at the expense of some of its members. For example, the most stable and long-lasting societies in human history—ancient Egypt and China—were grounded on myths of the naturalness and rightness of master-slave relationships. One of the stabilizing mythologies of modern Western cultures concerns the proper roles for men and women. Part of this sex-role mythology involves macroscopic concepts about one's proper social place. At least since the early years of the Industrial Revolution, when factories began to replace home manufacture, Western societies have perpetuated the assumption that man's primary activities should take place outside the home and woman's actions would be limited to the home. Man's responsibility is to represent his family to outsiders by making business decisions obtaining an adequate family income and so forth. Woman's responsibility is to provide a safe, nurturing haven from the pressures of the outside world, both for her husband and for her children. Eventually this economically and socially convenient division of action became regarded as natural (that is genetically ordained), inevitable, and morally right.

As this macroscopic sex-role mythology developed, it encompassed a complex, microscopic group of appropriate characteristics for each realm of action. Man's world demanded that its residents develop traits of independence, rationality, assertiveness, activity, task-orientation, and strategic skills. Woman's place required the opposite characteristics of dependence, emotionality, submissiveness, passivity, person-orientation, and openness. In a curious self-fulfilling cycle, acculturational processes prepare males for one world and females for another. Eventually social myths create "empirical" evidence to support themselves. The residents of the male world have "male" characteristics and the residents of the female world have "female" ones. Once a certain set of attributes is perceived as natural, it provides people with a stable and predictable basis on which to interpret their own and others' actions and a comfortable set of parameters within which to make their own choices about how to act. But when individual members of the society choose to act in alternative ways, or when the social and economic conditions that once supported the mythology change, the traditional myths no longer meet the needs of either the culture or its members. During times of social change, people often find that they cannot simultaneously conform to the traditional mythology of their culture and act in ways which meet their own individual needs, goals, values, and roles. They face complicated double binds—pressures and constraints which simultaneously tell them to act in different and incompatible ways. These double binds lie at the center of the relationship between sex roles and communicative action in organizations.[6]

SEX ROLES AND ORGANIZATIONAL SUCCESS

For decades both organizational theorists and employees have been trying to delineate the factors which contribute to success. Typically, organizational success has been defined in financial or status-related terms. "Successful" people are those who have large salaries and/or have obtained the symbols of high status—formal rank, autonomy, or tangible symbols of superiority. A number of factors, some of which are a function of random processes (like luck), have been identified as determinants of success. The most important of the nonrandom factors are *power* and *mobility*. Both these elusive factors depend primarily on an employee's ability to create strategic *perceptions* of themselves. In general, traditional notions about sex roles give male employees more opportunity to create the impression that they possess power and are mobile.

Determinant of Organizational Success 1: Power[7]

As explained in Chapter 7, power is in the eye of the beholder. It is the perception that some employees are better able to obtain their goals than others. Although a number of potential bases of power exist, there are four primary communicative processes through which perceived power is created.

Power Process 1: Demonstrating One's Appropriateness   People who demonstrate attributes perceived as appropriate to their profession, organization, and rank generally are more powerful than those who do not. In general, people perceive that professionals, especially managers, must be *rational* decision makers. Perceptions of rationality include personal control of emotional responses and avoidance of emotional considerations in decision making. People who react emotionally are seen as nonprofessional; people who attend to emotive or value-related factors during decision making are seen as "not tough enough to manage." Acculturation prepares us to perceive males as rational and females as emotional.[8]

Sex-role stereotypes create perceptual sets through which we (1) *attend* to events and actions which confirm our predispositions and (2) *interpret* the events and actions we observe in ways which support our perceptual sets. For example, when male and female managers exhibit the *same* behaviors, their actions often are *interpreted* differently. Males who adopt "human relations oriented" leadership strategies are seen as analytical and forceful, whereas women who use these approaches are seen as open-minded and nurturing.[9] In addition, because we learn that rational actions are appropriate for men (and emotional displays are not) and emotional actions are appropriate for women (and rationality is not), it is easier for males to adopt aggressive, calculating postures than it is for females. Thus, men can more readily appear to be "professional" and more often will be perceived to be so. Males have wider access to this appropriate professional characteristic.

Gender-related differences in the ability to create an appropriate professional image are complicated further by typical male and female patterns of communicating.[10] The images that people create of themselves depend on both the content and form of their communication. Certain communication patterns create impressions of weakness, insecurity, passivity, and limited competence. Other modes of communicating connote competence, power, assertiveness, and security (see Figure 12.3). Women tend to use "weakening" strategies more frequently then men. More important, when women do use weakening modes of communication, others tend to perceive them as less capable than when they do not. In effect, the weakening strategies elicit or accent traditional sex-role stereotypes about female emotionality and powerlessness. However, weakening strategies used by males have no significant effect on their images. Since males do not face a stereotype which accents

FIGURE 12.3 Strengthening and Weakening Communicative Strategies

---

Weakening Strategies

Tag Questions: "X is true, don't you think?"
"We should do Y, don't you agree?"
Disclaimers: "I know I'm out of my area of expertise but. . . . "
"The data aren't all in yet, but. . . . "
"X is Y, unless there are interactive factors that I've
overlooked."
Making statements without including supporting evidence
Failing to organize arguments or develop clear statements

Strengthening Strategies

Making clear, structured, and supported arguments
Assertively speaking up
Interrupting or "talking over"
Controlling substantial amounts of conversational time

---

powerlessness, their use of weakening strategies does not provoke negative cultural images.

In addition to differing *forms* of communication, men and women tend to differ in the *content* of their communication. Women discuss home, family, and relationships; men discuss business-related topics (the economic situation, investment opportunities) or topics symbolic of male sex roles (competitive sports, sexual conquests). When men discuss family concerns it generally is with women employees, and the conversation typically focuses on the woman's family. The selection of conversational topics subtly reinforces traditional perceptions about male and female societal roles and professionals. When women discuss home and family it perpetuates the assumption that their real commitments lie outside the organization. When men discuss football it confirms their appropriateness to their organizational "team." The subtle effects of topic may be accompanied by less subtle topic-related communication strategies. For example, in mixed-gender conversational groups, men sometimes seem to use topic choice as a means of embarrassing or reducing the credibility of female professionals. Sports and sexual conquest become *more* prevalent topics when women are present; discussions of family life and sexual innuendoes may be used to "put women in their place." These strategies succeed because they generate patterns of communication which confirm traditional sex-role stereotypes.

Thus, for a number of reasons, male professionals find it easier to create the impression that they possess the characteristics generally expected of professionals. Males also can more readily provide evidence that they have the specific features desired in their organization. Members of the upper echelons of organizations typically are surrounded by people who are very much like themselves in background, experience, orientation, race, gender, religion, and marital status. As earlier chapters explained, there are understandable reasons for preferring associates who are like oneself. In all organizations one of the most important needs people have is to manage the uncertainty that surrounds them. If they can ensure that only people who are like them are promoted into the positions on which they depend most, they can reduce the uncertainty they face. In addition, communication is complicated by heterophily. The more homogeneous a group is, the lower are the chances that its members will misunderstand one another or become defensive when communicating. Information flows more rapidly among them, and distortion of information is reduced. Each of these effects—reduced uncertainty and improved exchange of information—is important to the functioning of all organizations and all units within them. They are *most* important for organizations which exist in turbulent environments and units which face complex decisions. Since the bulk of upper-level employees in American organizations are Caucasian, Protestant males, these understandable preferences mitigate against the promotion of persons of a different sex, race, ethnic background, religious affiliation, or educational background.[11]

Men also find it less difficult to demonstrate another major "appropriate" characteristic: loyalty to their organization and career. Loyalty is a nebulous concept. It cannot be demonstrated directly, but an employee can repeatedly signal that the organization is one's highest priority. Although the symbols of loyalty differ in various organizations, there does seem to be one commonly accepted way to demonstrate it: the sublimation of all other activities and relationships to one's career and one's working relationships. Consistently taking work home, seeking promotions or transfers when they would be disadvantageous to one's family and limiting social ties to business contacts all seem to be widely accepted indices of loyalty. In traditionally structured families, creating these impressions is possible. The professional's wife is available to serve as hostess, secretary, child-care specialist, and therapist. But for unmarried professionals or married women professionals, no one is available to play this "wifely" role.

Presumably the husbands of women professionals could assist in home activities. However, the studies of time allocation in dual-career marriages (summarized in Chapter 11) provide compelling evidence that husbands rarely do so. For example, Kathryn Walker and Margaret Woods found that the average total number of nonleisure hours (job plus work at home) of husbands whose wives work full time was eleven hours *less* than that of males in traditional households. Because their wives' incomes allow them to reduce overtime, abandon second jobs, or ease their efforts to "get ahead," husbands' job-related workload is reduced by an average of eleven hours per week. Even though their wives work full time outside the home, these husbands spend no more time doing home-related work than their counterparts whose wives do not work. As a result, their total workload drops whereas their wives' workloads increase significantly.[12]

Consequently, women professionals rarely have the opportunity to use generally accepted symbols of loyalty. Household demands prevent them from taking work home, and the absence of someone at home in the "wife's" role (hostess, secretary, nanny, and so on) precludes "social" symbols of loyalty. Similarly, meeting their husbands' career needs and fulfilling demands related to child care limit their ability to accept promotions and transfers. Even in relationships with egalitarian values, it is the wife's career that generally is interrupted by relocation.[13] Traditional sex-role stereotypes and the realities of job and family relationships combine to reduce women's ability to demonstrate the "appropriate" professional characteristics of rationality, similarity, and loyalty. Their ability to use this image-creating process to obtain organizational power is less than that of their male competitors.

Power Process 2: Using Influence Effectively   Power begets power. Once employees are perceived as capable of obtaining their objectives, they generally are provided with additional opportunities to exercise influence. However, to start the cycle, employees must be in an organizational position which provides some initial opportunity to exercise power. In part because of their career "choices" and in part because of the assignments they are given when they first enter an organization, women rarely occupy positions from which they can exercise significant influence.[14] Even supervisors in personnel, customer service, or secretarial and clerical pools (the units of organizations with significant numbers of women) have little formal influence.

In many cases women occupy positions in which their power depends on the support of males. Rosabeth Moss Kanter argues that the role of "executive secretary" is an excellent example of this kind of relationship. The executive secretary's formal and informal status is contingent on her supervisors' rank; she is promoted when he is promoted; she is perceived as "X's secretary" rather than as an individual; she depends almost wholly on his evaluations of her performance for advancement; and frequently she is at his "beck and call," a phenomenon illustrated by request for personal services, such as errands for him or his family. As long as she is *perceived* by other members of the organization as *dependent* on her supervisor, she will have virtually no opportunity to exercise influence in a way which generates personal power. When she successfully exercises influence, the credit is his; when she fails, the responsibility is hers.[15] Typically male employees are placed in positions which provide greater opportunity to exercise influence and develop independence. If successful, they will receive additional opportunities to exercise power.

Power Process 3: Performance   *Exceptional* performance is another avenue to power. To be exceptional, performance must be *visible*, perceived to be *extraordinary*, and important to *significant problems* faced by the organization.[16]

However, to perform organizationally significant tasks, one must be assigned organizationally significant tasks. The positions occupied by women usually do not involve this kind of assignment.

To be *visible*, high-quality performance must be *communicated* to powerful members of the organization and *perceived* as an example of an employee's competence. To a certain degree all employees' performance is communicated to other members of the organization through formal channels. Quarterly reports, intraorganization newsletters, and appraisal conferences all provide powerful employees with information about the performance of other employees. But equally important, information is communicated through informal networks. Because the informal networks that emerge in organizations tend to include only males, information about the success of female employees is not disseminated as rapidly or as extensively as for male employees. The problem is not so much one of "blowing one's own horn" as of having someone available to listen when the horn is blown. This disadvantage is reduced when a woman has male colleagues who are willing to talk about her performance with other males. However, this is effective only to a limited degree. Unless other members of the network have an incentive to disseminate the information further, relatively few people will become aware of a female employee's success.

Even when information is communicated to powerful members of the organization, it will not lead to increased power and prestige unless those members *perceive* that the performance provides evidence of *competence*. If success is attributed to factors outside the employee's control—luck, the assistance of other employees, or the effectiveness of the organization as a whole—rather than to one's skill and expertise, performance will not produce power. Not only is there evidence that evaluators tend to attribute the performance of women to external factors and of men to intrinsic skills, there also seems to be a tendency for supervisors to feel and express greater confidence in their evaluations of their male than their female subordinates.[17] When evaluators express a lack of confidence in their judgments about an employees' performance, the credibility of successful performance is reduced. The comment "good job, for a woman" or any equivilent statement diminishes the significance of the success and helps perpetuate the assumption that women only perform effectively in atypical cases. Since the *expectation* that excellent performance will continue generates power and prestige, any communication strategy which defines a woman's success as atypical will short-circuit the performance, power, and opportunity cycle. Sex roles influence perceptions; perceptions influence attributions of the reasons for performance; attributions either transform performance into power or reduce it to trivia.

Power Process 4: Forming and Maintaining Alliances   As explained in Chapter 6, a potentially important source of power is the formation of alliances with other employees. If employees who are outside an alliance perceive that it is stable and the combined power of its members is equal to or greater than their own, the alliance will provide its members with sizeable influence over others' actions. However, the existence of a powerful organizational alliance gives outsiders strong motivations to join it and/or destroy it. Alliances are informal creations and their power does threaten outsiders. And they are transient and inherently unstable creations. Yet they remain an important source of power for relatively powerless members of organizations, particularly women.

Person-centered alliances. Often the advice given employees by researchers and practicing managers does not coincide. However, there seems to be widespread agreement that successful employees are those who have been able to establish close, personal relationships with one or more senior employees early in their careers. From their *mentors* young newcomers gain access to *information* and *expertise,* which they are able to use to improve their performance and enhance their status and power. The mentor-mentoree relationship seems to have been particularly important to the success of women who have reached the upper echelons of their organizations.[18]

Employees gain information about their tasks and their organizations from mentors. Much of this information is informal and thus not available through formal channels. Some information involves broadly applicable principles such as information about organizational power and politics. Expectations about an employee's image and life-style are subtle and difficult to interpret. Nonrational aspects of decision making are difficult for newcomers to anticipate or manage. Without accurate information about these subtleties of organizational life, new employees can make accidental errors with serious consequences. Once newcomers are perceived as error-prone or politically insensitive, it becomes progressively more difficult for them to gain access to the available sources of power. Mentors also can provide information which helps newcomers cope with more specific problems. For example, stress can be managed by prioritizing tasks or ignoring conflicting role demands. However, these approaches require employees to have accurate information about the relative importance of their tasks and about the relative power of the people giving contradictory commands. Mentors can provide information about priorities and power relationships. They also can communicate norms about how conflicts are handled in a particular organization. Open and honest confrontation is not only doomed to failure but also is damaging to an individual's status if the organization accepts avoidance as the only legitimate means of managing conflicts. Mentors can provide information which keeps a newcomer from learning this lesson through trial and error.

However, like all interpersonal relationships, mentor-mentoree relationships are difficult to form and maintain.[19] Some organizations have attempted to formalize these relationships, assigning every newcomer to an official mentor. At least in our culture, where choice is a strongly valued part of relationships, formal arrangements have had only limited success. Normally it is the potential mentor who initiates the relationship. Potential mentorees can facilitate the process by visibly demonstrating their career goals and competencies; determining which persons in the organization have the relevant information, influence, and expertise; and responding favorably when those people begin to initiate relationships.

Once a mentor-mentoree relationship is established, the greatest problem it faces is the possible creation of an actual or perceived *dependency relationship*. To the extent that an employee's success is perceived as dependent on the mentor's sponsorship, advancement may be impeded. Perceived dependency relationships are not usually purposefully created. For example, when newcomers face a difficult conflict, their mentors may choose to intervene on their behalf. This action accents the mentors' power, the mentorees' powerlessness, and the mentorees' dependence on the mentors. A more productive way of helping is for the mentors to provide the mentorees with information about the situation, issue, and history of the conflict and to discuss available strategies. Armed with this information, the mentorees can then "fight the battle" themselves, thus learning conflict-handling skills and avoiding the perception that their success depends on their mentor's power. Perceived dependency is one of the reasons for newcomers not to form mentoring relationships with their immediate supervisors and to try to be part of a number of different mentoring relationships. In supervisor-subordinate relationships, there is a great tendency for mentors to intervene rather than inform, and the potential for others *perceiving* the relationship as dependent is increased. When an employee has multiple mentors, each mentoring relationship is less visible and the potential for being seen as dependent is reduced.

Mentor-mentoree relationships also are difficult to end. Almost always there will come points in a newcomer's career development at which certain mentoring relationships become unproductive for the mentoree. At these points both members must be willing to dissolve the relationship and focus their attention on other mentoring relationships. Although terminating relationships without creating lasting bad feelings is quite difficult, these relationships must be terminated successfully because the same factors that made the parties attractive allies make them formidable enemies.

The comments made about mentoring relationships to this point hold true for all such relationships, regardless of the gender of the people involved. Mentoring relationships are important sources of information, expertise, and power but must be managed carefully if they are to enhance an employee's success. However, pervasive sex-role stereotypes complicate the mentoring relationship in unique ways when the mentoree is female. Because so few women occupy positions near the top of organizational hierarchies, the vast majority of mentors will be male. People perceive other people and other people's relationships through deeply ingrained interpretive frameworks. Part of these frameworks involve expectations about sex roles and mixed-sex relationships. Two traditionally accepted roles for women are those of sex object and child or pet.[20] The two corresponding traditional male-female relationships involve sexual bonds and father-daughter ties. Stereotypes prepare outsiders to interpret ambiguous and partial information in ways which define male-female mentoring relationships as either sexual (rather than professional) or familial (rather than advisory). In both of these stereotypical relationships, the woman is cast in an inferior, passive, and dependent role. In neither relationship is she expected to act in an assertive, powerful, or professional way. Traditional sex-role stereotypes also complicate the mentoring relationship itself because they make it more difficult for the parties to know how to act toward one another or to interpret each other's actions. The relationship is strained and communication is less open and spontaneous than in male-male relationships.

Women-women mentoring relationships also are complicated by the interaction between traditional sex-role stereotypes and organizational characteristics.[21] Because women tend to work in the same units of organizations, it is likely that women-women mentoring relationships will involve subordinates and their immediate supervisors. Similarly, because a majority of women managers occupy relatively powerless positions, it is unlikely that they can obtain the kinds of rewards for their subordinates that male supervisors can. As Donald Pelz demonstrated, supervisors with low levels of power tend to have less satisfied subordinates than supervisors with high levels of power, especially when they adopt leadership strategies oriented toward human relations, which are preferred by female managers.[22] However, if the supervisor-mentor has high levels of personal power, she may become isolated from her subordinates-mentorees. During a series of seminars for women managers, Judith Bardwick observed that the women with the highest levels of competence, assertiveness, skill, and so on often became the targets of the group's hostilities rather than respected symbols of potential. Bardwick explained that the less powerful women coped with their situations by attributing their lack of organizational power to factors outside their control—overt discrimination, unequal access to education and training, or other impersonal factors. When confronted with a woman who *had* overcome all these external barriers, the less-powerful women could then only attribute their situations to their own inadequacies. They resolved their frustrations by projecting them on the more powerful members of the group. Kanter observed a similar dynamic, although the less powerful women in her studies were covertly rather than overtly aggressive.[23]

Women mentors may find it difficult to correct or chastize their female subordinates; thus the direction and guidance which makes mentoring relationships succeed is absent. Subordinates then may become unaccustomed to receiving feedback, may become hypersensitive to criticism, and do not develop the ability to respond productively to feedback. Because the supervisor is not directive she appears to other members of the organization to be not "tough enough to manage." Eventually, her power is reduced, and task-related communication between supervisor and subordinates breaks down. The information subordinates need to advance is denied them, and the supervisor is less able to perform effectively. Open, informal communication is particularly important to mentoring relationships and to supervisors who prefer human relations leadership strategies. For quite different reasons, both powerful and less powerful female mentors may find it difficult to initiate and sustain effective mentoring relationships.

Situation-centered alliances. Unlike mentor-mentoree alliances, which are based primarily on interpersonal attractions, situation-centered alliances are based almost completely on the power relationships and issues existing in an organization at a particular time and place. Alliances are created when a number of employees perceive that they (1) have insufficient power as individuals to effect the changes they desire, (2) have common interests which could draw them together in united action, and (3) would have sufficient power to achieve their goals if they worked together. Some alliances are issue-specific. A number of parties all perceive that a forthcoming proposal, policy, or action threatens (or could benefit) them in some way. They are bound together by the presence of that imminent threat or promise. For example, stockholders who generally are competitors may unite to defeat a merger proposal. Once the vote is taken they no longer have any compelling common interests, and the alliance dissolves. Other alliances are more stable and can be expected to remain stable over a wide range of issues and decisions. Their members may perceive that they always face a common enemy, as when two small units of an organization perpetually face competition for resources from a larger unit. Another enduring alliance may be formed when organizational members have tasks or beliefs which coincide so that events which help one also help the others. First-line supervisors may collaborate in helping one of their subordinates obtain a salary increase because they know that eventually they can use their subordinates' salaries as an argument to justify their own salary demands.

As explained in Chapters 6 and 9, regardless of how alliances are related to the issues, they are inherently unstable. This instability tends to harm relatively powerless members more than more powerful ones. Coalitions often cannot afford to lose a powerful employee's support and may redefine their goals in order to accommodate their powerful members. Keeping powerful people in an alliance also prevents them from joining other alliances and using their power against their old allies. But for low-power individuals, these constraints rarely exist. In short, to the extent that different members of a coalition have widely differing levels of organizational power, the coalition is unstable and the low-power members are most likely to be left out when alliances change and coalitions dissolve.

Women are placed in difficult positions by the dynamics of alliance formation and change. Because they are denied access to other sources of power, managing coalitions is more important to them than it is to their male counterparts. But because they generally have low levels of organizational power they are most vulnerable to shifts in coalitions. This vulnerability may be heightened by certain aspects of sex-role acculturation. First, women sometimes learn to interpret actions and relationships more in personal terms than in situational terms. If an alliance is *person-centered* this interpretation is appropriate and would lead women to act in ways which enhance the benefits of the alliance. But if it is *situation-centered*, interpreting the alliance in personal terms may be damaging.

Shifts in coalitions may be totally unexpected because the interpersonal relationship "seemed" to be stable. Changes in alliances may be interpreted as reflecting the other members' lack of personal integrity or the declining interpersonal closeness of the members' relationships. Traditional processes of acculturation also often leave women without the background and experience necessary for managing organizational politics (alliance formation and alteration). The popularity of books and training programs which deal with corporate "games" indicates that many professional women find organizational politics to be foreign, offensive, sometimes frightening, and often incomprehensible.[24]

In summary, there are four primary sources of power, and thus of success, in organizations. Complicated interactions among traditional sex-role stereotypes, communication processes, and the characteristics of formal organizations make it more difficult for women to gain access to these sources. In general, people perceive that males "naturally" (1) possess appropriate characteristics, (2) are able to play powerful roles effectively, (3) are successful performers, and (4) are valuable and knowledgeable members of alliances. Women are perceived as "naturally" lacking these attributes and thus must overcome important perceptual and communicative barriers in their efforts to gain power.

Determinant of Organizational Success 2: Mobility

Just as power begets power, the opportunity to advance upward through an organization generates increased opportunity for upward mobility. Advancement begets advancement in two ways. First, once employees are perceived as upwardly mobile, other employees begin to treat them in distinctive ways. Because they are likely to have progressively increasing formal power, they become sought-after allies. They receive assignments which allow them to demonstrate expertise, become legitimate topics of conversation among upper-level employees, and thus are more visible than other employees of the same rank. They find it easier to take a central place in informal communication networks. When they err, the failure is more likely to be attributed to external factors; when they succeed, the action is likely to be perceived as confirmation of their competence. Once an employee is labeled a "hot shot," "boy wonder," or "water walker," people begin to communicate with that person in ways which enhance access to organizational power and opportunities for further upward mobility.

Mobility also influences communication. These employees become more confident and assertive, seek out additional contacts and a more central role in communication networks, take on more challenging tasks, and are more willing to make decisions which involve moderate risks and large potential payoffs. In short, they begin to act and communicate like executives, at least as that term is defined in most organizations. Conversely, the lack of mobility generates communicative behavior which reduces opportunities for advancement. Kanter identified five frequent responses to the perception that one has little opportunity to move up.[25] At base each of these responses is an attempt to "save face" in situations in which an employee feels trapped. By becoming *satisfied with their roles* in their organizations, "trapped" individuals are able to resolve the frustrations that arise from having little opportunity to advance, but they become involved in tragic frames of reference from which it is difficult to escape.

Trapped individuals may also *project their hostilities* and frustrations onto other, less powerful members of the organization. Since the targets of this projection are usually the employees' subordinates, this response separates supervisors from their subordinates, isolating both groups from important sources of information and reducing their ability to perform successfully. People with low mobility may also respond by forming close relationships only with other trapped people. Conversation within these *failure-support groups* tend to focus on the members' common plight and the "fact" that their situation is not their fault. Although these private gripe sessions serve a cathartic function, they also isolate participants from employees who have sufficient knowledge and power to help them escape their traps. Stuck employees also may *nonproductively withdraw* from their work or from their associates.[26] Isolates rarely have access to either power or opportunity. Finally, trapped employees may *covertly resist change.* Having adjusted as best they can to their situations as they are, the prospect of change, even productive change, is threatening. But so is overt resistance. So the subtle resistance to change becomes the safest available response.

Each of these reactions is both common and understandable. People strive to create organizational realities within which they can protect and confirm their own individual identities. The problem is that each response leads to a self-fulfilling cycle. Isolation, alienation, and resistance to change all reduce other employees' perceptions of an individual's competence. Consequently, they further reduce opportunities for mobility, which increases feelings of being trapped, which makes maladaptive responses more probable, and so on.

Although this cycle is characteristic of all employees' reactions to being trapped, it is a greater problem for female employees for a number of reasons. Women tend to be located in units of organizations which have relatively "flat" hierarchies. For example, the number of organizational levels between the lowest-ranking and highest-ranking members of a clerical department usually is smaller than the number of levels in a production unit. With fewer levels there are fewer slots available when a higher-ranking employee is promoted or leaves the organization. In addition, fewer levels means that an employee can be promoted only a few times before reaching a middle management position. The numerical realities of pyramidal organizations means that the number of available positions drops off markedly near the middle of the hierarchy. The positions which do exist beyond the middle level involve the supervision of a number of departments which have very different functions. Although employees who have advanced through the production unit, for example, may have had substantial contact with and understanding of other departments, employees who have advanced through the clerical department may not have had this kind of contact. And even if they had, the *perception* that the clerical department is not central to the operations of the organization generates a preference for production-unit personnel in upper-level positions. When combined with the other factors discussed in this chapter (preferences for surrounding oneself with people who are homophilous and perceptions of what characteristics are required to be successful in upper management), these structural factors mean that women will have less opportunity than men. As a result, women face a greater potential for becoming trapped in mobility-reducing cycles.

The preceding sections of this chapter have painted a rather bleak picture of the impact sex roles have on the careers of women. The characteristics of organizations and acculturational processes combine in ways which reduce womens' access to the key determinants of organizational success—*power* and *mobility*. This combination sometimes leads women to employ communication strategies which both perpetuate sex-role stereotypes and complicate their problems. Unfortunately, a number of currently popular approaches to reducing these barriers may have a similar effect. But fortunately, there also seems to be a group of communication strategies which may help women offset the binds created by an interaction between stereotypes and organizational structures.

ORGANIZATIONAL COMMUNICATION AND SEX ROLES

In some cases, self-help books, training programs, and college courses simultaneously provide women with important advice but trivialize the barriers they face. Unless the limitations of this advice are understood, it may lead women to adopt counterproductive strategies. For example, one of the ways in which employees, regardless of their gender, can create the impression that they possess organizationally appropriate characteristics is by conforming to norms about attire, office decoration, and other nonverbal cues. To the extent that one's choice of dress or decor calls attention to itself, to the extent that they are perceived as being "abnormal," they accent an employee's "differentness" at the expense of her "appropriateness." In some cases observations of attire and other nonverbal cues constitute a large percentage of the information on which employees judge others, for example in initial selection interviews. For individuals who already are perceived to be "different" (that is, not white males), using nonverbal indicators which suggest similarity and avoiding those which accent differences is particularly important. However, the situations that "different" people face are so complex that altering nonverbal cues alone addresses only a small part of their relevant problems. This is not to suggest that employees ought not to attend to nonverbal indicators of organizational appropriateness, but they should not expect major changes to stem from their newfound ability to "dress for success."

A related counterproductive effect of advice involves "blaming the victim." People can legitimately be adjudged responsible for their situations only when they make unwise choices. Legitimate choice occurs only when persons have realistic options available to them *and* adequate information about their options. "Victim blaming" occurs when people are perceived to be responsible for the "choices" they make when they lack options or information. Traditionally, one of the most effective means of keeping relatively powerless people in powerless positions has been for powerful people to persuade them that they are responsible for their situations.[27] When powerless people blame themselves, they tend to accept their powerlessness and rarely confront their situations in ways which will enhance their power.

In some instances members of organizations overtly and openly communicate in victim-blaming ways. "*You* chose to teach grade school" or "*you* decided to concentrate on pediatrics instead of gynecology" overtly communicate that individuals are responsible for being in relatively low-paying and nonmobile careers when they really never had any legitimate choice in the matter.[28] In other instances, victim blaming is more subtle, for example, training programs "for women managers" may covertly communicate that the participants are there because they have failed in some way and now must rely on someone else to save them from their past sins. In some cases the mere act of attending the seminar or reading the book may communicate personal responsibility when the "responsibility" rests with social myths and organizational realities. An even more subtle version of victim blaming occurs when someone creates an inaccurate impression that a particular "solution" will eliminate the problem. For example, programs in the "effective management of time" recently have become very popular for professional women, for reasons that are all too obvious. Single women, especially those who are parents, and wives in dual-career families face extensive time demands. By developing a clear sense of their priorities and learning to manage time more effectively, they can cope more effectively with these demands. However, there is a point at which efficiency cannot be improved substantially. Professional women can be maximally efficient and still feel overloaded. Even a 20 percent increase in efficiency over the seventy-four-hour-per-week workload demanded of the "average" woman employed full time leaves her with sixty hours a week of work. But if she has been persuaded that overload is a function of *her* mismanagement of time, she may blame herself for her continued overload. She blames the victim.

Fortunately, there seem to be three general approaches that professionals can use to overcome problems related to sex roles. The first of these involves careful *self-monitoring* of communicative behaviors. Personas are promoted; persons are not (see Chapters 8 and 9). Personnel decisions are based on perceptions of individual performance and potential. All employees need to determine the features of the image linked to promotability in their organizations and attempt to present themselves in ways congruent with that image. Female employees must take particular care to communicate in ways which create and sustain an appropriate image and avoid communicating in ways which confirm traditional sex-role stereotypes. Male and female employees can continually monitor their communication and their interpretations of others' communication in an effort to avoid the effects of stereotypical sex-role perceptions.

The second potentially productive strategy is actively to seek out access to salient, important information. One means of doing this is by forming alliances with other employees, particularly mentors. A second general communication strategy generally is labeled *networking.* Some networks involve professional women who work in a large number of different organizations. Most major cities now have active womens' networks, many of which involve regularly scheduled meetings. These external networks provide women with a wide variety of different kinds of information and social support. Women who have felt overt discrimination or sexual harrassment gain support from women who have had similar experiences, obtain insight which prevents them from blaming themselves, and learn how other women have handled similar problems. Information about which firms have good records of advancing women and which have poor ones is shared. Advice about handling everyday work-related problems is obtained, and information about when and where job openings are imminent can be exchanged.[29] In short, all the information that males traditionally have gained through informal "good old boy" networks is disseminated through semiformal, external women's networks.

Other networks develop within firms. Internal women's networks potentially can provide all the task-related expertise and covert information about organizational power and politics that is available through other communication channels. Their disadvantage is that they can separate women from potentially supportive male allies. Upper level managers often develop paranoia about grapevines (informal networks). If the network excludes them, as womens' networks do, the tendency is for them to feel threatened and attempt to suppress the network. Defensive communication produces defensive communication, and employees who might have been cooperative allies become isolated from one another. However, if the usable information gained from internal networks is sufficient to offset problems of separation, involvement can be a productive strategy. Similarly, actively becoming part of broader informal networks of an organization is particularly important for women.

A final productive strategy is to provide other members of the organization with compelling evidence of one's performance and expertise.[30] Because women are not expected to succeed, and because their success tends to be attributed to external factors rather than individual competence, women must provide *more evidence and more consistent evidence* of their competence than men do. Research indicates that people use traditional sex-role stereotypes to draw conclusions about others most when they have limited amounts or ambiguous information about actual performance and competence. When we cannot be certain about how to interpret an action, event, or situation we fall back on our stable, predictable, perceptual sets. But when adequate information is available, preconceived notions tend to be less important aspects. For this reason, for example, male executives who have had substantial experience working with and evaluating the work of women show less of perceptual bias in evaluations than do males who have not had this experience. Clear, compelling, repeated, and consistent communication of the capacity to succeed in both current and possible future positions is perhaps the most effective strategy for female professionals.

CONCLUSION

One of the subtle but unquestionably important changes that has taken place during the past twenty years has been the growing proportion of women in the labor force. All realistic projections suggest that this trend will accelerate in the future. People all work for the same reasons—to support themselves and their families, to meet their needs for creativity and generativity, to form social and interpersonal ties. None of these motives is salient for one gender and irrelevant to the other. Social and economic factors of continued inflation, growing numbers of single-parent households, and continued deemphasis on extended families ensure that increasing numbers of women will seek employment as a source of financial support. One of the realities of contemporary Western society is that organizations are and will continue to be "coeducational." Another of the realities of postindustrial culture is that deeply ingrained sex-role mythologies are inconsistent with the contemporary needs, goals, and motivations of many people. Although the sex-role problems faced by all employees are substantial and resistant to short-term solutions, there are communicative strategies through which people can cope. But these strategies are not *solutions* in any meaningful sense of that term. As long as traditional cultural myths persist—and they have survived decades of social, economic, and technological change—and as long as organizations and organizational communication function as they do, differing degrees of organizational success also will continue. In the short term, communication strategies allow people to adapt strategically to various situations. But it is only in the very long term that communication strategies transform social and organizational situations in any fundamental ways.

Notes

1. The key source for the information summarized in the initial sections of this chapter is Ralph Smith, ed., *The Subtle Revolution* (Washington, D.C.: The Urban Institute, 1979). For more detailed treatments see Joseph Pilotta, ed., *Women in Organizations* (Prospect Heights, N. J.: Waveland Press, 1983), and the sources cited in Julia Wood and Charles Conrad, "Paradox in the Experience of Professional Women," *Western Journal of Speech Communication*, 47 (1983), 305–322.

2. Major salary differences seem to exist even in firms with strong affirmative action programs. Benson Rosen and Mary Mericle, "The Influence of Strong vs. Weak Affirmative Action Policies and Applicant's Sex on Selection Decisions and Salary Recommendations" (paper presented at the Academy of Management Convention, Atlanta, 1979).

3. Arthur Brief, Mary Van Sell, and Ramon Aldag, "Vocational Decision-Making Among Women" (paper presented at the Academy of Management Convention, Atlanta, 1979). This trend does seem to be less pronounced among younger women (Smith, *The Subtle Revolution*, pp. 49–53). It has provoked growing concern for finding ways to compute salaries according to the "comparable worth" of employees in different units of organizations.

4. Jane Trahey, *Jane Trahey on Management and Power* (New York: Rawson, 1977); Virginia Schein, "Sex Role Stereotyping, Ability and Performance: Prior Research and New Directions," *Personnel Psychology*, 31 (1978), 259–267; Katherine Bartol, "Male vs. Female Leaders," *Academy of Management Journal*, 17 (1975), 225–233; D. Day and Ralph Stogdill, "Leadership Behavior of Male and Female Supervisors," *Personnel Psychology*, 5 (1972), 353–360.

5. The summary presented in this section is quite abbreviated. More complete treatments of the general functions of social myths appear in Ernst Cassirer, *The Philosophy of Symbolic Forms*, (New Haven, Conn.: Yale University Press, 1957), vol. I, and Northrop Frye, *The Secular Scripture* (Cambridge, Mass.: Harvard University Press, 1976). An excellent discussion of sex-role myths is Elizabeth Janeway's *Man's World, Woman's Place* (New York: Dell, 1971).

6. These concepts are developed more fully in Wood and Conrad, "Paradox."

7. The best single treatment of many of the ideas presented in this section is Rosabeth Moss Kanter, *Men and Women of the Corporation* (New York: Harper & Row, 1977). A brief review of Chapter 7 of her book might clarify this section.

8. L. C. Hackamach and A. B. Solid, "The Woman Executive—There Is Still Ample Room for Progress," *Business Horizons* (April 1972), 89–93; E. B. Schwartz and J. J. Rago, "Beyond Tokenism: Women as True Corporate Peers," *Business Horizons* (December 1973), 69–76; Virginia Schein, "The Relationships Between Sex-Role Stereotypes and Requisite Managerial Characteristics," *Journal of Applied Psychology*, 57 (1973), 95–100.

9. Lawrence Rosenfeld and Gene Fowler, "Personality, Sex and Leadership Style," *Communication Monographs*, 43 (1976), 320–324; Linda Putnam, "Women in Management: Leadership Theories, Research Results and Future Directions" (paper presented at the Central States Speech Communication Association Convention, St. Louis, 1979).

10. See, for example, Patricia Hayes Andrews, "The Folk-Linguistics of Women's Speech," *Communication Monographs*, 48 (1981), 262–284; Ernest Bormann, Julie Pratt, and Linda Putnam, "Power, Authority and Sex: Male Responses to Female Leadership," *Communication Monographs*, 45 (1978), 119–155; David Dotlich and Dorothy McGlauchlin, "Perceptions of Opposite-Sex Managers in a Large Corporation" (paper presented at the International Communication Association Convention, Philadelphia, 1979).

11. Smith, *The Subtle Revolution*, p. 194. Also see Michael Geerken and Walter Gove, *At Home and at Work* (Beverly Hills, Calif.: Sage, 1983).

12. Katherine Walker and Margaret Woods, *Time Use* (Washington, D.C.: The American Home Economic Association, 1976).

13. See, for example, Robert Rapoport and Rhona Rapoport, *Dual Career Families* (Harmondsworth, Eng.: Penguin, 1971). Studies of the actual role of voluntary relocation in career success are available in "Banking and Women Managers," *Management Today* (February 1982), 53, and R. Viega, "Do Managers on the Move Get Anywhere?" *Harvard Business Review* (March-Apr., 1981), 20–22, 26–30, 34–38.

14. M. Susan Taylor and Daniel Ilgen, "An Investigation of Initial Placement Decisions" (paper presented at the Academy of Management Convention, Detroit, 1980).

15. Kanter, *Men and Women*.

16. Ibid.

17. Nina Gupta, Terry Beehr, and G. Douglas Jenkins, "The Relationship Between Employee Gender and Supervisor-Subordinate Cross-Ratings," (paper presented at the Academy of Management Convention, Detroit, 1980); Benson Rosen and Thomas Jerdee, "The Influence of

Sex-Role Stereotypes on Evaluations of Male and Female Supervisory Behavior," *Journal of Applied Psychology*, 62 (1977), 44–48; Howard Garland and Kenneth Price, "Attitudes Toward Women in Management and Attributions for Their Success and Failure in a Managerial Position," *Journal of Applied Psychology*, 62 (1977), 29–33; Donald Gardner and Chris Berger, "The Effects of Sex Stereotypes, Amount of Relevant Information and Awareness of Organizational Selection Practices on Sex Discrimination for a Managerial Position" (paper presented at the Academy of Management Convention, Detroit, 1980); Madeline Heilman, "The Impact of Situational Factors on Personnel Decisions Concerning Women" (paper presented at the Academy of Management Convention, Atlanta, 1979); Veronica Nieva, Sharyn Mallamad, and Ellen Eisner, "Sex Bias in Performance Evaluation Narratives" (paper presented at the Academy of Management Convention, Atlanta, 1979). Problems related to perceptions and explanations of success are the bases of the advice often given to women to enter careers in sales or merchandising. The assumptions is that these occupations provide employees with quantifiable and easily communicated evidence of *their* success. To the extent that objective data are available, differential attribution of success is a less serious problem.

18.   Margaret Hennig and Ann Jardim, *The Managerial Woman* (New York: Pocket Books, 1976); Laurie Larwood and Mindy Kaplan, "Job Tactics of Women in Banking" (paper presented at the Academy of Management Convention, Atlanta, 1979); Trahey, *Management and Power.*

19.   Kathryn Ring, "Behind Every Successful Woman. . . There's a Mentor," *Women in Business* (July-August 1978), 9–11; Jacqueline Thompson, "Corporate Survival: Make the Right Connection," *Essence* (August 1978), 82, 122–123.

20.   Janeway, *Man's World.* Also see Natasia Josefowitz, *Paths to Power* (Reading: Mass.: Addison-Wesley, 1980). Gail Sheehy examined the problems of ending mentoring relationships in *Passages* (New York: Bantam, 1974).

21.   Judith Bardwick, "Some Notes on Power Relationships Between Women," in *Beyond Sex Roles*, ed. Alice Sargent (St. Paul, Minn.: West, 1976), pp. 325–335. Also see Barbara Benedict Bunker and Edith Whitfield Seashore, "Sexuality, Support: Breaking the Sex-Role Stereotypes in Social and Organizational Settings," on pp. 364–370 of the same book.

22.   Donald Pelz, "Influence: a Key to Effective Leadership in the First-Line Supervisor," *Personnel*, 29 (1952), 3–11; Randall Sleeth and Luther Humphreys, "Differences in Leadership Styles Among Future Managers" (paper presented at the Academy of Management Convention, Atlanta, 1979).

23.   Bardwick, "Power Relationships Between Women."

24.   Betty Lyhan Harragan, *Games Mother Never Taught You: Corporate Gamesmanship for Women* (New York: Rawson, 1977).

25.   Rosabeth Moss Kanter, "The Impact of Hierarchical Structure of the Work Behavior of Men and Women," *Social Problems*, 23 (1976), 415–430.

26.   See Chapters 9 and 10 for distinctions between productive and nonproductive withdrawal.

27.   Martin Chesler, J. Crowfoot, and B. Bryant, "Power Training: An Alternative Path to Conflict Management," *California Management Review*, 21 (1978), 84–90; Elizabeth Janeway, *Powers of the Weak* (New York: Knopf, 1980).

28.   Of course, we are not maligning either of these career choices. We are suggesting that employees may use references to them as a means of blaming the victim.

29.   Networks also tend to span geographical areas. Members of networks in one city can gain information about career possibilities in another city, information which can be invaluable for wives whose husbands are in the process of considering a job change or if the husband's career is an important consideration.

30.   Hazel Ezell, Charles Odewahn, and J. Daniel Sherman, "Being Supervised by a Woman: Does It Make a Difference?" (paper presented at the Academy of Management Convention, Detroit, 1980); Madeline Heilman and Richard Guzzo, "The Perception of Causes of Work Success as a Mediator of Sex Discrimination in Organizations," *Organizational Behavior and Human Performance*, 21 (1978), 346–357.

Bibliography

Indicates particularly appropriate reading for graduate students.

Adams, J. The Structure and Dynamics of Behavior in Organizational Boundary Roles, in *Handbook of Industrial and Organizational Psychology*, Marvin Dunnette, ed. Chicago: Rand-McNally, 1976.

Albrecht, T. Coping with Organizational Stress. Paper presented at the International Communication Association Convention, 1982.

Albrecht, T., Irey, R., and Mundy, A. Integration in Communication Networks as a Mediator of Stress. *Social Work*, 27 (1982): 118–129.

*Albrow, M. *Bureaucracy*. London: Pall Mall, 1970.

Aldrich, H., and Herker, D. Boundary-Spanning Roles and Organizational Structure. *Academy of Management Review*, 2 (1977): 217–230.

*Allen, T., Tushman, M., and Lee, D. Technology Transfer as a Function of Position in the Spectrum from Development to Technical Services. *Academy of Management Journal*, 22 (1979): 694–708.

Andrews, P. H. The Folk-Linguistics of Women's Speech. *Communication Monographs*, 48 (1981): 262–284.

Argyris, C. *Personality and Organization*. New York: Harper & Row, 1957.

Arvey, R., and Ivanevich, J. Punishment in Organizations. *The Academy of Management Review*, 5 (1980): 123–134.

Bacharach, P., and Baratz, M. Two Faces of Power. *American Political Science Review*, 56 (1962): 947–952.

*Bacharach, S., and Aiken, M. Communication in Administrative Bureaucracies. *Academy of Management Journal*, 3 (1977): 365–377.

*Bacharach, S., and Lawler, E. *Negotiation*. San Francisco: Jossey-Bass, 1980.

———. *Power and Politics in Organizations*. San Francisco: Jossey-Bass, 1980.

*Bantz, C., and Smith, D. A Critique and Experimental Test of Weick's Model of Organizing. *Communication Monographs*, 44 (1977): 171–184.

*Baratz, M. *Power and Poverty*. New York: Oxford University Press, 1970.

Barber, D. *Power in Committees*. Chicago: Rand-McNally, 1966.

Bardwick, J. Some Notes on Power Relationships Between Women, in *Beyond Sex Roles*, A. Sargent, ed. St. Paul, MN: West, 1976.

Barnard, C. *The Functions of the Executive*. Cambridge, MA: Harvard University Press, 1938.

*Bartol, K. Males vs. Female Leaders. *Academy of Management Journal*, 17 (1975): 225–233.

*Bartos, O. J. Determinants and Consequences of Toughness, in *The Structure of Conflict*, Paul Swingle, ed. New York: Academic Press, 1970.

Bass, B., and Shakleton, V. Industrial Democracy and Participatory Management. *Academy of Management Review*, 4, (1979): 393–404.

*Bazerman, M., and Lewicki, R. *Negotiating in Organizations*. Beverly Hills, CA: Sage, 1983.

*Beehr, T. Perceived Situational Moderators of the Relationship Between Subjective Role Ambiguity and Role Strain. *Journal of Applied Psychology*, 61 (1976): 35–40.

Bem, D. *Beliefs, Attitudes and Human Affairs*. Belmont, CA: Wadsworth, 1972.

Bennis, W. Beyond Bureaucracy. *Trans-action*, 2 (1965): 31–35.

Benson, H. *The Relaxation Response*. New York: Avon Books, 1975.

Berg, I. *Education and Jobs*. New York: Praeger, 1970.

Berger, C., and Cummings, L. Organizational Structure, Attitudes and Behavior, in *Research in Organizational Behavior*, B. Staw, ed. Greenwich, CT: JAI Press, 1979, vol. 1.

Berger, P., and Luckman, T. *The Social Construction of Reality*, New York: Anchor Books, 1966.

Berk, B. Face Saving at the Singles' Dance. *Social Problems*, 24 (1977): 530–544.

*Bhagat, R. Effects of Personal Life Stress on Individual Performance and Work Adjustment. Paper presented at the American Psychological Association Convention, 1980.

Bitzer, L. The Rhetorical Situation. *Philosophy and Rhetoric*, 1 (1970): 1–14.

————. Functional Communication: A Situational Perspective, in *Rhetoric in Transition*, Eugene White, ed. University Park, PA: Pennsylvania State University Press, 1980.

Blackburn, R. Dimensions of Structure: a Review and Reappraisal. *The Academy of Management Review*, 7 (1982): 59–66.

Blake, R., and Mouton, J. *The Managerial Grid*. Houston: Gulf, 1964.

Blake, R., and Mouton, J. When Scholarship Fails, Research Suffers. *Administrative Science Quarterly*, 2 (1976): 93–96.

Blau, P. *On the Nature of Organizations*. New York: Wiley, 1974.

Bormann, E., Pratt, J., and Putnam, L. Power, Authority and Sex: Male Responses to Female Leadership. *Communication Monographs*, 45 (1978): 119–155.

*Brass, D. Structural Relationships, Job Characteristics and Worker Satisfaction and Performance. *Administrative Science Quarterly*, 26 (1981): 331–348.

*Braverman, H. *Labor and Monopoly Capitalism*. London: Monthly Review Press, 1974.

Brayfield, A., and Crockett, W. Employee Attitudes and Employee Performance. *Psychological Bulletin*, 52 (1955): 415–422.

*Brief, A. Differences in Evaluations of Employee Performance. *Journal of Occupational Psychology*, 50 (1977): 129–134.

*Brief, A., and Aldag, R. The "Self" in Work Organizations. *The Academy of Management Review*, 6 (1981): 75–88.

Brief, A., van Sell, M., and Aldag, R. Vocational Decision-Making Among Women. Paper presented at the Academy of Management Convention, 1979.

Bunker, B., and Seashore, E. Sexuality, Support: Breaking the Sex-Role Stereotypes in Social and Organizational Settings, in *Beyond Sex Roles*, A. Sargent, ed. St. Paul, MN: West, 1976.

Burgess, P. Crisis Rhetoric. *Quarterly Journal of Speech*, 59 (1973): 61–73.

Burgoon, J., and Burgoon, M. Message Strategies in Influence Attempts, in *Communication and Behavior*, G. Hanneman and W. McEwen, eds. Reading, MA: Addison-Wesley, 1975.

*Burke, K. *Attitudes Toward History*. Boston: Beacon Press, 1937.

*————. *A Grammar of Motives*. Berkeley, CA: University of California Press, 1945.

*————. *Permanence and Change*. New York: Bobbs-Merrill, 1965.

314

Bibliography

Burke, R., and Bradshaw, P. Occupational and Life Stress and the Family. *Small Group Behavior*, 12 (1981): 329–375.

*Burns, T., and Stalker, G. *The Management of Innovation*. London: Tavistock, 1961.

*Burns, T., Karlsson, L., and Rus, V. *Work and Power*. Beverly Hills, CA: Sage, 1979.

*Caldwell, D., and O'Reilly, C. Responses to Failure. *Academy of Management Journal*, 25 (1962): 121–136.

*Campbell, J. Systematic Error on the Part of Human Links in Communication Systems. *Information and Control*, 1 (1958): 334–369.

Campbell, J., and Pritchard, R. Motivation Theory, in *Handbook of Industrial and Organizational Psychology*, Marvin Dunnette, ed. Chicago: Rand-McNally, 1976.

Carey, A. The Hawthorne Studies: a Radical Criticism. *American Political Science Review*, 32 (1967): 403–416.

Cassirer, E. *The Philosophy of Symbolic Forms*. New Haven, CT: Yale University Press, 1957, vol. 1.

Chase, S. What Makes the Worker Like to Work? *Reader's Digest* (February 1941): 15–20.

Cherniss, C. *Staff Burnout*. Beverly Hills, CA: Sage, 1980.

Chessler, M., Crowfoot, J., and Bryant, B. Power Training: An Alternative Path to Conflict Management. *California Management Review*, 21 (1978): 84–90.

*Clegg, S. *Power, Rule and Combination*. London: Routledge and Kegan Paul, 1975.

*———. *The Theory of Power and Organizations*. London: Routledge and Kegan Paul, 1979.

*Cohen, M., March, J. and Olson, J. A Garbage-Can Model of Organizational Choice. *Administrative Science Quarterly*, 17 (1972): 1–32.

Collins, B., and Raven, B. Group Structure, in *Handbook of Social Psychology*, G. Lindsay and E. Aronson, eds. Reading, MA: Addison-Wesley, 1969, vol. 4.

Conrad, C. Organizational Power: Faces and Symbolic Forms, in *Communication and Organizations: An Interpretive Approach*, L. Putnam and M. Pacanowsky, eds. Beverly Hills, CA: 1983.

———. Power, Performance and Supervisors' Choices of Strategies of Conflict Management. *Western Journal of Speech Communication*, 47 (1983) 218–228.

Conrad, C., and Ryan, M. Power, Praxis and Person in Social and Organizational Theory, in *Organizational Communication Research and Theory*, P. Tompkins and R. McPhee, eds. Beverly Hills, CA: Sage, In Press.

Cooper, C., and Marshall, J. An Audit of Managerial (Di)Stress. *Journal of Enterprise Management*, 1 (1978): 185–196.

Cox, J. Symbolic Action and Satisfactory Choices. Paper presented at the Speech Communication Association Convention, 1980.

Cummings, L. Organizational Behavior. *Annual Review of Psychology*, 33 (1982): 541–579.

*Cyert, R., and March, J. *A Behavioral Theory of the Firm*. Englewood Cliffs, NJ: Prentice-Hall, 1963.

*Dachler, P., and Wilpert, B. Conceptual Boundaries and Dimensions of Participation in Organizations. *Administrative Science Quarterly*, 23 (1978): 1–39.

*Daft, R., and Macintosh, N. A Tentative Exploration Into the Amount and Equivocality of Information Processing in Organizational Work Units. *Administrative Science Quarterly*, 26 (1981): 207–224.

Dalton, D., Todor, W., Spendolini, G., Fielding, G., and Porter, L. Organizations, Structure and Performance: A Critical Review. *Academy of Management Review*, 5 (1980): 49–64.

Davis, K. Management Communication and the Grapevine. *Harvard Business Review* (January–February 1953): pp. 43–49.

*Day, D., and Stogdill, R. Leadership Behavior of Male and Female Supervisors. *Personnel Psychology*, 5 (1972): 353–360.

Deutsch, M. Conflicts: Productive or Destructive? *Journal of Social Issues*, 25 (1969): 7–41.

———. *The Resolution of Conflict*. New Haven, CT: Yale University Press, 1973.

Deutsch, M., and Krauss, R. Studies in Interpersonal Bargaining. *Journal of Conflict Resolution*, 61 (1962): 52–76.

*Dewar, R., and Werbel, J. Universalistic and Contingency Predictions of Employee Satisfaction and Conflict. *Administrative Science Quarterly*, 24 (1979): 426–447.

*Dohrenwend, B., and Dohrenwend, B. *Stressful Life Events*. New York: Wiley, 1974.

*Dolbear, T., and Lave, L. Inconsistent Behavior in Lottery Choice Experiments. *Behavioral Science*, 12 (1967): 14–23.

*Dooly, D., and Catalano, R. Economic Change as a Cause of Behavioral Disorders. *Psychological Bulletin*, 87 (1980): 450–468.

Dotlich, D., and McGlauchlin, D. Perceptions of Opposite-Sex Managers in a Large Corporation. Paper presented at the International Communication Association Convention, 1979.

*Downs, A. *Inside Bureaucracy*. Boston: Little Brown, 1967.

Downs, C., and Conrad, C. A Critical Incident Study of Effective Subordinancy. *Journal of Business Communication*, 19 (1982): 27–38.

Duncan, K., Gruneberg, M., and Wallis, D. *Changes in Working Life*. New York, Wiley, 1980.

*Druckman, D., ed. *Negotiation*. Beverly Hills, CA: Sage, 1977.

*Edwards, R. *Contested Terrain*. New York: Basic Books, 1978.

*Edwards, W. Subjective Probabilities Inferred from Decisions. *Psychological Review*, 69 (1962): 109–135.

*———. Utility, Subjective Probability, Their Interaction and Variance Preferences. *Journal of Conflict Resolution*, 6 (1962): 42–50.

*Emerson, R. Power-Dependence Relations. *American Sociological Review*, 27 (1962): 31–41.

*Etzioni, A. Organizational Control Structures, in *Handbook of Organizations*, James March, ed. Chicago: Rand-McNally, 1965.

Ezell, H., Odewahn, C., and Sherman, J. Being Supervised by a Woman: Does It Make a Difference? Paper presented at the Academy of Management Convention, 1980.

Farace, R., Monge, P., and Russell, H. *Communicating and Organizing*. Reading, MA: Addison-Wesley, 1977.

Farace, R., Taylor, J., and Stewart, J. Criteria for Evaluation of Organizational Communication Effectiveness, in *Communication Yearbook 2*, Brent Ruben, ed. New Brunswick, NJ: Transaction Books, 1978.

Ferner, J. *Successful Time Management*. New York: Wiley, 1980.

*Fishbein, M., and Ijzen, I. *Belief, Attitude, Intention and Behavior*. Reading, MA: Addison-Wesley, 1975.

Fisher, C. On the Dubious Wisdom of Expecting Job Satisfaction to Correlate with Performance. *Academy of Management Review*, 5 (1980): 607–612.

Fleishman, Ed., ed. *Studies in Personnel and Industrial Psychology*. Homewood, IL: Dorsey, 1961 and 1967.

Folger, J., and Poole, M. S. *Working Through Conflict*. Glenview, IL: Scott Foresman, 1983.

Bibliography

*Fox, F., and Staw, B. The Trapped Administrator. *Administrative Science Quarterly,* 24 (1979): 449–456.

Franke, R. The Hawthorne Studies: a Re-View. *American Sociological Review,* 44 (1979): 861–867.

*Franke, R., and Kaul, J. The Hawthorne Experiments: First Statistical Interpretation. *American Sociological Review,* 43 (1978): 623–643.

French, J., and Raven, B. The Bases of Social Power, in *Studies in Social Power,* D. Cartwright, ed. Ann Arbor, MI: University of Michigan Press, 1959.

Friedman, M., and Rosenman, R. *Type A Behavior and Your Heart.* New York: Knopf, 1974.

*Frye, N. *Anatomy of Criticism.* Princeton, NJ: Princeton University Press, 1957.

*———. *The Secular Scripture.* Cambridge, MA: Harvard University Press, 1976.

*Galbraith, J. *Designing Complex Organizations* Reading, MA: Addison-Wesley, 1973.

Gamson, W. *Power and Discontent.* Homewood, IL: Dorsey, 1968.

*Gardell, B. Alienation and Mental Health in the Modern Industrial Environment, in *Society, Stress and Disease.* L. Levi, ed. London: Oxford University Press, 1971, vol. 1.

*Garland, H., and Price, K. Attitudes Toward Women in Management and Attributions for Their Success and Failure in a Managerial Position. *Journal of Applied Psychology,* 62 (1977): 29–33.

*Gardner, D., and Berger, C. The Effects of Sex Stereotypes, Amount of Relevant Information and Awareness of Organizational Selection Practices on Sex Discrimination for a Managerial Position. Paper presented at the Academy of Management Convention, 1980.

Garson, B. *All the Livelong Day.* London: Penguin, 1977.

Geerken, M., and Gove, W. *At Home and At Work.* Beverly Hills, CA: Sage, 1983.

George, C. *The History of Management Thought.* Englewood Cliffs, NJ: Prentice-Hall, 1972.

*Giddens, A. *Central Problems in Social Theory.* Berkeley: University of California Press, 1979.

Goffman, I. *The Presentation of Self in Everyday Life.* New York: Doubleday, 1959.

*———. On Face-Work. *Psychiatry,* 18 (1955): 213–231.

*Goode, W., and Fowler, I. Incentive Factors in a Low Morale Plant. *American Sociological Review,* 14 (1949): 618–624.

Gooding, J. *The Job Revolution.* New York: Macmillan, 1972.

Goodnight, T., Crary, D., Balthrop, V., and Hazen, M. The Relationships Between Communication Satisfaction and Productivity, Role Discrepancy and Need Level. Paper presented at the International Communication Association Convention, 1974.

*Greene, C., and Podsakoff, P. Effects of Withdrawal of a Performance-Contingent Reward on Supervisory Influence and Power. *Academy of Management Journal,* 24 (1981): 527–542.

Guetzkow, H. Communication in Organizations, in *Handbook of Organizations,* James March, ed. Chicago: Rand-McNally, 1965.

*Guetzkow, H., and Gyr, J. An Analysis of Decision-Making Groups. *Human Relations,* 7 (1954): 367–381.

*Gupta, N., Beehr, T., and Jenkins, G. The Relationship Between Employee Gender and Supervisor-Subordinate Cross-Ratings. Paper presented at the Academy of Management Convention, 1980.

*Habermas, J. *Legitimation Crisis.* Boston: Beacon, 1970.

*Hackamach, L., and Solid, A. The Woman Executive—There Is Still Ample Room for Progress. *Business Horizons* (April 1972): 89–93.

Hall, D., and Hall, F. *The Two-Career Couple.* Reading, MA: Addison-Wesley, 1979.

———. Stress and the Two-Career Couple, in *Current Concerns in Occupational Stress,* C. Cooper and R. Payne, eds. New York: Wiley, 1980.

*Hambrick, D. Environment, Stategy and Power Within Top Management. *Administrative Science Quarterly,* 26 (1981): 233–271.

*Hanser, L., and Muchinsky, P. Performance Feedback Information and Organizational Communication. *Human Communication Research,* 7 (1980): 68–73.

Harragan, B. L. *Games Your Mother Never Taught You: Corporate Gamesmanship for Women.* New York: Rawson, 1977.

Hart, R., and Burks, D. Rhetorical Sensitivity and Social Interaction. *Speech Monographs,* 39 (1972): 75–91.

*Hart, R., Carlson, R., and Eadie, W. Attitudes Toward Communication and the Assessment of Rhetorical Sensitivity. *Communication Monographs,* 47 (1980): 1–22.

*Hatfield, J., Gatewood, R., Boulton, W., and Huseman, R. Moderating Effects of Worker Characteristics on the Communication-Performance Relationship. Paper presented at the International Communication Associated Convention, 1981.

Hawes, L., and Smith, D. A Critique of the Assumptions Underlying the Study of Communication in Conflict. *Quarterly Journal of Speech,* 59 (1973): 423–435.

Heider, F. *The Psychology of Interpersonal Relations.* New York: Wiley, 1958.

Heilman, M. The Impact of Situational Factors on Personnel Decisions Concerning Women. Paper presented at the Academy of Management Convention, 1979.

Heilman, M., and Guzzo, R. The Perception of Causes of Work Success as a Mediator of Sex Discrimination in Organizations. *Organizational Behavior and Human Performance,* 21 (1978): 346–357.

Hennig, M., and Jardim, A. *The Managerial Woman.* New York: Pocket Books, 1976.

Hirokawa, R. Improving Intra-Organizational Communication: A Lesson from Japanese Management. *Communication Quarterly,* 30 (1981): 35–40.

Holmes, T., and Rayhe, R. The Social Readjustment Rating Scale. *Journal of Psychosomatic Research,* 11 (1967): 213–218.

Horowitz, M. *The Stress Response Syndrome.* New York: Jason Aronson, 1976.

House, R. A Path-Goal Theory of Leadership Effectiveness. *Administrative Science Quarterly,* 16 (1971): 321–329.

*House, R., and Wells, J. Occupational Stress, Social Support and Health, in *Reducing Occupational Stress,* A. McLean, G. Black, and M. Colligan, eds. Washington, D.C.: U.S. Government Printing Office, 1978.

*Ivanevich, J. An Analysis of Participation in Decision Making Among Project Engineers. *Academy of Management Journal,* 22 (1979): 252–269.

*———. High and Low Task Stimulating Jobs: A Causal Analysis of Performance-Satisfaction Relationships. *Academy of Management Journal,* 22 (1979): 206–222.

*———. The Performance to Satisfaction Relationship. *Organizational Behavior and Human Performance,* 22 (1978): 350–365.

Jablin, F. A Re-examination of the "Pelz Effect." *Human Communication Research,* 6 (1980): 211–227.

———. Superior-Subordinate Communication, in *Communication Yearbook 2.* Brent Ruben, ed. New Brunswick, NJ: Transaction Books, 1978.

Janeway, E. *Man's World, Woman's Place.* New York: Dell, 1971.

————. *Powers of the Weak*. New York: Morrow-Quill, 1980.

Janis, I. *Victims of Groupthink*. Boston: Houghton Mifflin, 1972.

Johnson, B. *Communication: The Process of Organizing*. Boston: Allyn & Bacon, 1977.

Josefowitz, N. *Paths to Power*. Reading, MA: Addison-Wesley, 1980.

*Kahn, R. Conflict, Ambiguity and Overload, in *Occupational Stress*, A. McLean, ed. Springfield, IL: Chas. C. Thomas, 1974.

*Kahn, R., Wolfe, R., Quinn, R., Snoeck, J., and Rosenthal, R. *Organizational Stress*. New York: Wiley, 1964.

Kanter, R. M. The Impact of Hierarchical Structure on the Work Behavior of Men and Women. *Social Problems*, 23 (1976): 415–430.

————. *Men and Women of the Corporation*. New York: Basic Books, 1977.

————. *Work and Family in the United States*. New York: Russell Sage, 1977.

*Katz, D., and Kahn, R. *The Social Psychology of Organizations*, 2nd ed. New York: Wiley, 1978.

*Kay, E. Middle Management, in *Work and the Quality of Life*, J. O'Toole, ed. Cambridge, MA: M.I.T. Press, 1974.

*Kearns, J. *Stress in Industry*. London: Priory, 1973.

Kennedy, G. *Classical Rhetoric in its Christian and Secular Traditions from Ancient to Modern Times*. Chapel Hill, NC: University of North Carolina Press, 1980.

Kerr, S., and Slocum, J., Jr. Controlling the Performances of People in Organizations, in *Handbook of Organizational Design*, P. Nystrom and W. Starbuck, eds. New York: Oxford University Press, 1979, vol. 2.

*Komorita, S. Negotiating from Strength and the Concept of Bargaining. *Journal of the Theory of Social Behavior*, 7 (1977): 56–79.

Koontz, H. The Management Theory Jungle Revisited. *Academy of Management Review*, 5 (1980): 175–187.

Kotter, J. *Power in Management*. New York: AMACOM, 1979.

*Kreps, G. A Field Experimental Test of Weick's Model of Organizing, in *Communication Yearbook 4*, Dan Nimmo, ed. New Brunswick, NJ: Transaction Books, 1980.

*Kriesberg, L. *The Sociology of Social Conflicts*. Englewood Cliffs, NJ: Prentice-Hall, 1973.

Kuhn, T. *The Structure of Scientific Revolutions*. Chicago: University of Chicago Press, 1970.

*LaRocco, J., House, J., and French, J. R. P. Social Support, Occupational Stress and Health. *Journal of Health and Social Behavior*, 21 (1980): 202–218.

Larwood, L., and Kaplan, M. Job Tactics of Women in Banking. Paper presented at the Academy of Management Convention, 1979.

Lawler, E. *Pay and Organizational Effectiveness*. New York: McGraw-Hill, 1971.

Lawler, E., and Rhodes, J. *Information and Control in Organizations*. Pacific Palisades, CA; Goodyear, 1976.

Lawrence, P., and Lorsch, J. *Organizations and Environment*. Cambridge, MA: Harvard Business School, 1967.

*Lazarus, R., and Launier, R. Stress-Related Transactions Between Person and Environment, in *Perspectives in Interactional Psychology*, L. Pervin and M. Lewis, eds. New York: Plenum, 1980.

*Leary, T. *Interpersonal Diagnosis of Personality*. New York: Ronald, 1957.

Lee, J. Behavioral Theory vs. Reality. *Harvard Business Review* (May–June 1970): 47–60.

Likert, R. *New Patterns of Management*. New York: McGraw-Hill, 1971.

Lindblom, C. The Science of Muddling Through. *Public Administration Review*, 19 (1959): 1–21.

Locke, E. The Ideas of Frederick Taylor: an Evaluation. *The Academy of Management Review*, 7 (1982): 14–24.

———. The Nature and Causes of Job Satisfaction, in *Handbook of Industrial and Organizational Psychology*, M. Dunnette, ed. Chicago: Rand-McNally, 1976.

Locke, E., Saari, L., and Latham, G. Goal Setting and Task Performance: 1969–1980. *Psychological Bulletin*, 90 (1981): 125–152.

Louis, Meryl Reis. Surprise and Sense-making In Organizations. *Administrative Science Quarterly*, 25 (1980): 226–251.

*Lukes, S. *Power: A Radical View*. London: MacMillan, 1974.

Macarov, D. *Incentives to Work*. Beverly Hills, CA: Sage, 1981.

Mallinger, M. Effective Coping. *Small Group Behavior*, 12 (1981): 269–284.

March, J. The Technology of Foolishness, in *Ambiguity and Choice in Organizations*, J. March and J. Olson, eds. Bergen: Universitetsforlaget, 1979.

*March, J., and Feldman, S. Information in Organizations as Signal and Symbol. *Administrative Science Quarterly*, 26 (1981): 756–771.

*March, J., and Olson, J., eds. *Ambiguity and Choice in Organizations*. Bergen: Universitetsforlaget, 1979.

*March, J., and Simon, H. The Concept of Rationality, in *Human Behavior and International Politics*, D. Singer, ed. Chicago: Rand-McNally, 1965.

*Marwell, G., and Schmidt, D. Dimensions of Compliance-Gaining Behavior. *Sociometry*, 30 (1967): 350–364.

*May, K. Intransitivity, Utility and Aggregation of Preference Patterns. *Econometrica*, 22 (1954) 1–36.

McCroskey, J., and Peck Richmond, V. The Impact of Communication Apprehension on Individuals in Organizations. *Communication Quarterly*, 27 (1979):55–61.

*McPhee, R. An Ideal-type Theory of Organizational Coalitions. Paper presented at the Conference on Interpretive Approaches to Organizational Communication, Alta, UT, 1981.

*McPhee, R., and Cushman, D., eds. *Message-Attitude-Behavior Relationships*. New York: Academic Press, 1980.

*Mechanic, D. Sources of Power of Lower Participants in Complex Organizations. *Administrative Science Quarterly*, 7 (1962): 349–364.

Meyer, A. Mingling Decision-Making Metaphors. *Academy of Management Review*, 9 (1984): 6–17.

*Meyers, H., Kay, E., and French, J. R. P. Split Roles in Performance Appraisals. *Harvard Business Review* (March–April 1965): 21–29.

Miles, R. Human Relations or Human Resources. *Harvard Business Review* (July–August 1965): 43–161.

———. *Theories of Management*. New York: McGraw-Hill, 1975.

Miles, R., Meyer, A., and Coleman, A. Organizational Strategy, Structure and Process. *Academy of Management Review*, 3 (1978): 546–562.

Mintzberg, H. *The Nature of Managerial Work*. Englewood Cliffs, NJ: Prentice-Hall, 1980.

Mintzberg, J. *Structuring in Fives*. Englewood Cliffs, NJ: Prentice-Hall, 1983.

Monge, P., Edwards, J., and Kirstie, K. The Determinants of Communication and Communication Structure in Large Organizations, in *Communication Yearbook 2*. Brent Ruben, ed. New Brunswick, NJ: Transaction Books, 1978.

*Muchinsky, P. Organization Communication: Relationships to Organizational Climate and Job Satisfaction. *Academy of Management Journal*, 20 (1977): 592–607.

Mulder, M. Power Equalization through Participation? *Administrative Science Quarterly*, 16 (1971): 31–38.

*Mulder, M., and Wilke, H. Participation and Power Equalization. *Organizational Behavior and Human Performance*, 5 (1970): 430–448.

Nehrbass, R. Ideology and the Decline of Management Theory. *Academy of Management Review*, 4 (1979): 427–431.

Niehouse, O., and Massoni, K. Stress—An Inevitable Part of Change. *S.A.M. Advanced Management Journal* (Spring 1979): 17–25.

Nieva, V., Mallamad, S., and Eisner, E. Sex Bias in Performance Evaluation Narratives. Paper presented at the Academy of Management Convention, 1979.

Nishiyoma, K. Japanese Quality Control Circles. Paper presented at the International Communication Association Convention, 1981.

Nord, W. and Durand, D. What's Wrong with the Human Resources Approach to Management. *Organizational Dynamics* (Winter 1978): 13–25.

Olson, J. Local Budgeting, Decision-Making or Ritual Act? *Scandinavian Political Studies*, 4 (1970): 85–118.

*Ouchi, W. A Conceptual Framework for the Design of Organizational Control Mechanisms. *Management Science*, 25 (1979): 833–848.

———. Markets, Bureaucracies and Clans. *Administrative Science Quarterly*, 25 (1980): 129–141.

———. *Theory Z*. Reading, MA: Addison-Wesley, 1981.

Ouchi, W., and Jaeger, A. Type Z Organization. *Academy of Management Review*, 3 (1978): 305–314.

*O'Connor, E., and Barrett, G. Information Cues and Individual Differences as Determinants of Perceptions of Task Enrichment. *Academy of Management Journal*, 23 (1980): 697–716.

*O'Reilly, C. Variations in Decision Makers' Uses of Information Sources. *Academy of Management Journal*, 25 (1982): 756–771.

*O'Reilly, C., and Anderson, J. Trust and Communication of Performance Appraisal Information. *Human Communication Research*, 6 (1980): 290–298.

Pacanowsky, M., and O'Donnell-Trujillo, N. Organizational Communication as Cultural Performance. *Communication Monographs*, 50 (1983): 126–147.

*Palmer, R. *Hermeneutics*. Evanston, IL: Northwestern University Press, 1969.

*Pascale, R. Communication and Decision-Making Across Cultures. *Administrative Science Quarterly*, 23 (1978): 91–110.

*Payne, R. Epistemology and the Study of Stress at Work, in *Stress at Work*, C. Cooper and R. Payne, eds. New York: Wiley, 1978.

———. Stress in Task-Focused Groups. *Small Group Behavior*, 12 (1981): 253–268.

Pelz, D. Influence: A Key to Effective Leadership in the First-Line Supervisor. *Personnel*, 29 (1952): 3–11.

*Perelman, C. *The Idea of Justice and the Problem of Argument*. London: Routledge and Kegan Paul, 1963.

*Perelman, C., and Olbrechts-Tyteca, L. *The New Rhetoric*. Notre Dame, IN: Notre Dame University Press, 1970.

Perrow, C. *Organizational Analysis*. Belmont, CA: Wadsworth, 1970.

*Pettegrew, L., Thomas, R., Ford, J., and Costello, D. The Effect of Job-Related Stress on Medical Center Employee Communicator Style. *Journal of Applied Psychology*, 66 (1981): 428–443.

Pettigrew, A. Information Control as a Power Resource. *Sociology*, 6 (1972): 187–204.

———. On Studying Organizational Cultures. *Administrative Science Quarterly*, 24 (1979): 570–581.

*Pfeffer, J. *Organizations and Organization Theory*. Marshfield, MA: Pitman Publishing, 1982.

*———. The Bases and Uses of Power in Organizational Decision-Making. *Administrative Science Quarterly*, 19 (1974): 453–473.

*———. Power and Resource Allocation in Organizations, in *New Directions in Organizational Behavior*, B. Staw and G. Salancik, eds. New York: St. Clair Press, 1977.

———. *Power in Organizations*. Marshfield, MA: Pitman Publishing, 1981.

*Pfeffer, J., and Salancik, G. *The External Control of Organizations*. New York: Harper & Row, 1978.

*Pierce, J., Dunhan, R., and Blackburn, R. Social Systems Structure, Job Design and Growth Need Strength. *Academy of Management Journal*, 22 (1979): 223–240.

Pilotta, J., ed. *Women in Organizations*. Prospect Heights, NJ: Waveland Press, 1983.

Pines, A., Aronson, E., and Kafry, D. *Burnout*. New York: The Free Press, 1981.

Pondy, L. Organizational Conflict: Concepts and Models. *Administrative Science Quarterly*, 12 (1967): 296–320.

Poole, M. S., and McPhee, R. Bringing Intersubjectivity Back In: A Change of Climate, in *Communication and Organizations: An Interpretive Approach*, L. Putnam and M. Pacanowsky, eds. Beverly Hills, CA: Sage, 1983.

Poulton, C. Blue Collar Stressors, in *Stress at Work*, C. Cooper and R. Payne, eds. New York: Wiley, 1978.

Putnam, L. Women in Management: Leadership Theories, Research Results and Future Directions. Paper presented at the Central States Speech Association Convention, 1979.

*Putnam, L., and Sorenson, R. Equivocal Messages in Organizations. *Human Communication Research*, 8 (1982): 114–132.

*Putnam, L., and Wilson, C. Development of an Organizational Conflict Instrument. Paper presented at the International Communication Association Convention, 1982.

*Rapoport, A., Guyer, M., and Gordon, D. *The 2 × 2 Game*. Ann Arbor: University of Michigan Press, 1976.

Rapoport, R., and Rapoport, R. *Dual Career Families*. Harmondsworth, Eng.: Penguin, 1971.

———. *Dual Career Families Revisited*. New York: Harper & Row, 1976.

*Raven, B., and Kruglanski, A. Power and Conflict, in *The Structure of Conflict*, Paul Swingle, ed. New York: Academic Press, 1970.

Redding, W. C. *Communication Within the Organization*. New York: Industrial Communication Council, 1972.

*Rhenman, E., Stromberg, L., and Westerlund, G. *Conflict and Cooperation in Business Organizations*. New York: Wiley, 1970.

Ring, K. Behind Every Successful Woman . . . There's a Mentor. *Women in Business* (July–August 1978): 9–11.

*Robbins, S. Conflict Management and Conflict Resolution are not Synonymous Terms. *California Management Review*, 21 (1978): 67–75.

Roberts, K., Hulin, C., and Rousseau, D. *Toward an Interdisciplinary Science of Organizations*. San Francisco: Jossey-Bass, 1979.

Bibliography

Roberts, K., and O'Reilly, C. Failures in Upward Communication: Three Possible Culprits. *Academy of Management Journal*, 17 (1974): 205–215.

Rogers, E., and Argawala-Rogers, R. *Communication and Organizations.* New York: The Free Press, 1976.

Rogge, E., and Ching, J. *Advanced Public Speaking.* New York: Holt, Rinehart and Winston, 1966.

Roloff, M. *Interpersonal Communication: the Social Exchange Approach.* Beverly Hills, CA: Sage, 1981.

Rosen, B., and Jerdee, T. The Influence on Sex-Role Stereotypes on Evaluations of Male and Female Supervisory Behavior. *Journal of Applied Psychology*, 62 (1977): 44–48.

Rosen, B., and Mericle, M. The Influence of Strong vs. Weak Affirmative Action Policies and Applicant's Sex on Selection Decisions and Salary Recommendations. Paper presented at the Academy of Management Convention, 1979.

Rosenfeld, L. Self Disclosure Avoidance. *Communication Monographs*, 46 (1979): 63–74.

Rosenfeld, L., and Fowler, G. Personality, Sex, and Leadership Style. *Communication Monographs*, 43 (1976): 320–324.

Rousseau, D. An Assessment of Technology in Organizations. *Academy of Management Review*, 4 (1979): 531–542.

*Rubin, J., and Brown, R. *The Social Psychology of Bargaining and Negotiation.* New York: Academic Press, 1975.

*Schein, V. The Relationships Between Sex-Role Stereotypes and Requisite Managerial Characteristics. *Journal of Applied Psychology*, 57 (1973): 95–100.

———. Sex Role Stereotyping, Ability and Performance: Prior Research and New Directions. *Personnel Psychology*, 31 (1978): 259–267.

*Schriesheim, C., and von Glinow, M. The Path-Goal Theory of Leadership. *Academy of Management Journal*, 20 (1977): 398–405.

Schwartz, E., and Rago, J. Beyond Tokenism: Women as True Corporate Peers. *Business Horizons* (Dec. 1973): 69–76.

*Segovis, J., and Bhagat, R. Participation Revisited. *Small Group Behavior*, 12 (1981): 299–328.

Seidenberg, R. *Corporate Wives, Corporate Casualties?* New York: AMACOM, 1973

*Selye, H. *The Stress of Life.* New York: McGraw-Hill, 1956.

*Sgro, J., Worchel, P., Pence, E., and Orban, J. Perceived Leader Behavior as a Function of Trust. *Academy of Management Journal*, 23 (1980): 161–165.

Shaw, J. An Information-Processing Approach to the Study of Job Design. *Academy of Management Review*, 5 (1980): 41–48.

Shaw, M. *Group Dynamics.* New York: McGraw-Hill, 1971.

Sheehy, G. *Passages.* New York: Bantam, 1974.

Shepard, J. On Alex Carey's Critique of the Hawthorne Studies. *Academy of Management Journal*, 14 (1971): 23–32.

*Sillars, A. Stranger and Spouse as Target Persons for Compliance-Gaining Strategies. *Human Communication Research*, 6 (1980): 265–279.

Simon, H. *The New Science of Management Decision.* New York: Harper & Row, 1960.

Sims, H. Further Thoughts on Punishment in Organizations. *The Academy of Management Review*, 5 (1980): 135–138.

Sleeth, R., and Humphreys, L. Differences in Leadership Styles Among Future Managers. Paper presented at the Academy of Management Convention, 1979.

*Slovic, P., Fischhoff, B., and Lichtenstein, S. Behavioral Decision Theory. *Annual Review of Psychology*, 28 (1977): pp. 1–39.

*Smart, C., and Vertinsky, I. Designs for Crisis Decision Units. *Administrative Science Quarterly*, 22 (1977): 640–657.

*Smircich, L., and Chesser, R. Superiors' and Subordinates' Perceptions of Performance. *Academy of Management Journal*, 24 (1981): 198–205.

Smith, D. Theoretical and Research Problems with the Concept of Utility. Paper presented at the International Communication Association Convention, 1980.

Smith, R., ed. *The Subtle Revolution*. Washington, D.C.: The Urban Institute, 1979.

*Sofer, C. *Men in Mid-Career*. Cambridge, Eng.: Cambridge University Press, 1970.

*Stagner, R., and Rosen, H. *Psychology of Union-Management Relationships*. Belmont, CA: Brooks-Cole, 1965.

*Staw, B. Knee Deep in the Big Muddy. *Organizational Behavior and Human Performance*, 16 (1976): 27–44.

*Staw, B., and Ross, J. Commitment to a Policy Decision. *Administrative Science Quarterly*, 23 (1978): 40–52.

*Stogdill, R. *Handbook of Leadership*. New York: The Free Press, 1974.

*Strauss, W. Some Notes on Power Equalization, in *The Social Science of Organization*, H. Levitt, ed. Englewood Cliffs, NJ: Prentice-Hall, 1963.

*Tedeschi, J. Threats and Promises, in *The Structure of Conflict*, P. Swingle, ed. New York: Academic Press, 1970.

Tegar, A. *Too Much Invested to Quit*. New York: Pergamon, 1980.

Thomas, K. Conflict and Conflict Management. In *Handbook of Industrial and Organizational Psychology*, Marvin Dunnette, ed. Chicago: Rand-McNally, 1976.

*Thomas, K., and Walton, R. *Conflict-Handling Behavior in Interdepartmental Relations*. Los Angeles: UCLA Graduate School of Business Administration, 1971.

Thompson, J. Corporate Survival: Make the Right Connection. *Essence* (August 1978): 82, 122–123.

Thompson, V. *Modern Organizations*. New York: Knopf, 1963.

*Tichy, N., Tushman, M., and Frombrun, C. Social Network Analysis for Organizations. *Academy of Management Review*, 4 (1979): 507–519.

Trahey, J. *Jane Trahey on Women and Power*. New York: Rawson, 1977.

*Tushman, M. Impacts of Perceived Environmental Variability on Patterns of Work-Related Communication. *Academy of Management Journal*, 22 (1979): 482–500.

Tushman, M., and Nadler, D. Information Processing as an Integrating Concept in Organizational Design. *Academy of Management Review*, 3 (1978): 613–624.

*Tushman, M., and Scanlan, T. Boundary Spanning Individuals. *Academy of Management Journal*, 24 (1981): 289–305.

U.S. Department of Health, Education and Welfare. *Work in America*. Cambridge: M.I.T. Press, 1972.

*van Maanen, J., and Schein, E. Occupational Socialization in the Professions. *Journal of Psychiatric Research*, 8 (1971): 521–530.

*Vecchio, R. An Empirical Examination of the Validity of Fiedler's Model of Leadership Effectiveness. *Organizational Behavior and Human Performance*, 19 (1977): 180–206.

———. Worker Satisfaction and Performance. *Academy of Management Journal*, 23 (1980): 479–486.

Viega, R. Do Managers on the Move Get Anywhere? *Harvard Business Review* (March–April 1981): 20–22.

*von Neumann, J., and Morganstern, O. *Theory of Games and Economic Behavior.* New York: Wiley, 1947.

Walton, R. *Interpersonal Peacemaking.* Reading, MA: Addison-Wesley, 1969.

Wardwell, W. Critique of a Recent "Put Down" of the Hawthorne Studies. *American Sociological Review,* 44 (1979): 861–867.

Ware, B., and Linkugel, W. They Spoke in Defense of Themselves. *Quarterly Journal of Speech,* 59 (1973): 273–283.

Watzlawick, P., Beavin, J., and Jackson, D. *Pragmatics of Human Communication.* New York: W.W. Norton, 1967.

*Weber, M. *The Theory of Social and Economic Organization,* T. Parsons, ed. New York: Macmillan, 1947.

*Weick, K. *The Social Psychology of Organizing,* 2nd ed. Reading, MA: Addison-Wesley, 1979.

*Weiner, B. *Achievement Motivation and Attribution Theory.* Morristown, NJ: General Learning Press, 1974.

*Westerlund, G., and Sjostrand, S. *Organizational Myths.* New York: Harper & Row, 1979.

Wofford, J., Gerloff, E., and Cummins, R. *Organizational Communication.* New York: McGraw-Hill, 1976.

*Wood, J., and Conrad, C. Paradox in the Experience of Professional Women. *Western Journal of Speech Communication,* 47 (1983): 305–322.

Wood, J., and Pearce, B. Sexists, Racists and Other Classes of Classifiers. *The Quarterly Journal of Speech,* 66 (1980): 239–250.

*Wood, M. Power Relationships and Groups Decision-Making in Organizations. *Psychological Bulletin,* 79 (1973): 280–293.

*Woodward, J. *Industrial Organization: Theory and Practice.* London: Oxford University Press, 1965.

Wren, D. Scientific Management in the U.S.S.R. *The Academy of Management Review,* 5 (1980): 1–12.

Zalzenik, A. Power and Politics in Organizational Life. *Harvard Business Review* (March–April 1971): 51–59.

Zimbardo, P. *Shyness.* Reading, MA: Addison-Wesley, 1977.

Acknowledgments (*continued from p. ii*)

Exerpts on pp. 74 and 107–108: From *Theories of Management* by Raymond Miles. Copyright © 1975. Reprinted by permission of McGraw-Hill Book Company.

Excerpts on pp. 82, 96–97, and 113–115: From *New Patterns of Management* by Rensis Likert. Copyright © 1961. Reprinted by permission of McGraw-Hill Book Company.

Excerpt on p. 94: From "Behavioral Theory vs. Reality" by James Lee. *Harvard Business Review* (March/April 1971). Copyright © 1971 by the President and Fellows of Harvard College; all rights reserved. Reprinted by permission of the *Harvard Business Review*.

Excerpts on pp. 101–102: From "The Hawthorne Studies: First Statistical Interpretation" by Richard Franke and James Kaul. *The American Sociological Review*, 43 (1978). Reprinted by permission of the American Sociological Association.

Excerpts on pp. 103 and 177: From "Power and Politics in Organizational Life" by Abraham Zaleznik. *Harvard Business Review* (May/June, 1970). Copyright© 1970 by the President and Fellows of Harvard College; all rights reserved. Reprinted by permission of the *Harvard Business Review*.

Excerpt on pp. 106–107: From *Communication and Organizing* by Richard Farace, Peter Monge, and Hamish Russell, pp. 160 and 161. Copyright© 1977. Reprinted by permission of Addison-Wesley Publishers, Reading, Massachusetts.

Excerpt on p. 154: From *The Social Psychology of Organizing* by Karl Weick. Copyright© 1977. Reprinted by permission of Addison-Wesley Publishers, Reading, Massachusetts.

Excerpts on pp. 178, 181, and 195–198: From *Power in Organizations* by Jeffry Pfeffer. Copyright© 1981. Reprinted by permission of Pitman Publishers.

Excerpt on p. 227: From *The Presentation of Self in Everyday Life* by Erving Goffman. Copyright© 1959 by Erving Goffman. Reprinted by permission of Doubleday and Company, Inc.

Excerpt on pp. 283: From "The Social Readjustment Rating Scale" by T. M. Holmes and R. H. Rahe. *Journal of Psychosomatic Research*. Copyright© 1967 by Pergamon Press, Inc. Reprinted by permission of Pergamon Press.

Excerpt on pp. 284–285: From *The Two-Career Couple* by D. Hall and F. Hall. Copyright© 1979. Reprinted by permission of Addison-Wesley Publishers, Reading, Massachusetts.

AUTHOR INDEX

Author Index

SUBJECT INDEX

absenteeism, 118
accountability, 25
acculturation
  and myths of rationality, 149
  and organizational power, 187–188
  and sex roles, 292–294
accuracy of information, 50–55
across-the-board salary increases, 61
acting in organizations, 228
actions
  constraints, 138
  guidelines, 11
  parameters, 11
actor view of employees, 202
ambiguity
  reduction of, 149
  strategic, 235
ambiguity management, 149
  and advancement, 195
  function of communication, 12–14,
    140–141, 147–164
  processes, 48
apologia, 230–231
army metaphor for organizations, 16–17
artificial languages, 49
assembly lines
  as barriers to communication, 39–40
  and worker alienation, 39
attire
  and organizational cultures, 213
  and victim blaming, 306–307
attribution
  of meaning, 48
  of success or failure, 61
audiences, 171, 201, 237
  analysis of, 201–204
  hidden, 204
  and power of appeals, 202
  and power relationships, 204
authority
  charismatic, 36–37
  legal, 37
  traditional, 36
  Weber's concept of, 15
autonomy, 38

behavior modification, 61
belief-behavior relationships, 118

blaming the victim, 306–307
boundary role elements, 136
bureaucracy, 15, 74
bureaucratic organizations, 35–37

career paths, 215–216
causal relationships
  among communication, satisfaction, and
    performance, 115–120
  between satisfaction and performance, 87
chain of command, 34, 47, 90
choice making, 3, 55, 59, 118, 125
  and goals, 152
  incomplete information and, 141
  intransitivity, 151
coercion, 250–251
command function, 8–10, 47
commitment to failing policies, 156
communication
  anxiety, 113
  cathartic, 202
  channels, 88
  climate, 124
  emergent patterns of, 164
  expressive, 171, 202
  functions of, 7–15
  and hiding of motives, 158
  informative, 171
  instrumental, 5, 171
  modes, 236
  needs, 54
  networks, 69, 89, 105–107
  overload, 52, 113, 136
  processes, 6
  recurring patterns, 138, 166, 201, 215
  rhetorical, 172, 202
  and sex roles, 289–301
  significance of, 4
communication skills
  adapting to situations, 219–238
  analyzing situations, 175, 200–218
  message-creating, 175
  self-monitoring, 307–308
  strategic adaptation, 175
compensating for recurring communication
    breakdowns, 55
competition and advancement, 69
compliance, 76

status differences in and accuracy of communication, 50–51
stories, 160
strategic attitudes, 219
strategic communication, 80
stress, 64, 113, 260–288
  communication and, 261
  costs of, 260
  definition of, 262
  dynamics of, 261–273
  families and spouses, 281–288
  life changes and, 282
  middle managers and, 263–264
  moderating factors, 266–269
  perceptions and, 261
  performance feedback and, 266
  personalities and, 261
  physiology of, 262, 269–270
  role ambiguity, 266
  supportive communication, 267, 282
  Type A vs. Type B behavior, 267–269, 282
stress and dual career couples, *see* dual career couples
stress management, 273–280
  base lines and, 278
  comic frames and, 275–276
  individual strategies, 275–280
  intervention strategies, 279–280
  mortification and, 276
  organizational strategies, 273–275
  personal programs of, 280
  preparation as, 276–279
  relaxation and, 279–280
  systematic assessment and, 277–279
  tragic perspectives and, 276
  victimage and, 276
stressors, 261–266
  communication anxiety, 263
  communication overload, 263, 264
  constraints, 263
  deadlines, 265
  decision-making, 263
  demands for action, 263
  external pressures, 263–265
  family demands, 281–283
  internal pressures, 265–266
  pressures exceeding resources, 263
  relationship to stress, 262–266
  relaxation as, 261
  role conflict, 264
  task characteristics, 263, 264–265
  threshold levels, 262, 266
  underload, 264
  working conditions, 263
  work overload, 263–264

stress responses, 269–273
  adaptive-maladaptive continuum of responses, 271–273
  behavioral responses, 271–273
  escalating cycles, 273
  fight vs. flight responses, 271
  physiological responses, 262, 269–270
  range of, 278–279
  strategic vs. pathological withdrawal, 271–272
  syndrome, 269–271
structural distortion of information, 47, 48
supervision
  close, 96
  loose, 96
support
  from interpersonal relationships, 74, 101
  in work groups, 77
supportive communication, 75, 83–84, 124
  and group rewards, 102
  limits to, 101–105
supportive supervision, 101–103
symbols
  of professionalism, 160
  of rationality, 172
systematic soldiering, 27–28, 42
System 4, 97, 113
system rewards, 61
systems, organizations as, 45
systems-contingency type of organization, 120, 133–147

tasks
  complexity, 141
  learning task skills, 215
  range of response options, 141
  structure, 144
Taylor's four principles of scientific management, 29–33
Taylor's great mental revolution, 28–29, 80
technologies
  changes in, 41
  large batch, 142
  process production, 142
  production, 142–143
  small batch, 142
T-groups, 103
Theory X and Theory Y, 81
time-motion studies, 30
trained communication incapacity, 48–50, 97
training programs
  and scientific management, 30
  functions of, 60
translation, 50